SUPERVISORY HANDBOOK

SUPERVISORY HANDBOOK

A Management Guide to Principles and Applications

MARTIN M. BROADWELL

JOHN WILEY & SONS

New York   Chichester   Brisbane   Toronto   Singapore

Library of Congress Cataloging in Publication Data:

Broadwell, Martin M.
  Supervisory handbook.

  Includes index.
  1. Supervision of employees.   2. Personnel management.
I. Title.

HF5549.B8573   1985   658.3'02   85-723
ISBN 0-471-88783-8

Printed in the United States of America

10 9 8 7 6 5 4 3 2 1

CONTRIBUTORS

Martin M. Broadwell heads the Center for Management Services, which specializes in conducting in-house training in the fields of instructor training, supervisory and management skills, and development and training of technical instructors. He taught school in Ohio and worked with the Bell System for nearly 20 years as an engineering manager, personnel director, and training director. In 1968 he started Resources for Education and Management, Inc., now a worldwide mail order house handling packaged supervisor, management, and audio visual training programs. Dr. Broadwell's writings include over one hundred and fifty articles and a dozen books. Several of his books have been standard texts for a number of years in organizations around the world. He has consulted for over 20 years in the field of instructor training and supervisory development and has designed and conducted development programs in Italy, England, India, Nepal, Hong Kong, Japan, Germany, Poland, Greece, Australia, and South Africa.

Paul H. Chaddock is currently Senior Vice President of Personnel and a member of the Executive Committee of Lechmere, Inc., a New England hardgoods chain. He was Vice President of Organization Planning and Development for Dayton Hudson Corporation, the parent of Lechmere. Mr. Chaddock has several published articles and has contributed to several books in the field. He is on the Personnel Board of Directors of NRMA, the Board of Directors for the Associated Grantmakers of Massachusetts, and the Board of Governors of ASTD. He is a graduate of West Virginia

Wesleyan College. He specializes in individualizing executive development, organizational development, organization planning, institutionalizing the development process, and performance measurement systems.

Stephen L. Cohen is Executive Vice President of Assessment Designs, Inc. He received his B.S. from Hobart College and both his M.S. and Ph.D. from the University of Tennessee. Dr. Cohen has worked for Pitney Bowes, Allstate Insurance, and Union Carbide in various personnel research and development capacities, in addition to having served on the faculty of the University of South Florida. He has consulted with numerous government and industry organizations in the area of personnel selection, appraisal, and training systems and has written and presented extensively on these subjects. He is currently editor of the *Journal of Assessment Center Technology* and an editorial reviewer for the *Training and Development Journal*. He is a member of the International Assessment Center Congress Advisory Committee, the National Society for Performance and Information, American Society for Personnel Administrators, and the American Psychological Association and is a licensed consulting psychologist.

M. Thaxter Dickey has roots deep in fundamental and traditional values, especially in individual freedoms, which attracts him to the study and teaching of economics. After four years of majoring in physics and math at Florida State University, he earned a degree in psychology and business administration at Western Kentucky University, followed by both a Masters and Doctorate at the University of South Florida in the fields of industrial and organizational psychology, with minors in economics and management. He is presently an instructor at Florida College in the fields of business administration and social sciences, and consults with local and national organizations in personnel selection and program evaluation.

Olice H. Embry, Jr. is Professor of Management at Columbus College, The University System of Georgia. He holds two Bachelor's degrees in mathematics and business administration from

Presbyterian College in Clinton, South Carolina and the M.B.A. and Ph.D. in Business Administration from Georgia State University in Atlanta, Georgia. He is the author of two books and numerous publications in the management and computer information management fields. He is an active consultant and trainer in the Southeast in supervisory training.

Fredric D. Frank holds a B.A. degree in psychology from Michigan State University and M.S. and Ph.D. degrees in industrial psychology from Wayne State University. He has been instrumental in the development and implementation of a large number of selection and development programs for a variety of organizations, both in the private and public sectors, in the United States and internationally. Dr. Frank has published extensively in the human resource field and is the author of several books in the area. He is an active speaker at various professional conferences and was formerly on the faculty at Bowling Green State University, and the University of Central Florida. He is Executive Vice President of Assessment Designs, Inc., in Orlando, Florida.

Robert Hays is both a professor and a consultant. He has taught technical writing at Southern Tech, Marietta, Georgia, for more than 30 years. He has also served as a consultant to more than 50 companies and agencies and has conducted continuing education programs at more than 30 colleges. His publications include four books (two on technical writing) and over a hundred articles. He has supervised an industrial group preparing manuals and has written numerous proposals. He holds a master's degree in education from Emory University, with an additional year of graduate study in English.

Matt Hennecke is a manager of management development for Arthur Andersen & Co. in St. Charles, Illinois. He has worked for and consulted with several organizations on the subjects of human resource planning and executive/management development and is a regular national training conference speaker. He has published articles in both the *ASTD Journal* and *Training Magazine*.

Ruth Sizemore House received her Ph.D. degree from the University of Georgia and has coauthored three books on training and management. Dr. House has contributed articles to professional journals and has conducted seminars and training programs. Her clients include AT&T, Gulf Oil Company, both the U.S. Navy and U.S. Army, and Georgia State University School of Business Administration.

Cabot L. Jaffee is President of Assessment Designs, Inc., a leading human resource management consulting firm. He received his B.A. from New York University, his M.A. from Columbia University, and his Ph.D. in psychology from Florida State University. He began his career with AT&T as a Personnel Research Analyst, responsible for the Bell System Assessment Centers. After leaving AT&T, Dr. Jaffee taught at the University of Tennessee and the University of Central Florida, while consulting with numerous organizations in the area of assessment. In addition, Dr. Jaffee was a member of the task force which developed assessment center standards for practitioners. Dr. Jaffee has authored some 10 books and numerous articles on various aspects of leadership and assessment center technology. He has spoken at national meetings and conferences and teaches a course on the assessment center method at the University of Michigan.

Bill Johns has over 35 years of experience in the field of personnel and labor relations. Currently he is the Industrial Relations Manager for Georgia Kraft Company. His interest in people management has led him to a major role in the development of labor for supervisory and managerial positions in the Woodlands Division of Georgia Kraft Company. He specializes in succession planning and presupervisory training. He has also generated one of the most successful accident prevention programs for forestry and woodlands operations in the United States. Mr. Johns has also worked for Ampex Corporation and Kimberly-Clark Corporation, and is a graduate of the University of Alabama.

Linda M. Lash has over 13 years of sales, supervisory, and training experience, having designed and conducted training seminars on product knowledge, selling skills, supervision, and management techniques. She has had articles published in *Training Magazine* and has appeared at national conferences in the United States for ASTD and *Training*. She has put her skills to work in designing, training, and implementing a number of sales territory organizations in Europe and the Near East.

Joel D. Ramich is Corporate Director of Training and Development for Siecor Corporation, Hickory, North Carolina. Previously he worked for Corning Glass Works, where he held plant level positions as Shift Supervisor, Training Coordinator, and Assistant Personnel Supervisor. He worked in Poland for two years, serving as Personnel and Training Manager for a television plant start-up near Warsaw. He has provided consulting and training for other projects in Great Britain, France, Germany, Mexico, China, and the U.S.S.R. Mr. Ramich has also served as Corporate Manager of Production and Maintenance Training, a position from which he was instrumental in developing and implementing Corning's overall productivity and quality improvement strategy. He has published articles in several professional journals and has spoken at various training and productivity conferences throughout the United States.

Robert A. Rock was educated at Dartmouth College and gained experience by developing and executing two substantial training assignments in the U.S. Navy during World War II. He had some 37 years of supervisory and managerial experience in the field of industrial relations, including labor negotiations, personnel, training, and affirmative action. He was instrumental in designing and implementing one of the largest presupervisory programs in the United States for Georgia Kraft Paper Company; he is now retired from Georgia Kraft after serving for an extended period as Vice President of Industrial Relations.

Irwin A. Scherman is a career civilian personnel director with the Department of the Army, presently serving at Fort Sheridan, Illinois. His career spans the Atlantic, with assignments in the United States and Germany. During his time in Germany he served as the Chief Training Officer for several years, and moved to Deputy and Acting Civilian Personnel Officer, with total personnel responsibilities. He has been nominated for and awarded a number of citations for outstanding work in community relations, training, and personnel. His essays have been acclaimed in competitions throughout the worldwide network of personnel people in the Department and read at ceremonies at the Pentagon. He is a member of the Commanding Officer's Executive Staff at Ft. Sheridan.

PREFACE

A lot of people have put a lot of good time into producing this volume of topics. Each is an expert in the field he or she wrote about. Each has put in a labor of love. The task was formidable: Put down as much as you can in a chapter, about a subject you'd like to write a whole book about! Each chapter represents what each author would say if he or she had only a few minutes to tell the most important thing to be said about the subject under discussion. They all did well.

I have made no attempt to exhaust the list of topics relevant to supervisors, or to exhaust each topic that is treated. A number of topics were considered but left out; there were some hard choices made, and the topics that survived did so because they seemed to best fit the scope of the book. Some subjects were left out because they were *too important*. For example, the matter of motivation—as a topic—was omitted because it simply couldn't be reduced to one chapter with any justice. But almost every other chapter deals with it as it relates to the subject being discussed in that chapter. There are other topics which fit this same pattern.

I have also made no effort to have the writing fit a single pattern or style. Since I did not intend that a person would read the entire book chapter by chapter, it seemed more practical to let the authors use their own styles.

My intention is that the book will serve as an encyclopedic reference so that a supervisor or manager can look for a specific chapter when there is a specific problem to be solved. Hopefully, each person will find several relevant topics for his or her own use and help. To the extent this works, the book has met its goal of being a handbook and guide, not the final word on every subject included.

MARTIN M. BROADWELL

Decatur, Georgia
April 1985

ACKNOWLEDGMENTS

To name the people who contributed to this book would be only to repeat the names of the authors. I would like to tell of those who took precious time to do their writing, those who got their work done ahead of schedule, those who rewrote to accommodate a different idea or a changed mind (and did it with graciousness), and those who stepped in and delivered excellent products when others had to drop out at the last minute. I won't mention their names, but they know who they are, and they must know how grateful I am for their support. Thanks!

I can mention Dianne Caudill, because it was Dianne who sometimes prodded, sometimes encouraged, sometimes took on emergency typing jobs, who sometimes gently lifted me out of lethargy or despair and brought me back to reality. It's a good feeling to have somebody who always has the big picture but can also handle the smallest of details with ease and efficiency. Thanks, Dianne!

MMB

CONTENTS

SECTION 8. SAFETY CONSIDERATIONS

SECTION 9. PERSONNEL CONSIDERATIONS

SECTION 10. EMPLOYEE RELATIONS

INTRODUCTION

1

THE ROLE OF THE SUPERVISOR IN THE ORGANIZATION

MARTIN M. BROADWELL

There is much that is unique about the job of the supervisor in the organization in comparison to any other job or level. Obviously, there is a big difference between the first level of supervision and the nonsupervisory job of the hourly worker. The difference isn't as marked, but still exists between the supervisor and the nonsupervisor who is not an hourly worker—or as we say, "covered employee"—such as certain engineering, computer, and other technical people. Because of the difference in *roles*, there is a difference in the nature of supervision at the first level from that at all levels above that position. It is not the purpose of this chapter to deal with these differences, but to point out the uniqueness of first-line supervision.

ATTITUDE TOWARD THE JOB

If first-line supervisors come up through the ranks, they see their first challenge as changing their perspective of the job itself. For all of their past work history they've been measured on how well they are performing on the job, meaning *how much work they are doing*. Now the measure is how much work their *people* are doing. Their success depends upon how well they motivate their people, how much they are able to get their people to do—how well they motivate and delegate. Their job changes drastically from one of doing to one of getting the job done through others. While their past skills will help them in technical decision making, the new job requires an entirely new set of skills, most of them in the area of human or interpersonal relations.

In the midst of this new challenge, they will find themselves frustrated when the job is not done correctly, not done quickly, and not done with "spirit." No matter how diligent they might have been before they took on the assignment of supervisor, and no matter how well they performed, they must take a new, proprietary interest in the job that they've never had before. Before, there was someone else that higher management looked to to get the job done. When the whistle blew, it was either time to go home or work overtime. The decision was left to the individual: "Do I or don't I want to work longer to complete the job?" Now, there is no such question to be asked. If the job is not complete and it's necessary for it to be done by a certain time, it is the supervisor who is working to get others to stay and finish. The supervisors can't do it themselves, hence the frustration.

First-line supervisors will also find a different perspective on the job—the perspective from an organizational standpoint. Perhaps for the first time the supervisor now wonders if the job is laid out properly, if there should be some changes in procedures, if the standards are too high or too low. These weren't considerations when this person was an hourly worker. Now they are major concerns. The concerns look both ways—up and down. The supervisor may wonder if management is asking too much—more than can be accomplished in the time allowed—and at the same time may wonder if the employees couldn't be doing a bit more than they are.

One final matter that is important to supervisors is the sometimes lost feeling of now knowing what to do as precisely as when they were hourly workers, when they may have been superb at doing every phase of their jobs. In fact, this may have been one of the prime reasons for their promotions. Not only did they know the jobs, but the jobs were spelled out in detail. If there was a question, the worker could look up the procedure in the manual and see pictures, know exactly which steps to take, which adjustments to make, and come away with feelings of satisfaction of a job well done. In their new job as supervisor, there is seldom that kind of complete confidence. For one thing, there is no manual or handbook that gives all the answers. The answers that do appear in the personnel policy manual deal only with specific, measurable things, such as the policy on overtime, on discipline, and on things like tardiness and absenteeism. Even in all these areas there is a feeling of nebulousness—an absence of exactness. Yet the hourly people reporting to these supervisors expect fairly exact answers, and certainly consistent answers. When they ask, "Can I take the afternoon off?" they want a very exact "yes" or "no," not a "maybe," or "I'll see."

ATTITUDE TOWARD SUBORDINATES

For most new supervisors, a proper perspective toward the people under their supervision is the hardest thing to develop. It is often the case that these people were actually peers not too long ago. They were lunch and break mates, joint carpoolers, friends and buddies on the weekend hunting and fishing and shopping trips. Now they are expected to take orders, do work on time, and meet the expectations of someone who was—until recently—"one of them." This new perspective is hard to come by, for obviously there doesn't need to be an overnight, drastic difference in the relationship, yet there is an overnight, drastic change in the role of those becoming supervisors. The supervisors find it difficult to walk in one morning and announce, "Now we will no longer be friends and buddies; we will no longer have the same relationship. You will now treat me with the respect and dignity due a supervisor." A few have tried it and there is little success to show for their efforts.

In spite of all this, we still find that there has to be a noticeable difference fairly soon in the relationship between the supervisors and the subordinates. Fortunately, there is something that helps the process along. Even if the supervisors do not act any differently, the *workers* will begin to act differently immediately. It's as if the supervisor has a big sign hanging around his or her neck— "BOSS!"—the moment the announcement of the promotion is made. Subordinates won't be quite so quick to criticize in front of the newly appointed supervisor; there will be some uncomfortableness in discussing things around the boss. The astute supervisor quietly takes advantage of this, building on the separation, rather than trying to tear it down. Rather than getting the reputation of acting like the "big shot," supervisors let the hourly workers make the separation.

ATTITUDE TOWARD THE BOSS

When people "break" the ranks of the hourly workers, or even the ranks of nonsupervisory, exempt positions, and become supervisors, they enter into a new world of what we call *management*. Their organization may not use management terms in their titles, but they have one thing in common that makes them "management" people. They are part of the team that has the responsibility for instituting and even enforcing the views, policies, and procedures of the organization's planners, directors, and top decision makers. Where before they were being told what to do, and expected to carry out the actual work, now they belong to that group whose major role is getting others to do the work. They've crossed an imaginary line and are now on a different "side." They now have to support management policies and directions as a *job responsibility*. They may not believe in the policies, they may not like the decisions that have been made, and they may privately complain about the way the organization is being run, but on the job they must support these policies and decisions and do everything they can to make them work!

That puts them in a different relationship with their bosses. They are now in a position of being on the bosses' side when a disagreement arises. They may discuss their differences privately with the boss, but they can't publicly take issue with him or her. The boss now becomes an object of ambivalence: the boss gives instructions and yet is part of the same management structure, that is, is on the same *side* as the supervisors. This isn't to suggest that all of this presents insurmountable problems. It's an accepted way to operate, it makes a lot of sense, and organizations have run smoothly in this manner for years. It is a consideration, though, and will sometimes present problems, especially for the newly appointed supervisors. The main thing to keep in mind is that things work better if everyone thinks in terms of a *total* team, made up of management, supervision and hourly workers, with whatever technical support personnel are needed.

ATTITUDE TOWARD PEERS

The supervisor has a role to play with peers that is unlike other roles played in nonsupervisory jobs. In some unhealthy organizations the role is misunderstood to the extent that there is a strong political play going on throughout the organization. To an outsider, it would seem that these supervisors are in competition with each other, even more bitterly than with the actual competition in some cases. In healthy organizations there is a view of team effort that says, "We're all here to support the goals of the organization. How can I help you?" The support can be seen when there is a problem of some kind. Supervisors from one section or department immediately respond with offers of assistance, including people, money from their budget, materials, or any other kind of help they have to offer. When one group is hurting, all groups share in the pain and do what they can to alleviate the suffering. On the other hand, in the unhealthy organizations there is a quick retreat when somebody is having a problem. Others hasten to point out, "We've got our own problems—don't look to us for help." There is in-fighting over money, people, space, time—all kinds of things that should be shared for the good of the overall organizational goals.

It is difficult for supervisors to set their own rules, if they are counter to the norm for the rest of the organization. It is even more difficult if there has been no particular thought given to what role to play, and the supervisors have just settled into the normal, accepted, nonsupportive role that everyone else is adopting. When it comes time to change, there is not only the need to change roles, but an even harder task of changing habits! Ideally, one should be able to see that being a supervisor means being a part of the total organization, meaning that the whole is no stronger than the weakest part of the organization. If this view is held in the beginning, really believed, and practiced from the start, then the job is an easier one. There is an easy settling into the role of getting the job done by cooperation, not competition. It works best if everyone is in agreement on the role the peers are playing; but even if there is not full understanding, as many as can should work under the ideal of getting along as a team, rather than as adversaries.

GETTING THE JOB DONE THROUGH OTHERS

As we've seen, the role of the supervisor is to get the job done using others' skills. This in itself requires certain skills. There are more than can be discussed here, but we can look at the ones that are likely to be different and more difficult than those skills used before becoming a supervisor. They include delegating, training, controlling, communicating (orally and in writing), motivating, and appraising and assessing potential. We can't go into detail on each, nor develop skills in this chapter, but we can look at the use of these skills by supervisors.

This is not to suggest that other things aren't important, *and new,* to the supervisor. There are things like problem solving and decision making, analyzing situations, being perceptive, talking with people in interviewing situations, planning and organizing, conference-leading, and so forth. The list could go on, and each item would be important, sometimes even critical. However, there are some other, basic skills that are used everyday, and are new enough to most supervisors that they need to be discussed. For example, conducting meetings is difficult for those who haven't done it before, but compared with delegating, which has to be done all day, everyday, supervisors need to have delegation skills much sooner and with more mastery. Interviewing is a critical skill, but it isn't something that is done everyday as writing and talking to people are, so oral and written communication has to be learned well and quickly.

Delegating

Delegating something to somebody is the essential element in getting work done through others. There are some questions to be answered when we consider the role played by the supervisor in this function: What do we delegate? What shouldn't we delegate? To whom do we delegate? How do we delegate? The first role for the supervisor in delegating is the decision maker's role. Decisions have to be made about what to delegate. This means the supervisor makes a specific decision that certain things will be done by others and that certain things won't be delegated. Since our purpose here isn't to explore these skills in depth, but rather to explore the *role,* we can only say that the decision-making role in delegation is one of the hardest to learn, and one that can make the job easy or hard, depending on whether the delegation is done well or poorly.

Deciding what to delegate is the first decision that must be done well. We delegate those things that we have the authority to do ourselves and the authority to delegate to others. We delegate things that are routine and do not require special knowledge that only we have that can't be imparted quickly. We delegate those things which will provide growth possibility for subordinates, but only when there is little chance that serious consequences will result from poor performance. (We take risks, but we calculate the degree of risk.) We delegate those things that can be done more appropriately at lower levels, things that could easily be done by us but will provide us with some relief when the subordinate does it. It will also provide the subordinate with challenge and growth opportunity. We delegate things where there is greater skill at the lower level, such as a skills/knowledge assignment that fits the person's background or experience.

Deciding not to delegate is sometimes a more demanding skill and requires more ability at decision making than just delegating anything and everything. For example, we do not delegate those things that are given to us to do, with sole responsibility and accountability assigned to us by someone above us. We avoid delegating things that are in anyway related to discipline or morale. We never want to delegate things that call for giving rewards or reinforcement to others. Obviously we don't want to delegate things that are of a confidential nature, where information has been entrusted to us for our use. We try to be most careful when we delegate matters that pertain to the developing—in the form of teaching or counseling—employees. We also try to avoid delegating things that might either cause a problem between people or departments, or matters that involve trying to repair damage in relations between departments or work groups. Finally, we should never delegate things that pertain to safety or safety training, or that in some way can harm a person or equipment.

The third decision is to whom to delegate a task. The cardinal rule for any delegation is to try our best to get the work done at the lowest level where there is the skill to do the job. Next, we delegate to people who need to grow, who will take the risk, and who have the potential to do a successful job. We rarely should delegate to people just to show them they can't do the job. We should avoid delegating to people who don't "deserve" the recognition and reward of increased responsibility. Simply put, the role the supervisor plays is deciding if people have earned the right to have their jobs enriched, and the right to get the recognition that might come from the delegated assignment. The other side of that is that we always delegate to people who have demonstrated the ability and the desire to take on the additional assignment. While we delegate to people who have potential and who have shown they can handle assignments, we don't want to overload or overwork good people.

When we delegate, we should make certain that we make the assignment clear, both as to what is to be done and the standard or expectation of the finished product. We tell what, then we tell how well, then we devise ways of giving feedback concerning the results we want. If we ask someone to do a job that is normally ours to do, we should make sure they know how they will be evaluated. There should be strong support so that the risk isn't so great a factor that we don't get solid results. Again, there should be feedback to the employee along the way so that he or she can measure the progress being made.

Training

What is the role of the supervisor in the training and development activity? Simply put, the supervisor has the sole responsibility to see that employees are trained to do their jobs. The person who does the training may vary, but the responsibility to see that it happens, and happens well, is the supervisor's. The supervisor's function is to see that training is recognized as a part of the natural development of the employee, not a nice thing that may or may not happen.

Controlling

Controlling serves two functions: (1) It tells us how well we're doing; and (2) it tells us what changes, if any, need to be made from what has happened. Supervisors have to see that controls exist, and that existing controls function. For example, if there is a budget, then the supervisor should always be watching to see whether the budget is being followed, and if not, finding out why not. Supervisors also need to see that information is forwarded up the line to middle management so any necessary action can be taken. Finally, supervisors have the job of feeding information to the workers to let them know how well they are doing with regard to controls.

Communicating

It is perhaps improper to speak of "communications" as a separate entity, requiring a separate role. A much better approach would be to describe the use of communicating skills in connection with the other skills we've been talking about. For example, we talk about training or controlling; most of that is done with some form of communication, either written or spoken. We use the word *feedback* frequently, and that's no more than one of the major requirements of good communicating. When we delegate something to someone, it is a matter of *telling* them what we want them to do, how we want it done, and what we will do to measure their performance. All that telling is just communicating at work. When we report the results of last month's production or sales or the number of customer complaints, we usually do it in *writing*. We may even include a memo or cover letter. That's *communicating*.

What, then, is the role of the supervisor in all of this? The supervisor's role is to see that things are understood, as opposed to just seeing that things are said or written. It isn't enough that we have fulfilled an obligation to write something to someone or to tell somebody something. Our job isn't finished just because someone *can* understand what we've written or spoken. It is our role as supervisors to see that what we communicate is *not misunderstood*. We have to devise ways of getting enough feedback to tell us that people do understand it. If we find ourselves saying to someone, "Don't you remember, I told you yesterday to do it this way?" we're out of our role. It isn't our job to exonerate ourselves by proving that something was said. It is our job to see that the message was actually received in the form and substance we wanted it to be received, and that the required action (if any) is taken.

Motivating Employees

What is the supervisor's role in getting employees excited about their jobs, about quality, about customer relations, about working together as a team? Easy question to answer: "Make it happen!" The answer is much easier than the action required to get things happening. There is much known about how to motivate people, but the main role of the supervisor is to accept the responsibility for the employees' behavior. If they aren't doing their jobs right, then the supervisor has the first role of counseling the employees, doing those things that provide motivation on the job, letting the employees know how we see their work, disciplining them as necessary, then moving them out of the organization if they don't meet the expectations of the organization.

The important thing to remember about motivation is that it is not the role of the supervisor to get rid of employees! To a large extent, it is a form of failure when an employee is fired after having been interviewed, selected and trained and then worked on a job for a while. Somebody, somewhere, most likely made a mistake: either we hired the wrong person, assigned the person to the wrong job, did our training poorly, or the person had a poor motivator for a boss! While it is obvious that not every employee is salvageable, nor is it worth it to salvage some of them, for every one we can get to be a productive, satisfied, motivated employee, we have saved the organization considerable time and money. And that's the role of the supervisor all the time!

Appraising and Assessing Potential

There are two parts to the appraising and assessing function, as the words suggest. First, we appraise how the employee is doing on the present assignment; then we speculate and formulate an idea of how the employee would do on another assignment, one different from the first. That's the role of supervisors in these activities: seeing that we know how an employee is doing and deciding how we think the employee will do on another job. It's a frightening but necessary job in many ways. Supervisors have a certain amount of power in their hands when they make a judgment as to how an employee is doing. Usually, such judgments go into records, they are in writing, they affect decisions about promotions, raises, and other forms of recognition. Whole families will be affected by the decisions made about how a person is doing or what the person's capabilities are. To the extent we are accurate, the organization prospers; to the extent we are wrong, both the organization and the employee suffer. The supervisor's role is one of striving for the highest degree of accuracy, based on as much reliable information as possible, then doing everything possible to document and validate the information. If appraisals are dreaded, it ought to be for the awesome responsibility, not the drudgery of the assignment.

CONCLUSION

There is a uniqueness about the job of supervisor. It is a different job than any other in the organization. The primary difference is in the roles that have to be played by supervisors. It is not a single-role assignment, but a many-faceted one. There are skills required to play the roles. There is a great deal hanging on the expertise with which these roles are played. Done poorly, not only does the organization suffer, but so do many people. Done well, great and wonderful things happen, and good impressions are made that last for years and years!

SECTION

2

PRESUPERVISORY CONSIDERATIONS

CHAPTER

2

PRESUPERVISORY TRAINING

BILL JOHNS
ROBERT A. ROCK

Proper preparation of employees to assume the duties and responsibilities of supervision is uncommon. Long-term rewards are available to the organization which, through presupervisory training, establishes good attitudes among its future supervisors. Learning to supervise people can be done on the job without presupervisory training, but it is mixed with the frustrations of job problems and the lack of experience in handling them effectively. One of the keys to such rewards is to conduct the training outside the normal pressures of the job. Once philosophies and techniques have been studied and experienced in the training environment, the opportunity to apply them on the job becomes less anxiety-packed.

PHILOSOPHY

Supervisory training in general is often undertaken with a view to presenting a certain volume of information to the trainees and assuming that they are somehow now "trained." But such thinking ignores the reality that we may not have trained them for reasons that are consistent with the trainees' reasons for learning and, therefore, like a stray arrow, the training misses the mark and fails to achieve its objective.

Presupervisory training philosophy should recognize the supervisor's position as a key link in an organization. Such training must be viewed as an investment and, as with any investment, plans laid and expectations clearly thought out as to what is expected from the investment.

A commitment to a presupervisory program should recognize that no amount of work gets done that is not done or controlled by people. Therefore, to insure the quality and quantity of work becomes the responsibility of the supervisor. To aim at excellence in the quality of supervision is a necessary step in developing a philosophy of presupervisory training. A training philosophy that is directed at the trainees' desire for self-fulfillment through the exercise of their authority as supervisors for the mutual benefit of the subordinates and the company must be made obvious to the trainees. Show them what's in it for them!

Training should make the supervisor's job *easier!*

DEVELOP A MODEL

Clearly the planning phase of the program is critical and should be done deliberately and should include the expertise of one with experience in the techniques of teaching, communicating, and dealing effectively with human nature.

Set Specific Objectives

As usual, we must begin by deciding what conditions we want to exist when the training is over. The objectives should be clear, meaningful, and measurable, and we should be able to visualize in our mind the way things will be at the end of the training when the trainee is promoted to a supervisory position. Objectives might include the following.

1. *Develop an Adequate Number of Employees Who Have Become Qualified for Promotion to a Supervisory Position.* The size of the group to be trained will depend on the anticipated needs of the organization for a specific period of time in the future, say, five years. Depending on conditions, the past five years may offer some guidance as to the needs of the next five years. The age and health of present supervisors and the growth or decline of business are factors that would be relevant to the size of the trainee group. The group should not be unrealistically large. If only 10 new supervisors are anticipated for the next five years, it would be wasteful and possibly demotivational to some to train 50 people. On the other hand, all trainees will not be successful in the training. Allowances should be made for dropouts and those who do not measure up to expectations during training.

2. *Provide a Source of Qualified Minorities and Females for Promotion to Supervisory Positions.* The program should result in the availability of trained minorities and females who can move into supervisory jobs as opportunities present themselves. Where compliance with legal standards have not been met in first-line supervisory personnel, it is desirable to include minorities and females in the trainee group in order to provide capable, high-quality candidates for supervisory vacancies.

3. *Increase the Effectiveness of First-Line Supervisors.* This may be done by: (1) reexamining the jobs and more clearly defining the primary responsibilities; (2) designing the training to develop specific skills needed to perform the jobs; and (3) including both principles of supervising and "how-to-do" techniques in the training to maximize the ability to apply the skills on the job.

Develop Measures for the Objectives

In order to determine whether the training has been effective, we must have some method of determining if our objectives have been achieved. The question is: what are the trainees able to do after the training? Can they express relevant policies; plan for effective use of manpower; effectively trouble-shoot operational problems; sift through information to uncover relevant facts in investigations; listen to ideas of others, including subordinates; administer discipline fairly to one and all; motivate subordinates by making the job itself more meaningful to them? These are some of the measures of the effectiveness of a supervisor. While they can all be summed up by the question, "Can the supervisor get the job done well, safely, and willingly through others?" we need to be more specific than that in setting measures for the objectives.

Trainees should be tested at various times during the period of training. Questions should be designed to test the trainees' knowledge of matters that they must know to be effective supervisors; they should not be academic questions. Some trainers will tell the trainees what questions will be asked on a test as a means of emphasizing the importance of some matters over others. The logic of this is that it is important for the trainee to learn, and if this method causes the trainee to "latch on" to certain concepts, then the objectives are met.

Performance appraisals of trainees during training are another effective way of measuring progress toward objectives. These appraisals should be realistic, factual, and, wherever possible, encouraging.

Construct Supervisor Job Analysis

The supervisor's job must be analyzed in terms of the major and minor responsibilities in order to determine the content of the training. Does the job require the supervisor to train, hire, discipline, and evaluate subordinates? Then the program should include sessions on techniques of training, interviewing, investigating, and so forth. Left to their own devices, new supervisors could find themselves in serious trouble in each of these major responsibility areas if they have not had some advance training in these skills. In approaching the task of analyzing the job, care should be taken not to live in the past, but to anticipate changes in the work environment, in technology, in work force size and makeup, as well as any other changes that may occur in the future. Our aim is to improve the caliber of future supervisors over those of the past.

Design Training Program Content

The content of the program may vary depending on local circumstances, but there are certain subjects that are important to a supervisor in practically any circumstance.

1. *The Organization.* All supervisors (thus presupervisory trainees) should be knowledgeable about how the organization is structured, who the key managers are in each department, what the basic functions are of each department and how their units' activities fit into the whole picture, the management philosophy of the organization if there is one (and if one does not exist, top management should develop one and communicate it to all levels of management), the organization's specific objectives, and any other general information about the organization.

2. *Accident Prevention.* The most effective tool for supervisors to use to establish good labor relations, productivity, efficiency, longevity, and cost reduction is accident prevention. Properly administered with generous amounts of patience, accident prevention is the ideal avenue open to supervisors to demonstrate a true, caring concern for the well-being of employees both on and off the job. The objective is to create a climate in which employees respond positively to the supervisor.

3. *OSHA (Occupational Safety and Health Act).* Supervisors must know how their actions, or failure to act, can adversely affect their organizations, how inspections are conducted, and what to do or say if an OSHA inspector shows up.

4. *Unions.* Whether an organization is unionized or not, supervisors should be aware of the company's attitude toward unions and what is expected of the first-line supervisor in dealing with the union, or what his or her role is in maintaining a non-union status.

5. *Equal Employment.* If first-line supervisors have a role in the employment process, they should be thoroughly trained in

the legalities of dealing with applicants for employment. If first-line supervisors are not involved in the employment process, they should be thoroughly trained in the pitfalls of discriminatory activities in the day-to-day routine of a supervisor, including their responsibility to support the organization's affirmative action plan. Failure to insure that supervisors are effective in this area can be very costly and time consuming.

6. *Fringe Benefits.* Most employees have short memories or a limited ability to remember provisions of the organization's benefits package. First-line supervisors should seek to develop a reputation among their employees that they are the ones who can answer questions or can get an answer. Being effective in this way tends to reduce the employees' dependence on a third party such as a union. Therefore, supervisors must have at least a general knowledge of the benefits package and know where to get specific answers.

7. *The Supervisor's Role.* Supervisors need to develop many different skills in order to carry out their role as supervisor, and among the first things they must learn is the role of the supervisor. It may sound strange, but it is critical for trainees to have spelled out for them just what their role will be. Most presupervisory trainees have been "doers" all their lives. Now they must be effective in getting the job done through others. In order for supervisors to get the job done through others they will need training in communication, performance appraisal, leadership, motivation, interviewing, discipline, and how to train their workers for successful performance. Obviously, each of these skills could be a chapter in itself.

Design Methods of Training

The conduct of training is as important as the content. If supervisors get bored with the training they receive, they may conclude that being a supervisor is going to be boring. Presupervisory training can be exciting and filled with expectations. Just as small children can be prepared to eagerly look forward to starting school, or can dread the idea, so too can presupervisory trainees be prepared.

Training sessions should be crisp, snappy, versatile, and comfortable. The alternate use of films, chalkboard (or easel board), slides, lecture, and discussion will help to insure this interest. Meetings do not necessarily have to be short, but they should not become endurance tests. One-hour training sessions are not likely to produce much learning. Sessions lasting four to six hours provide time for in-depth discussion of major skill areas.

Above all, training sessions should be designed with the trainees in mind, and this means their active participation where the opportunity to make discoveries is programmed into each training session. Retention of knowledge or information is improved when the trainee "makes a discovery." Pride is involved.

Rome wasn't built in a day and we do not develop good supervisors overnight. Five-day training programs designed to cover soup to nuts have for the most part been a waste of company money and employees' time. The objective is to teach a new way of life, and this will take time. If we are unwilling to invest a year or two in the training and development of people who may be supervisors for the next 20 or 30 years, we may be burdened with mediocrity at best and inefficiency and failure at worst.

Develop Qualifications for Trainers

A poor trainer is not likely to produce well-trained supervisors. Therefore, care should be taken to insure that all trainers are well qualified. This means knowing the subject with authority, being able to communicate their knowledge to the trainees, possessing patience in dealing with those who may be slower learners, possessing some significant enthusiasm about their subjects, and being able to secure feedback from trainees to determine if learning is taking place.

Trainees are typically critical of trainers who don't know their subjects, who are dry and speak in a monotone, and who don't seem to care what the trainees think. So major attention should be given to developing or securing well-qualified trainers.

One trainer may not be knowledgeable in all of the skill areas that go into the content of the program, and therefore several trainers may be needed. Team teaching has much to recommend it, including the change of pace it affords the trainees and the improved quality of training due to the use of specialists in different skill areas.

Trainers should remember that trainees may not be familiar with technical or slang terms common to the trainer. Simple, understandable language by the trainers will earn the gratitude of those they are leading; at the same time the trainers need not be concerned that they are talking over the heads of those who may learn more slowly.

Trainers should have enough managerial experience to be able to speak with some authority. Where possible, trainers should be exposed to a seminar or training session designed to acquaint them with *effective* training techniques. Knowing the subject and understanding good training techniques do not necessarily come packaged with the same experience.

Unless a trainer has significant experience in developing training materials, it is better to have this function done by someone with expertise. Failure to have well-developed and well-coordinated materials may result in little or no change in behavior among the trainees. The preparation of training materials should be done with one eye on how attractive the material is to trainees, and the other eye on the behavior expected at the conclusion of the training.

Select Trainers

Several characteristics share top billing when selecting trainers. Interest, desire, and knowledge are critical. To *want* to perform this task as opposed to *having* to will be very obvious to trainees. Trainers who are pressed into service against their wills will waste a good deal of the company's money, and no change in behavior is likely among trainees.

As mentioned earlier, knowledge of the subject is critical. It may become necessary to have several trainers in order to have someone speaking with authority on every subject. The schedule should be arranged so that trainers do not feel the pressures of their normal duties and therefore hurry through the material so they can get back to their jobs. In selecting trainers it is desirable for trainers to see the task as an opportunity for them to spread their knowledge and expertise among others and thereby create for themselves a great deal of job satisfaction. There is much truth in the old saw that "if the student hasn't learned, the teacher hasn't taught." Thus, the selection of trainers becomes one of the first priorities in any training program. Long-range thinking should be applied here. The best material in the nicest environment is not likely to produce changed behavior among trainees if a poor trainer is at the helm.

Develop Qualifications for Participants (Trainees)

There must be some standards used in the selection of participants in a presupervisory program. In order to steer clear of any charges of discrimination, the criteria for participation should be readily attainable by minorities and females, though not necessarily *all* minorities and *all* females.

1. *Minimum Service Requirement.*   It may be desirable to have a minimum service requirement so that the trainee has some basic knowledge of the operation upon which to build. Knowledge of the jobs in this operation is important if this candidate is a potential supervisor of the area.

2. *Present Performance.*   While good operators do not necessarily make good supervisors, something can be learned about the candidates by a thorough look at what kind of performance they have given on their present and past jobs. Have they been conscientious about production, cost, quality, safety, and people? Have they demonstrated a willingness to listen to others? Have they shown any interest or ability in solving problems, both people and operating? Do they have even temperaments? Have they shown any signs of leadership? Have people followed their suggestions even though they had no authority? Have they been able to demonstrate a fairness that does not permit undesirable or illegal discriminations? Is their performance improving rather than showing no progress? What have they done to indicate there is something of the self-starter in them? Have they engaged in any self-development activities such as night school or correspondence courses?

These are some of the questions that might be asked to uncover what qualities each candidate for training might have. The responses will probably give some indication as to their desires to become supervisors.

3. *Attendance.*   When selecting trainees, attendance should be considered. A poor attendance record in the past will not be a particularly positive recommendation for the future. However, care should be exercised to fairly evaluate past attendance records.

4. *Emotional Stability.*   A prime requirement for a supervisory training candidate is emotional stability. Do candidates sound off at the drop of a hat? Do unimportant things upset them? Are they easily confused by excitement? Are they moody? Do they exercise any discretion in considering who is present when they "sound-off"? Where are their loyalties? Of course, evaluation of some of the responses to these questions will be subjective, but in many cases there is a clear record that is very helpful in evaluating a candidate.

Design Participant Promotion Policy

Obviously, if considerable time and money is to be spend on pre-supervisory training, there should be some plan for utilizing those who demonstrate greater potential. While no guarantees can or should be given to the participants, a policy of promoting from within should be spelled out in a formal policy. This is important both to the trainees and to provide policy guidance to the organization's managers who are responsible for selecting first-line supervisors. Nothing is as discouraging to a good trainee as to have a supervisory vacancy filled by someone not in the presupervisory training or hired from outside the organization. (Later in this chapter we will deal with the manager's role in selecting trainees.)

Participants should be utilized as substitute supervisors in cases of vacation relief and on other occasions when regular supervisors are absent.

Develop Policy for Participant Replacement

In the event that one or more of the original trainees should drop out of the program for any reason, it may be necessary to decide whether to replace them with new trainees. This may be considered at the time of initial selection. One method would be to select several alternates. However, the matter of whether to make a replacement may depend on how far the training has progressed. The program content and its arrangement may dictate that a second class be started at a later date. Ordinarily, the material would build on itself as the training unfolds, and if a replacement trainee comes into the program at the halfway point, his or her comprehension of some of the material probably would suffer from having missed some basic concepts covered earlier.

As indicated earlier, dropouts should be anticipated in determining the size of the original class. This should minimize the need to consider replacements.

Design Process to Select Participants

If a promotion policy is developed which requires promotion from within, and then only from among presupervisory trainees, the process of selecting trainees becomes critical. It becomes a preliminary selection of your next first-line supervisors.

Depending on the organization's status in its efforts to comply with equal employment laws, it is well to insure that the selection process yields an appropriate number of female and minority trainees. This may be partly accomplished by making provision for employees to nominate themselves. Candidates should also be nominated by the supervisory force.

Nominees should be interviewed by the coordinator of the presupervisory training program to determine their interest and potential. Further, if the company policy is for immediate supervisors to make the final decision as to whom they hire or promote, then consultation between the coordinator and the manager of the unit in which the candidate now works is essential. This amounts to the hiring supervisor affirming that the presupervisory candidate would be an acceptable candidate for a permanent first-line supervisory vacancy in that manager's unit. Failure to have this commitment from a unit manager could result in accepting candidates into the presupervisory training program who are unacceptable to their managers for a supervisory vacancy in the future. In short, this agreement on candidates for training tends to eliminate conflict when a permanent vacancy occurs.

Select Participants

Participants should now be selected using a consistent set of objective requirements. In order to avoid any legal conflicts, it is wise to document the reason why each successful applicant was chosen and why each unsuccessful applicant was not chosen. This administrative procedure will tend to minimize the subjective reasoning in the selection process.

If the training is designed to provide supervisory candidates for a wide geographical area, such as statewide, it would be well to have trainees from across the area. If a prediction can be made with a high degree of accuracy as to where vacancies will occur for first-line supervisors in the future, this would give guidance as to the number of trainees to pick from each part of the area. If the training is for one location, such as a local plant, this becomes unnecessary, except that you may want to have a good distribution of trainees from among the various departments.

Trainees should be notified in writing that they have been selected. The notice should provide details as to starting date, time, place, and length of the training session. The supervisors of the successful candidates for training should receive similar information. The more information the supervisory force has concerning the training activity of their own employees, the more support the training effort will receive.

Begin Training

Since there is much truth in the old adage that first impressions are lasting, every effort should be made to see that the training begins in such a way as to clearly communicate to the participants that we are to be involved in a major undertaking which could have a favorable impact on their whole career.

Several areas are important if the trainer is to get things started on a positive note. First he or she should create a friendly, informal atmosphere which encourages two-way communication. This task falls to the trainer and unless the trainer causes it to exist, it probably will not happen. Second, the seriousness of the program should be emphasized. The plant manager, or other top executive, should be invited to welcome the trainees and to voice his or her support for this milestone in the trainees' working lives. The trainer should emphasize the importance of regular attendance, even to the point of asking trainees to schedule vacations around the training sessions. A standard of attendance should be established which would be required for successful completion of the program. The sessions should begin and end on time according to the established schedule. A schedule of the entire program, giving dates, time, place, and subjects of the session should be given to each participant.

It should be remembered at all times that the trainees are not participating for the purpose of doing the organization a favor. They are there in hopes that there is "something in it for them." Any of a number of tactics can be used to make this point. One very successful approach is for the trainer to tell the class that they will not be expected to accept everything they see and hear in the class just because the trainer said it or they saw it in a film. Rather, they should ask themselves this question about the material being covered: "Is this the way I would like to be managed?" The trainees should be told that if the answer is "yes," they will be expected to accept the principle under discussion and adopt it as a guide to how they would supervise others. There are other approaches, but this is one.

The Classroom

Many of the participants will be uncomfortable in a classroom environment because they are accustomed to physical activity rather than strictly mental activity. Therefore, the trainer is challenged to "keep it lively" and at the same time not go too fast. Using a variety of teaching aids will greatly aid in this problem: easel-board flip charts using colored ink pens, films, lectures (brief ones), individual tasks, small group tasks, and role-playing. These all tend to be very educational when compared to straight lecturing.

The length of each session is a matter of individual consideration. Two- to three-hour sessions would probably be a minimum. Six-hour sessions broken by a lunch break are not too long. However, "soaking" time is important. Week-long sessions of eight-hour days usually do not accomplish much. But one day per month gives time to apply or experience the subjects discussed in class. *Don't get in too big of a hurry to finish the training.* Remember you are training would-be lifelong supervisors! You can afford to be deliberate! Much training money is wasted in haste.

A session should not run more than one and one-half hours without a brief (five- or ten-minute) break.

Opinions vary, but small groups of 10 or 12 trainees offer a better opportunity for one-on-one guidance. With a group this size it is easy to arrange the classroom so that everyone can see everyone else. Ideal is the "V" (or inverted "V") with the open, or wide, part of the "V" at the front.

The quality of the meeting place, of the chairs, tables, materials, and of the trainer will reflect the quality of supervisors you are expecting to turn out.

The classroom should also be a place of encouragement. The trainer will have many opportunities to correct or disagree with opinions and responses by the participants, but encouraging them to "think further" or "tell me more" rather than showing up their faults will be very encouraging to the trainees.

The trainer should always be guilty of repetition when it comes to major points. He or she should find occasions to repeat the principle in session after session and within sessions. Much learning and remembering takes place the second and third time around.

The language of the classroom should reflect the environment the trainees work in; that is, terminology and examples should be relevant to the trainee's workplace, not to some other industry.

On-the-Job Practice

Some way should be found to provide on-the-job experience for the trainees at some point in the program. Vacation relief, illness relief, and so forth are good opportunities for practical experience. If this is not possible, then the trainees should be given an assignment to work with a first-line supervisor from time to time.

Evaluate Training Effectiveness

It is at this point that probably more training dollars are wasted than any other place. We train people with the expectation that people are going to learn something about supervising people and that there will be a change in behavior which reflects this new knowledge. Several methods of evaluating the training are suggested.

1. *Testing.* To inform the trainees that there will be periodic tests helps to establish a certain accountability on the part of trainees. Failure to test would normally leave them with the idea that this is just another training program.

Test questions should be especially relevant to the trainee if he or she becomes a supervisor. Testing for purely academic reasons risks discrimination charges if minority, female, or older trainees do poorly on the tests. But if the test questions reflect the reality of a supervisor's day-to-day job, you are improving your basis for selection later.

One tactic used in testing to help insure learning and to give appropriate emphasis to things that are important and definitely should be learned, is for the instructor to indicate during the training certain things the class can expect to see on a test. The trainee is likely to take better notes on these items and study them carefully for the tests. Repeating important questions on subsequent tests also reflects their importance.

In considering this approach to testing, it should be remembered that the instructor is not in a contest with the trainees. Rather the idea is for the trainees to *learn!* If they recognize the importance of certain material and thus study and remember it better, then the goal is achieved.

2. *Opinion Surveys.* Before-and-after opinion surveys are helpful in determining whether the trainees are making the transition from hourly employees to management. Professional assistance should be retained in the development of an appropriate opinion survey. By all means, the responses should be anonymous! You are looking at the training and how the group responds.

3. *Individual Participation.* Unless the trainer is receiving feedback during the training session, he or she is missing a very important tool in evaluation. This in-class tool allows the trainer to detect how the individual trainee is thinking and reasoning and what changes are taking place in his or her process of reasoning. This is one reason for keeping the class size small.

4. *Training Aids.* The trainer should be tuned-in to the trainees to such an extent that he or she senses which type of training aids and tactics the trainees are most responsive to and thus are most effective. The trainer should maintain flexibility in order to use those aids that are affecting learning and retention the most positively.

Post-Training Development

When the classroom training is completed, it is almost normal to think that "school is out" and to pay little or no attention to the trainees. However, opportunities should be provided for self-development activities such as outside courses, subscriptions, mailing-list articles on specific supervisory subjects such as safety, discipline, budgeting, and so forth. This gives an additional opportunity to evaluate the trainee in terms of his or her initiative.

The post-classroom training should include an in-depth tour of the whole facility so that these candidates for supervisory jobs have an appreciation and understanding of the whole process and how one unit's work fits into the whole.

Promotion to Supervisory Jobs

It should be remembered that the newly promoted first-line supervisor is still a rookie and needs guidance. This is best done by the immediate supervisor of the first-line supervisor. This is a time for understanding and assistance and patience.

WORKING WITH UNIONS

While the union is not a partner as such in this activity, it is very desirable to have the support of union leadership. Therefore, informational meetings early in the process are important. Failure to have them may result in resistance that could torpedo the project.

Before the selection of participants begins, the training process and objectives should be explained to the union leaders, and their ideas and suggestions solicited. Requesting the support of the leadership will normally be a positive factor in giving the program widespread appeal. The leadership should understand that they may even consider self-nomination, if not otherwise nominated by managers. The union leadership could also be influential in encouraging self-nomination of its members. The more competition that develops to "be selected," the better.

What happens in the classroom will inevitably find its way back to the union leadership. Therefore, the content of the classes should be realistic, honest, and straightforward, conveying the message that first-line supervisors are not taught to be the opponents of unions, that good human relations does not involve secrets, and that the training reflects a philosophy that recognizes the dignity of the individual, the importance of work and production in the economic system, and the challenge that supervision offers to those who choose to move up the economic ladder.

SPECIAL
CONSIDERATIONS

3

MANAGING IN THE FEDERAL SECTOR

IRWIN SCHERMAN

Two supervisors were engaged in a rather heated discussion over whose job was more difficult—the one supervising in a unionized industry in the private sector or the one supervising in a large federal agency. Finally, one turned to the other and said, "Look, you'll never understand how hard it is to get things done when you really can't control your people. They just about laugh in my face if I say I'm going to have them fired. They know about all the red tape I have to go through, and chances are that someone up in personnel will come up with a dozen reasons why it can't be done!"

Do you know which of the two supervisors made those comments? It's probably a matter of perspective, since most supervisors in either of the two work environments have either heard or made similar statements and can relate to them quite well. The truth of the matter is that as we moved away from a simple entrepreneurial society—the mom-and-pop grocery store with three or four employees—into one containing large multinational corporations plus a large federal sector with about three million employees, management has seen its right of "absolute discretion" disappear. The reasons these changes have occurred are due to many sociological, economical, and psychological factors. The purpose of this chapter is not to try to understand how we got where we are, or, as a society, whether we are better or worse for it; rather, the intent is to accept the fact that federal managers work within the framework of a system established by Congress in the form of law, by the Office of Personnel Management (OPM) in the form of regulation, or under the watchful eye of a union which has won concessions at the bargaining table.

Each of us has our personal opinion of how good or bad any constraint is, and I don't choose to argue the goods and bads, or strengths and weaknesses of federal personnel law. Instead, I offer this advice: Forget about your personal likes and dislikes; accept the fact it is the system in which you as a federal manager must operate; spend the necessary time to learn it so it doesn't consume you, and, in turn, make it work for you. The following pages will address some of the major areas of personnel management and highlight problems that managers frequently encounter in each area. I'll try to offer some insight into each of these areas—things as a manager that you *can* do! Hopefully, with some additional insight you won't feel quite as constrained or restricted in carrying out your role as a manager of people. The most effective supervisors I have encountered have two things in common: first, they don't spend their time crying about the system and how frustrating it is; and secondly, they know, understand, and employ the many facets of federal personnel management—use the rewards and motivators—and enjoy the respect, confidence, and loyalty of their employees.

Now, let's take a look at that multifaceted term *personnel man-*

agement in the federal sector and see if we can identify ways to make its execution easier.

GETTING YOUR PEOPLE HIRED

Probably the three areas that are managers' greatest sources of frustration with "the system" and the personnel office are hiring, firing, and pay. The frequent lament is: "I can't hire who I want. I have to take from their list of people when they *finally* get around to sending me names. If I pick someone who doesn't work out, they won't let me fire the person, and when I get someone who really is good, they won't let me upgrade the job to keep the person. So any way you cut it, as a supervisor I lose!" If things were really that way I guess I'd say: "Okay, let's pack it in. Turn on the gas and stick our heads in the oven." At times the system can seem quite formidable, as if designed to hinder rather than help. So while hiring in the federal sector is not as simple as going down to some local gathering place where people looking for work congregate, pointing to three people and saying, "You're hired! Welcome to the federal work force," or as simple as just putting up a sign in your window saying "Clerk Wanted," a great deal of managerial frustration can be eliminated with some understanding of the basics of recruitment.

As a supervisor, you have a great deal of effect on the amount of time your positions stay vacant and the quality of people referred to you for consideration. As a supervisor you want the very best candidates referred to you when recruiting to fill a position. How can you insure that this happens? How can you have input to the referral process at the beginning and not just at the end as the selecting official? By taking the time and becoming involved! The relatively small investment you make up front can pay big dividends in assuring that you get to consider the right—by your standards—people to fill your jobs.

The filling of any job in the federal sector is the result of people applying in response to an announcement. What is in the announcement will determine in large measure the qualifications possessed by the people applying and ultimately referred. All federal agencies are required to have crediting plans which contain job-related criteria, that is, the skills, knowledge and abilities (KSAs) that would be possessed by an individual likely to succeed in the job you are trying to fill. As the supervisor over that position, you know what your expectations are of that position, which means that you are in the best position to know and describe the desired KSAs, not a staffing specialist in the personnel office who may only have a peripheral understanding of your job's requirements. Confer with the staffing specialist and insist that *your* requirements are spelled out in the announcement, not just the minimum qualifications that the specialist extracts from an OPM handbook, or KSAs from another job that has the same title as yours but may be quite different. For example, personnel staffing specialists are placed in the GS-212 series. Yet some perform at the operating level and do the actual hiring, while others occupy staff jobs and are concerned more with program management and development. So while each is in the GS-212 series, the qualities needed for successful performance could and in fact are quite different. If you're content to leave it to others to determine what your needs are, you have little reason to complain if you don't get applicants with the quality you're seeking.

Rule number two, *don't*, repeat *don't*, subscribe to the old axiom, "A warm body is better than nobody at all." If you stacked the bodies of supervisors who bought into that poor bit of logic and later came to regret it on top of each other, it's doubtful if the Empire State Building could hold them all. Poor selections made in haste to fill a job not only don't satisfy your requirement to get a job done, but prove counterproductive since the supervisor inevitably must then deal with a performance problem. Unless your agency has some unique regulation, you don't have to hire from the first or any other numbered referral list that is provided. In filling jobs, most agencies will first utilize their internal merit promotion policy. This allows present agency personnel to have first consideration for a job being filled. The key word here is "consideration." As a general rule, no one has any entitlement to a job. So, if you are given a referral list containing only internal candidates and after reviewing their qualifications and interviewing them you don't feel you have the right match for your job, *return* the list and tell the personnel office to reannounce the job and make a wider search. Repeat the process until *you* are satisfied that you have the right person for the job. It takes more time, but you will be much happier in the long run.

As noted earlier, supervisors and managers complain bitterly about the time it takes to hire a new person. One agency has a goal of 60 days for the personnel office to fill nonprofessional job vacancies. Thus, on the one hand your personnel office can take pride if it is filling jobs on an average of 45 days; but for you as a supervisor, 45 days without someone to do a particular job can put a large burden on you and the others in your organization. On the other hand, the personnel office is required to perform a number of legitimate functions, that is, review the job for accuracy and currency, advertise the position (usually a minimum of two weeks), rate and rank candidates (a time-consuming process, particularly when 25 or more people have applied for the vacancy), prepare a referral list, allow time for the supervisor to interview and arrange for a release date, and handle any other problems that may crop up along the way. So what's the answer? Grit your teeth and bear it? No, there are some very positive steps that you as a supervisor can take to materially shorten the time your position is vacant.

For starters, try to anticipate vacancies. No, you're not expected to have a crystal ball. But frequently you can be well down the road—if not all the way—to filling your job by the time it is vacated. It takes some preplanning but doesn't require crystal-ball gazing. Have you ever had the spouse of a military member as an employee? Most military people rotate on a three year basis and receive orders for their new duty assignment as much as six months in advance. There is nothing wrong with asking these employees to let you know when their spouse has orders and approximately when they will be departing. You can initiate an "anticipated recruitment" action at that time, even four or five months in advance, without knowing the exact date your present employee will be leaving. This affords the personnel office plenty of lead time to find good candidates and avoids your feeling that you need to make a quick selection to fill your vacancy (you know, the "warm body" syndrome). You can proceed with all the steps, up to actual selection, without even knowing when your job will actually be vacant. When you find that out, you only need to formalize the selection; the release date is set, your present employee can depart on Friday, and the replacement can arrive Monday morning. It sounds almost too simple to work, but it does. Try it! Better yet, if your budget allows, you may even be able to bring your new employee on board a week or two before the present incumbent departs to provide for on-the-job training by your present employee.

This approach isn't limited only to dealing with spouses of military personnel. What about the individuals who announce in January that they plan to retire by the end of the year? Or the female who announces her pregnancy and further indicates that she will be resigning when the baby arrives? Or maybe the situation where you find yourself completing supervisory appraisals for excellent employees who are looking to further their careers, and you know it's only a matter of time until they are selected for promotion to a higher grade? These are just some of the situations where you can do a pretty reasonable job of anticipating vacancies. You might be thinking, "But what if my employee doesn't leave, then what?" No problem. Just tell the personnel office to cancel the action. No selection was made, no job was committed.

Two other areas that warrant consideration in helping to acquire and retain a quality work force are the labor market for the jobs you typically need to have filled, and the turnover rate you experience. Let's look at a "worst case" situation. Suppose that you are in charge of a section in a finance office and have 20 GS-5 accounting technicians. Another agency right down the street also has accounting technician jobs, but those are graded GS-6. The labor market is very healthy, so people aren't banging down your door for those GS-5 accounting technician jobs. Because of the agency with the higher grades down the street and the competitive nature of the labor market, you find yourself with a 25% annual turnover rate. You're losing one out of every four employees, and every four years you've completely turned over your work force. You find yourself constantly telling your boss—who is constantly telling you, "We need more, quicker"—that the turnover is killing you. No sooner do you hire someone, get them trained, and producing, then they up and leave for higher grades somewhere else.

On the surface it seems like a hopeless situation. Stability in an organization is important; it builds continuity, fosters a spirit of team work, and enhances productivity. High turnover rates demoralize an organization. Employees develop a "so what" attitude. Management tends only to look at solving today's problems, paying little if any attention to long-range planning. The focus is on the here-and-now. Get the work out! Get the job done now! In fact, one questions if the word *organization* is actually the right word to describe the entity, since *organization* usually implies some degree of cohesiveness.

What, then, can managers do in this situation? Obviously, one option is to do nothing and continue to tread water, hoping that the tide will change. That's usually about as effective as hoping that the agency down the street with those GS-6s will close up or move out of town. Not too likely. A second option is to oppose the people in the personnel office who are responsible for classifying the jobs: "Can't they understand what they're doing to me? They just don't understand our situation." Chances are the personnel office has looked at those GS-5 jobs time and time again and concluded that the level of work just isn't there to support a higher grade. A realization that many managers find difficult to accept is that there are other organizations that perform work at a higher level than their organization does. Two different organizations may be equally busy, but it's level of difficulty that drives the classification train. You may not like the classification system or agree with how the standards for a particular series are written, but, in reality, how much impact are you going to have to get a classification standard changed? Supervisors should follow a basic law that says: "I won't expend my time, effort, or energy on areas where I cannot effect change. Rather, I will channel my attention into those areas where I can make meaningful change occur."

You may be thinking that we've strayed afield from the basic problem—getting and hanging on to a work force—but we haven't. It's just that experience has shown that many managers feel they are limited to two courses of action when faced with the problem of hiring and retaining a work force—do nothing, or oppose classifiers—and they end up with no change in their situation. How about expending some energy in a positive direction that may well produce some positive net results?

For starters, accept the fact that your jobs are GS-5 and the ones down the street are GS-6. Accept the fact that you will probably lose a certain percentage of your staff each year to those GS-6 jobs. You can't change or control that. What you can change and control is who you hire and what they do. Rarely, at any grade level, do people spend all 40 hours performing duties at the grade for which they are paid. In other words, your GS-5s aren't all performing GS-5 level work 100% of the time. Chances are they may be spending as much as 30% of their time on GS-3 or GS-4 level work. It's normal and happens with all jobs. And because the work is parceled out in this fashion, managers automatically assume they must have only GS-5s to get the job done.

Be honest now and think for a minute: when was the last time you sat down and took a personal look at how many hours those GS-5s spend on work that truly requires GS-5 level skills and abilities? Have you been too busy fighting classification standards which you *can't* change, instead of looking at work assignments which you *can* change?

We began discussing this hypothetical situation by saying there were 20 people in the unit. That equals 800 hours of work per week. If we discover that 30% of the work—240 hours—is at a level not requiring GS-5 skills, that equals six people who can be GS-3s or GS-4s. If we can break down the work into GS-3 and GS-4 components, our organization might now show three GS-3s, three GS-4s and 14 GS-5s. This is a totally different organizational structure than what we started with, and the benefits should start to become apparent. Our GS-5s are now doing the highest level work for which they are being paid and it's a safe bet they are finding their jobs more interesting. (See if anything happens with your sick leave rate). You now have a career ladder built into your organization: the GS-3s have promotion potential to the GS-4 level and the GS-4s have promotion potential to the GS-5 level. You have also now created some in-house resources to fill future vacancies, which greatly reduces the time to accom-

TABLE 3.1
Salary Dollars

Present Structure
20 GS = 5s, step 4, @ $14,707 = $294,140

Proposed Structure
14 GS = 5s, step 4, @ $14,708 = $205,898
 3 GS = 4s, step 4, @ $13,143 = $ 39,429
 3 GS = 3s, step 4, @ $11,710 $ 35,130
                                 $280,457
Reduction in salary costs = $14,683

plish future recruitment. This approach may not stop the turnover problem entirely, but it will slow it down dramatically and afford the organization a much higher degree of stability and continuity.

Another factor to consider is salary dollars. Your organization is budgeted for 20 GS-5s. For budgeting purposes the fourth step of the GS-5 grade level is normally used. Currently, that's $14,707 per employee, or $294,140 for the unit. But look at Table 3.1 and see what happens under the revised structure. The new structure results in a savings of $14,683 annually to accomplish the same amount of work. With most federal government organizations, the staffing levels are never enough. If that's the case with your unit, just think of the selling power you now have to hire an additional person. Your restructuring means you can have another person in your unit—2087 hours of work—without spending any more money than your agency has budgeted for you right now. And there's even more opportunity to fully utilize your budgeted salary dollars if you're willing to take the time to look at your turnover rate.

In our initial example we said the organization was experiencing a 25% turnover rate. That means that five people must be replaced each year. A reasonable assumption is that in a strong labor market (a seller's market—plenty of jobs available) it would take the personnel office 70 days to fill each vacancy. Some simple arithmetic shows that's 350 days of vacancy, when no budgeted dollars are being used to pay salary. Are you letting those dollars sit there going unused while you're fighting the system? Let's hope not. Put those dollars to use by hiring an extra person. Even when you have all 20 spaces filled, you should be actively recruiting to fill a twenty-first space based on your past turnover rate. The people in your comptroller's office, or wherever the purse strings are held in the organization, will have little to quibble over if you request that additional person and are able to demonstrate how he or she can be paid. This procedure is commonly known as "utilizing hire lag." And through its use, we now have the services of 20 people for a full year and have actually increased productive hours by 2087.

In looking to restructure the organization, you don't have to do this on your own. Help is available. Remember those classifiers in the personnel office that you used to take issue with, the ones who didn't understand your situation? Well, they're really not bad folks. Ask them to come over and sit down with you and help you restructure your organization, assist you in identifying the GS-3 and GS-4 level work. Tell them you want to establish some lower-graded positions to provide for intake and career progression. You'll think you're dealing with a totally different group of classifiers. (The truth is you're not, it's just *your* perspective that has changed.) Instead of opposing these people, you're now asking them to share with you some of their professional expertise. You're recognizing them as being able to make a positive contribution to your organization. You'll find in most cases they will jump at the opportunity to show you that they want to and can help. They will identify for you the various levels of work being performed and provide you with assistance in developing new position descriptions at the various grade levels. So instead of clashing with a staff resource, you've put it to work for you, rather than against you.

You'll also notice a difference in the service you receive from the staffing specialist who serves your organization. Few things are more frustrating to a staffing specialist than to keep filling and keep filling the same positions over and over and over again. When the staffing specialist sees that you are trying to help yourself by anticipating vacancies, restructuring your positions to allow for entry-level hiring, and looking at turnover rates and utilizing hire lag, how can the staffing specialist help but think, "Now there is a supervisor who is trying to resolve a problem and get the organization on its best footing. I really want to help that person all I can." When that staffing specialist gets inundated with recruitment actions and has to decide which ones to pursue first, care to guess who gets the priority?

Supervisors involved with this style of management are soon recognized as shrewd money managers. Top management, involved with deciding how the agency's money gets distributed, can't help but take notice of supervisors who achieve greater productivity with no increase in costs. Those supervisors make everyone in the agency look good! And when those supervisors say, "I need more money in next year's budget and with it I can accomplish the following," you can be sure that their requests fall on sympathetic ears. If there is more money to be had, you know who's going to get it. The examples shown above are not just nice theoretical concepts. They are practical approaches to solving common problems experienced by large numbers of supervisors in the federal sector. They are regularly employed by those supervisors who tend to get the best appraisals, the monetary awards, and ultimately the promotions. They are creative solutions employed by supervisors who have long ago figured out, that they won't fight the system, but will learn it.

Who Do I Pick for the Job?

We've discussed the hiring process and the benefits that can be achieved through restructuring. One familiar question frequently asked is, "How do I know which person I should select for the job?"

While perhaps falling short of being the "perfect system," the system used to screen and qualify applicants for a federal position is considerably more sophisticated than that employed in the private sector, in many instances. Yes, we all know the story of employees who are told they don't meet the qualifications for a higher-graded job in their office. The boss and the employee come screaming into the personnel office complaining: "How can you say he or she isn't qualified? They've been doing the job for the last two months since it's been vacant. I don't care what the OPM standards say about needing so many years of formal education to qualify for the series this position is in, I'm telling you they're doing the job and doing it well." And they may well be. However, if the personnel specialist suggests that perhaps the job is misclassified, that it doesn't really require the services of a professional in the particular field and should approrpiately be placed in the technician series, and probably be reduced in grade accordingly, the conversation usually ends up with the supervisor offering one last thought about either the bureaucrats in the personnel office, the bureaucrats at OPM, or the bureaucracy in general (sometimes, if on a good roll, the supervisor will include all three). The point here is not to delight in supervisory frustration—as a supervisor, I empathize more often than not—but rather to emphasize that there is a well-defined, well-thought-out and, in the overwhelming majority of cases, efficient system to insure that the individuals referred do possess the technical expertise necessary to perform the jobs for which they're hired.

When dealing with a work force of almost three million people, such structure is a necessity. Without it, we would have little more than the "spoils system," and chaos would reign. So, whether we know of some real or perceived inequities, let's not get hung up on this issue, but, once again, accept the fact that qualifications are spelled out quite distinctly for most jobs, and that the individuals on the referral list you receive are qualified to perform your job. How then do you go about selecting that one person from a list of five or six people? How do you decide which person will fit in best in your shop or office? How do you decide which person you want to entrust, in part, with your career? (After all, as supervisors, we sink or swim based on how well our people perform.) How do you decide which individual will give you the kind of performance you're seeking? One answer, of course, is the interview. Another is a discussion with previous supervisors. Both of these provide excellent avenues for obtaining data and should be used. But just like looking at a map with all the streets clearly marked, if we don't know where we're going—or in this case truly know what we want—having the answer in front of us doesn't help very much. What is being suggested is that we need to do some soul searching about ourselves, to see if we can pinpoint, based on our own value system, what we perceive as the successful employee.

No attempt is being made here to put labels of right or wrong, good or bad on any set of values. Rather, the intent is to recognize that different sets of values exist and that when there is a meshing of values between those being supervised and those doing the supervision, the likelihood of a productive relationship that is rewarding to both parties is greatly enhanced. Look at this example:

Mike is the supervisor. He's a no-nonsense, by-the-book type of person. The work day officially starts at 7:30 A.M. and Mike can be counted on to be at his desk ready to begin work at that time. So can all of his employees except one—Fran. And Fran is giving Mike fits! More often than not, it's closer to 7:45 before Fran is at her desk. And if that isn't bad enough, the lunch hour situation really irks Mike, too. Everyone knows that lunch is from 12:00 to 12:30. But does that mean anything to Fran? If she's in the middle of something when someone says, "Going to lunch today Fran?" more likely than not she says, "Not right now." Frequently it's 1:00 P.M. when she'll announce, "I'll be back in a few minutes, I'm going to grab a sandwich." At 1:15 P.M. she's finished her sandwich and is back working. As the others depart at 4:00 P.M. punctually, Fran says, "See you in the morning. I just want to finish up this report before I go," which may mean another hour or so. As Mike relates the story: "Her work is tops, but she has got to learn to observe the rules. I'm going to call her in and give my 'or-else' lecture. Rules are made for *everyone* to follow."

Is Mike right? When Fran says at the counseling session, "But Mike, you know I outperform every other person in the section," is she "right" in not following the rules?

Or what about Natalie, who supervises Marty. She just finished telling a supervisor in another department who was considering talking to Marty about a job in his section that she didn't feel Marty was very motivated.

It seems that Natalie would be labeled as a "rising star, on a fast track." Her career has advanced rapidly. Promotions have come quickly and have been well deserved. She's bright, hardworking, goal-oriented, achievement- and career-minded, and gives her all to the requirements of the job. Staying late or taking work home at night is not unusual for her, and her bosses know that she can be counted on to turn out a quality product regardless of the obstacles encountered. Marty, on the other hand, is quite different. He has been in the section for a number of years. He knows the work well enough to be considered for a supervisory position. However, he has never applied for one. He is dependable and will complete his assignments on schedule as long as no extra hours are involved. The only time he'll work late is if a project can have absolutely no slippage in the time for completion. His completed work, while almost always technically accurate, hardly ever shows any creativity. However, he is always receptive to suggestions made by others on ways that result in his turning out a better job. Marty observes all the rules and is respected and well liked by his peers. They come to him for advice, and he will gladly share his technical expertise. As Marty tells it, "I give a full eight hours of work every day. I try to be conscientious and do my very best. I like my job, the office, and the people. But at 4:00 P.M. I want to leave and go home and enjoy my family. I'm not interested in being a supervisor. That means working late in the evening, giving up some weekends, and traveling. The extra money isn't enough to compensate for what I have to change in my priorities of life's important things. To those who are interested in earning more money, having a title, or enjoying organizational prestige, I say more power to them. It's just not where it's at for me."

Is Natalie correct in her assessment that Marty is not motivated? Is Marty correct in setting his priorities the way he has?

There's no one correct answer to whether Mike is right in saying the rules must be observed by all, or whether Fran is right in saying her output exceeds everyone else's and that's what is important, or whether Natalie is right in tagging Marty as not being motivated, or whether Marty is right when he says going after the brass ring is not as important as other things in life. These defy any one correct answer because any answer that is given is based on the perception of the person giving the answer. If Marty worked for Mike and Mike was asked by a prospective supervisor about Marty's performance, more likely than not Mike would extol Marty's virtues, that is, he's stable, dependable, loyal, competent, observant of rules. Conversely, if Fran worked for Natalie, what would Natalie be saying? You got it: "A hard charger, a go-getter, motivated, lots of potential, should have a bright future!"

Hopefully, the point being made is rather apparent. To maximize the possibility that those we select will perform in a manner we judge acceptable, we need to first make sure that we recognize what our value system tells us is good and bad or right or wrong. When we have done that, we can then structure our interview questions to include not only questions that relate directly to the job, but also questions that will give us some insight into the person as well. If you are someone who is satisfied with your position in the organization, how are you going to react after hiring someone like Natalie with her big aspirations? Will you feel threatened, seek to stifle her growth, keep her under close control? Or can you feel comfortable giving her breathing room, take satisfaction in watching her develop, encourage her to go after the next promotion and leave you? In the two examples, we had situations of two good people working for the wrong type of boss, which probably will result in four unhappy people.

Since the employee doesn't control the selection process, the burden of responsibility rests with the supervisor. If strict adherence to rules is important to you, tell this to the candidates at the interview. Let them know what your expectations are. As the supervisor, you have the right to establish the ground rules for success under your supervision. However, you also have a responsibility to spell out those ground rules before someone accepts your job. Remember, each person has his or her own value system and I'm going to assume yours matches mine unless you tell me otherwise.

Getting an understanding of a prospective employee's values or, in the language of the day, "where they're coming from," is not really difficult. It doesn't require a degree in psychology, and you need not worry about asking why they love their mother or hate their father. Instead, some rather easy and straightforward questions can help you gain insight. For example, ask: Describe, without naming names, the best one or two bosses you ever had; what, specifically, made them good bosses? The kind of responses you'll get will usually run along these lines: "Oh, I liked this one particular boss over all others because he treated everyone fairly and equally. Nobody got any preference. He was strict but fair." Or you'll hear, "I really enjoyed this one boss because she gave you a job to do and left you alone to do it. She was really easy to work for, never hassled you as long as your work was done on time."

Another good question is: Of all the jobs you've ever had, which one did you like best? Why? Answers you'll get will run along these lines: "That's easy. It's when I worked for ABC Company. The work was very exciting. There was almost no room for error and you could really feel good about completing a job and knowing that what you did was perfect or just about perfect." Or you might hear, "I guess the best job I ever had was when I worked for XYZ Company. Your assignments were given to you in broad, general terms and you had to work out the solutions yourself. It really made you think because you got to work pretty much on your own. I guess it was the independence that I liked."

Another question I like to use at the conclusion of the interview: If I only could remember one thing about you from this interview, what would you hope I'd remember? Responses you'll get will include: "I'm hard working," "I'm loyal," "I'm ambitious," "I'm a quick learner," "I'm willing to assume responsibility," "I like challenge," "I'm committed to my job," "I'm goal oriented" and so forth.

As you can see, each of these questions allows us to see a little deeper into the person we're interviewing. When we've identified what's truly important to us, we can use these kinds of responses to help us make a better match in terms of the personality traits we can best relate to and feel comfortable with. Additionally, when we define our job requirements and expectations, these responses materially assist in improving the match. To fill a job which requires exactness with someone who has told us that they enjoy working on conceptual problems probably wouldn't result in a very long relationship.

While the interview is the most important step in the hiring process, checking out our tentative selectee with former supervisors is important, too. A call to a former boss doesn't allow us the same opportunity to look at the former boss's value system that we have when we look at ourselves or interview a candidate. Therefore, we must be careful in the kinds of questions we ask and how much weight we give the response. When a former boss says that he or she didn't find the individual we're thinking of hiring "motivated," we need to know if we're talking to a Natalie- or a Mike-type supervisor. When that supervisor says the person is not motivated we need to ask, "Could you be a little more specific?" Or if that former boss says the person was "really outstanding," we need to ask what kinds of things he or she did that made the former boss regard him or her so highly? When we go just a little deeper with these former bosses, we can then perhaps see a little bit into how they view the world of rights and wrongs and goods and bads.

Today, as managers, we find ourselves in a rather enviable position. When we attempt to fill our jobs, we see many highly qualified and talented people looking for employment and seeking careers in the federal service. This permits us to be more selective than in the past. As supervisors, we need to better understand ourselves and to use that information in putting together a work force that we can understand, appreciate, and motivate. When we do, we markedly increase the odds that we will be satisfied as supervisors, that our employees will find satisfaction in working for us, and that our supervisors will be pleased with the job we are doing for them.

The selection process will never be perfect, but we can make it better by investing some time in the hiring process. Remember, be it public or private sector, it's always easier to hire than fire.

RETAINING YOUR EMPLOYEES

As managers, we all want to hire "good people" and hang on to them forever. We have enough to be concerned about without having to worry about hiring someone new and then getting them trained to do the job. But, as we know, the real world doesn't operate that way. Turnover in an organization is normal and, many times, healthy. When we have turnover, it gives us the chance to infuse new blood into our work unit, to be exposed to new thinking and fresh ideas, if we are willing to be receptive. The problems come not from turnover, but from excessive turn-overs. What's excessive? Is it 10% or 20% or 40%? Numbers alone won't give you the answer. They're just one measure. A better answer, perhaps, is that when people are moving in and out so fast that we are unable to have any stability or continuity, when production and quality fall, and when we're unable to get our job done on time and morale is low, then turnover is excessive. When we find that we are spending more and more time hiring and training than tending to our other supervisory responsibilities, that's excessive! And when turnover is excessive we have a prob-lem. We need to explore the reasons and see what we can do as supervisors to correct the situation.

Earlier we looked at a situation where employees were going down the street for a higher-paying job with another agency. While not denying that higher-paying jobs will attract a certain percentage of people, the very affluence of our society in general clearly shows that money (or more money) alone will not be the sole determinant in making people move en masse to other jobs. While it may sound reasonable on the surface, all the current re-search dealing with people and their jobs just doesn't support that rationale. In fact, the research done by Frederick Herzberg, Abraham Maslow, and Douglas McGregor, plays down the sig-nificance that money plays in motivating and retaining a work force. While it's true that federal salaries do not match those in the private sector, to belabor that issue is to ignore the fact that what does keep people happy in their jobs and motivates them are the tools available to every federal supervisor. What are some of the things that your employees regard as being important? Challenging work assignments. Recognition and appreciation for a job well done. And who controls these things? You, the super-visor! We've already discussed earlier the way work is assigned and how it can affect costs and turnover. But a decision has to be made to do these things.

While generalizations can often get one in trouble, one that is pretty safe is that the federal manager has as much if not more latitude in utilizing recognition devices than a counterpart in the private sector. Supervisors frequently say, "But we can't afford to give away lots of money for cash awards." When was the last time you sat down and wrote a letter of appreciation to an employee for doing a particularly good job? When was the last time you prepared the paperwork for a certificate of achievement or some other noncash award your agency has? What's your ratio of telling your employees when you're unhappy with their performance to telling them about the good job they did?

Each agency has a cash awards system, and the amount of money that can be paid is usually far more liberal than the amounts paid under similar programs in the private sector. Ask among your private sector manager friends how many are in a position to recommend up to 15% of an employee's salary as the amount for a cash award for outstanding performance. You'll be very surprised at how much asking you'll do before someone says, "I can." Yet that amount is available for federal supervisors to recommend.

When discussing awards, supervisors often complain, "Oh, but I don't have time to do all the paperwork that has to be done." Of course paperwork must be done, but it is seldom as fearsome a task as it's made out to be. Sit down with the person responsible for administering the program and let him or her walk you through the steps. You'll be pleasantly surprised at how easy it is. Think about this for a moment: Have you ever watched other supervisors receive awards and honestly felt that you should have received one too, but your boss was too busy or couldn't find the time to do the paperwork for you? How did you feel toward the other supervisor's boss? How did you feel toward your boss? Don't forget, you're a boss too!

REMOVING AN EMPLOYEE

We've looked at the hiring process and the advantages of structuring jobs to provide for career growth and opportunity for your employees, we've explored a variety of issues to be considered to enhance the odds of making a good selection, and we've reviewed some of the things that make people stay on the job and want to perform well. However, even when all these things are happening in the right proportion, every supervisor will sometime encounter the employee who doesn't respond, the employee who, for whatever reason, just cannot or will not perform in a satisfactory manner.

If ever there was a myth that needs destroying it's the one that says, "You can't fire a federal employee." It deserves to be destroyed not only because it's false, but because in many instances removing a federal employee is easier than removing an employee in large, private sector corporations. (Recently I spoke with a middle manager from one of the largest United States corporations— in the top 10 of the Fortune 500. I asked him what authority he personally had to fire an employee who worked directly for him. He laughed and said, "Almost none! And if they've worked for the company at least five years it never happens. Bad for the corporate image! We transfer them to another job somewhere else within the company.")

Prior to the passage of the Civil Service Reform Act of 1978, removal of a federal employee was a difficult chore. When accomplished, it was a feat which the supervisor and the personnel specialists could reflect on with a rather well-deserved sense of pride. Not pride in terms of, "Well, we finally got rid of him," but pride in the sense that they had successfully worked their way through a maze of regulatory and procedural requirements that frequently trapped even the most expert personnel specialist. Many cases were lost on the appeal of some minor or trivial procedural requirement which in no way affected the merits of the case or were harmful to the employee. Because of these situations and the overwhelming amount of proof required of the employer, supervisors understandably shied away from removal actions.

The Civil Service Reform Act drastically changed all of this. So, while supervisors can't just say, "You're fired!" the removal process is far less cumbersome and tedious than it once was. For supervisors to now feel that it's easier to live with a bad situation than to take the time to change it is unwise. The effort and time spent to remove an unsatisfactory employee is decidedly less than tolerating the poor performance; and the odds of having the action sustained are clearly in management's favor. Old lessons learned are hard to dispel, so a myth prevails even though the rules have changed.

Two significant changes included in the act were the introduction of mandatory performance standards for all employees and a lowering of the supporting documentation required on the part of the agency to sustain a removal action. Written performance standards are now required for each employee. They function as a management tool that can be viewed as a double-edged blade. On one side they are extremely positive. When well written, they serve to clearly delineate for both the employee and the supervisor what is expected from the employee in order to be considered satisfactory performance. Well-written standards will show how much, how well, and how frequently something should be accomplished. They remove the guesswork about what is expected of them that too many employees have frequently labored under. The primary purpose of performance standards is a positive one—a statement of expectations.

However, when standards are reduced to writing and provide measurable goals, subjectivity—long the basis for performance appraisals—is removed and replaced with a much higher degree of objectivity. Both the supervisor and the employee can look at results and see if the employee did in fact measure up. Equally important, so can an appellate body such as the Merit Systems Protection Board, the agency charged with reviewing removal appeals.

Each employee's standards must contain at least one element that is considered *a critical element. A critical element* is any part of an employee's job that is of sufficient importance that performance below the minimum standard established by management requires remedial action and denial of a within-grade increase, and may be the basis for removal or reducing the grade of an employee. What this means to you as a supervisor is that if employees cannot or do not perform a portion of their job which you deem as essential, you have the basis to consider removal.

A decision that an employee is not performing at a satisfactory level is usually the result of the supervisor watching performance deteriorate over a period of time, or observing the failure of an employee to ever successfully perform an important part of the job. Because most people do not enjoy confrontation, and many supervisors feel that counseling an employee must inevitably lead to confrontation, they choose to do nothing until the situation becomes intolerable.

As a first step, supervisors have a responsibility to all their employees to sit down and discuss performance on a periodic basis. Performance problems should be addressed as they occur. Employees are entitled to this feedback. Since most employees are desirous of performing well, some early discussion may well result in improved performance, without confrontation. It's not at all unusual for an employee to respond, "Oh, is that the way you want it? No problem." Unless we convey our assessment to our employees, we can't hold them totally to blame when we are dissatisfied with the job they are doing. While this counseling is an informal action, the supervisor should prepare an informal memo of the meeting, outlining the items discussed and describing any assistance offered by the supervisor. The employee should also receive a copy. The memo, although informal, serves some very useful purposes. First, it provides a written record months down the line when memories fade, and avoids dialogue such as:

SUPERVISOR: "Well I told you that the quality of your typing had to improve."

EMPLOYEE: "No you didn't. You just mentioned that you wanted the filing to be done daily not weekly. We never even talked about my typing."

Secondly, should the supervisor ultimately give the employee an "unsatisfactory" rating on a performance appraisal, the memo serves to document that counseling had been given earlier.

Finally, there is the psychological impact on the employee. The fact that the supervisor has made a written memo alerts the employee that the supervisor is serious.

After the counseling, the supervisor needs to pay close attention to the employee's work. The supervisor should provide a steady stream of feedback to the employee. If the employee's work is improving, the supervisor needs to insure that the employee knows it. The supervisor needs to be supportive of the employee's effort to improve. But what if the performance doesn't get better? Then what?

If the employee's work continues to be unacceptable in at least one critical element, or if the supervisor rates the employee "unsatisfactory" at the end of the rating period, the employee must then be informed as to which critical elements are not being performed satisfactorily. The employee must then be given a reasonable period of time in which to bring performance up to at least the minimally acceptable level for the element's standard. What is reasonable? There is no fixed answer. It will depend on the job. However, a period ranging from a minimum of 30 days to a maximum of 90 days will cover almost all situations. During the time that the employee has been given to improve performance, the supervisor must also assist the employee in appropriate ways. This might take the form of classroom training, intensive coaching, assistance from another skilled employee, or any other reasonable means to bring the work up to an acceptable level. If at the end of the stated time the work is still unacceptable, the supervisor has two choices. One is to reassign the employee out of the job they cannot perform into another job at the same grade level or to a job at a lower grade level for which the employee is qualified. If no such job is available, then the supervisor must proceed with a removal action.

The employee is now given a "Proposed Notice of Removal for Performance." The employee is informed in writing of the specific instances of unacceptable performance and the critical element(s) involved with each instance. This notice must be given to the employee 30 days before the removal can be affected, and the employee must be given an opportunity to respond either orally, in writing, or both.

At the conclusion of the notice period, the individual designated as the deciding official (this individual must be at a higher level than the supervisor proposing the action) then has 30 days in which to decide whether the employee should be removed. If the decision is to remove, it can be accomplished any time after the 30-day advance notice period.

A few words about documentation needed to remove an employee are appropriate, since this is probably the area that makes most supervisors hesitant about proposing removal. As noted earlier, the Civil Service Reform Act has greatly reduced the burden on management to document and prove its case for a performance related removal. What then is necessary in terms of documentation?

First, examples of the employee's work which failed to meet the established standard for minimally acceptable work should be available. Second, the supervisor should have records available which show the time given to the employee to produce an acceptable work product, examples of assistance given to the employee during this time frame, samples of the work produced during this period, and a record of the procedural steps followed during the proposal and decision phases of the action. It can't be overly stressed that the documentation need not be excessive. It must only be sufficient to reflect that the removal is based on cause, that is, unsatisfactory performance.

Each year since the passage of the act in 1978, more and more supervisors are learning that removing poor performers from federal service has become far less demanding. It is considerably easier than continuing to tolerate the poor performers and the organizational problems they create.

The beginning of this chapter spoke of the fact that as managers in the federal sector we operate under a prescribed set of laws, rules, and regulations. If we only focus on what we view as the constraints to our freedom to manage, we start to feel that the tail is wagging the dog. The intent of this chapter has been to get federal managers and supervisors to see the latitude available to them under the system, and to see that by exerting some energy, initiative, and creativity they can manage as effectively as their skills permit.

Is managing in the federal sector different from managing in IBM? Of course it is. But so is managing in Ford different from managing in IBM, just as managing in Proctor and Gamble is different from managing in IBM, Ford, or the federal government. Each is a separate entity having its own rules, regulations, customs, cultures, and values. Each of these entities have successful and effective supervisors, and they are so because they have learned the system and not allowed themselves to be consumed by it.

To do the things described in this chapter will require change on the part of many supervisors. It's often said that change doesn't come easily, that people only change when they perceive it's in their best interest.

How about "success instead of survival" in supervision?

CHAPTER

SUPERVISING IN A PRODUCTION ENVIRONMENT

Part A. Managing in a Union Environment

BILL JOHNS

An old professor once said, "Companies get the kind of unions they deserve." While it may sound like just a catchy phrase, it turns out to have enormous significance to those who find themselves with managerial responsibility in a unionized organization. In this chapter we will explore two concepts that might exist as one approaches the task of managing in a union environment. In each case readers should understand that the climate in which they find themselves is a result of the stones they have laid and mortared day by day or the stones they have removed day by day. But in both cases the wall you build or tear down will take time and patience.

The "wall" is that barrier that sometimes gets built between labor and management, and it is up to us as managers whether we build the wall higher and thicker, whether we prevent it from being built, or whether we dismantle it, hence the idea that a company gets the kind of union it deserves.

THE ADVERSARY CLIMATE VERSUS COOPERATION

How does the adversary climate develop where unions represent the workers? Some think it is natural for this conflict to exist between supervisors and workers. As we shall see later in this chapter, that idea is both ridiculous and immature. But there are reasons for the presence of an adversary climate, and they are all made by people.

THE POWER SYNDROME

Many managerial people cannot resist the urge to demonstrate the power of their position. The power, or authority, of the supervisor must be utilized, but it is the manner in which it is used that can, day-in and day-out, add building blocks to the wall. The human will tends to resist that authority that is exercised for the purpose of "showing the subordinate who is boss," and a lack of cooperation tends to result. It must be remembered that the supervisor's job is to get the job done through other people, and when a worker resents the manner in which the boss uses his or her authority, cooperation is not likely.

But why do supervisors fall into this trap of "lording it over the workers"? The basic reason is that they have not matured in their understanding of human nature. They feel that somehow this positional authority makes them better than, or personally superior, to the workers. Clearly, most people resent this view when it is held by someone else.

But this may be a problem for the supervisor who means well and who truly believes that this is the way to motivate people. Or this supervisory style may come from a higher-level superior who insists on harsh treatment of the workers by a subordinate supervisor.

The result is all the same. Employees begin laying stones on the wall by devising ways to "get even." The supervisor who depends upon the authority of his or her position to get the job done will frequently be a poor supervisor in the categories of leadership, communication, discipline, and motivation. We will deal with each of these categories.

THE LABOR AGREEMENT

Of primary importance for all supervisors operating in a unionized situation is a clear concept of the labor agreement. The labor agreement is a legal contract which binds both parties and imposes certain limitations on management's right to manage. The contract is more than a simple "gentleman's agreement." Seldom will you find a labor contract that is fully desirable to any given supervisor. Its very nature will cause it to contain provisions that are not "what I would have agreed to." But we must remember that the labor contract is the result of collective "bargaining," a give-and-take process. Compromise is at the root of the bargaining process. But we should distinguish between compromise and expediency. When management surrenders its right to manage in the bargaining process, it has no one to blame but itself. Be that as it may, once an agreement is reached, it is the responsibility of supervisors to abide by the provisions of the contract. The fact that we do not like a provision, or think it unfair, is quite beside the point. We must be obedient to its terms.

There are two areas where supervisors and managers fail in working under a labor agreement. First, they may try to ignore a provision which they think unduly limits them in carrying out their responsibilities. It is true that certain agreements place administrative or procedural burdens on supervisors, but ignoring those responsibilities only leads to the development of a suspicion on the part of workers that the supervisor is trying to renege on the agreement. The company's good faith begins to be questioned and stones are laid for the foundation of the wall. The wall always has stones marked "lack of trust" at its base. Second, supervisors fail in working under a labor agreement by their generosity in going beyond its provisions. This is sometimes done in an effort to be a "good guy," or it may be done accidentally. Whatever the reason, supervisors should be as diligent in their efforts to not go beyond the agreement as they are to live up to all of their obligations under it. Where exceptions are made to the provisions of the agreement, employees frequently use that as the basis for future expectations. For example, when you decide to give a turkey or a ham to each employee at Christmastime and next year you don't do it, they want to know, "Where's my turkey?"

Obviously, supervisors must be acquainted with the labor agreement to the extent that they know what it requires of them in their daily activities.

LEADERSHIP

Those who fill positions of supervisor or manager who do not have a self-image of themselves as a leader are likely to travel a very rough road. We say self-image because if the self-image as a leader is not present there will be no actual leadership.

Unfortunately, there is no formula or set of specifications that a company can lay down that insures that an individual will be a successful leader. That should not deter us from dealing with the problem of developing leadership qualities.

One characteristic of a good leader is that he or she must be willing to make decisions. In a union environment it becomes especially important for a supervisor to be willing to make decisions. The failure to do so usually results in a gradual loss of respect for that supervisor among subordinates. The shop steward is not likely to follow, very long, a supervisor who can't or won't make a decision. After all, decision making is what management is all about. The quality of decisions we make as supervisors is a product of our experience, and if we do not make better decisions as we become more experienced, then we are going backwards and the organization will suffer.

Employees want to be led. And they want to be led by a person who inspires confidence. That's what leadership is all about: getting people to willingly do things that lead to the accomplishment of the company's goals. A supervisor cannot afford to look to the shop steward for leadership. When this happens, he or she is failing as a supervisor. The steward has a role and we will discuss that presently.

Another characteristic of a good leader is integrity. While it is true that people who did not have a great deal of integrity have been successful as leaders, they are not successful without contributing stones to the wall that divides. There truly is no substitute for integrity. When we finally lay down our life's work, we will all want to look back and be able to say that we did it with a sense of responsibility and fairness to those under our supervision.

What is integrity? It is believing and acting according to a code of values that speaks of fairness, honesty, truth, and unity. We are expected to be fair to those who work for us and those we work for. We are expected to honestly deal with all those we come in contact with. If we are willing to be truthful in all of our dealings, we will begin earning the respect of superiors and subordinates alike. Finally, we will be a unifying force in our jobs, a force that begins taking stones off the dividing wall and replacing them with a sense of trustworthiness. The writer is aware that these are values that are often discarded in today's business world, but the fact that they are discarded in no way affects their value, nor does it affect the truth of them.

Can you apply such a code of values in a union environment? Well of course we can and should. On the matter of integrity we should ask ourselves the question, "Do I want to manage with integrity because I have to or because I want to?" If we fail to manage with integrity in a union environment, the inevitable result will be greater pressure from the union for us to give up more and more of our managerial prerogatives, and that is particularly destructive.

COMMUNICATION

Good communicating skills are essential in a union environment. The first requirement of a supervisor in this area is a willingness to share information with those in official positions within the union, as well as with subordinates. In some cases supervisors are reluctant to share information with union people because "It's none of their business." While that may be true, the mature, improvement-oriented supervisor will not be influenced by this kind of concern.

One of the items consistently listed by employees as important to them on their job is to feel that they are "in" on what's happening. People do not like to feel left out, and they especially do not like to be made to feel left out deliberately. Again, the result is resentment—another stone on the wall.

But stones are removed from the wall when we show union officers various courtesies through good communications. Being sure that the appropriate union officer(s) know the details of a bulletin board announcement before it goes on the board has several advantages. First, it offers the opportunity to answer questions that might arise. Second, it provides an opportunity, because of the courtesy, to get official union support for the matter being announced. Third, we may have overlooked some important consideration that this kind of communication might reveal. But if we are a bit too proud to accept an idea from the union, we can be sure we will live to regret it. While it is true that the union does not have a *right* to tell you how to manage, it is also true that people seem to be more rebellious when we talk about our "rights" and more cooperative when we talk about our "responsibilities."

Thus the courtesy of sharing information with union officers tends to build trust and confidence, while a failure to do so results in mistrust and animosity. It is truly surprising how favorably people react when they feel they are being taken into your confidence. It's like a pat on the back, a well-done, a thank you, all rolled up in one. Remember, companies get the kind of unions they deserve. We must begin to realize that we have some control over what our union relationships are to be like.

DISCIPLINE

A very greatly mistaken idea exists in some quarters that we can't discipline people in a unionized organization. This idea fails to take into account several realities.

First, all people need and want discipline. The "need" is often more apparent than the "want," but they both exist. Our failure to use discipline gives rise to employees (and unions) believing that their conduct is acceptable. There are many examples of how we need and want discipline. Not very many of us would feel comfortable about getting our families loaded into the family car and starting out on our cross-country vacation trip if there was no speed limit on the highway. No, we are grateful for a speed limit that improves our chances of a safe arrival. In addition to wanting the speed limit, we sometimes find that we need that speed limit to keep ourselves in check.

A second reality is that supervisors are unsuccessful with discipline because they ignore rule violations right before their eyes. And even worse, they break the rules themselves. The various unions pride themselves in standing up for the workers. If supervisors are not consistent in the enforcement of rules or break the rules themselves, they need not look for any sympathy from the shop steward. On the contrary, they will build the adversary relationship stronger and stronger.

Disciplining employees is difficult, and therefore becomes a battleground between labor and management, because of the inability of the supervisor to investigate properly and develop all of the relevant facts in the case. We often have a blind spot to facts that support the employee's side of a situation, and because we are so determined to "teach a lesson," we ignore, or fail to uncover, some important information. Instead of seeing ourselves as prosecutors whose job it is to prove the employee guilty, we

should see ourselves as judges who determine the guilt or in-
nocence of an employee based on the relevant facts. To achieve
this we must develop two arts: the art of asking questions and
the art of listening. These two arts, when properly practiced, have
a way of rapidly destroying dividing walls.

STATE OF MIND

Our state of mind has a great deal to do with our success as a
supervisor in a union climate. If we expect our people to perform
poorly, our own actions will contribute to the workers ultimately
performing poorly, because we will tend to treat them according
to our expectations. This has its roots in the idea that if the employees belong to a union, then their interests are somehow contrary to the interests of the supervisor. Further, if we expect unionized employees to complain about every little problem and file
grievance after grievance, then we can be sure of developing quite
a backlog of grievance meetings.

On the other hand, if we as supervisors can combine the leadership characteristics mentioned earlier with a positive expectation
that we and the workers have a mutual goal, namely to earn a
good living for ourselves and our families while doing quality
work, the results are likely to be surprising. The most militant
worker or union officer is not immune to being well thought of
by the supervisor.

Where adversary relationships exist between labor and management, we would be well advised to review the history of how
that relationship developed. One of the first discoveries we will
make is that it developed step by step, incident by incident, over
an extended period of time. Common sense should tell us that
such a situation will not be reversed overnight. The same process
that led to its development can be reversed to build a strong team
effort. But patience is the first requirement. This is an ideal area
for the application of managing by objectives.

We should ask ourselves, "What do we want the relationship
to be like one year from today, then two years from today, and
five years from today?" Measure progress in terms of reduction

in grievances filed, reduction in absenteeism, reduction in turn-over, increase in production, reduction in cost, reduction in waste, increase in ideas from employees, and so on. All of these reflect the labor relations climate in an organization.

It is strongly recommended that where relations between labor and management are strained, management examine honestly its own state of mind regarding the union(s). The solution to any relationship problem must begin with one party making a constructive change in its state of mind. Understand that we are not suggesting weakness. Weakness is not respected by labor unions. But some supervisors confuse obstinacy with strength and wisdom.

Supervisors in unionized organizations often complain about work rules and various conditions they must meet in supervising their crews. We should remember that unions enjoy no rules, procedures, benefits, or wages that were not granted by management. As was stated earlier, the labor agreement is simply a series of limitations on management's right to manage. If there is a moral here, it is that those responsible for reaching agreements with unions should be wise enough and farsighted enough to be able to visualize where a particular agreement is leading.

A sad commentary on many unionized organizations is that frequently union officers, including stewards, are more knowledgeable of contract provisions than supervisors. This can lead to supervisory errors in decision making that can lead to controversy. Thus, the supervisor should have a clear understanding of the limitations placed on his or her by various agreements.

One last thought on the supervisory state of mind. There is an inclination at times to allow the workers to be thought of as the union's people. Now the question is: "Who can best represent 'your' employees—you or the union?" The answer should be clear. Supervisors are in the best position to represent the interests of the workers. They are the ones with the authority. They are the members of management. They are the most knowledgeable of the problems. In short, they are where the rubber meets the road and they should think of the workers as *their* people, and go to bat for them. The long-range view of supervisors should be one of representing their people so well that a third party becomes unnecessary. When this view is effectively used, it may not result in the elimination of the union, but it will certainly make dealing with the union a more civilized experience. This will not be accomplished if supervisors have an "anti-union" state of mind.

SUMMARY

The way we believe will determine the way we act. If we believe in the dignity of the individual, and if we are concerned about the well-being of people who have been entrusted to our supervision, it will not make a great deal of difference whether employees have chosen to be represented by a union or not. But if we picture the union as an adversary, we are probably going to act in such a way as to insure that a climate of conflict exists.

We should be conscious of the building stones represented by our acts on a daily basis. The fact is that we can help build the wall of separation or we can be the primary force that removes it. The choice is ours. We must lead with integrity. We must communicate with open-mindedness. We must discipline with the aim of correcting, not punishing. And we must be loyal to the legitimate goals of our organization, without being overcome with the power given us by virtue of our position.

Part B. Managing in a Nonunion Environment

BILL JOHNS

In order to successfully manage in a nonunion environment, it is important to understand one's own motivation for wanting a nonunion arrangement; and in order to reach an appropriate reason for such motivation, a fairly good understanding of unions is essential. Otherwise it would be like being opposed to traveling in an airplane without knowing the advantages and disadvantages.

A union exists for a basic purpose, and that is to advance the welfare, or well-being, of the membership. There are all kinds of philosophies and theories of unionism, but essentially it is an economic force whose purpose is to exercise its strength to gain improvements for the workers. In the process of achieving its basic goal, the union—through the process of collective bargaining—is able to gain concessions from management which have the effect of placing certain limitations on management's right to manage. This in and of itself is not necessarily harmful, depending on the areas and extent to which management makes concessions.

If management is willing to assume the full range of managerial responsibilities and carry them out in a manner which demonstrates a knowledge of human nature and a true sense of fair play, then employees will give little support to the idea of needing an agent to represent them. Indeed they will see their immediate supervisor as their agent.

In many respects, managing successful in a nonunion shop is more difficult than managing with a union, and we will deal with this idea in some detail.

WHY EMPLOYEES JOIN UNIONS

There are, no doubt, many reasons why people join unions. Most of these give us some guidance on how to manage in a nonunion shop.

It may be that the predominant reason for people joining a union is to satisfy a very basic need to "belong." Practically all people must satisfy this need one way or another. Some find their needs met at home, or in churches, civic clubs, athletic teams, fraternal groups, or at work.

Because work is the place where people spend the second-largest segment of their lives, it becomes important for them to meet this need for belonging at work. The person with the best opportunity to help meet this need is the immediate supervisor. If the supervisor is alert to this opportunity, he or she will innovatively devise many ways to insure that the subordinate is made to feel that he or she belongs. Failing this, the employee will cast around to see where he or she can "belong." Unions have long recognized this need and have even gone so far as to call themselves "brotherhoods!"

People also join unions because they feel that they are relatively poorly paid or have substandard benefits.

But it is likely that more people join unions because of the manner in which they are treated by their immediate supervisor than for any other single reason. In other words, in an election to determine whether a union shall be the bargaining agent for employees, the individual employee is likely to be casting a vote for or against his or her supervisor.

In a general sense, people join unions because they feel that their problems can be resolved more effectively if there is a body behind the complaint than if a single employee is trying to get the problem settled on his or her own: strength in unity.

So often, then, the reason employees join unions points back to the first-line supervisor and how that supervisor manages the job. Thus we will direct our attention to how the first-line supervisor manages to successfully maintain a nonunion environment.

THE INFORMED SUPERVISOR

Employees need answers from time to time and they need direction in their work. If they do not get information and direction from their supervisors, then they will look elsewhere, namely to a union representative.

A very practical question for a supervisor to ask is: "If we can get answers for a union steward, why can't we get answers for the individual employee?" Why let a union steward get the credit for solving the employee's problem when the supervisor could get the credit? Management must recognize the sensitive position of the first-line supervisor and provide an information system and training program that keep supervisors adequately informed, so that the supervisor becomes the person employees look to for information and guidance. For this to work, we must be aware of a strange bit of human nature that afflicts some managers and that is to hoard information as a status symbol: "I have greater status than you because I know something you don't know." The basic principle involved here is that management, middle and top, must recognize the need to be supportive of first-line supervisors.

Obviously a supervisor cannot be a walking dictionary and have a ready answer for every question, but he or she should know, through proper training, where to get answers. When first-line supervisors begin to develop the reputation among their subordinates that they are truly interested in their subordinates and their concerns, and will respond on a timely basis, then they begin to eliminate the need for a third party to represent their employees.

This leads us to the next characteristic required of supervisors to insure a nonunion shop.

THE CARING SUPERVISOR

The business climate is all too often characterized by the highly impersonal attitude of both workers and supervisor. Some would say, "That's the way it ought to be." That could be. But in this writer's view, this is the germ from which suspicions grow, and suspicions are the bricks out of which the wall between labor and management is built.

There is no rule of labor relations that says that people cannot truly care about each other and still run a successful enterprise. On the contrary, when people are made to feel that their supervisors care about their personal safety, on and off the job, when they are interested in the achievements of their employees' children, and in the successes and tragedies of families, then they will experience a reaction by these employees to the concern the supervisors have demonstrated.

The supervisor's job, at any level, is to create a climate in which subordinates respond positively to his or her leadership. Supervisors can create a highly authoritarian climate which often results in a response of resentment, or they can create a climate of personal caring and concern in which people tend to respond with their best efforts.

An ideal vehicle for the establishment of this climate is the safety program on the job. When supervisors are able to demonstrate to their subordinates that they are primarily concerned about the safety of that employee instead of "production at all costs" or "a good safety record," or any other performance standard which just makes the supervisor look good, then they will find that the employee's response will be favorable.

(Please notice, as we look at various characteristics of good supervision and management, that we are, one by one, eliminating the reasons for an employee to want a union to represent him.)

As we talk about *caring* and *concern* on the part of the supervisor, we are not talking about "Mr. or Ms. Milktoast." When supervisors continually talk to subordinates about production, they convince them that production is the top priority on their lists. If, on the other hand, they talk constantly to subordinates about their personal safety, supervisors will convince the employees that their safety is the most important thing to them, and this, as a matter of human nature, causes the employee to have a positive attitude toward those supervisors. This occurs over a period of time, say six months to one year. It does not develop overnight any more than production-consciousness develops overnight.

Finally this personal concern for people must be genuine. If supervisors are not sincerely concerned about their people, they will err in trying to make it appear that they are. They will look like fakes and, of course, would be.

THE FAIR SUPERVISOR

Anyone who has ever observed a picket line where employees were on strike against their employer has probably seen signs carried by the pickets that read "Unfair." Most complaints by employees against their employer have at their root the idea that the employee has been treated unfairly. "Fairness" can be a most difficult reputation for a supervisor to achieve, because fairness involves a certain emotional subjectivity. In other words, if I am the one who feels unfairly treated, I may not be able to see all sides to the situation as well as I see my own side.

The supervisor has a good chance of becoming a "fair" supervisor when he or she is able to consider each employee as an individual, and at the same time be consistent in his or her judgment with all employees. A reputation for fairness is achieved only over an extended period of time and is usually accompanied by the reputation that "you always know where the supervisor stands." We will say more about that later.

It has often been observed that some parents can spot bad behavior in other children but cannot, or will not, recognize the same behavior as undesirable in their own children. This same problem faces the supervisor. There are almost always some employees whom you mentally tend to favor, if not actually. But these employees cannot be allowed to exhibit behavior that would not be allowed in any other employee.

WAGES AND BENEFITS

Many companies believe, erroneously, that better pay and higher benefits will maintain nonunion status. This is presumably based on the idea that if you pay people enough money, other problems will disappear. Nothing could be further from the truth. Time and time again we have seen employees receive pay increases, either individually or collectively, in hopes that they would be "motivated" to higher levels of productivity, only to find them producing, temporarily if at all, slightly more than before the increase.

The prevailing practice among unionized plants of granting the same pay increase for all employees in a job classification, or worse, for all employees in the organization, is on its face discriminatory and discourages individual excellence and initiative. If all employees in a classification are granted the same increase in pay regardless of their performance, why should a poorly motivated person stretch himself or herself to excell?

This practice of granting the same pay increases to all employees is born out of real or imagined failures of supervisors and managers to equitably compensate individuals for their performance. Often the cry of favoritism is heard. This is clearly one hazard around which management must steer in a nonunion plant. A system of individual performance appraisals is essential if fairness is to be achieved where no labor agreement exists to prescribe pay increases. The individual performance appraisal has the additional advantage of providing the supervisor with the opportunity to "hear-out" the employees and their concerns about job, career, personal development, promotional opportunities, and so forth.

COMMUNICATIONS

Unlike a unionized organization where certain communication processes are required, such as grievance procedure, notification of reprimands and discipline, informational meetings and such, the nonunion environment presents a considerable challenge to management to be self-disciplined. Our good judgment is not challenged as much on a highway with clearly marked and enforced speed limits as it is where there is no speed limit and no enforcement to keep us alert. Likewise in a nonunion plant it is often easy to ignore those things which we "do not have to do." But we will ignore a good communications network at considerable risk.

First, there must be a free flow of necessary information within the management team. We have already referred to the hoarders of information who think they raise their own status because they possess information which others do not have. This thinking is particularly irrational when we consider that a supervisor's job (at any level) is to get the job done through other people. Where employees are not fed information they need to perform satisfactorily, or information that would reflect a respect for their interest in knowing, we will only succeed in alienating them. For instance, employees are particularly offended to read something in the local newspaper about their company and hear it for the first time there or from friends not associated with the company. Granted, there are times when circumstances make it impractical or even unwise to make a private announcement to employees before a public announcement in the media.

The flow of information upward, downward, and laterally in an organization may be poor due to a lack of consideration of the needs of other supervisors, or a lack of understanding of how important it is to people to feel "in" on things.

As managers move up in an organization, they sometimes lose sight of the importance of information to those at the bottom of the ladder. Or to amend a phrase, "They can't see the people for the trees." This is not unnatural, since the problems demanding attention at the executive level tend to be less people-oriented and more economics-oriented.

The task of insuring openness of communication with management is not a simple task, but it is the starting place.

Next, attention must be focused on communicating effectively between first-line supervisors and hourly, or production, workers. With regard to managing in a nonunion environment, this is the critical area. Supervision in its barest essentials is communicating. The ability and willingness to be a good communicator will take the first-line supervisor a long way in his or her efforts to get the job done through other people. It will cover many shortcomings in other skill areas. It is the primary requisite for the successful first-line supervisor.

But what philosophy should guide a supervisor in setting out to be a good communicator and meeting the needs of the employees without the intervention of a third party?

Strange as it may seem, if supervisors would communicate well, they must be good listeners. We seem to be automatically drawn to people who will listen to us and make us feel that our comments and/or problems are the most important things to them at that time. We may, in fact, have other problems that are far more important, but we must build a relationship with each employee that speaks of a willingness to listen to his or her problems, ideas, suggestions, comments, criticisms, and successes. By demonstrating a positive attitude as a good, patient listener, we are reflecting the self-worth of the employee. Among other things, our task as a supervisor is to promote the development of a self-image of self-worth among our subordinates. When an hourly employee begins to develop a positive self-image as a result of his or her supervisor's communicating skills, union organizers might as well pick up their coats and hats and find greener pastures elsewhere because they have little to offer such an employee. Techniques for developing a positive self-image are a whole other story, but suffice it to say that if supervisors expect quality work from their people, they must first convince them that they are quality people; and supervisors do not accomplish this by running them down privately or publicly, but by building them up in such a way that they begin to be dissatisfied with less than their best performance because "quality people don't do junky work."

Much has been said about the "open-door" policy in nonunion plants. Call it what you will, it is important for people to feel that there is an appeals process available to them, and that it works. Union organizers make very effective use of the idea that a union can provide a grievance procedure "to make management listen to your complaint." It is well to consider a system that assures the employees the appeals process found in a grievance procedure. We are going to hear employees' complaints with or without a union, so why not do it in a manner that does not involve giving up other management rights to manage, as a labor agreement inevitably does. We must understand again that a union thrives on its role in the adversary relationship. The first-line supervisor's task is to take away that selling point and provide a climate where employees can discuss their problems person-to-person and feel a sense of equality in the process. The union evens things up with the steward sitting with the aggrieved employee. But the supervisor can assure the employee of a fair hearing and retain the worker's sense of dignity, if not increase it. Supervisors must have a genuine desire to fill this role for this technique to succeed. If they are just trying to get the employee off their backs, they may soon be meeting with a union steward.

It is often difficult for a supervisor to give employees bad news or information that will not be popular. Too many people are obsessed with being a "good guy" and thus are unwilling to "tell it like it is." Earlier we spoke of supervisors developing a reputation of people knowing where they stand. This reputation is never awarded to supervisors who sugarcoat their communication, thinking that the crew can't take straight talk. Not only can they take it, they respect it, but not if supervisors continually blame others for decisions they think will be unpopular with the workers. To be willing and able to present unpopular policies and decisions to the workers builds credibility among subordinates.

HIRING

Proper selection of workers is not more or less important in a nonunion situation than where a union exists. The obvious purpose of hiring is to get desirable people on your payroll who either have the skills required or are trainable with normal training effort. One of the hazards to avoid in the nonunion plant is the hiring of the agitator, the troublemaker, the rotten apple in the barrel. Of course, you want to avoid this kind of applicant in any case, but especially in the nonunion plant. The logic here is that this kind of employee on your payroll is a disturbing influence and you are subjecting yourself to the threat of being unionized by such an employee. It's almost blackmail.

Second, the very good intentions of first-line supervisors are sometimes undermined by the malcontent. It is a very unnecessary evil that you don't want. But it remains the serious task of the people who make hiring decisions, whether they be personnel or first-line supervisors, to do meaningful reference checks in order to weed out undesirable applicants. A good rule is to be safe rather than sorry. In other words, it is better to miss a good employee through not being able to get reliable information on his or her work history than it is to accept a poor applicant.

It is surprising how little factual information is used in some cases before a hiring decision is made. Workers are sometimes hired on a basis no more substantial than a hunch or appearance. Past performance is what we need to know about, and we need to talk to someone who knows that applicant better than we do. A wise employer will approach the hiring decision much like marriage: It's forever. Nobody wants to get stuck with a lemon forever. So investigate thoroughly before deciding.

The hiring process should recognize the value of first impressions. You want that newly hired person to get a first impression of your organization that gives him or her a picture of a good place to work, a fair place to work, a profitable place to work, a secure place to work. All of these things will work against the efforts of a union organizer.

SUMMARY

If the reader has drawn anti-union conclusions from this chapter, then he or she has missed the point. The intended aim here is to demonstrate the substantial burdens on supervisors, particularly first-line, who manage in a nonunion environment. In most particulars, there are more difficulties to overcome there than in the unionized plant. The rules of the game and the boundaries are not as clearly drawn as with a labor agreement. So greater self-discipline is usually required.

The writer is not concerned with the aims, successes, or failures of union organizers, but with the development of successful managing techniques in given circumstances. The nonunion environment offers an excellent opportunity for supervisors and managers to utilize important life principles and philosophies, the rewards of which are tremendously satisfying when peaceful and harmonious working relationships result.

SUPERVISING IN THE RETAIL INDUSTRY

PAUL H. CHADDOCK

Supervision is a challenge regardless of industry. Supervising in the retail business is particularly complex because of the nature of the business itself. In order to understand that statement, we'll examine some of the characteristics which make the retail industry unique and then focus on the retail supervisor's responsibilities in light of these characteristics.

CHARACTERISTICS

"People-Dependent"

Unlike many businesses, retail is "people-dependent." All retailers can buy from the same suppliers, can use the same architects to design stores, and have access to the same advertising media. As customers, however, you and I are conditioned to shop again and again at that retail establishment which provides us the best value. Value is very individual. To some, it can mean the best price. To others, it can mean having a large assortment to choose from. However, to most customers, it means experiencing the most pleasant shopping environment. What is the most critical ingredient in a successful shopping environment? For most of us, it is the way we are treated as customers.

Therefore, it is the interaction of customer and salesperson that has a lot to say about how we determine whether that retail establishment provides us with value. What are our expectations as shoppers when it comes to interfacing with salespeople? We want someone who is knowledgeable, someone who is courteous, someone who is helpful, and someone who is responsive to our needs.

Now that makes pretty good sense and really doesn't sound that unique in terms of supervisory challenges. It is only unique when you think about the makeup of the work force that one typically finds in a retail establishment. With the exception of professional, commissioned, full-time salespeople found primarily in specialty stores or in specialty departments of major stores, most of the people who are in sales jobs are part-time employees. They are "second" wage earners. Typically, they are students who are attempting to finance part of their education, or they are spouses, both male and female, who are working for some short-term cause. Oftentimes it's to finance a vacation, a place in the country, or some other financial objective which has required a second income for a relatively short period of time. This means that the work force most supervisors in retail deal with is very perishable. This results in high turnover of the primary worker in most retail stores—the salesperson.

Variability

Another characteristic of the business is variability and long work hours. In those states which allow retail establishments to be open seven days a week, it normally means that the retail store is open approximately eighty hours. Even if the work force is made up of forty-hour workers, the typical workweek, it means that there would be two completely different work forces staffing a store in a course of one seven-day period. The supervisor probably works a different shift every week and would therefore have limited contact with each of the employees. It becomes difficult to know the employees, to train them, or to respond to their needs if the supervisor only touches them for a portion of the workweek.

Most retail businesses are constantly changing. The merchandise or products offered often change because of season, style, fashion, or technology. This year's spring fashions for men may be made from different or new fabrics. The new televisions have features which allow them to be used as monitors for computers because of technological advancements. Running shoes now come with tread to suit a variety of running or sporting needs, each tailored to a specific customer target group. These examples mean that training of this highly flexible and rather temporary work force is a major and constant challenge. How to keep up with the changes in the business is no small obstacle for both the supervisor and the salesperson.

To this point, we have concentrated on the salesperson as the employee to be supervised. There are, however, many other employees required in a retail establishment. There are stockpeople, cashiers, credit people, customer service people, maintenance people, and delivery people, just to mention a few. This means the supervision, training, and hiring challenges for most retail supervisors are further complicated since there is a variety of jobs and skills to respond to in a typical retail store. The communication requirement is to be clearly understood with all employee groups. The supervisor has to be as effective a counselor with the delivery driver, who may be a minimum-wage employee with a limited vocabulary, as with a full-time, professional, highly compensated, articulate, women's fashion salesperson. Being able to give instructions to a wide range of employees with the same degree of effectiveness is key.

Knowledgeable Customers

Another factor that makes retail supervision and training a challenge is that the customer is increasingly knowledgeable. Most shoppers come to the store to meet specific purchasing needs. This means they have a specific product in mind when they enter the store. What they are seeking, therefore, are answers to their product-comparison questions. Which is the best value? Which will best meet my needs? Which will last the longest? Which product has the most features and will serve my needs the longest?

This more-informed customer has come about because of several reasons. Advertising has certainly contributed to the knowledge level of customers. The focus of advertising frequently is to compare the product advertised with others being offered, in terms of special features, reliability tests, price, or newness. The customer entering the retail establishment has more information at hand today than in the past. Once in the store, customers are looking for answers to their product-comparison questions. The demand upon supervision is to provide salespeople with that ever-changing product-comparison information.

Less Time for Shopping

Another phenomenon affecting the retail business today is that people typically have less time available for that necessary activity called shopping. An ever-increasing number of families have more than one prime wage earner. For those purchases requiring agreement between principal wage earners, mutual shopping time is at a premium. Whether it be husband and wife deciding which is the best television set, or parents determining which is the best furniture for their child's room, the shopping experience is a "time poor" activity. The customer is demanding quick answers, a convenient shopping environment, and easily accessible sources to answer their questions. The demands upon supervision again include assuring knowledgeable, helpful, responsive salespeople.

Employee Demands

Another challenge for supervisors in retail comes from employee demands. Again, because there are multiple wage earners in a family, or because the employee may have another full-time job, those who work in a retail establishment will often require flexible hours. Their requirements for variable schedules may not match the requirements to staff the store during the eighty or so hours a typical store is open. Matching employees' flexible work schedule requirements to the store's flexible staffing requirements, to insure that the store has adequate coverage, makes staffing scheduling a particularly difficult chore.

Employees also want the opportunity to influence how the job is done. Today's work force is better educated, more independent, and wants the opportunity to influence how their jobs are accomplished. Successful supervision, therefore, may require negotiation between supervisor and employee in the methods employed to get the job done.

Technology

Another phenomenon which is increasingly affecting the retail supervisor is technology. The typical machine used today to accept the customer's payment for a purchase involves much more than the classic cash register did. Customers want to charge their purchases from a variety of credit card sources. Point-of-sale equipment is used not only to record the amount of the sale, calculate the taxes, and accept the cash or check, but also to record information regarding the type of merchandise purchased. This is input to the inventory system, the accounts receivable system, the sales audit system, and so on. This technology adds a new training burden to most supervisors in retail. Technology may also be threatening to the older, longer-service employee who is used to more simple or even manual methods. Helping employees successfully deal with and accept change is the key to obtaining the advantages this new technology can provide. New standards for accuracy and speed cause additional employee demands.

This new technology produces many useful products for the supervisor. Reports of yesterday's business are readily available today. Inventories are automatically credited. Purchase orders are automatically written when inventory levels get to minimum quantities. Cashier productivity is automatically calculated because the register transaction can capture the employee's number along with merchandise sold and the amount of the sale.

Security and Loss Prevention

It appears that security and loss prevention are increasingly important concerns for most retail management personnel. Society seems to be breeding an increasing number of people who think it's okay to steal from a retailer as long as one doesn't get caught. Pilferage from both employees and customers costs American retailers billions of dollars each year. One to three percent of most retail companies' total sales is lost through "shortage." This shortage is caused by both stealing and errors in paperwork transactions involving the buying, receiving, or selling of merchandise.

Interruptions

A key retail supervising challenge is to learn how to "manage by interruption." The retail environment is almost noncontrollable. What happens day to day or even hour by hour is impossible to predict. Weather can keep customers away, or bring them in unexpectedly. An unplanned delivery truck arrives with merchandise which must be received and put away on the day two stock people call in sick. The number of staff you assigned at 9:30 A.M. to the selling floor to cover the department is not adequate at 10:30 A.M. because twice as many customers as normal are in the store. An unhappy customer takes 30 minutes to satisfy, which throws the morning schedule all out of sync. Because the business is affected by the weather, unexpected customer flow and on and on, the supervisor is constantly needing to rearrange priorities, reassign employees, and make frequent short-term decisions.

RESPONSIBILITIES OF RETAIL SUPERVISORS

To this point, we have talked about demands on the supervisor in face-to-face supervisory situations, such as dealing with employees on the selling floor, helping customers, or just being present during store hours. But handling people issues is only one dimension of a retail supervisor's total responsibility. There are tremendous amounts of paperwork, book work, and non-people-related challenges which are a part of a supervisor's workweek. Keeping up with receipts of merchandise, taking inventory counts, changing prices, insuring that orders are placed, reading about new product introductions, keeping up with new legislation which could affect the business, and other demands make it almost impossible for supervisors to spend more than a fraction of their time actually on the selling floor supervising people. These multiple demands make it imperative to have some process for setting priorities. Often supervision is a reactionary, fire-fighting activity. Someone once said that the prime role of a manager is to solve problems. Whoever said that certainly had a reactive view for the role of supervision. Reacting does demand a tremendous amount of supervisory energy. Being proactive, determining new directions, establishing plans, is perhaps the most valuable role a supervisor plays. However, with the time demands as described above, it makes it very difficult for supervisors to set aside the necessary thinking or planning time in a typical work day.

The demands on the supervisor in retailing are particularly complex. It is uniquely a people-dependent business. Work force stability is very temporary. Many people are in the work force as second wage earners. Turnover is constant. Long hours, variable work schedules, and seasonality make staffing a unique challenge. Changing customer demands requires knowledgeable and responsive salespeople, convenient and efficient shopping experiences. Employee demands for flexible hours and the opportunity to influence how their job is done also create supervisory pressures. Technology, theft, and other causes of shortage also add to the complex challenge. Let's now address some of the specific responsibilities a retail supervisor faces.

Instilling Attitudes

One of the most important challenges a supervisor has is instilling attitudes in salespeople that are consistent with customer expectations. If a retailer has built its business on customer service, then making service an employee priority is critical. It means hiring people who are interested in providing service to the customer. It requires reinforcing employees for making the trade-off decision of service to a customer over stocking the shelves. Keeping shelves full of merchandise is important. Stock work frequently consumes much of the time a salesperson works. A customer may come in at a time that interrupts that stock work. Helping the salesperson understand that a customer question is a welcome interruption to stock work is not easy. Salespeople frequently find the boss—you—putting pressure on getting the shelves straightened, the new merchandise displayed, or the prices changed, and, therefore, look upon the customer's presence as an obstacle to getting their work done. From a customer's point of view, a salesperson is expected to be responsive, courteous, pleasant, and available to answer questions, no matter how insignificant. Instilling your desire to have the customer properly served, even when doing stock work, is not easy. It appears to the salesperson as an apparent conflict. Taking time at the beginning of a working relationship to explain how to set such priorities when customers are present is an important part of a new salesperson's orientation. If the company has built its reputation because it is an inexpensive place to buy merchandise, then instilling a low-expense, no-frills attitude among employees is a priority. Establishing a supervisory posture consistent with the company's set of values is a key to success. Retail stores can be driven by a variety of dominant values: individual customer service versus self-service; clean but low cost versus a plush store; a quick and efficient shopping environment versus a leisurely, more social shopping experience. Understanding the prime company value is key to acceptable employee performance.

Training

Supervisors often overlook the importance of an up-front investment in training time for new employees. This may be caused by a variety of reasons. So much of the job of salesperson or stockperson is responding to customer questions and to instructions given by the supervisor. In other words, the job is to do what you are asked or told to do. Because the supervisor is frequently giving such short instructions early in the employment relationship, the need for training may not be that apparent, except for more obvious applications such as operating a cash register or filling out a sales slip. Another factor has to do with expense. For most retailers, over 50% of their total operating expense is payroll. This causes a very high concern to use payroll dollars or employee time for any activity other than merchandising or dealing with the customer. For many supervisors, retailing is a very short-term-focused job. Thus, initial job-training time may be seen as a frill or unnecessary expense. Related to this management perspective is the issue that staff additions usually occur only after the need for that staff is already very acute. If these factors postpone or eliminate complete initial training, the objective of satisfying customer expectations can be in serious jeopardy. Using new people without proper training can cause numerous supervisory challenges later on, the most serious one being a mishandled customer.

Initial training is a complex supervisory challenge. The new person must understand department operations, how to ring the cash register, how to change prices, where the inventory being received should be stocked, and on and on. Orienting the person to all of the types of merchandise being sold must be covered in the early days of employment. This must include not only where it is, but what it is. Explaining company policy, starting hours, break times, pay practices, and handling returns are just a beginning list of initial orientation and training subjects.

Training is not only a challenge for the new salesperson, but is an ongoing responsibility of most retail supervisors. Training is a constant requirement because new products are frequently brought into the selling assortment. Prices frequently change. Policies, department procedures, seasons, and competition are but a few of the forces which will make daily operations frequently change. Other types of training include proper selling-technique training, how to handle returned goods, housekeeping duties, and proper use and placement of signs. What are some of the techniques successful retail supervisors employ to meet some of these training challenges?

Frequently, supervisors employ a "buddy" system. This means pairing up an experienced salesperson with a new employee. This can be an effective method of relieving the supervisor of the actual training task. It certainly is an opportunity to positively reinforce a long-service employee who has acquired expertise over time. There are some limitations to this method. There is no assurance the "buddy" will provide training in the same manner as the supervisor. There is no easy method to evaluate the effectiveness of the training. It is usually after the supervisor finds the new person making mistakes that he or she becomes aware that training was less than perfect.

Another method is to use vendors' representatives. The vendors are usually very knowledgeable about the products they sell. Asking vendors to spend time with salespeople on the sealing floor can be a very valuable means of training people in product knowledge. Again the limitations involve the use of quality and time: Are the vendors' representatives willing to come when all of your salespeople are present? How will they train the salesperson who wasn't scheduled during a vendor's visit? Do vendors explain the features of their product in terms of positive buying reasons or do they do it in a way which knocks their competition? Customers, are not interested in learning the bad points of one product in favor of the good points of another product; rather, they are interested in learning what features of the product satisfy their particular buying needs. The quality of training is somewhat questionable when accomplished by vendors who may have very self-serving interests in mind.

Another method for training in product information is to use the packaging which accompanies the merchandise. A "fact" tag may be affixed to a product to describe features, specifications, and prices. If fact tags are not used, the outside of the package or the instruction booklets with most products can be valuable training tools.

Another technique is on-the-job training. Here the supervisor becomes the instructor. The supervisor explains how to do something, demonstrates how to do it, asks the new employee to verbally describe doing it, then the employee does it with supervisory guidance, and finally does it without the manager's assistance. This is a very effective way to help people learn to perform specific job functions. It is, however, time-consuming for both parties. It obviously works best in a one-on-one situation. If the supervisor is faced with training many new salespeople, such as at peak staffing periods like Christmas, the on-the-job technique is not very efficient.

Because the supervisor's job responsibilities require frequent selling-floor presence, the salesperson is almost constantly able to observe his or her behavior. This makes the supervisor an ever-present model. This unusual public presence puts pressure on the supervisor to perform consistently with the instructions being given the salesperson. The role of "model" presents an opportunity to train, but also gives the employee a unique chance to see if "practice matches preaching."

Training as a key management skill does not mean being a formal classroom instructor. Classroom training may be appropriate when large groups of employees are hired, such as at Christmas time. Most retail stores will almost double their work force for the Christmas season. This may, indeed, require a supervisor to take on a classroom instructor-type responsibility. If so, there should be some skill and confidence in developing training objectives, teaching outlines, and training materials, so the training need is met. This training may require feeling comfortable using audiovisual aids, lecturing, conducting discussions, or providing demonstrations. Training, however, will probably most often be of a more individual nature. This is because employees normally will be hired one at a time. Employees tend to be hired for unique or special job responsibilities: a housewares salesperson; a cashier; a door guard. Therefore, a one-on-one teaching method will more frequently be used. The supervisor needs to be comfortable using on-the-job training techniques, the buddy system, observing and coaching, and other individual methods.

Staffing

The subject of staffing was previously mentioned. Finding people to fill the required jobs in a retail store is not an easy task. It is becoming increasingly difficult. Fewer and fewer people are in the category of part-time, variable-work-hour employees. Fewer and fewer teenagers or young adults are entering the work force and are thus available to work in a retail store. The supply necessary to staff may increasingly become scarce.

Determining Job Specifications

Most important in staffing is determining the job specifications required for any position. People are often interviewed before the supervisor has really thought through the requirements a successful candidate should have. Up-front time invested by the supervisor in thinking through the performance required, the education necessary, and the skills needed will make recruiting more efficient and effective. Generating candidates is another important part of staffing. Putting an ad in the local newspaper, a poster in the window, or using an employment agency are three fairly obvious ways to generate candidates. The industrious supervisor may also use guidance counselors in local schools, local community social groups, or the state unemployment office to generate a source of candidates. Meeting the challenge of staffing first requires determining the specifications required and then, finding sources of candidates to produce a variety of people to pick from when filling the job.

Screening and Interviewing

After candidates are available, the job of screening and interviewing begins. It is very important to find people who are willing to work the schedule required for the position. Oftentimes, the retail sales or stockperson job requires odd hours. Shoppers mostly do their buying during two or three hours in the middle of the day, in early or late evening, or on Saturdays and Sundays. This makes for a particularly broken-up and unusual workweek. Finding people who are available to work those kinds of hours is not easy. So once you find people who are available for the hours required, who have the background of education or experience, and who are particularly good at interfacing with the public, the task of staffing is met.

Managing a Diverse Work Force

Speaking of staffing, supervisors are frequently required to hire and manage a diverse work force. There can be full-time commissioned people who demand a different mode of supervision from the part-time, minimum wage, hourly person looking for a short-term job. Professional commissioned salespeople frequently are the prime wage earners in a household versus the second wage earner as described in the other salesperson profile. Being able to satisfy the expectations and needs of these two diverse groups presents a unique challenge for the manager. Oftentimes the former is a very interested, professional, highly motivated employee. Frequently the latter is only working for the money and really is not interested in a professional, long-term employer-employee relationship.

Scheduling

Another dimension of staffing has to do with scheduling. There is a phrase often used in supervisory circles called staffing to "customer presence." What this means is determining when the greatest numbers of customers will be in the store and trying to schedule staff during those peak periods. The amount of money spent in payroll is a key expense budget item. Having excess people on the selling floor when customers are not present is an unnecessary use of payroll dollars. On the other hand, having too few people will cause customers to not be served and, therefore, be unhappy with their experience in the store. The first step in scheduling is to determine customer shopping patterns. This can be done by observing, over periods of time, the number of customers in the store by day and by hour. Keeping track of these quantities of customers will develop a customer-presence pattern. This will frequently be different by day of the week and by week of the year. Customer presence will also be affected by the amount of advertising being used. If advertising is successful, it will frequently draw people in great quantities for short periods of time. Anticipating the proper number of salespeople required on the floor will be an important ingredient in meeting customers' shopping experience expectations. Once the typical or base pattern by hour, by day, and by week has been developed, you are now ready to establish a staffing schedule.

A key to successful staff scheduling is to allow employees to have an opportunity for variety in their weekly schedule. This may mean posting a schedule and letting the employees choose their work schedule for the coming week or month. Some employees for whom this is a second job may have limited flexibility in their availability. They may require the same schedule week after week so it does not interfere with their full-time job, going to school, or some other inflexible obligation. The overall objective, of course, is to use payroll dollars as wisely as possible while at the same time staffing to customer presence.

Evaluating Employee Performance

Another difficult challenge is evaluating employee performance. Good performance evaluation systems begin with clearly outlined performance expectations. If an employee understands what is expected and has been given the tools and the training, evaluating performance becomes relatively simple. However, many supervisors make the mistake of trying to evaluate against some soft or subjective criteria. This makes the evaluator and the evaluatee most uncomfortable. The retail business has a unique opportunity for objective performance measurement. There is a tremendous amount of quantifiable work involved in a retail store. Examples of this are sales dollars, cartons put away per hour, sales rung per hour, cartons priced per hour, cartons received per hour, unit transactions per hour, and on and on. Determining what are proper measures for each job supervised is step one in establishing a performance evaluation system. If it is determined that unit sales per hour is a fair measure of a successful employee's performance, then those quantifiable goals should be communicated to the new employee. This not only provides the supervisor with a standard against which employee's performance can be measured, but it gives the individual employee something to shoot for. Setting up the performance evaluation system should also include determining the priority job responsibilities for each person. A written list of responsibilities, measures, and priorities should be given to the employee at the beginning of the evaluation period. These can become the standards against which performance is evaluated, training is measured, and perhaps even hiring and staffing are determined. Much has been written on conducting performance reviews and, therefore, that topic won't be covered in this chapter. It is, however, important to note that retailing provides many positive opportunities to objectively evaluate employees.

Interpersonal Relations

Being skillful in interpersonal relations is a major supervisory responsibility. So much of the supervisor's job is involved with interfacing with another person. That person could be a peer, a boss, an employee, a vendor, or a customer. Being comfortable and competent in the skill of communications, both orally and written, is required. Asking good questions, being a good listener, being able to give clear directions and instructions, providing positive reinforcement on performance, giving corrective feedback when necessary, interviewing, coaching, and persuading are examples of the dimensions of interpersonal skills necessary.

Making Good Use of Time

One very difficult dimension of a retail supervisory job is making good use of one's time. The demands upon a retail supervisor are many. The customer who is unhappy, the customer who needs information, the employee who is new, the employee who needs discipline, the peak period when too few employees have shown up, and on and on. It appears to many supervisors that it is one crisis after another. Priority setting is a very important supervisory skill. Knowing how to make the trade-off decision between that seemingly urgent question or demand and some longer-term, proactive, behind-the-scenes-type task is also part of the job. Coming up with criteria for making those priority decisions is important. So often supervisors err on the side of making decisions on behalf of the business at the expense of a particular customer. Oftentimes, as a customer, you will see managers preoccupied with changing the prices, taking inventory, or straightening the shelves, and it appears that when you ask a question you are "interrupting" something terribly important to that supervisor. Obviously this can be very frustrating. It is not easy for most retail supervisors to remember that being interrupted by a customer is important. Helping employees understand this same set of rules is also a challenge.

Merchandising

Merchandising is one of those job responsibilities that needs to be defined in each company. In some companies, very specific standards for setting up a department and displaying merchandise are established. This means the job of the supervisor is to implement the merchandising plan. In other companies, it is up to the individual supervisor to figure out the best way to display and locate merchandise within his or her department. It is only after understanding the merchandising philosophy and the techniques to be employed that the supervisor can successfully be a trainer of employees.

Housekeeping

Housekeeping, or storekeeping, as it sometimes is called, is another important supervisory responsibility. This involves learning the housekeeping standards that insure the shopping environment is clean, organized, and most attractive. This may involve understanding how signs are to be displayed, where special displays are to be constructed, how the merchandise is to actually be shown on the shelf or hung on the rack. In some companies, there is a process called plan-o-gramming which is used to insure that every department has a similar look. This process insures that stores which are part of large chains have a consistent look. There are obvious economies to the overall operation of a store. Plan-o-graming provides customers with a familiar shopping environment no matter which store in the chain they visit. Understanding how plan-o-grams work and how to implement them are important skills for the supervisor to acquire.

There are many unique operations to be learned. For example, it is important to understand the policy for handling customer returns. Teaching employees when to accept a returned piece of merchandise and when not to requires important judgement. The balance between taking something back for which the company may not be able to receive credit versus making a happy customer is sometimes a fairly complex decision. Thoroughly understanding the philosophy behind the policy and communicating that concept to employees is an important responsibility. Learning how to take inventory, how to receive merchandise, and how to store it in a stockroom are but a few of the store-operating procedures necessary to learn and train.

Managing Expenses

Developing a sense of expense management is also very important in most retail supervisory situations. Knowing how to develop a budget, how to manage expenses to insure you are staying within that budget, and understanding how to report results may be demanded of a supervisor. These procedures are usually unique to each company and, therefore, must be thoroughly understood in order to insure that employees operate within expense guidelines.

Problem Solving and Decision Making

Probably one of the most important skills for supervisors is in the areas of problem solving and decision making. Problems come in a variety of situations. There may be problems relating to merchandise, to the customer, resolving conflicts between employees, learning when to say no to a customer, how to set a department to support a promotional event; these are examples where problem-solving and decision-making skills play key roles. So much of the retail supervisor's job is responding and reacting. The true manager of retail circumstances is one who knows how to plan and be proactive so many problems can be avoided. Teaching employees to make decisions, to solve problems within company guidelines, and to provide good customer service pays big dividends.

Building Stability

How to build stability in an organization which is naturally unstable is probably one of the more difficult responsibilities the retail supervisor has. The organization is unstable for the reasons pointed out above: a temporary work force; turnover; variable work hours; seasonality of the business. All of these factors contribute to the retail environment's constantly being in a state of change. But if the supervisor is to provide an organization which consistently gives good customer service, it is important to build a sense of stability and predictability into that retail supervisory situation.

Helping the employee have a sense of affiliation to the team and belonging to the company will go a long way in getting the employee to make decisions and behave within the guidelines and policies of the company. This sense of affiliation is an important one to instill. It can occur because the employee is made to feel important—a key link between the retail store and the customer. He or she must have a sense of personal value while on the job. The employee gets those kinds of positive feelings from the direction and feedback of the supervisor. It is, therefore, important to show that input is welcomed. Employees can be recognized in many nonfinancial ways for the contributions they make. This sense of overall pride can be built in employees if they feel that what they do makes a difference and that what they say has meaning. The supervisor who understands these dynamics and cultivates this environment will build stability and consistency in the organization. Someone has said that many retail employees are unloyal. *Unloyal* is distinguished from *disloyal*. *Unloyal* simply means that there is no sense of belonging or feeling of obligation to the organization because the employee sees the relationship in a rather temporary manner. That doesn't mean the employee is disloyal or dishonest or destructive or out to do anything to deliberately hurt the company, but it does mean that he or she doesn't do anything to enhance the company or expend any energy above and beyond what is actually demanded of him or her. Making the unloyal employee excited has great payoff. Just as customers repeatedly come to a store where they feel valued, employees will work in a positive way for an organization in which they feel a sense of value. Finding unique ways to make that happen is a key supervisory skill for the retail manager.

SUMMARY

Retail is a people-dependent business. This means a customer cannot usually avoid being in contact with some retail employee, whether it's the stockperson, salesperson, or the cashier. It's almost impossible to have a retail experience as a customer without coming into contact with somebody. The challenge of retail supervision is to make employees competent in all their job requirements and sensitive to customer needs.

SUPERVISING LOW-SKILLED WORKERS

MARTIN M. BROADWELL

There are a number of things that need to be considered when talking about supervising those who have minimum skills and who do minimum-skills work. We'll look at both the positive and negative sides in this chapter. Considering the problem areas first, we'll identify them, then discuss them in more detail—along with other problems that may arise—and show how the problems can either be eliminated or minimized.

The problems:

1. *Incorrect Assumptions.* First and foremost in the problem area is the fact that many supervisors make quite incorrect assumptions about people who have low skills. These assumptions

lead to erroneous conclusions and faulty actions by the supervisors, often compounding or even creating problems.

2. *Personality Differences.* Those with low skills tend to have personalities which differ from other employees, due to factors that include background, environment, and previous job experience.

3. *Less Motivation.* For many reasons, low-skilled workers often are less motivated to exert themselves in areas such as problem solving, decision making, job innovation, attendance, tardiness, and actual job performance.

4. *Unenriching Jobs.* A job that requires little or no skill often has little in it that will serve to offer job enrichment opportunities.

5. *Personal Dress Habits.* The supervisor has a problem adapting to the personal dress habits of many low-skilled workers. Other workers may be offended by both, appearance and dress habits.

6. *Low Self-Esteem.* Most low-skilled workers show few positive feelings toward their own ability to be different than or to do better than they are now. This leads to an acceptance of their "fate."

7. *Poor Education.* It isn't always a lack of intelligence but a lack of education that makes it difficult for the supervisor—and others—to communicate with the low-skilled worker, both in normal conversation and during training and coaching sessions.

8. *Lack of Job Opportunities.* The low-skilled worker is less likely to be afforded a chance to move upward in the organization, simply because of the low skill, but also because of the lack of exposure opportunity.

9. *Past Job Experience Problems.* Previous supervisors may have sown some bad seeds about this worker's habits or abilities; discipline may have been sporadic, overused or poorly administered, leaving the worker with bad work habits for the present assignment.

The individuals:

1. *Typically Nontypical.* A major problem in dealing with the low-skilled worker is the fact that there is no "typical" worker in

this category. There are some things that many have in common, but there is no such thing as a typical low-skilled worker.

2. *Lack of Work Ethic.* Because of previous work efforts, family traits and influences, and some failures, the low-skilled worker often lacks a satisfactory work ethic, either with regard to the job itself, or with regard to tardiness and absenteeism.

3. *Poverty Background.* Because of the lack of skills in the family and among those the worker associated with during the growing-up period, there isn't the need to "be like my parents." There may be a drive to *avoid* being like them, but often workers' views of what they can and can't be is cloudy.

4. *Health Care.* The low-skilled worker comes with less concern about insignificant illnesses and injuries, sometimes leading them to overlook minor medical care. This may lead to more serious illness.

Personality:

1. *Belligerence.* While not all of low-skilled workers fit the pattern, there is the possibility of belligerence in this worker. If there is a feeling that the world is either "against me" or "owes me a living," there will most certainly be some belligerence.

2. *Defensiveness.* One result of being "pushed around" from one job to another, because of the lack of a salable skill, is that the worker may become defensive. He or she might strike back without any apparent reason.

3. *Passiveness.* Probably the most common trait found in the unskilled or low-skilled worker is one of just not appearing to care about anything. This passiveness may be a shield, or the person actually may not care about anything as far as the job is concerned.

4. *Unskilled in Interpersonal Relations.* While the more skilled workers may work a little harder at getting along with the boss and other workers, the low-skilled worker may be pleasant enough at times, but will certainly not be attempting to use interpersonal skills in dealing with workers, supervisors, or customers.

Viewpoint:

1. *The organization.* The structure of the organization may escape the low-skilled worker altogether. Certainly there will be little

appreciation for the levels and authorities and nuances of organizational structure and politics.

2. *The Home and Family.* Frequently the low-skilled worker has a different viewpoint toward the roles played by parents and family members than the higher-skilled worker has. There will be affection and care, but there may be a somewhat different view with regard to the patriarchal or matriarchal roles.

3. *Other Workers.* The low-skilled worker may tend to be a loner, or at least make little effort to "win friends and influence people." There will be a typical clannishness between the low-skilled workers, just as there is with the higher-skilled ones.

4. *Life-Style.* Frequently the low-skilled worker will have a few friends who are in the same boat, but not be so inclined to worry about self-improvement. As a result, there is less effort to have a life-style that matches that of higher-skilled workers, although there may be a desire to have "nicer" things. Low-skilled workers' value systems will almost certainly be different from those of supervisors and higher-skilled workers; theirs is frequently a "here-and-now world."

SOLUTIONS ARE COMPLEX

Strangely enough, the solution to dealing with the low-skilled worker is often more complex than working with the more trained and capable workers. One obvious reason is that so much about the lesser-skilled worker is different from those who supervise them. Looking back over the nature, characteristics, and viewpoints of these workers as mentioned above, we can see that there are many differences between them and those who would normally supervise them. Low-skilled workers are one group from which there isn't likely to be much promotion from within the ranks, especially to a position of supervision. In almost every other area of work—skilled, technical, operational maintenance, sales, clerical, and so forth—there is a good likelihood that there will be some upward mobility to the supervision ranks. Among the low-skilled, there is very little likelihood of this happening. We've already seen that this lack of opportunity works against motivation, but it also creates a gap between the supervisor and the worker, because the supervisors have never actually experienced the life and work of the low-skilled people. There is sometimes a lack of empathy, sometimes a lack of appreciation, and sometimes a complete lack of understanding of the causes and circumstances that put the low-skilled people where they are.

Another factor that complicates the job of supervising the lower-skilled people is the fact that often the supervisors of such workers are not as frequently considered as candidates for training as are supervisors of other employees. There are several reasons for this, including the nature of the kind of businesses and industries that have large numbers of low-skilled workers. Such organizations frequently do not have fully established training and development departments. The training is usually considered only a part of some "more important" activity, such as labor relations, safety, or personnel. In such cases, supervisory training is either not done or is done by poorly qualified trainers.

Poor training, together with other factors, many times results in another damaging factor: the kind of supervisors chosen to supervise these workers, the lack of training, and the lack of experience in the job being supervised together create a total lack of understanding of the worker. Worse yet, it probably causes the supervisor to even look down on the worker, to feel disgust with the apparent lack of self-motivation and desire for improvement, and to have no interest in helping the workers improve themselves. This feeling quickly becomes apparent to the workers and further reduces their interest and motivation on the job.

These are not insurmountable problems, though they may appear difficult and complex. The most difficult task—and the thing most helpful in solving the problem—is for supervisors to gain an understanding of the workers. The purpose of this chapter is to increase that understanding by breaking the problems down into some finite bits. As we go back over the problem areas we will try to give solutions that are practical and workable, things that have worked for others in similar situations.

INCORRECT ASSUMPTIONS

We've seen enough by now to understand why there are wrong conclusions drawn by the supervisors as to the nature and traits of the low-skilled workers. It is not true to say that all of these workers are lazy, unambitious, dirty, immoral, that they lack family feelings, have no intelligence to move upward, cannot handle more challenging jobs, or have no interest in bettering themselves. While it may be true that many of them have not *shown* typical signs of ambition, it is not true that they could not learn to exert themselves and show interest in accepting more responsibility.

It is also a false conclusion to say that all of these less qualified people are the product of their environment or their "up-bringing." Society has not produced all of these people, who, in other circumstances would be bank presidents, corporate giants, and managing directors of large endeavors. While environment and society have played a part, more than anything, they are in control of their own destinies. It is no more accurate to blame society for all their problems than it is to credit *only society* for the success of the bank presidents, corporate giants, and managing directors. However, they *do* live in the world around them; they have either gotten or not gotten things from their family, friends, and neighborhoods, and this makes them a part of what they are today. It would be wrong to conclude that they are what they are, and that's that. We have to believe—as we do about anyone—that there are things a supervisor can do to get the most from the employees, and that employees have the potential to be better than they are. Supervisors have to accept that there is a difference in performance under good and bad supervision, and that supervisors differ in their skills at supervising. Supervisors can be better; the logical conclusion from this is that *workers can be better accordingly*.

The solution to the problem of incorrect assumptions is to try to eliminate *all* of the assumptions, if possible. Accept that these people have human natures much like everyone else, hence can be motivated, changed, and supervised in much the same way as other employees, regardless of background and skill. After trying to use the various skills offered in this book and others, and finding that the best efforts don't work on certain people, then it is safe to draw some conclusions about *those people*, but not the class of people referred to as low-skilled.

PERSONALITY DIFFERENCES

Perhaps it is not fair to refer to the differences as being "personality" differences. Whatever it is that we call personality—humor, moods, reaction to things, body language, approaches to other people, and so forth—all of these things tend to be regarded as a person's personality. When a person has worked around other low-skilled workers, been treated as someone without much to contribute, often been paid minimum wages, and has had poor supervision for most of his or her life, it has an effect on the personality. Some retain a sense of humor and an attitude that life is worthwhile on the job, but many don't. Some view the boss as a pleasant personality, one who offers congenial friendship possibilities, but most don't. Some work at getting along even with the malcontent, but many won't. Some learn to show their appreciation for the even minimum wages, but most don't. Some will play the game of being pleasant to the boss, though not feeling it, but most won't. There will simply be some personality differences.

What can be done? There is no question but that the supervisor is the one who has to deal with, make allowances for, and try to overlook the differences. A degree of tolerance is needed here. Some make the mistake of just writing the people off as insignificant, or as people who will be here today, gone tomorrow, so there's no need to worry about them. That's the easy way out, but not the most productive. The first positive step is to accept the fact that these people play a key role in getting the job done, no matter how little they may be paid or how unskilled they are. They are not there because the organization wants to be in the welfare business, taking these unskilled people off the streets. They are there because they are needed to reach the goals of the organization. If they are not there, there will be a vacancy. Someone else will have to be hired to take their place. Considering their importance to the goals of the organization, they are worth some time on our part to see that they fit well into the work plan.

Next, the supervisor must realize that no matter how little skill they have, they bring a brain with them each day they come to work. They bring physical abilities with them. The most unskilled worker we have may be able to fix a lawnmower at home, repair a sewing machine, cook a very good meal, or put a fantastic wax job on a car. This being true, we need to find out what their skills may be, if for no other reason than to give them some positive reinforcement in something. Having recognized their abilities, their potential to think, their skills in some areas, we now have something to converse with them about. We can ask them questions, we can talk about something they are interested in, and we can begin to see them more as human beings with problems and pleasures and activities outside the job.

Finally, we don't have to try to make them over. We don't have to have them become like us, or like everyone else. We need to see them as they are, find common ground to discuss things, and find out that we can carry on reasonable conversations with them. It also lets them know that we can discuss things they are interested in, and that we aren't all that difficult to converse with either. Nothing is more likely to work than asking them something about their job to indicate that we feel they know as much or more than we know. No matter if we're addressing an entry-level clerk or a ditchdigger, when we say, "Tell me how you get that to work that way," we've opened the way for some further conversation!

LESS MOTIVATION

If we can accept that the source of most motivation comes from the job itself, we have only to look at the jobs being done by low-skilled workers to see that there is less opportunity for motivation here than with any other level of employee. The job is just a simple one, with little challenge, and few places for real decision making. It is usually repetitious; it is boring; it gives little room for problem solving. In addition, it offers little in the way of job security, so that even in those "maintenance" items there is little to be offered. The pay is usually low, the working conditions are not very often above average, the benefits may be about average, and the hours will not be exceptionally good. In other words, there will not be any motivation coming from the things that surround the job. If the motivation isn't coming from the job or from the things around the job, then there isn't much left to produce the necessary incentive for working well.

That's where the challenge comes in for the supervisor! That's where *skill of supervision* becomes important. There are some things that can be done and they aren't too difficult; they can be done by any supervisor and they will work on almost anybody. They don't cost any money and don't require any change in the job structure or in job titles or responsibilities. It does require a change in *perception* of the job by the employee and probably by the supervisor. We've already seen that the job may not seem important to the worker, but it is important to getting to the goal of the organization. Handing empty buckets to someone isn't very exciting or challenging until we ask the employee if there's a better way to handle the bucket, or if the buckets could be handed all at one time, or if the job could be made easier by having the buckets stacked somewhere else. The perception of the job could be changed if the supervisor pointed out that getting the buckets from one place to another is vital to the whole assembly operation and showed the employee where the buckets went from his or her action to the next operation. When a new employee comes on board, the supervisor who asks the experienced worker to show the new person the way to do the job effectively and error-free has two employees who see that the boss thinks this is an important job. The experienced employee has developed a little pride in the activity; the new employee sees that this is something the boss wants done correctly because it is necessary to getting the job done.

The problem with all of this is that many supervisors fail to see that everybody wants to feel they are good at something, better than somebody else at something. All we have to do is listen to these same low-skilled workers at break or lunch, and we see them describing how they were better at doing something than one of the other workers: "I can drink more than you, spit further than you; my car was a better buy than yours; I've had more trouble than you; I raised better tomatoes than you; my back hurts more than yours." All people everywhere seem to have this desire to "stroke their egos." Little children in the sandpile can be heard saying the same thing: "My castle is better than yours; my truck is bigger than yours; I can pour more sand on my head than you can; my Daddy can beat up your Daddy." Let's note that the idea isn't to try to trick the employees into *thinking* their job is important. The *supervisor* has to *believe* that the work is important before any of this will work.

UNENRICHING JOBS

"Job enrichment" is akin to motivation in that it looks to the job for the best motivational results. There is little that can be done to add related tasks to a low-skilled workers' job to enrich it, so the supervisor will have to find other means of getting enrichment. We've seen that the supervisor has a good chance of motivating workers by letting them see that the job is important. The job can be enriched by letting the employees become involved in some of the decision-making activities. Many supervisors have found that the employees get enthusiastic about making suggestions when their suggestions are truly listened to. Sometimes there is even a committee—a group of people who stand around and talk, rather then go to a committee room—that discusses ways of speeding up the operation, smoothing out the activities, saving time or money, changing to meet certain customer requirements, and so forth. The idea is that the worker is closest to the job, hence can give more firsthand information on what can and cannot be done.

PERSONAL DRESS HABITS

Many times the supervisor is unprepared for the kinds of clothes worn by the unskilled worker. Because there has often been little opportunity for these workers to "dress up," there may be little interest in appearance. This may be apparent in either the way the clothes are worn or the kind (color, style, fit, and so forth) that are worn. Work clothes are always acceptable in jobs for which they're appropriate, of course, but sometimes the problem is that the work is done around customers or in areas where other employees are dressed in more "acceptable" clothes. This is always a delicate situation and can be troublesome from both the low-skilled workers' standpoint and that of the other employees. It is difficult to go to an employee and say, "I'm sorry, but your clothes look terrible!" Even when we don't use those words, the message comes out the same. What do we do?

One simple, but probably costly, solution is to supply uniforms, then have some requirements for cleanliness of them, or have the organization do the washing and keep clean ones on the job. Another solution is to give employees a laundry allowance, with standards for cleanliness. Such a solution is often worth the hassle, just to assure proper appearance. If it is handled properly, and the employees are told what is being spent on the clothing, this can serve as a pretty good incentive.

Another approach is to have a dress code that is distributed and posted—and enforced. It doesn't have to require the expenditure of money, such as by saying that the employees must wear certain colors or styles of clothes, but it can require a degree of neatness or cleanliness. It can also specify that hose or socks be worn, that sandles are prohibited, or that shoes must be free of visible mud or dirt when entering the buildings. The written and enforced code should have a basis in logic and necessity, not just be something to satisfy a whim of the supervisor who happens to like a particular style or color. It serves as a means of discussing the appearance of the workers, and is something that can be mentioned on the day of employment or during orientation.

The simplest approach is a straightforward one in which the supervisor goes to the employee whose appearance is not satisfactory and has a frank discussion. If muddy boots are a problem, and the appearance could be offensive to the customers, then this can be so stated. It should be done with candor and kindness. It can be softened by stating that the supervisor is aware that the job is one that requires working in adverse conditions and that not everyone likes that kind of work environment. The supervisor can express appreciation for the willingness to work under these conditions, and then point out that there are reasons for having a different dress or apparel, and give logical reasons. Ask for help in meeting these requirements. Be firm but not harsh.

LOW SELF-ESTEEM

Supervisors find that lower-skilled employees seem to make less effort to advance than employees at any other level. One reason seems to be that workers at this level often have a very low view of their own abilities to be better or move up. They expect to fail at jobs they aren't familiar with or haven't done before. Often their life is one of many failures, hence they more often expect failure than success.

The answer to overcoming this is to build some successes, trying to change the self-image. Supervisors have a problem with this because they can't always think small enough to realize how small a success is needed to classify as a "success" with these people. One of the best approaches is to just give verbal support to things they are now doing. We can say, "Hey, I like the way you do that," and the "that" is something they have been doing right all along. We can do an even better job by saying to someone who is new or not familiar with a certain operation, "Joan, how about showing Sue how to handle this, will you? You've always done it pretty well." If we do this kind of thing long enough, with enough sincerity, the dividends will be quite satisfactory.

POOR EDUCATION

There is no way we can make up for a lack of education. If people cannot read or do simple calculations, we can't teach them these skills overnight. There are many places in most large towns where adults can learn basic skills. If these are not available, or if an employee isn't interested in taking such classes, then we have to deal with it on the job. Two things to remember: (1) lack of education is not a sign of lack of intelligence; and (2) lack of education is not the same as lack of experience and job knowledge.

We have to work hard at understanding that these people come to us without the advantage of a good education for many reasons. We don't even have to know the reasons, nor are they important. What we do is determine as best we can the level of their ability to understand things about the job, education aside. Does the person have the ability to comprehend the basic steps involved in operating this machine? Can the person understand my instructions—couched in simple terms—on repair and maintenance of the equipment? If reading is a problem, I make allowances by telling instead of assigning reading activities. Next, I build on job experience wherever possible, to give some of the successes discussed above in connection with low self-esteem. I get an idea of the person's intelligence by gauging the experience level against what it takes to really understand and do the kinds of things this person has done.

Supervisors of the poorly educated can avoid anything that looks like making fun of illiteracy. Correcting the person's grammar isn't going to build much rapport. Talking about the advantages of being able to read the specifications might be a better incentive.

LACK OF JOB OPPORTUNITIES

At least two things have to be overcome in improving the low-skilled workers' job opportunities. First, we have to see that the employees have an opportunity to learn more skills, if at all possible. We give them the chance to fill in for somebody else, we let them have time to learn another operation, and we give them praise when they are close to successful. Next, we try to give them some exposure to others who might have openings for someone to learn another job. We can send the person to them, saying, "I've got somebody who's doing a good job for me—see what you can do with them." It is very difficult for them to get exposure, even when they're doing very well, because the lower-skilled jobs rarely get into the appraisal systems.

PAST JOB EXPERIENCE PROBLEMS

Overcoming bad habits is a major task for any supervisor, especially when the habits were accepted in previous jobs—or even
developed there. When low-skilled workers come to us from poor
supervisors, we have the difficult job of overcoming the bad supervision as well as all the bad things learned under that supervision. It can be a long, drawn-out situation. We have to start by
stating what we expect, encouraging the employees to try the new
way, giving praise when there is success, minimizing the failures
by urging them to try again, and practicing a great deal of patience
and tolerance. Part of the problem may be that the employees
have learned to distrust supervisors. To remedy this, we have to
have some good, constructive conversation, building up the employee's confidence in us, both as a person and as a supervisor.

INDIVIDUAL TRAITS AND PERSONALITIES

Now let's look at some of the individual traits and personalities
of these workers, with some suggestions on overcoming the problems that arise from them.

Typical or Not?

Someone has said, "All generalities are false, including this one."
Well said! However, we do have to start somewhere, and what
we've done here is to look at some of the commonalities of this
class of worker. Some of the things we've said are not so much
a function of the type of employee as a function of the type of
job. The job itself either breeds habits and characteristics into people or attracts certain types of people. In either case, supervisors
have to deal with the situations as they find them. The best thing
for the supervisor to do is to make a very diligent effort to take
each employee as he or she comes, trying not to classify them
into broad groups, but seeing what they have and haven't got as
far as the things we've talked about in this chapter. If the person

fits one of the problem areas, we try to use the solutions suggested. If not, we go on to another problem.

Lack of Work Ethic

Many times one of the most frustrating characteristics of low-skilled people may be the lack of interest and concern about either being on time or coming to work at all. Not all are like this, but many are. Some of this stems from not having steady work in the past. Sometimes they are accustomed to work only a few days a week, hence have other activities outside the job. Because of their low pay, and low skill, they are often just "pick-up" employees, doing something different each day or each week. This lack of steady work or steady assignments reduces their feelings of belonging. It gives them the appearance of having a poor work ethic.

Another characteristic is the need to be told when to do each activity and perhaps even how to do it. When the work is done, they may well wait for another assignment, leading us to we say they have no sense of responsibility. They may be responding to the kind of jobs and supervision they've had in the past.

How do we change all of this? Only by having some rules, sticking to them (with some tolerance and understanding), and reinforcing any good things we see happen. Quiet talks, giving reasons for the need for regularity in the job and showing the advantages and consequences of continued good performance, will more likely succeed than anything else.

Poverty Background

The background of low-skilled workers often reflects the kind of parents or home-life situation they came from. They may not have had very good role models, so there is not only the lack of work ethic, but a lack of life-goal or career objective. They may not have learned to handle money very well. They may have a good sense of how to live *within* the framework of poverty, but no idea of how to exist *outside* of it. This not only adds frustration, but builds on the low self-esteem problem talked about earlier.

The only thing the supervisor has to do, usually, is help the workers adjust to the newer life style. There may be the need for counseling on how to handle money, sometimes even how to open a bank account or how to avoid time payments too large for the income expected. Again, this is a touchy thing, and help should be offered not imposed.

Health Care

If low-skilled workers have come from environments where they have not had good medical advice, they may present a problem for the supervisor in that they don't take good enough care of themselves on *minor* problems, hence have more serious ailments as a result. Supervisors must learn to detect areas of neglect, offering help in contacting doctors, if necessary, and making sure the employees take advantage of whatever medical service and assistance is offered by the organization. If the employee is frequently absent for minor illnesses, supervisors should be concerned about the health problem rather than about just the absenteeism and the job problems.

Belligerence

One thing that is difficult for supervisors to learn in dealing with any employee, and it is especially true—for some reason—with low-skilled employees, is that nothing in any work agreement ever requires the employee to like the supervisor, the organization, or the job itself. When employees get belligerent, the supervisors somehow want them to start to like things about the job. What they need to look for is whether or not the employees are doing their work. If the job is being done and other employees are not being affected adversely—as far as performance is concerned—then the supervisor must just let things go as they are.

On the other hand, if the work is being neglected or other employees are being interfered with, then action has to be taken. The action must always be directed toward the work, not the employee. Supervisors must make certain that the employees know that it is the poor performance that is the trouble and the source of displeasure, not the employee personally. Set standards and deal with those who do not meet the standards.

Defensiveness

It is natural for these workers to sometimes get defensive as a means of covering for the perceived mistreatment they've experienced over the years. In different jobs under different supervisors, they've perhaps gotten the idea that they are being picked on unjustly. They haven't gotten much positive reinforcement so they have reason to believe some of the things. They aren't in a position to command much respect and they don't get very much. They don't do any kind of a job that means that higher-level people come around and know them. They get untrained supervisors, who may be very autocratic in nature. They have been fussed at, ordered around, never given much status, and at some point find that being defensive is a more comfortable way to live than just being submissive.

The job of the good supervisor in such cases is to not be offended by the defensive reaction of the employees, but to offer encouragement and positive reinforcement whenever possible. We have no obligation to make up for any mistreatment in the past, but we can see that it doesn't continue. We can remember that each of these employees is an individual with feelings and problems and families and needs. We don't have to solve all the problems, but we can try not to be part of additional problems. There is no reason for us to make an exception to the work rules for any of our employees, if we really want to continue to be fair, but we can be understanding when there is some room for doubt or flexibility. While we don't want to let out employees ever take advantage of us, neither do we want to take advantage of them. "Fair but firm" is the order of the day, for all our employees.

Passiveness

The thing most often heard from supervisors about low-skilled employees is that "they just don't care." For all the reasons we've seen so far in this chapter, they certainly give that indication, and perhaps have some reason to be that way. The truth is, though, that they *do* care about a lot of things. Part of their defensiveness is not letting the caring show. They will respond to good treatment, though the response may not appear as appreciation. They will respond to being asked their opinions, though the response may come out as only a shrug of the shoulders while they're giving their opinions. They will improve their attendance and on-time rate when we recognize their positive contributions and show them the importance of the job, though they may not come charging in and showing great smiles of excitement. What we have to do is use the skills we know will work and look at output and production and job performance, rather than outward changes in appearance and attitudes.

Interpersonal Relations

Supervisors often become distressed over low-skilled employees who show no concern for the customers, act arrogantly towards the boss and other employees, appear sullen and noncommunicative, and generally exhibit poor interpersonal relations. Without any customer-relations training, many of our employees do a poor job, and without any employee-relations training, our employees often fail to handle their relationships well. The low-skilled employees are neither trained nor usually held accountable, and would probably not respond to the training very quickly anyway. What does the supervisor do?

First, we should try to see that this type of employee is not put into situations where there is much customer contact, since we will not be training the employees and they will rarely figure out on their own how they should act. Next, we may not need to put much emphasis on employee relations, since most often the low-skilled worker is relating with other such employees—and they have less trouble relating to each other than they do with those of higher-level skills or jobs. Next, we should have group meetings to discuss the importance of our customers to the organization, letting the workers know that all of us depend on the customers for our wages and for the continuance of our jobs. We also ask them for ways we can improve our image with the customers.

The general awareness created by this discussion and implementing suggestions will help a lot in our efforts to improve the low-skilled workers' behavior in front of customers.

As far as relations with the employees and the boss are concerned, we may have to work harder to improve these. If confrontations get to be serious, then we may have to take a heavy hand, going to the root of the problem and setting some stern standards of conduct. (We can do this with customer relations, too, but it is usually easier to get the employees aware of customer-relations problems than it is to get them to see the importance of getting along with co-workers. If the spats and quarrels are not all that significant, and some of the workers aren't on good terms with other employees, and this doesn't hurt the job performance, we may do well to leave it alone.

VIEWPOINT

The Organization

Employees with the lower-level skills aren't very impressed by the hierarchy of the organization, and don't need to be. There's little to be gained by their understanding the politics of the departments and managers and different work groups. In many ways, they may be much better off and better employees for not being involved or interested in these things. There may be occasional embarrassment when one of the workers fails to be impressed by one of the big shots who comes along and speaks to them, but we can learn to live with that. If we know in advance that one is coming our way, we may want to suggest that this is an important person who has some bearing on our jobs and the money and maybe we should try to be nice to them. It shouldn't be a big issue, of course.

The Home and Family

By now we see the reasons for some of the viewpoints the low-skilled workers have toward their families and their role in the family. We do wrong if we think they don't have compassion, that they don't worry about their children getting in trouble or being sick, and don't feel any responsibility for the family. It may be that we just assume some things about them and put all of the workers in the same category. One thing we might do is have a conversation with them about their family, asking them how many children they have at home, what their ages are, and a few things about them. We will get a much better picture of their viewpoint by doing this than by just assuming some things.

Other Workers

We have seen that they will not treat other workers in the way we would like, and that sometimes this may cause a problem. Part of the difficulty is that they feel little need to get along with others, especially those with higher levels of skills. They don't relate with them and they sometimes feel that these people are part of the cause of their own poorer estate. They will exercise their own clannishness, and the best thing we can do is let that alone unless there is some reason to change it. We don't force people to associate with people just because we think it is nice.

Life-Style

We can be of some assistance to low-skilled people in handling finances and developing savings efforts, but we should be careful not to try to formulate a plan for them that suits *our* life-style. Their thought processes are centered around living from one day to the next, with little regard for how much they will have at retirement time. They pretty much live on the installment plan, and can pay for very few things with saved cash. They pay high interest for what they purchase. We probably don't like that, but we will not be very likely to change it. Our best rule is to offer advice, not try to run their lives. One important thing we can do for them is to let them know if there are any savings plans or stock options or other money-making or savings programs operated through the organization. We can also point out the benefits of the hospitalization and other insurance programs available through the organization's benefit program. It's not enough to have all these people in a large auditorium, with other employees asking in-depth questions and getting complex answers, and let it go there. We must take the time to explain carefully and sometimes simply what the programs are and what they will do for the employees.

CONCLUSION

We've seen that it is difficult to understand all the ramifications of supervising low-skilled workers, who are likely to be far different from us in life-style, thought processes, and behavior on the job. It is a difficult task to properly supervise such workers. But they do an important job, and we need them. For that reason, it's worth the effort to become more skilled at dealing with them. There is payoff, some of it visible, but not all of it. If we watch production and performance and see it improving, then we have to be satisfied that we've done the organization a good service by giving them employees who are doing a better job because of what we have done as supervisors. That should be satisfaction enough!

CHAPTER

7

SUPERVISING TECHNICAL AND PROFESSIONAL PEOPLE

RUTH SIZEMORE HOUSE

Do you face your role as technical manager with these unanswered questions distracting you?

1. What's so special about supervising technical and professional people?
2. What is the role of a technical supervisor?
3. How can I maintain a positive outlook in a technical environment?

7.1

4. How can I build an effective technical team?

5. How can I keep that team working smoothly?

6. How can I help my technical group communicate effectively with nontechnical people?

7. How can I handle temporary disruptions to minimize losses in productivity and morale?

8. What should I look for in training and development opportunity for my technical people?

Matt Stephens, a new technical supervisor in a nationwide firm, has been going over these questions again and again. He'd accepted his new position with some misgivings. He'd heard that technical managers find out the hard way that technical employees are "a different kind of animal." As one computer department manager put it:

> Programmers have pretty well been the masters of their own destinies throughout the decade. They have been well paid; they have named their hours of work; they have hopped from job to job with impunity, leaving behind deskfuls of chaos; they have been wined and dined, coddled and humored, promoted and pampered. If ever a group of employees rose to Cinderelladom overnight, the computer specialists were that group. They were immune to control; they were immune to discipline; they were immune to competition. [Snyders and Lasden, 1982: 47]

Matt had read about high levels of conflict in technical management positions: his evening management classes at the university referred to a manager as "the person in the middle." And his professor had reported that research managers demonstrated the highest levels of role conflict (Miles and Perrault, 1976: 40). Furthermore, role conflict correlated with a host of undesirables like tendency to leave the organization, delay in decision, frustration, tension, sense of threat and anxiety, psychological withdrawal, sense of futility (House, 1982: 15).

And he'd heard how difficult it would be to get technical and non-technical people to work together: "Those people may be brilliant, but nobody else in the company can understand what they are talking about." "Those guys want to get ahead. Trouble is, they're not willing to get along with anybody in the process—not even top management!"

Matt's misgivings aren't unusual. No wonder. Those three themes weave in and out of a technical manager's day-to-day interactions:

The ways technical and professional people are like/different from others.

The conflict that characterizes the technical manager's position.

The need for effective interface between technical and non-technical people.

Matt will supervise 17 technical/professional people. Six work on R&D projects, three design sequences for production and develop product standards, and eight inspect for quality assurance. They vary in skill and experience, but each person has some unique skill or knowledge to offer to most projects. Some of Matt's employees are loners, others enjoy discussing new information and techniques. There is the usual conflict and jealousy that exists in most job situations, and there's also some reluctance to work as a team. Advancement opportunities are fairly limited in the organization, and there's one rather frequent complaint: "Where do we go from here? What's the payoff for doing a good job?"

Several of Matt's concerns center around Bill Norman, a talented and experienced technical employee. Bill knows the jobs, has handled all of them at one time or another. There is little that's new that he doesn't know about, though he doesn't do very much reading or research. He says he prefers getting the information by listening to others and observing.

Bill prefers a job that allows him to be on a team, but he only rarely will be the leader. He has a hard time sitting through the "rules-setting" stage of organizing the team: he prefers to "get on with it." On several occasions Bill's interest has dropped sharply on projects where there was considerable paperwork or delay while projects were going through the red tape of approval. He wants things delegated to him and seems to work better when he has considerable authority. He may make excuses that management "sandbagged" the project when on-time completion is doubtful or when errors surface.

Let's review Matt's research on his questions and see how he can apply what he finds to his dealings with Bill.

1.   What's so special about supervising a technical or professional person?

Technical people were people before they were technical—even engineers, even computer programmers. So, like other people, their needs may move up and down Maslow's hierarchy. Like other people, they need good feedback, they will respond to positive reinforcement, they will have highs and lows. And according to one technical consulting firm, they share many qualities of the "new breed" of employees when compared with employees several decades ago. They

Are less likely to be "in awe" of upper management,

Are more technically specialized,

Are more demanding of a pleasant job environment,

Expect respect for personal values,

Show more loyalty to their profession than to their employers (Snyders and Lasden, 1982:35).

And—like many of us—they are likely to cope with stress by eating (Renwick and Lawler, 1978:60).

Technical people do share distinguishing characteristics as a group. Interviews with over 600 data processing professionals showed they had a relatively high need for professional growth, coupled with a relatively low need for social interaction (Snyders and Lasden, 1982:35). (The conflict these create emerges again: that low need for interaction could really limit opportunities for professional growth—and certainly opportunities for advancement that are likely to require some social visibility.)

There's good reason to believe that the performance of research and development professionals improves when

Their authority comes from expertise rather than from formal position,

They can openly express their differences,

They feel encouragement to take calculated technical risks (Aram and Morgan, 1976:1135).

But the impatience of technical people with nontechnical staff throws hurdle after hurdle in the path of efficient and painless interaction in the organization.

This information will give Matt some ideas about getting to know Bill.

First of all, Bill was a person before he was technical. So Matt should do what he can to get to know Bill *as an individual*. That means Matt should find out what Bill perceives as rewarding (like delegated authority) and as punishing (like red tape). Then he can try to follow some of those necessary red-taped assignments with assignments that allow Bill to exercise some authority rather than to meticulously follow someone else's rules. (Notice that the rewarding activity *follows* the grueling one.)

Like many technical people, Bill likes to have tasks delegated to him rather than to work under close supervision. Since Bill is a top professional, Matt can afford to leave a variety of decisions in Bill's hands. He can allow Bill a longer time span of discretion (length of time between giving an assignment and reviewing that assignment). When a decision is one that only Matt can make, he can be sure to get technical input from Bill first. It's important in these situations for Matt to make it clear at the outset that he will make the decision but that Bill's input will influence the decision.

When Matt's decision differs from Bill's opinion, Matt should be prepared for open disagreement. To be sure he's hearing Bill's opinion accurately, he should be able to summarize it to *Bill's* satisfaction. He can explain his decision, he can acknowledge that it was a difficult one, but he need not defend his need to make it. Nor should he attack Bill's opinion in an attempt to justify his own.

Bill's impatience with paperwork may overflow into impatience with the typist or the administrative staff processing it. There won't be a quick fix for this problem. Of course Matt can respond to some specific incident directly. But over the long term the model of his own behavior is likely to have the most impact. He can be sure that the nontechnical people on his staff know the technical vocabulary they need to survive in the organization and know exactly how their own work fits in. When technical terms aren't necessary, he won't use them; they can seem like a secret code designed to keep the uninitiated in their place! Above all, he can encourage. He can give immediate, positive feedback for jobs well done. For those jobs not so well done, he can give feedback that is specific, nonjudgmental, and clearly related to the task (not to the employee's lineage, anatomy, and so forth).

2.   What is the role of the technical supervisor?

Matt summarizes the primary role of technical supervisors in just one word: interface. Interface between members of his technical team, interface between his group and the rest of the organization, interfere between technical and nontechnical people—these will require the largest part of his time. He is the interface that permits communication between these components—incompatible as they may seem at times.

As the interface between his technical team and the rest of the organization, Matt must constantly be on the lookout for links between organizational goals and the talent of his people, then pass that insight on in both directions. What management decisions are deadlocked over technical issues that Bill Norman could help clarify? What opportunities for growth might open up to Bill as a result of his participation?

At the same time, Matt must translate to his technical people the marketplace decisions and pressures that top management must face: real-world issues that may impede or even overrule technical know-how. The translation must strike a balance: too little said may promote dissatisfaction with management; too much said may discourage technical effort. For example, Matt will try to encourage Bill's acceptance of management reality but *not* fuel complaints about "sandbagging."

Matt's translation to management of the needs and pressures

of his people must be equally balanced. He should give management the technical information they need to evaluate the tradeoffs. They should know how marketplace decisions will affect technical quality. They should know how cost or time limits will affect product performance and human performance. They may need to know how a technical person like Bill feels administrative delays affect technical progress. And Matt is the one to translate Bill's complaint, "The guys at the top have sandbagged us again" into realistic "If . . . then . . ." information that can help with a decision:

"Our best technical people tell us that another day's delay will keep us from meeting XYZ's deadline. That means we'll be facing some fines unless we make the decision now. If we delay, we're sure to get fined; if we give the go-ahead now, we can meet the contract deadline."

Throughout Matt's interface activity, he can emphasize the "larger team" approach. He can do that through the feedback he gives: "Bill, your suggestion to revise the production sequence saved the company $xxxxx in overtime," or "Bill, your idea to buy that new equipment would be just right for engineering, but we'll need to wait until production can budget comparable equipment for their shops."

Matt can encourage team effort by emphasizing team performance rather than by comparing the performance of individual team members: "We caught the production problem in time to change the sequence *before* it caused any delays," *instead of* "Bill, you've beat John's long-standing record for the fastest turnaround from inspection to solution."

And you can encourage team effort by delegating some decisions to the group. You may need to set some parameters first, of course, but why not let the group decide

How to adopt flexible scheduling and still be sure there's always someone available to provide technical assistance.

How to make shift assignments fairly (if this decision hasn't been made already by a union.

How to schedule adequate "alone time" for heavy technical work and still allow for helpful give and take.

Group decisions can become increasingly effective if you provide team members with skill-building opportunities in group problem-solving techniques like

Brainstorming.   A technique to generate the greatest possible volume of ideas to later be evaluated against suitable criteria.

Force-Field Analysis.   A technique for visualizing and assessing the forces supporting change and the forces resisting it.

Synectics.   A technique using analogies to get maximum benefit from interdisciplinary groups.

3.   How can I maintain a positive outlook in a technical environment?

Keeping a positive outlook in a technical environment can be tricky for a manager. For one thing, there are those stereotypes to contend with. While Matt makes every effort to get to know Bill as an individual, he must also realize that others may see him as the stereotypical engineer, "hacker," or researcher. And if Matt has a technical background, they may very well see him the same way. His capability as an interface unit is likely to soon come in handy. When he represents Bill's ideas or his own to upper management, he must take the time to translate first. He can't leave to chance the relationship between what he wants and the bottom line for the organization: he will spell it out for upper management.

Matt's ability to relate the needs of his technical group to the bottom line will also help prepare him for shifts in priorities that management is bound to make from time to time. Upper management's goal is to compete for resources and for the market; without Matt's translation for Bill, Bill is likely to see his only goal as the pursuit of technical excellence.

Now and then the two goals are bound to clash. If Matt keeps on top of how things happen in his organization—how money moves and how control moves—he'll more likely see the clash coming. He'll be in better shape to let management know

The costs of abandoning a current project.

The value of potential breakthroughs in the current project.

The application of current project development to the new priority.

He'll be in a better position to let Bill and other team members know

The cost of continuing the current project,

The application of current project developments to the new priority.

The effect of the shift on their activities, and their job security.

How can Matt handle the stress of constantly being the "person in the middle"? Good stress management maintenance may determine his ability to function during a crisis: regular exercise, regular relaxation, regular sleep, nutritious meals, and avoidance of chemical dependencies can help give you a sound baseline for stress management. Deep-breathing exercises, muscle relaxation exercises, self-talk in response to your own "catastrophizing" can help give the extra dose of energy and control you need during a crisis.

4. How can I build a technical team?

Matt's technical group is varied: Bill Norman is talented and experienced. He's likely to be a good team member, but not much of a leader. He's impatient with administrative procedures and is likely to resist decisions imposed by an authority figure. Sam Johnson has 13 years of technical experience in three different hi-tech industries. He prefers to work alone. He has a high need for advancement, but rejects the idea that interpersonal skills will affect his move up the organizational ladder. He openly exhibits his disgust when any of his technical innovations is "put on hold" because it doesn't support current management goals. Alice Whyte is a bright new hire just out of college. She is certainly capable, but has little work experience. She seems to want to learn everything at once and be given decision and project authority immediately. Although other staff members recognize this as a "stage" many young graduates go through, they're a little put off by what seems like aggressiveness. (Alice, no doubt, sees it only as enthusiasm.) As a result, she often has to "play 20 questions" to get helpful information from more experienced technical people.

The situations Matt must deal with are likewise varied. Matt feels he has very little influence over some management decisions. Some administrative decisions, in fact, come as a complete shock to him, such as the decision to reassign group parking allotments and locations. Sometimes Matt feels he has more control. Management defines some pretty rigid parameters, but usually honors his decision.

Many decisions are clearly delegated to Matt. He may need to explain them to management, but he's never had to actually defend them. And there are a number of decisions management will never hear about. These decisions affect only the internal operations of his division.

To deal with these varied people and varied situations, Matt needs a flexible management style. He'll need to recognize those situations in which he'll simply tell his people about a management decision. With staff members of Bill's disposition, he may be able to *sell* the decision—use an inductive approach to win support *without* misleading the employee about the decision or the decision maker. He will likely choose to *sell* his employees on those decisions he makes which are defined by rigid management parameters. Or he may choose to *consult* with his staff first and then decide. That's what he's most likely to do when he has more leeway. And there may be operations decisions within the division for which he *joins* his group as an equal member, agreeing beforehand to honor the group's decision.

His technical people and his work situations aren't governed by any fixed formulas. So Matt will probably look at a variety of management models—and draw on at least several of them—when he looks for examples of management techniques he wants to practice. The more useful ones are likely to have several things in common:

A way to be sure expectations are clear: Matt's expectations of his employees *and* their expectations of him.

A way to unobtrusively provide positive reinforcement for jobs well done.

A way to engineer feedback that is immediate, measurable, visible, goal-related, and self-administered. (That last characteristic is a critical one. If Matt wants his group to run on "automatic," he needs to be sure the employees *themselves* have some way to know how well they're doing.)

A way to handle emotionally loaded situations that builds understanding of the other person's point of view yet clearly establish Matt's point of view or that of upper management.

Skill in handling emotionally loaded situations will be especially helpful when Matt encounters some of the typical hazards in technical management: technical competition among group members, withholding information or ideas, impatience with nontechnical people, isolation, variety in jobs and the personalities that match ("thinkers" versus "doers").

5. How can I maintain a technical team?

Matt's concerns with Alice Whyte comes down to this: Alice has the technical ability to handle many technical tasks; but she's not ready for the accountability and the authority that must go with responsibility for delegated tasks. How should his delegation style be different for Alice than for Bill Norman? For someone with high motivation and low experience like Alice, Matt should just explain the details, be available when she needs help, and check progress in subtle ways. For someone with high motivation and high experience like Sam Johnson, Matt can *leave him alone.* No tracking is necessary. If he needs help, he'll ask for it.

For Matt's employees with low motivation and low experience, Matt will need to explain what needs to be done and how to do it. He will probably write out details. He'll point out specific checkpoints and do constant, obvious checking. And for those with low motivation and high experience, Matt should explain the importance of the task, sell the project, and keep checking at regular intervals. These employees may lose interest easily.

If Matt's general mangement style is to effective, he'll need to be aware of some specific pitfalls that pose hazards to technical managers. At one one end of the scale, there is resistance. Resistance may show up clearly as open hostility, but it can be disguised in many forms: demand for details, demand to give details, concerns about the "real world," instant agreement (abdication), administrative red tape, exaggerated time or money pressure. Usually, resistance stems from concern about some kind of loss of control. Usually, the best antidote is reassurance and support. That's right, support: even when group members are blocking the progress of the group, they need reassurance and support for their team membership. Otherwise the sense of threat from perceived loss of control is likely to grow and the resistance likely to intensify. Confidence and a good management style will enable Matt to provide that support without undetermining his own position or the importance of other group members.

At the other end of the scale is the pitfall of "group think." "Group think" results from the *absence* of *dis*agreement. In turn, it can result in the acceptance of an unsound strategy or the release of an unsafe product. "Group think" is most likely to occur in a highly cohesive group striving for concurrence. It's accompanied by an illusion of invulnerability (which results in willingness to take excessive risks), shared stereotypes, rationalization, an illusion of morality, self-censorship, an illusion of unanimity, direct pressure on those who suggest disagreement, and mind guarding.

You can steer around this pitfall by bringing in an outside opinion, asking each member to be a critical evaluator, avoiding direct leadership, and making it clear you want all alternatives explored.

Maintaining your team, like establishing it, will require flexibility: the use of models, not rigid formulas.

6. *How can I help my group communicate with nontechnical people?*

Because they have devoted so much energy to their technical development, technical people may feel awkward dealing with anything that can't be measured—such as emotions. One nationally known counselor feels strongly that awkwardness with emotions complicates interpersonal relationships with technical people. In fact, she's writing a book on marriage for couples in which one person is a scientist/engineer. Her husband, an engineer, characteristically suggested she call it *The Engineer and the Twit!*

Of course, technical people were people before they were technical: Matt can expect them to be more *like* other people than different from them.

But he should still look for

Failure to recognize the emotional components of an issue.

Persistent logical problem solving in the face of emotional (not logical) situations.

Unrealistic expectations that nontechnical people will be in awe of and knowledgeable about their technology.

Impatience with nontechnical people and nontechnical issues.

The model of Matt's own behavior is likely to be his most powerful tool for influencing his staff. He can be sure his nontechnical staff understands the nature of the work done in his division. He can be sure they understand the necessary technical terms. And he can be sure that he himself

Uses plain English when technical terms aren't needed.

Provides positive reinforcement and feedback of the same quality he gives his technical people.

Clarifies expectations: the nontechnical persons' expectations of him, his expectations of the nontechnical person, and his expectations of the relationship between technical and nontechnical people.

7. *How can I help my group handle specific situations?*

Throughout Matt's supervision of his division, there are likely to be changes that will affect group morale and group performance: breakthroughs, upward mobility, changes in membership, loss, and disappointment.

In his poem, "If," Rudyard Kipling identifies several signs of emotional stature:

If you can dream—and not make dreams your master;
 If you can think and not make thoughts your aim,

If you can meet with Triumph and Disaster
    And treat those two imposters just the same.

Bill can enjoy the triumph of a breakthrough to the hilt. But then he'll help his staff prepare to face other challenges—some of which will seem mundane by comparison. Remember the astronaut who became dependent on alcohol and drugs after walking on the moon because he felt there was nothing left for him to look forward to? After the glow of a breakthrough has worn off, technical staff may sink into listlessness and boredom. Again, it's a time for encouragement by

Putting the less dramatic achievements ahead into perspective.

Giving positive reinforcement more frequently and for smaller steps well done than you normally would.

Watching for signs of burnout and being ready to discuss the emotional issue with individual employees.

Most other changes have stress built into them—even changes for the better such as upward mobility. Research in sociology and psychology ranks upwardly mobile people as high risks for stress-related illnesses, divorce, and suicide. The "fair-haired" person who outpaces others in advancement may face as many difficulties as the one who falls behind.

Changes in group membership will also add stress to the technical team. After someone has come into the group or someone has left the group, Matt will probably see the group revert to an earlier stage of development—more concerned about objectives, ground rules, leadership. If the group loses a beloved member, Matt can expect to see other team members go through stages of grieving. Grief might also result from another perceived loss or great disappointment. Before team members accept the loss, they may express denial, anger, and depression or bargaining for —. Even if these feelings don't show (and technical people may have trouble expressing them), Matt can be sensitive to the fact that they are likely to be churning beneath the surface. He can make himself available to his staff in case they want to talk. He can simply invite them to talk, but for those who have difficulty expressing their feelings, he may be most helpful by being visible—at the water cooler, at lunchtime, getting a cup of coffee, arriving early and starting each employee's day off with an individual "Good morning!"

8. What should I look for in training and development—technical, management, and interpersonal?

Regardless of the kind of training, it's a good idea to look for out*comes* rather than out*lines*. Outcomes are usually preceded in a course description by an expression such as "After this session, participants will be able to," or, "when you have completed this course, you will be able to . . . ."

If Matt wants his employees to gain new *knowledge* as a result of the training or other development activity, he should look for objectives such as these:

Recognize five different kinds of errors in the typical Basic language program.

Compare the economic considerations for exceeding minimum tolerances in the Alpha project by 12%.

Identify the three most often used lubricants in food processing and list why each meets FDA standards.

If he wants his employees to gain a new *skill*, he should look for objectives that match the skill he wants them to use back on the job such as:

Diagnose the seven most probable errors in laboratory processing where lasers are used, and identify each as it occurs in controlled experiments.

Operate the hexagonic diamometer to a tolerance standard of 0.012 grams under normal field conditions.

Wire the electrical harness for a six-cylinder 425 engine to demonstrate correct computer readouts on the Harvey V-5 Analyzer.

If Matt wants employees to gain a new *attitude*, classroom training isn't likely to deliver what he wants. Although course objectives may read," Be sympathetic to the management point of view," about the best he can hope for is *awareness*. There's a big step between intellectual awareness and the desired emotional response, and many variables come to bear on that step. Matt can provide information that will bring about awareness, he can provide models of and practice for interpersonal skills that sharpen the awareness, but whether that awareness results in empathy or in anger is largely in the hands of the trainee, not the instructor.

Matt is more likely to be successful in changing someone's *behavior* than in changing someone's *attitude*. So he'll try to identify the specific behaviors that would demonstrate the desired attitude, and plan his training and development around those behaviors.

Classroom work isn't the only development option. Rotating assignments and on-the-job instruction are two other good options in some cases. Regardless of the development activity Matt selects, he'll want to find out

How new information will be presented.

How new skills will be demonstrated.

How new information will be applied in the activity.

How new skills will be practiced in the activity.

How the employee will find out how well he is doing *during* the activity.

What he should look for and reinforce when the employee returns to his or her regular job.

Matt summarized what he found about technical management in this checklist, which you might want to keep handy as a reminder:

1. To supervise technical and professional people I will take special care to

   Know each employee as an individual.

   Delegate decisions when possible or get technical input before I make the decisions I can't delegate.

   Accept—perhaps even encourage—open expression of disagreement.

Model cooperative behavior with nontechnical people.

2. My role as a technical supervisor requires me to act as an interface unit. Specifically, it requires that I

    Link bottom-line organizational goals with the talents of the people I supervise.

    Translate management pressures for my technical people.

    Translate the needs and pressures on my technical people for management.

    Emphasize the larger team approach.

    Emphasize team performance.

    Delegate some decisions to the group.

3. To maintain a positive outlook, I will

    Combat stereotypes.

    Prepare for shifts in priorities.

    Manage stress.

4. To build a technical team I will use a flexible management style that includes

    A way to clarify expectations.

    A way to give unobtrusive positive reinforcement.

    A way to provide feedback that is immediate.

    Measurable, goal-related, and self-administered.

    A way to handle emotionally loaded situations.

5. To maintain a technical team I will

    Adapt my delegation style for individual team members based on experience and motivation levels.

    Give support even to resistant team members.

    Guard against "group think."

    Retain a flexible management style.

6. To help my group communicate with nontechnical people I will provide a model in which I

    Use plain English.

    Give positive reinforcement and quality feedback.

    Clarify expectations.

7. To help my group handle special situations like break-throughs and changes in membership I will give encouragement by

Putting less dramatic achievements in perspective.

Giving positive reinforcement more frequently and for smaller steps than usual.

Noticing signs of stress or burnout in my employees.

Being visible to employees and available to discuss emotional issues.

8. When I consider training and development activities for the people I supervise, I will find out

What the outcomes of the experience are likely to be.

How new information will be presented.

How new skills will be demonstrated.

How new information will be applied in the activity.

How the employees will learn how well he or she is doing *during* the activity.

What I should look for and reinforce when the employee returns to his or her regular job.

REFERENCES

Aram, J. D., and C. P. Morgan. "The Role of Project Team Collaboration in R & D Performance." *Management Science* 22, no. 10 (June 1976):1127–1137.

House, Ruth, S. "Increase Training Benefits: Decrease Role Conflict." *Performance and Instruction* 21, no. 15 (June 1982):14–15.

Kipling, Rudyard. "If." In *One Hundred and One Famous Poems* edited by Roy J. Cook. Chicago: The Reilly and Lee Company, 1958.

Miles, Robert H. and William D. Perrault. "Organizational Role Conflict: Its Antecedents and Consequences." *Organizational Behavior and Human Performance* 17, no. 1 (1976):19–44.

Renwick, Patricia A. and Edward E. Lawler. "What You Really Want From Your Job." *Psychology Today* 11, no. 12 (1978):53–118.

Snyders, Jan, and Martin Lasden. "Managing Programmers to Work Harder and Happier." *Computer Decisions* 12, no. 10 (October 1982):34–48.

CHAPTER

SUPERVISING A SALES FORCE

LINDA M. LASH

The task of supervising a sales force is like no other supervisory job and is, in fact, a supervisor's nightmare. Salespeople switch from job to job often and are motivated only by money. They spend as little time on the job as they can get away with, and are hopeless at administrative details and routine paperwork. When they do work, they spend their time servicing existing customers instead of selling new ones. Worst of all, they can always be found on the golf course in the middle of a business day and will insist they made the big sale on the seventeenth hole.

For the new supervisor just promoted from the ranks of the sales force, for the experienced production supervisor now given a sales force to manage for the first time, and for the experienced sales force supervisor, the challenges of supervising a sales force may seem just this way. Coming to grips with each aspect of the supervisory role involves all of the known supervisory and management principles, plus a few special considerations. The following pages contain the 17 most frequently asked questions by both new and experienced supervisors of sales forces, plus thought-provoking suggestions and special considerations to help in dealing with the supervision of a sales force.

1.   *How do I recruit and select the best salespeople?*

Good salespeople have good selling skills; they are good at selling, including selling themselves for a job. The supervisor has only to select the one who has done the best job of selling himself or herself for the job.

Finding the hiring the best person is not always easy and does demand the supervisor's time in recruiting (placing ads, contacting an employment agency, passing the word around the existing sales force that there is a vacancy, and so forth) and in interviewing.

Good techniques for interviewing salespeople will involve asking about previous sales experience, the track record or number of sales made in the previous experience, and why the salesperson has left or wishes to move from the previous job. An interesting and revealing interviewing technique is to ask the applicant to sell something during the interview, even if it is something simple like the chair in the interviewing office. This is particularly useful in interviewing your people just embarking on a business career or in interviewing those who have not held jobs in selling before.

Before embarking on recruiting and selecting the best person, it is critically important to know what skills are necessary for the job and what kind of applicant should be hired. If the personnel department or sales management do not offer detailed instructions and advice on this, supervisors can create their own personal specifications by listing in order what skills and knowledge are most important for the job and by looking at existing employees who are performing well.

2. Should I pay a salesperson a salary or straight bonus?

Paying a salesperson a salary that does not vary by performance (amount of sales) does not stimulate a salesperson's strong achievement and recognition needs. Some companies combine this practice with the practice of terminating low performers, which stimulates only security needs. Other companies combine this practice with sales contests which carry travel, monetary, or other rewards that work toward stimulating achievement and recognition needs in the corporate environment.

Some companies pay salespeople no salary, a very small salary, or a small salary that is deducted from commissions. Commissions, bonuses, or incentives form the major part or the total of a salesperson's compensation in this instance, making a strong appeal to a salesperson's achievement and recognition needs. However, if a corporate decision causes the product to be of poor quality or uncompetitively priced for a period of time, if the economy takes a nosedive, or if the marketplace suddenly has no need for the product, the best salesperson will be the first to find another job, out of necessity.

A good compensation package for a sales force combines elements of security (possibly a salary above minimum wage and unemployment compensation levels) and elements that appeal to achievement and recognition needs (bonus, commission, incentives, contests, rewards), as well as any tools the salesperson needs to perform the job (company car, demonstration samples, uniform, status symbols, and so forth).

The toughest job for sales managers who work in a company with other types of employees may be to get approval for the right compensation package for the sales force. Common pitfalls include:

1. A bonus cap which stops bonus payments at quota or at 125% of quota, forcing the best salesperson to stop making calls after the tenth month of the year.
2. A bonus linked primarily to the company's profit performance if the salesperson is allowed only to influence revenues.

3. A bonus package that is introduced late in the year, that is too complex to be understood by the sales force, or that is kept secret from the sales force.

The most important part of the justification must include the numbers, that is, linking additional sales and revenues to additional bonus payments ("If we sell 1000 more widgets, we can pay $1000 more bonus").

3. Should I give a salesperson a company car?

If the salesperson's job requires traveling to visit potential and existing customers, most companies provide a company car as an essential tool needed to carry out the job. Unlike other job tools which are useful to an employee only in the corporate environment, a company car can be used for personal travel and can give an employee a status symbol to boost morale.

Some companies make a practice of giving their sales force attractive new cars each year as a means of attracting good salespeople. Others extend this benefit to allow salespeople to purchase the car personally after one to three years at book value (even if the car is leased, this may be possible).

Some companies view the company car as an advertising opportunity and have cars painted in company colors, with advertising messages, or with the company name and logo. This generally makes the car less desirable for use on a personal basis.

In some sales jobs, the company car is essential to transport clients. Here the dilemma is to provide practical luxury, a nice car that is recognized as value for money, to present a practical but quality image to clients.

4. What is the best way to train a new salesperson?

A new salesperson will almost certainly require training for product knowledge to be able to sell the product, and may require training in selling skills in order to sell the product in the manner expected.

As with any new employee, a new salesperson deserves training to enable him or her to do the job correctly. Not training new salespeople almost always costs more money—in mistakes, in missed sales opportunities, in lost accounts, in company loyalty, and in turnover, to name a few.

Many companies run their own internal training courses for new salespeople, focusing on training for product knowledge or combining it with training in selling skills. Other companies use external training courses. Whatever is available, a good sales supervisor will make use of it and send new salespeople for training as soon as they are hired. The cost of an uncovered territory is almost always less than the cost of not training a salesperson.

Some companies offer no training programs and expect that the sales supervisor or manager will train new salespeople. Training or helping the new salesperson do his or her new job will require the supervisor to devote some time to this activity, and that time must be devoted to the salesperson on the first few days of employment.

Whichever method is used for training, the same basic training principles should apply:

1.   The sales person will need to know exactly what the job is—what territory is to be covered, what constitutes good performance or bad performance, and what the objectives, targets, or quotas are. Whether this information is conveyed in a classroom, in a letter from the personnel department, or in a discussion in the sales supervisor's office, the salesperson must know and understand what is expected.

2.   The salesperson will need to know what the guidelines and policies concerning the job are—how expenses are handled, where the office is and what its hours are, what tools can be used in the job, when salary increases are given, what the benefits are, what departments are available to help, and so forth. This information might be read in company manuals, discussed in a classroom, or explained by the supervisor.

3.   The salesperson will need to know about the product—its features, advantages, and benefits; how much it costs; how it compares to competitors' products; what customers it is designed for; how it is ordered, delivered, and serviced, and so forth. It is important that salespeople learn this information well and dem-

onstrate their knowledge, whether the demonstration of knowledge is done in a classroom or a supervisor's office. Teaching aids are essential—price lists, charts of benefits, customer leaflets, order forms, and samples of the products (either samples the salesperson can try or a visit to where the product is in use).

4. The salesperson will need to know how to sell the product—where customers can be located, what the benefits are for various market segments, how to approach potential customers, what questions to ask in fact finding, what methods and sales aids to use in presenting the product, what closing techniques are best, and how to overcome customer objections. While some new salespeople will already have these standard selling skills and be able to apply them easily to a new product in a new company, some may have to be trained or refreshed. Practice and demonstration are important to show learning of selling skills, whether it is a case study and role-play with video playback in a classroom, or a simple role-play practice in the supervisor's office.

5. How can I supervise a sales force and still handle my own portfolio?

Many companies assign their sales supervisors or sales managers a portfolio or sales territory to handle in addition to their management duties. The key factor in handling this dual role is how the company perceives the dual role. If the sales supervisor's incentive compensation or targets are based solely on the handling of the supervisor's portfolio or territory, then the supervisor knows that supervisory duties are clearly secondary or can be neglected. If the sales supervisor's incentive compensation or targets are based solely on the sales made by the sales force being supervised, then the supervisor knows that his or her own portfolio or sales territory is clearly secondary or can be neglected.

If, however, the sales supervisor's incentive compensation or targets are based squarely on both the sales made by the sales force and the sales made by the supervisor in handling his or her own territory, the company expects that both roles will be handled successfully by the sales supervisor.

If the sales supervisor can take the bird's eye view of this dual situation, he or she will see that there is a group of people working to achieve agreed-upon targets or sales. If one of the group is clearly below his or her target, then that person requires supervisory guidance or time from the supervisor. If that person is a salesperson, the supervisor takes time from handling his or her own territory to help the salesperson. If that person is the supervisor, then the supervisor must devote more time to handling his or her own territory. It may be necessary to take this bird's eye view on a monthly, a weekly, or even a daily basis.

Organization of time is an important factor in handling this dual role successfully. Depending on the management style of the company, the following ideas may be used:

1.   The sales supervisor can apply time and territory management techniques to the "dual" territory—that of selling and that of supervising—by dividing time between the two roles and making a time plan of the activities that must be done in both "territories."

2.   The sales supervisor can divide his or her own territory or portfolio and assign it to the sales force. This is a rugged test of supervisory abilities since the supervisor is putting his or her own incentive rewards in the hands of the sales force supervised.

6.   What is the best way to measure a salesperson's performance?

Stated simply, the best way to measure a salesperson's performance is on the basis of the number of sales made. Sales contribute to the company's revenues and profits and, under a good compensation package, reward and motivate the salesperson.

The number of sales made, however, may lead to several other considerations:

1.   The sales force must have a clear understanding of what constitutes a sale made. Is it when the customer verbally says yes, when the customer signs an order or agreement, when the goods are delivered, or when the customer pays? Are canceled or unrealized orders deducted? This understanding is important so that the sales force knows exactly what constitutes their job.

2.   If a number of products are being sold by the sales force, there may be a quota for each different product, the quota being linked to the company's profit margins on each product. Again

the sales force must have a clear understanding of the quotas for each product and why these quotas were established.

3.   Sales reporting methods should be clear and simple so that sales made are counted the same by the sales force and by management.

4.   The number of sales made can be influenced by the size and opportunity factor of a given sales territory, by the available selling time, by the quality or price of the product, by the economy, or by any number of factors outside the salesperson's control. For this reason, it is critical to set individual targets for each salesperson and to measure performance against those targets.

Setting targets, quotas, or objectives at the beginning of the selling period for the number of sales to be made, and agreeing upon them with each salesperson, provides the basis upon which to measure a salesperson's performance. This avoids the subjectivity of measuring performance based on personality traits or selling techniques, and focuses on the key issue at hand—namely selling—as opposed to support activities such as punctuality, number of calls made, or administrative details.

It is critical that the compensation package, incentives, contests, and rewards all have the same basis—namely sales made—so that performance is not only measured but rewarded and recognized on the same premise.

7.   How can I get a salesperson to improve record keeping and do proper reports?

Salespeople often view their jobs as primarily selling. Administrative details are often secondary in importance to the salesperson and are therefore not done as well, as accurately, or as timely as management might want.

The records that a salesperson keeps on customers or accounts help the salesperson to sell and service customers better. Poor record keeping of this sort will ultimately be reflected in the number of sales made and in the number of accounts lost. In an ideal situation where the number of sales made is the basis for incentive compensation and is the measure of performance, poor customer record keeping will be a part of the appraisal process as both su-

pervisor and salesperson work together to find ways of improving
the number of sales made. One other consideration is the type of
records the salesperson is required to keep. If these records are
designed centrally by the company, they may be complex and
detailed, requiring that the salesperson be trained in how to use
them correctly.

Salespeople are hired generally on their ability to sell and not
on their power of the pen. Complex and lengthy sales reports,
even when done by a good writer, take time away from selling.
The easiest reports to write are those which state simply and
clearly what the salesperson knows most about, namely what he
or she did. In a system where goals and objectives are agreed
upon at the beginning of a selling period (usually a year), reports
can simply report on progress against those goals or objectives.
Some companies use a simple two-copy report form successfully.
At the beginning of the month (or other time period), the salesperson gives the supervisor the first copy, which shows what the
planned activities for the month are, including the number of sales
to be made. At the end of the month, the salesperson gives the
supervisor the second copy, which shows what activities were
done during the month, including the number of sales made.

If the compensation package (and contests and rewards) is
geared to the number of sales made, and the reports and records
required of the salesperson are kept simple and focused on this
goal, there is a good chance that record keeping and reports will
be accurate and timely, since the salesperson will need the customer records to generate sales and will need the report to know
how he or she is doing.

8. How can I get a salesperson to organize the territory and call on new accounts instead of servicing existing accounts?

There are many good books and good training courses devoted
to sales territory organization for various industries. Some companies use swing work load plans where a selling year may have,
for example, four swings with different areas of emphasis and
where accounts are visited with a certain frequency between
swings. Other companies use geographical territory organization
with call frequency levels for new and existing accounts based on

potential volume. The important aspect is to have an organized plan for the sales force and to communicate with the sales force through sales meetings, internal bulletins, discussions, and training to insure understanding.

The syndrome of calling on existing accounts and neglecting prospecting or finding new accounts may have its basis in the method of territory planning used, in the compensation package and incentive plan, or in the sales force's own motivation. Salespeople may call on existing accounts because their territory plan demands a certain call frequency level on these accounts, leaving little time to call on new accounts or on accounts buying from competitors. If the compensation package does not force salespeople to prospect and bring in new sales, the sales force may stick to acquiring renewals and selling more to existing accounts. Social needs may also be a factor as salespeople call on their favorite accounts to insure that the product has been delivered satisfactorily. Good territory planning and balanced compensation packages can remedy this syndrome.

9. How can I get a salesperson to make more sales calls per day?

The number of sales calls a salesperson can make in a day depends greatly on the geographic distance or traveling-time distance of the territory. The territory might be two city blocks in Chicago, the entire state of Texas, or the Far East. Each type of territory, plus the method of transportation the salesperson is authorized to use to cover that territory (is a car used to cover the whole state of Texas?), as well as the nature of the product itself and the salesperson's own motivation, all have an influence on the number of sales calls in a day.

Consequently, enabling the salesperson to make more sales calls per day may involve:

1. Restructuring the territory—making the territory itself smaller distance-wise, eliminating frequent calls to distant locations that do not yield significant opportunities, and so forth.

2. Authorizing a different method of transportation—using train or airplane when faster than automobile, using public transportation when faster than walking, using business-class or first-

class air travel when selling time is short in distant locations, and so forth.

3. Providing streamlined sales aids—giving salespeople a good sales presentation package, structuring demonstrations to cover the key benefits in the most expedient manner, insuring that demonstration items can be set up quickly and work properly the first time, and so forth.

4. Reducing administrative details—keeping reports simple, providing specialized staff to handle service questions and other non-selling activities, not requiring sales persons to spend time reporting in to the office in person or by telephone, and so forth.

While the question of how to get a salesperson to make more sales calls per day is asked often, sales supervisors should ask themselves why it is important for a salesperson to make more calls. If one salesperson makes nine calls and two sales while another makes three calls and three sales, the supervisor has to face the basic question whether number of sales or number of sales calls is more important. Sales calls cost a company money—transportation expense, salesperson's time—while sales bring a company revenue and profit.

This basic question then leads to the basic compensation package and targets or objectives set for salespeople. If targets or objectives focus on sales made and the compensation package rewards sales made, then the task will automatically appeal to an average salesperson's natural motivation to achieve, and the salesperson will make the number of sales calls in a day that allows him or her to achieve and be rewarded.

10. *How do I know what a salesperson is doing out in a remote location?*

Salespeople in remote locations, without the benefit of a sales supervisor on site, can and do present a special challenge. The most common exposure is the traveling corporate executive who just happens to visit that remote city and find that the salesperson has not yet been in the office at 9:30 A.M. or is on the local golf course.

When supervising a sales force in a remote location, it is crucial that sales targets be agreed upon and that progress against those targets is reported to the supervisor accurately and on a timely basis. Reporting need not be elaborate but should report the facts. If the target was to sell 100 widgets last month, the report should say how many were sold and why. Communication between the salesperson in the remote location and the supervisor is essential, and the supervisor must devote time to reading and following progress reports.

Good reporting enables the supervisor to visit the locations where assistance is required instead of simply visiting all remote locations according to an established schedule. The ideal situation may involve visiting or contacting remote locations where supervisory assistance is required and those salespeople who ask for the contact themselves. A good technique is to read progress reports and communicate with the salesperson about the report, to demonstrate that it has been read and is important. This good communication allows the supervisor to counter the traveling executive's criticism with good performance reports (or disciplinary action).

11. How can I get a salesperson to close the sale?

It is no accident that many sales training courses and sales training films are devoted to the subject of getting a salesperson to close the sale or ask for the business correctly and at the right moment. From the high-pressured, door-to-door encyclopedia salesperson whose first statement may be the close, to the young salesclerk in a department store's cosmetic department who may never have to say a closing statement at all, there is clearly a wide range of opinions on how to close and when to close. There is agreement, however, that sales must be made and that closes must be done in some fashion.

The most powerful weapon for getting the sales force to close the sale is to agree upon challenging targets, quotas, or goals, and to link compensation to the achievement of those targets, quotas, or goals. If the quota is too easy, the salesperson can afford the luxury of visiting a potential customer several times before closing the sale. If the quota is too difficult, the salesperson may feel trapped into closing the sale too quickly or may avoid calling on potential customers who are felt to be too difficult to sell.

Training and coaching can help salespeople to learn to close effectively and at the right moment. Accompanying the salesperson on a live sales call can enable the supervisor to discuss with the salesperson when and how the close could have been made. Proper training and coaching, particularly if videotaped role-plays are used, can allow the sales person to adopt a method of closing which is suitable for him or her. A method which has often doomed a sales force is a company's enforced, "canned" close, particularly if it is a direct, pressurized close.

12. What are the best kinds of sales aids?

Sales aids are anything a salesperson uses during the sales contact to help prove the benefits of the product to the customer or to show customers what the product will do for them. Good sales aids used effectively can save selling time and improve the number of sales made. A sales aid might be a demonstration of the acutal product, such as a vacuum cleaner or a microcomputer; a short audiovisual presentation of the product's features and advantages, such as a videotape of a computer installation or a nuclear reactor; a presentation book containing detailed product specifications, delivery dates, and an actual contract to be signed; or just a simple chart showing the advantages of the product.

The best sales aids, then, are those which help prove the benefits of the product to the customer or which show customers what the product will do for them. It is essential that the sales aid work correctly—that the vacuum cleaner does indeed pick up the dirt on the customer's carpet and make the carpet look new. It is essential that the sales aid be set up easily and quickly—that the microcomputer just plugs in quickly and is ready to go. Sales aids should truly be an aid to the salesperson in showing or demonstrating something that could not be described as well by in a salesperson's words, as opposed to a videotape or book that simply delivers the salesperson's presentation.

The best sales aids are those which are personalized to show the benefits to the customer being sold. With proper fact-finding, a salesperson can use a good sales aid to say, "Our product will save your company $2000 and here's how."

13.   Do sales contests have value?

Sales contests appeal to a salesperson's strong achievement and recognition needs and can therefore be powerful motivators.

Sales contests can also satisfy corporate goals, such as selling off a discontinued product line or achieving a profitable level of sales on a new product line.

There are some pitfalls to avoid:

1.   If the sales contest is geared to reward achievement of normal daily goals and targets, it becomes part of the standard compensation package and has to be continued or repeated. ("But I've *always* earned the $5000 prize.")

2.   If the sales contest offers a prize, the prize must be something each individual would like to have. (A trip to Tahiti may not be the most desirable prize to a parent trying to find the money to keep three children in college).

3.   Recognition includes not just winning but having others know you've won. A good sales contest is supported by publicized recognition in the company environment (mentioned in company news publications, a plaque for the office wall, and so forth) and in the personal environment (a plaque for the den at home, a prize that friends or family can share, and so forth).

4.   Contest rules should be clear to all and known to all. It makes winning that much sweeter.

5.   An obvious consideration is that the contest promote sales geared to corporate objectives. The contest becomes even stronger as a motivator when the supervisor can clearly explain the benefits. ("The person who wins will receive a $2000 cash prize plus the right to say he or she saved the corporation from writing off $75,000 in discontinued widgets.")

14. How can I present a salesperson from taking our client lists to a competitor?

In most countries, there are laws that forbid an existing employee from selling or providing client lists to competitors, and these laws work well in protecting companies.

The laws are not so clear or prevalent for employees who leave one company and take that company's client lists to a competitor. While files or lists or physical evidence can be protected within the law, it is very difficult to protect what useful information is stored in a departing salesperson's memory. It is impossible to protect sales contacts that have developed into trust or even friendship. While some companies negotiate employment contract with executives which prevent them from working in the same industry for a competitor within two to five years after leaving, there remains a large risk when good salespeople go to a new company in the same industry with their experience, their friendships and contacts, and their knowledge of customers who need the product.

The best protection is to be able to keep good salespeople happy in their current company. Some aspects to consider are:

1. Are compensation packages and incentive plans as good or better than those of competitors?
2. Are benefits as good or better than those of competitors?
3. Does the management style and appraisal system of the company communicate clearly to the sales force that they are important and valued employees?

These items need to be verified and questioned on a continuing basis to protect good employees from moving to competitors.

15. Do sales meetings have value?

Sales meetings can be held for any number of reasons—to reward and recognize performance, to enable salespeople from remote locations to meet each other, to show the sales force a company's head office or production plant, to communicate company goals and objectives, to launch a new product, to train the sales force, or to accomplish several of these objectives simultaneously. The important aspects are that there is a reason for the meeting, that the reasons be known to the salespeople, and that the cost of the meeting and its expected benefits compare favorably to the cost of taking the sales force away from selling for the length of the meeting.

In organizing a sales meeting, it is important to plan in advance and to select participative methods linked to the meeting's objectives. The objectives of the meeting should be communicated to the participants, and a good feedback evaluation technique is to ask participants in writing before they leave to indicate how well they feel the objectives were met.

In some companies, sales meetings are the official method of launching new products and doing training. If learning is to occur, it is important to consider the number of participants and what methods will involve them the most. Workshop sessions, demonstrations, and role-plays are effective techniques.

16.   How can I get a salesperson to go after the 'big sales'?

Some salespeople persist in selling small accounts, in selling small orders or partial orders of the product to many customers, or in selling small revenue-producing or small profit-producing orders, causing their supervisors to wonder why they never go after the "big sales."

One of the possible sources of this problem may be the compensation package or the incentive plan. If the compensation package consists of straight salary, there is no special reward for the "big sales." The salesperson may perceive the small sale or partial order as easier to make and will look to make lots of small sales to satisfy his or her own achievement needs. This is also the case if the incentive plan rewards solely on the basis of the number of sales made in terms of the number of customers sold (regardless of the size of the order). Changing the compensation package or incentive plan to reward salespeople for the "big sales" can make a salesperson go after these kinds of sales. If compensation packages cannot be changed, then sales contests, rewards, or recognition of some sort, even on a local level, may be used with success.

A second possible source of this problem, even when incentive payments weigh heavily in favor of the "big sales," may be lack of confidence. The salesperson may view small sales as easier to make or may have a proven record of being very successful at small sales. A salesperson gets his or her biggest kick out of making sales. On the other side of the coin, salespeople do not like the answer "no," and only those with confidence are able to shrug off a series of "no" answers. Confidence is generally a result of knowledge in selling—knowledge of the product, knowledge of oneself, and knowledge of selling skills. Restoring confidence may include additional training, coaching, or accompanying the salesperson on calls to both large and small accounts.

Avoiding sales calls to large accounts or to customers with potentially large orders can also be a performance trait associated with those who do not really wish to be in the field of selling or those who are holding a selling job until they find another (usually in a different field). Training and coaching may assist these people in learning the selling trade, or the supervisor may simply accept their performance in making small sales.

One aspect that has to be considered is why "big sales" are important. While a group of salespeople at a cocktail party may be discussing the biggest sale they made last month, a company's view may be different. From a company viewpoint, the most desirable sale may be the one that produces the most revenue, the one that produces the best profit margin, the one that produces the most profit, the one that gains market share, the one that sells off a discontinued product line, the one that gives the company president more status, or the one that improves the company's image in the community. With some products, small sales are more profitable than large sales with volume discounts. It is important that company objectives be communicated to the sales force, even to the point of being reflected in the compensation package, so that the sales force knows which kinds of sales are important to make.

17.   What really motivates a salesperson?

A truly good salesperson gets his or her biggest kick out of making a sale and being rewarded for it. Thus, achievement and recognition needs are prime motivators of good salespeople.

Second on the list is a feeling of social acceptance, the good feeling that comes when salespeople visit their favorite accounts or have a good encounter with a new account. Because salespeople generally make a profession of communicating with other human beings, social needs are particularly strong and may require special attention.

Good sales supervisors devote themselves to providing the opportunities for salespeople to fulfill their achievement, recognition, and social needs. Below are some key elements of the right environment that are often overlooked:

1. Providing a quality product at a competitive price and insuring the sales force knows this, so that salespeople can achieve sales (it is difficult to sell an Edsel).

2. Providing a compensation package that rewards and continues to reward and recognizes achievement (there is no further motivation to sell if a salesperson has reached the quota or bonus limit).

3. Agreeing upon sales targets that are challenging but not impossible to achieve (motivation is highest when targets are viewed as 50% achievable).

4. Providing simple results-oriented measurement and reporting methods that require a minimum amount of administration (keep the salesperson out on the street selling instead of in the office doing paperwork).

5. Having flexibility or using creativity to offer special benefits that are of value in the job but that also appeal to social needs (the golf club membership fee may be cost-justified in terms of motivation and sales made during play).

6. Using a leadership style that makes the most of a salesperson's results-oriented drives and that encourages self-discipline and self-measurement.

The task of supervising a sales force is like no other supervisory job and is, in fact, a supervisor's fondest dream. Given the right product, compensation package, and results-oriented leadership, salespeople will produce amazing results, calling on new accounts and completing simple, routine paperwork quickly and promptly. Top performers will continue to turn in results and surpass all expectations as will average performers, while low performers will either change dramatically or resign for a cushier job, leaving space to hire another top performer. Best of all, a good sales supervisor will be happy to see one of his or her salespeople playing the eighteenth hole in the middle of a business day as the supervisor is completing the seventeenth hole where, of course, both made big sales.

PERSONAL MANAGING

CHAPTER

MANAGING CHANGE

MATT HENNECKE

Management textbooks of the past rarely, if ever, had a chapter devoted to the discussion of change. There simply was no pressing need. Of course things were changing, but not at an intolerable rate. Most managers and supervisors felt themselves quite capable of making whatever minor adjustments were necessary to keep pace with the rest of the world. Life was basically predictable and frequently boring. Most employees stayed with their employers for their entire lives, and many supervisors and their subordinates developed lifelong friendships nurtured by years and years of loyal service. Company missions were clear and the status quo assured.

Like it or not, those days are gone. Today we are bombarded with changes that are often drastic and mostly unpredictable. Look around for just a few minutes at all the changes that have occurred in the last few, short years. The "open office" concept has ushered in offices that are like tents. They can be taken down, folded up, and moved anywhere in a matter of minutes. Companies are centralizing, decentralizing, merging, and divesting every 15 minutes. This country's system of measurement is changing from pounds and ounces to grams and liters, from Fahrenheit to centigrade. People will kill for a conversion table. The slide rule has followed the dodo bird into extinction and been replaced with the pocket calculator and the personal computer. Employees' attitudes toward work and their employers have changed, with obvious effects on supervisors everywhere. The United States economy of late has taken us all on a financial roller coaster ride, complete with breathtaking peaks and frightening valleys. The long-standing societal roles of men and women have been altered and blurred. Entire organizations are galloping into the future with no sense of where they've been or where they're going. Stress levels among supervisors and subordinates alike have reached frightening levels.

Short of becoming a hermit, there is no escaping the rushing torrent of change. All of us may soon lose our grip on the last vestiges of order and be swept away by that swollen river of change that leads unerringly into the future. Already many of us have faced and survived changes that few of our ancestors ever even imagined. To support that contention, read through the following list of experiences and place a check mark by any you may have had during the last few years:

_____Had a job change

_____Used a computer

_____Had a female supervisor

_____Was involved in a company reorganization

_____Lost a job due to company bankruptcy

_____Had a divorce

Except for those unfortunate enough to have lived during the Great Depression, most of our ancestors would have been unable to check a single one of the above experiences, yet many of us have had such experiences—several times.

While changes will continue at an alarming rate in all areas of existence, a real concern for supervisors has to be the changes that are happening within an organization. Not surprisingly, many supervisors would rather not have the responsibility of managing change. They'd rather just let change happen. It's true that change is difficult to face, but it's certainly worse to ignore it. Sadly, many supervisors will have to be dragged kicking and screaming into the future. The alternative? The alternative is to develop a strategy for handling change—to plan, direct, and control change. Obviously, this not an easy task, but supervisors who learn to cope with change and plan for it will have a real advantage over those who don't. They'll have an edge which can mean advancement and career success. The decision is yours. You can either learn to manage change or be managed by it, because change will go on regardless. If you're equal to the task, then this chapter should help lead the way.

CHANGE ACCEPTANCE VERSUS CHANGE RESISTANCE

Some supervisors attribute change resistance among employees to good old-fashioned stubbornness. When Yaz Gummer, the flagpole painter, resists your efforts to get him to use a scaffold, you might assume he's just being stubborn. Or, when Elba Tobar insists on using the old manual typewriter instead of the new improved Laser Letter Layer you just purchased, you may be convinced she's just being spiteful. Stubbornness alone, however, is rarely the cause of change resistance—it may be instead a by-product or a symptom.

Other supervisors believe that people are basically resistant to change, but this too is probably not true. Not all change is bad, and not all change is resisted. The problem is one of being able to know when change will be accepted and when it will be resisted. The situation is further complicated because humans are both the most adaptable creatures in existence and the most stubborn. Let's look at an example of change resistance and change acceptance in action:

Daisy Dimknot had been supervisor of the personnel department for Belchmoor Frozen Foods for only seven months when she decided to initiate a cross-training program for her department. She allowed the idea to steep for a few days and then approached her boss, Sid Flapper, and explained that by having all of her subordinates cross-trained she could continue to maintain high productivity levels. Not surprisingly, Sid wanted to know how cross-training would help. Daisy, who had expected the question, patiently unfolded her idea. A cross-training program would alleviate the problems that came about whenever someone called in sick or went on vacation. After all, if all of the record clerks knew who to do all of the jobs in the department, then everyone could be used as backup whenever necessary. At first Sid was skeptical, but Daisy persisted and Sid, not wanting to miss his Caribbean cruise, finally gave in. After wishing her boss sunny skies and warm seas, Daisy called a staff meeting to make assignments for the cross-training program. Within two weeks absenteeism in Daisy's department was at an all-time high, and productivity had plummeted to new lows. Realizing she was losing the battle, and fearing a career casualty, Daisy abandoned the program and in a few days things were back to normal.

Daisy, confused by the failure of her brilliant idea, was, to say the least, leery about initiating any changes in her department from that day on. A few months later, however, she was reading an industry publication that gave a glowing report of a new record-filing system that had been installed at Phabulous Phoods. She decided the idea was so good that she just had to try it in her department. Again she went to Sid, and again he grudgingly gave her the go ahead. Six weeks later the system was in place and except for a few bugs was functioning beautifully.

Why had Daisy's early attempts at change been unsuccessful and her later attempts successful? The reason was simple. Daisy's subordinates for some reason didn't want any part of the cross-training program, but were ready for a filing system to replace the outdated one they had struggled with for nearly five years.

One of the baffling aspects of change management is knowing when change will be accepted and supported by subordinates, and when it will be resisted. Why do subordinates sometimes welcome changes (and in some cases demand them) and at other times drag their collective feet?

The reason some changes are accepted and others are not is because all of us from childhood on have developed and perfected our skills at internalized cost-benfit analysis. A two-year-old child contemplating a bath—which constitutes a change from her more playful endeavors—does a quick cost-benefit analysis and inevitably concludes that the cost of taking the bath in terms of lost playing time outweighs the benefit of being a clean, shiny baby. The result? Resistance. The teenager, faced with the prospect of moving to a new community because of his dad's job change, does a quick, internalized cost-benefit analysis and decides that the cost of leaving his friends far outweighs the benefits of the move. The result? Resistance. Or, the secretary, when considering the change her boss is demanding in the office filing system, does a cost-benefit analysis and concludes that the cost of initiating the change (that is, extra work, overtime, frustration) exceeds the benefits (happy boss, more efficient department). The result? Resistance. A principle is at work in all three cases: attempts to initiate change will be difficult and perhaps impossible if, in the minds of those affected by the change, the benefits of changing do not meet or exceed the costs. In Daisy's case, the cross-training program had come out on the short end of the cost-benefit analysis, while the new filing system had apparently been viewed by her subordinates as more beneficial than costly.

FIVE CHANGE PHASES

Although the research on change and the effect of change is still in its infancy, there seem to be roughly five phases that people pass through whenever they are faced with change. The five phases are illustrated in Figure 9.1.

The speed and ease with which subordinates pass through these phases depend largely on their assessement of the benefits and costs of changing, their ability to adapt to change, and their readiness for change. The management of change is further complicated because no two subordinates are likely to proceed through

THE CHANGE CYCLE

FIGURE 9.1.   The Change Cycle

the five phases at the same pace. In fact, some may even get stuck in one of the phases and need your assistance in finally moving to the support phase. An explanation of each phase follows:

Phase One: Fear

Whenever we are faced with unexpected, unexplained change, fear is likely. If you, for instance, walk into the plant or office tomorrow and discover your desk has been moved down into the basement, you'll probably feel a pang of apprehension. What's your desk doing down there? Who ordered it moved? Are you fully vested in the company pension plan? Is your resume ready for mass mailing? What you're experiencing is fear, dread, terror, dismay—and change is the cause.

Fear is an interesting emotion, that, uncontrolled, can turn a usually normal, rational person into a blithering, white-knuckled wreck. Obviously, it's in the supervisor's best interest to help his or her subordinates through this phase as quickly and painlessly as possible. But how? We'll get to the how, but first, it's important to be able to distinguish between specific fears and nonspecific fears.

Specific and Nonspecific Fears

Specific fears are fears that are distinct and identifiable because they are stated or inplied in conversation with a subordinate. Nonspecific fears, on the other hand, are feelings of apprehension or foreboding that are not easily expressed. A specific fear of an impending reorganization might be stated like this: "I don't like this talk of reorganization—we've got to stay centralized so we can keep control over our field offices." Such a fear is specific because the actual cause of the fear is stated. The employee is afraid of losing control over the field offices. A nonspecific fear, however, might be stated like this: "I don't know. I just don't like the idea—it scares me." The fear is certainly present, but the real cause is hidden. The point is, you can only help someone overcome his or her fears if they have been specifically identified. So, the first demand on the supervisor is to help subordinates specifically identify the fears associated with any proposed change. Once nonspecific fears are changed into specific fears, they're much easier to manage and resolve.

The fears felt by anyone experiencing change can be numerous and diverse, but some basic fears often surface. By being aware of these basic fears and planning for them, the effective supervisor should be able to diffuse or resolve them quickly and with a minimum of effort.

Fear of the Unknown

Many people are afraid of change, especially if it takes them by surprise. Consider how you might feel if an announcement was made by the president of your organization that your company was being purchased by some Saudi Arabian conglomerate. You wouldn't know what to expect. Or, what would be your reaction if your boss walked into your office tomorrow and told you to pack your bags—that the Brazilian office needed someone familiar with Gyrogizmo Afterburners and your name was at the top of everyone's list? Among all of the other emotions you'd be feeling would be one we could loosely define as "fear of the unknown."

You'd be asking yourself questions like: Do they have refrigerators in Brazil? Plumbing? Bugs? Can the wife come along? What about the kids?

All of us would like a little warning, and maybe an explanation. Anything is better than not knowing what to expect. When faced with an unexplained change, most subordinates will retreat into that which is known and familiar, and no amount of coaxing by a supervisor is likely to get them to be supportive of the change.

What does that mean to you as a supervisor? It means you need to patiently explain the likely results of a change so as to eliminate the subordinate's fears of the unknown. If the subordinate knows why the change is necessary, and knows how the change will affect him or her, then the unknown is replaced with the known and the fear is reduced.

Fear of the Loss of Routine and Predictability

The reason most of us reminisce about the "good old days" is because in retrospect they seemed predictable. Routine and predictability are the things from which habits are made, and whether we are willing to admit it or not, all of us have habits. Good or bad, habits are old friends and we usually come to their defense whenever they are under attack. Like those favorite pair of worn-out shoes, or that old baseball mitt signed by Scrubby Jackson, there is a certain comfort associated with well-worn habits. Change, that vile and frightening enemy, strangles our habits and slaughters our routine. The new shoes and the new mitt just don't feel right, and we lament their loss and mutter about how "they don't make things like they used to." In short, change is uncomfortable and frustrating because it strips us of our routine.

The feeling of frustration and the sense of discomfort associated with change and the loss of routine and predictability is easily demonstrated; the next paragraph will be printed from right to left instead of the traditional left to right. To understand the text, you will have to start at the right side of the page and read to the left. Then, when you get to the last word on the left side of the page, you will have to go back to the right side of the page and begin reading from right to left again. Ready?

to right from read Chinese the that aware probably are us of Most
an get ,ever if ,rarely people speaking-English but , left
enough difficult it's us For .habit the develop to opportunity
.left to right less much ,right to left from read to how learning
were it if uncomfortable and disturbed quite be would we Obviously
all on now from that officials government by announced suddenly
we doubt a Without .way this typed be would magazines and books
.change such any resist would

You were probably able to read the paragraph without too much trouble. The real difficulty probably came in changing from one line to the next. Now we'll try the same paragraph again, but this time not only will the text run from right to left, but the letters of the words themselves will be in reverse order.

ot thgir morf daer esenihC eht taht erawa ylbaborp era su fo tsoM
na teg ,reve fi, ylerar elopoep gnikaeps-hsilgnE tub, tfel
hguone tluciffid s'ti su roF .tibah eht poleved ot ytinutroppo
.tfel ot thgir ssel hcum ,thgir ot tfel morf daer ot woh gninrael
erew ti fi elbatrofmocnu dna debrutsid etiuq eb dluow ew ylsuoivbO
lla no won morf taht slaiciffo tnemnrevog yb decnuonna ylneddus
ew tbuod a tuohtiW .yaw siht depyt eb dluow senizagam dna skoob
.egnahc hcus yna tsiser dluow

How was that? This time the pace was certainly much slower, and the frustration and discomfort were higher. We can read the material, but it difficult because of the reading habits we have developed over the years. Imagine, then, what it must be like for a subordinate who is asked to alter or eliminate some work habit.

Time, patience, and practice can be very helpful in assisting subordinates in developing new habits and new routines. Supervisors should be willing to provide the needed time, display the necessary patience, and allow the required practice.

Fear of Potential Incompetence

No one likes to feel incompetent, yet change has a way of doing just that. When Wilma Fermock, the dispatcher for Vroom Trucking, is told that the Master Datagasher Computer will be installed to replace the 17 file cabinets that she has filled to capacity during the past 32 years. She is going to feel incompetent. For 32 years she has been the expert, the only one who could find the old invoices and manifests for the trucking company, and for what? Once the computer is installed she'll be starting all over again. In her own mind it'll be like the first day on the job, and she's afraid. What if she fails?

There is no easy way to help subordinates overcome the fear of incompetence. The nature of change is such that it will force us to learn new skills and for a time there will be a loss of competence. The solution for helping subordinates overcome this fear is to allow mistakes, and to keep subordinates looking forward to the competence they will develop, rather than looking backward to the competence that has been lost.

The more a supervisor can reduce or eliminate the fears associated with change, the less formidable will be the resistance to change. So, to effectively initiate change, the knowledgeable supervisor will first remember that fear is the emotion that drives change resistance, and then discover and attempt to resolve the fears that always accompany change.

Phase Two: Resistance

There is, perhaps, no greater frustration faced by a supervisor than resistance by his or her subordinates to some change over which he or she has no control. If your company decides to automate the assembly line that you supervise, then you probably have no choice but to follow orders. What will you do if you face stiff resistance from your subordinates? Punish them? Fire them? The likely result of such harsh measures is usually greater resistance. What is the solution? We'll get into solutions a little later; for now suffice it to say that resistance is rare among subordinates who themselves have a say in change, and who themselves suggest ways to initiate change.

Change resistance can take many forms. There is active resistance, passive resistance, intentional resistance, and unintentional resistance. Each type can be equally frustrating to a supervisor. A discussion of each follows:

Active Resistance

Active resistance to change is certainly the most noticeable and the most volatile: Witness the active resistance to the Vietnam War during the sixties and seventies—riots, bombings, draft evaders, demonstrations. Much of the activity was in response to proposed or actual changes in foreign policy and world affairs. Resistance was high and respect for authority was low.

In organizations, the same active resistance to change is also possible, and may take the form of sabotoge, strikes, and violence. When robots begin replacing our friends on the assembly line, one method of reducing the stress and frustration we feel is to sabotage the robots. When economic constraints force a company to lay off 300 workers, the change may cause a retaliatory strike or walkout by the rest of the company's employees. Change is often unpleasant and the resulting resistance may be equally unpleasant.

Passive Resistance

Passive resistance, while not as explosive as active resistance, can be just as frustrating and counterproductive to an organization. It can take a variety of forms including absenteeism, turnover, and slowdowns. Unlike active resisters, who are more obvious about their dissatisfaction and often vocal in their opposition to change, passive resisters are often subtle and inconspicuous. If they don't like some change, they may call in sick or quit. Because passive resisters are less obvious in their opposition to change, a supervisor may never be sure if an increase in absenteeism and turnover is caused by some change or not. It's difficult for a supervisor to overcome change resistance if he or she is not sure there is resistance.

Intentional versus Unintentional Resistance

For our purposes it is important to understand the difference between intentional and unintentional resistance. Intentional resistance is just that—intentional. When subordinates decide that some proposed change is not to their liking or causes them some fears, and they then act either actively or passively to resist the change, we've got intentional resistance. Unintentional resistance, on the other hand, is the result of being unfamiliar with the demands and duties associated with the change.

To illustrate, consider Phil Waxgag, a reporter for the Davenport Gazette. He has been told by his boss, Gabby Lloyd, that the Gazette needs someone to write the obituaries for the next two months in the absence of Karl Phazzbod who is recovering from malaria. Phil, who is a 10-year veteran of the newspaper, doesn't want the job even if it's temporary, but his boss insists. Unhappy with the temporary job change, Phil is purposefully late with the daily copy for the entire two-month period.

According to our definition, Phil is being intentionally resistant to the change. The result is an intentional slowdow. Now consider Meg Preshot. She has been a messenger for the Gazette for seven months and has been begging for a chance to do some real reporting. Imagine this time that Gabby approaches Meg with the two-month, temporary obituary assignment. Meg is ecstatic and begins writing immediately, but because of her lack of skill the daily copy for the next two months is late.

In both cases change has caused a slowdown in the turnaround time for finished copy, but in Phil's case the slowdown was intentional. In Meg's case it was unintentional. Why is it important to know the difference between intentional and unintentional resistance? Because each must be handled differently. Phil probably needs a lecture. Meg certainly needs practice. The point is this: the type of resistance faced by a supervisor will provide a clue to the proper way of handling it.

It's the supervisor's best interests to assist subordinates in quickly passing through the resistance phase. Resistance, whether intentional or unintentional, is always counterproductive. Intentional resistance is probably best handled through negotiation with the resister, or by simply making the benefits of changing outweigh the costs. Unintentional resistance can best be resolved through patience and by allowing sufficient time for the subordinate to practice any new skills associated with the change.

Phase Three: Compliance Resignation

Having passing through the resistance phase of our change model, most subordinates proceed to a phase marked by compliance or resignation. By this time they have usually given up on intentional resistance, and have had sufficient time to adjust to the change and get the practice so as to overcome unintentional resistance.

This phase is marked by the realization that the change is here to stay and little is to be gained by continued foot dragging. There continues to be a longing for and reminiscing about the old way of doing things, but subordinates begin slowly to comply with the demands of the new situation. They resign themselves to the situation, though they probably still don't like it. This phase can be especially prolonged if subordinates' fears are not addressed early in the change process.

Unfortunately, many supervisors are content to let their subordinates get stuck in phase three. As long as there is no resistance they feel there must be support, but such is not the case. Subordinates who are allowed to stay in the compliance/resignation phase are rarely motivated to do more than the minimum, and are frequently ready to leave the company when the first opportunity presents itself. Theirs is grudging compliance.

In order to encourage subordinates to accept (phase four) and ultimately support (phase five) the change, supervisors must continue to monitor the feelings of their subordinates. Adjustments must be made in the changed situation wherever necessary to convince subordinates that their best interests are being considered at all times. Weekly grievance meetings can give subordinates an opportunity to air their persisting fears, or make suggestions for streamlining or adjusting the change they've been asked to make. Only when those nagging fears are addressed, and needed adjustments made, will subordinates begin to accept change.

Phase Four: Acceptance

After management has done all it can to make subordinates feel comfortable with the changes they've experienced, considerable time will still be needed before subordinates begin to accept the change. It is not unusual for months or years to pass before the change seems less like change and more like routine (of course, the time needed will depend on the magnitude of the change.) Fortunately, time is on the supervisor's side. Given enough time, even the most obstinate subordinate will finally accept the change—it may be 54 years, but acceptance will occur! Your responsibility is to speed the process along. Here again, this is done by being attentive to the feelings and fears of your subordinates. By listening to them and letting them generate ideas and solutions to any of the change-related problems that may arise, they will more quickly come to accept the change.

The acceptance phase is marked by a willingness on the subordinates's part to abide by and endure the change without complaining. This phase is distinguished from phase three by a lack of longing for the old way of doing things. Subordinates who progress to this phase no longer talk about the "old way" and seem comfortable with the change. The acceptance phase, then, is an interim phase between the complaining and grumbling of phase three (compliance/resignation) and the genuine support of phase five.

One word of caution: it is possible, especially early in the acceptance phase, for subordinates to actually slip back into phase three—a phenomenon known as "phase regression." How does this happen? One explanation may be that since not all subordinates pass through the phases at the same pace, a phase two or phase three subordinate's complaining will influence a phase four subordinate to actually become less accepting of the change. The challenge to a supervisor is to track all subordinates through the phases and provide rewards to subordinates who progress to the acceptance phase. Certainly, subordinates who are rewarded for their acceptance of needed changes will be less likely to regress.

Phase Five: Support

The final phase of our change model is the support phase. This phase may never be reached by some subordinates. They will be content to accept the change, but may never wholly support or defend it. Newer subordinates, however, seem to move much more quickly through the first four phases then long-term subordinates, and are more likely to reach the support phase than their tenured colleagues. This phenomenon is easily explained: newer employees have fewer preconceived notions about how things should be done, and have fewer established habits and routines than long-term employees. Hence, change is not quite so frightening nor difficult to accept and support.

Subordinates who reach the support phase have come full circle in their feelings about the old way of doing things compared to the new. They are now as willing to support and defend the new way of doing things as they were the old. They may even find themselves defending the change. Phase five subordinates are active in their support, whereas phase four subordinates accept change passively.

GUIDELINES FOR INITIATING CHANGE

The effective supervisor, recognizing all of the difficulties associated with managing change, should remember the following guidelines for initiating change:

1. *Create an Awareness for the Need to Change.* Long before decisions are made regarding change, the effective supervisor will discuss the need for change and keep subordinates aware of the changes going on in other organizations.

2. *Let Subordinates Diagnose the Situation and Recommend the Change Direction.* If subordinates are involved in the process of initiating changes, they are more likely to suggest and accept changes.

3. *Help Subordinates See How the Proposed Change Will Affect Them.* This step may be difficult because it requires some predictions of the affects of change. A little effort expended here, however, may save considerable effort later.

4. *Listen to and Resolve the Fears and Concerns of Your Subordinates.* The discovery and resolution of fears and concerns early in the change process will virtually guarantee speedy movement through the five change phases.

5. *Use the Cost-Benefit Analysis to Your Advantage.* Whenever possible, make the benefits of changing far outweigh the costs. By rewarding subordinates for their commitment to and support of needed changes, they win and so do you.

6. *Monitor the Progress of All of Your Subordinates Through the Five Change Phases.* Each subordinate is different and has different needs and concerns. Constantly seek suggestions and support of the change and keep track of each subordinate's location on the five phase model.

THE CLYDE STAPLEJAW CASE

The following case study will serve to reinforce some of the concepts discussed in this chapter. At times throughout the case you'll be asked to respond to questions related to the material we've covered. The answers to the questions will follow the case study.

Clyde Staplejaw worked at Dollop Industries and had done so for nearly 20 years. He was the Senior Machine-Fixer and had developed a reputation as the fastest and most efficient troubleshooter in the company's long and healthy history. Clyde was always called on to fix the most severe mechanical breakdowns, and on many occasions had been called in to troubleshoot during the graveyard shift. Clyde was a master. No one else could coax the machines to do the things he could. His worn yet steady hands could do some amazing things with belts and pulleys. He always talked in a low, encouraging voice to the ailing mechanical patient who happened to come under his loving care. The other Machine-Fixers, mere amateurs by comparison, always spoke in amazed whispers about Clyde. He was their idol. Over the years Clyde's tremendous skills had earned him the nickname "Fixer."

Dollop Industries had been using the same machinery for well over 13 years and top management was secretly discussing the possibility of purchasing new equipment. The old equipment seemed adequate, but Dollop's major competitor, Xambofizz Incorporated, had just installed new equipment and Dollop's owner was afraid Xambofizz was out to steal some of Dollop's best customers by offering faster turnaround on their version of the Widgetmasher 420—Dollop's best selling item.

At 9:00 A.M. on Monday morning, Dollop's top mangement met to discuss the need for new equipment and after some lively discussion decided to purchase new equipment. Just before the meeting adjourned at 11:10 A.M. strict orders were issued that there should be no leaks about the decision to employees until all of the details of the purchase were finalized. By 11:15 A.M. everyone in the plant was talking about the new equipment.

Clyde was worried. It had taken him a long time to develop his skill, and now some "newfangled machines" would be purchased. What was wrong with the Gasmulcher 5000s? They had been good to him and to the company. After all, Dollop was still the leading manufacturer of Widgetmashers, weren't they? Who needed the new Spiffyspark machines anyway?

All Clyde could think about was the loss of both his reputation and his advantage over the younger, less experienced Machine-Fixers.

Questions

1. What kind of fear is Clyde experiencing? Specific or nonspecific?

In dread, Clyde went to his supervisor to complain and was assured the company had no plans to purchase new equipment. Three days later Clyde and the other Machine-Fixers were in a training session at Spiffyspark headquarters in Mooselipp, Idaho. They had two weeks to learn how to perform maintenance on the soon-to-be-installed Spiffyspark machines. Resentment quickly replaced Clyde's respect for Dollop Industries.

Getting the machines running was not easy. The start-up deadline came and went and still the Spiffysparks were silent. The training had helped, but there were so many new things to learn.

2. In what phase of the change cycle is Clyde?

3. Is Clyde's resistance at this point intentional or unintentional?

Clyde grumbled about the new machines and lamented the loss of the Gasmulchers. He started "forgetting" his tools and became more and more difficult to find when some mechanical problem came up. His anger lay just beneath the surface and frequently erupted when his supervisor walked by. In retaliation for the "dirty deal" he'd gotten from the company, Clyde began "fixing" the Spiffysparks. He overtightened the sweezy nuts and intentionally undergreased the kingpin coil. In no time the machines began wheezing and hacking uncontrollably and production finally came to a standstill. Clyde's hope was that the company would soon realize its mistake and bring back the Gasmulchers.

4. What kind of resistance is Clyde now exhibiting?

Weeks passed and still the company refused to get rid of the Spiffysparks. Production levels were abysmal and a few top managers had their heads lopped off. In the meantime, Clyde found himself getting less and less angry and more and more intrigued by the internal workings of the new machines. He had to admit they were pretty amazing. He couldn't figure out how they worked, though, so he spent much of his time disassembling and reassembling one of the standbys. He convinced himself his growing knowledge of the Spiffysparks would be useful in finding out new ways to "fix" them.

5. Clyde is moving into what phase of the change cycle? How do you know?

One night, two months later, Clyde got a call from the plant. Apparently the flapper panel on one of the Spiffys (which they had come to be called) had sprung a leak and was spraying Gammergoo all over the place. No one could figure out how to turn the crazy thing off. Clyde grudgingly agreed to drive down to the plant and see what he could do. When he arrived, he quickly located the problem and soon had the machine working. As he put away his tools, one of the Machine-Fixers (who had tried and failed to solve the problem) complained to no one in particular that the machines were just no good—that they were expensive pieces of junk. Instead of agreeing, Clyde began defending both the machines and Dollop Industries for keeping pace with the new technology.

6. *Now where is Clyde in the change cycle?*

7. *Where in the change cycle is the complaining Machine-Fixer?*

The Answers

Answer to Question 1: Clyde's fear is specific. He's afraid of losing his reputation and with it his advantage over the other Machine-Fixers.

Answer to Question 2: Clyde is probably somewhere between phase one (fear) and phase two (resistance). Either response could be correct. It's not always easy to pinpoint a person exactly.

Answer to Question 3: At this point Clyde's resistance is unintentional because it's the result of a lack of knowledge and practice with the new machines.

Answer to Question 4: This is good old-fashioned sabatoge and is, therefore, intentional resistance.

Answer to Question 5: Clyde is probably moving into phase three (compliance/resignation). He is still complaining about the new machines, but regardless of his threats, he will probably no longer sabatoge the machines.

Answer to Question 6: Clyde is in phase five (support) as indicated by his defense of both the machines and the company. Though we have no indication from the case itself, at some point Clyde went through phase four (acceptance). Remember, phase four is a passive, uncomplaining phase.

Answer to Question 7: The complaining Machine-Fixer is probably in either phase two (resistance) or phase three (compliance/resignation). If he sabatoged the machine, then he's in the resistance phase. If, on the other hand, he really did attempt to correct the problem with the machine, then he is probably in the compliance/resignation phase.

CHAPTER

10

TIME MANAGEMENT

MATT HENNECKE

By picking up this book, turning to this chapter, and reading what follows, you are making a commitment of your time in order to learn more about managing your time. As a rule, people make commitments to satisfy needs. We make a commitment in marriage to satisfy a need for companionship. We make a commitment to an employer to satisfy a need for work, achievement, and money (and all that it will buy). So, let's assume your commitment to reading this chapter also arises because of a need: a need to gain control of your time.

If you are like most people, time management constitutes a real problem. All of us have to face the forces that constantly compete for our time and energy. Most of us have to work, so our employers demand some of our time; and if we have families they

10.1

too demand and need some of our time. Then there is sleeping, eating, recreation, the demands of church activities and civic responsibilities, all of which compete for the few hours we have each day. It's no wonder that we so frequently seek help in learning better how to manage our time.

To customize this chapter to your particular time-management needs, there will be occasions when you may be asked to respond to questions or to engage in various activities. You'll be tempted to read past the questions or activities, but try to overcome that temptation. Just as each of us has a different set of fingerprints, we also have different time-management problems. So, the more we analyze our time problems, the better we'll be able to solve them. Ready? Let's start with a simple question:

What are the total number of hours in a typical work week (if there is such a thing) that you think you could save through more effective management of your time? Are you able to come up with a number? Typically supervisors like yourself will do some rough calculations and arrive at a figure somewhere between four and eight hours per week. Regardless of the number you came up with, any number greater than zero is incorrect. That's right, incorrect. You see, it's impossible to "save" time. You can only "spend" it more effecively. Time is not like money that can be stashed away in a local savings and loan for future use. All of us will spend exactly 168 hours per week, no more and no less. So while we cannot save it, we can spend it more effectively.

Let's assume that the average number of hours that most people can "spend" more effectively is four per week. You may have indicated more or less. But if four hours is a fair average, then we can approximate the annual cost of wasting time.

Most working Americans work an average of 50 weeks per year (assuming two weeks for vacation). If we multiply four hours by 50 weeks per year we get 200: 200 hours wasted per year per working American. That may not seem like much, but if we then multiply that 200 hours by an average hourly wage, say $5 per hour, we get a total of $1000. Then, if we multiply $1000 by the number of working Americans, roughly 40 million, we get an annual loss of $40 billion! Forty billion dollar's worth of wasted time each year! And that's low by most accounts. Many estimates of the annual cost of wasting time are two to three times larger!

In order for you to effectively tackle your own time problems, you've got to have a plan—a systematic approach for first identifying your time problems and later solving them. To do this you should approach your time problems the same way you would approach any problem, and that's by using the same problem-solving method you use in tackling the other problems you face.

THE TIME-PROBLEM-SOLVING MODEL

If you are familiar with the traditional problem-solving model, you will remember there are usually five steps. First, you identify the problem; second, you identify the causes; third, you determine solutions; fourth, you implement the solutions; and finally, you evaluate your progress. With a few minor changes, we can make the model a time-problem-solving model as illustrated in Figure 10.1.

Now the real work begins, and that is proceeding through all five steps. The remainder of this chapter will help you do just that.

Step One: Identifying Your Time Problems

Before you will get anywhere in solving any time problems, you must first identify the problems. You may be thinking that you've already identified the problem—you have too much to do and too little time in which to do it. But that's not specific enough. Imagine getting some work done on your ailing automobile and then asking the mechanic to explain the problem. Instead, he hands you a bill for $347.50 and says, "Well, the car wasn't working." Obviously, that wouldn't satisfy you. You would want to know what wasn't working—specifically! Well, the same is true of time problems.

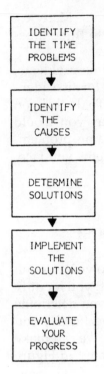

FIGURE 10.1. Time-Problem-Solving Model

You need to identify the specific things that are robbing you of your precious time.

The best method for uncovering time problems is through the use of a time record log. Now, some of you are probably ready to bail out of this chapter at the mere mention of a time record log. A time record log sounds like a lot of work, and the last thing you need now is another project, right? Wrong. The only way you will ever find out exactly what is devouring your time is by keeping track of where your time goes. Here's a guarantee: if you will keep a time record log for just three days, you will have 80% of the work behind you, because suddenly it'll be clear what your real time problems are. A sample of a time record log is provided on the next page for your use. Follow the instructions and fill out the log religiously. See you in three days.

Instructions:

1.   Enter your name, the day, and the date at the top of the time record log. Try to begin your record in the morning.

2.   Record your time usage in 15-minute intervals. Obviously, during some 15-minute intervals you may be doing the same thing. For instance, you may be in a meeting for two hours. During other 15-minute segments you may be doing several things (for example, using the telephone, dictating a memo, walking through the plant, and so forth). As much as possible, try to record all that you do. The more detailed you are, the more useful your log will be.

3.   Make sure to record your activities *as you are doing them*. Don't wait until the end of the day to try to remember. Try not to generalize—go for detail. Be brutally honest about your activities. Remember, nobody but you has to see the completed log.

4.   Be certain to record *all* interruptions that may occur during the three days. This may include things like telephone calls, drop-in visitors, crises, and so forth.

5.   Leave the two right-hand columns blank for now. You'll receive instructions later on how to complete them.

Step Two: Identifying Your Time-Problem Causes

The second step in the time-problem-solving process involves identifying the true causes of your specific time problems. In other words, you've got to know what's causing the problems before you can take appropriate action to correct them. Too often we fall into the trap of trying to eliminate a symptom instead of a cause. If, for instance, a man goes to his doctor complaining of a persistent headache, the doctor, rather than simply prescribing some painkiller and sending the man home, will probably check to see if there is some deeper reasons for the headache—some cause for the symptom. The same principle applies to time-management problems; if we want, we can treat the symptoms, but that's not as effective as getting to the real causes.

Now that you have completed your time record log, it's time to go back over the three-day period and see how well you are

TIME RECORD LOG

NAME_____ DAY_____ DATE_____

TIME	ACTIVITY	INTERRUPTION	COLUMN A		COLUMN B	
7:00			I	E	U	I
7:15			I	E	U	I
7:30			I	E	U	I
7:45			I	E	U	I
8:00			I	E	U	I
8:15			I	E	U	I
8:30			I	E	U	I
8:45			I	E	U	I
9:00			I	E	U	I
9:15			I	E	U	I
9:30			I	E	U	I
9:45			I	E	U	I
10:00			I	E	U	I
10:15			I	E	U	I
10:30			I	E	U	I
10:45			I	E	U	I
11:00			I	E	U	I
11:15			I	E	U	I
11:30			I	E	U	I
11:45			I	E	U	I
12:00			I	E	U	I
12:15			I	E	U	I
12:30			I	E	U	I

Continued on next page

FIGURE 10.2.   Time Record Log

TIME	ACTIVITY	INTERRUPTION	COLUMN A		COLUMN B	
12:45			I	E	U	I
1:00			I	E	U	I
1:15			I	E	U	I
1:30			I	E	U	I
1:45			I	E	U	I
2:00			I	E	U	I
2:15			I	E	U	I
2:30			I	E	U	I
2:45			I	E	U	I
3:00			I	E	U	I
3:15			I	E	U	I
3:30			I	E	U	I
3:45			I	E	U	I
4:00			I	E	U	I
4:15			I	E	U	I
4:30			I	E	U	I
4:45			I	E	U	I
5:00			I	E	U	I
5:15			I	E	U	I
5:30			I	E	U	I
5:45			I	E	U	I
6:00			I	E	U	I
6:15			I	E	U	I
6:30			I	E	U	I
6:45			I	E	U	I
7:00			I	E	U	I

currently using your time. In other words, you have to begin the process of identifying the causes of your time problems. You already may be amazed at where your time actually goes, and the number of interruptions you face during the day. It's been estimated that most supervisors are interrupted an average of every 10 minutes, and that few ever have an uninterrupted period of time longer than 20 minutes!

Internal versus External Time-Problem Causes

Most of us are quick to blame others for our time problems. We say things like, "My boss controls my time," or, "If the stupid telephone would just stop ringing then I would have plenty of time." These statements indicate a tendency on our part to attribute time problems to things outside of our control, that is, *external* causes. It may come as a surprise to learn that for most of us, between 80–90% of our time problems are not external at all, but internal, that is, within our control.

Obviously, the amount of control we might have over any situation will vary considerably, but as long as we have some control, we should use it to manage our time more effectively. Let's look at a few examples that will illustrate more clearly the difference between internal and external time problems.

Suppose you are sitting at your desk trying to figure out next week's schedule when the telephone rings. Since most organizations frown on supervisors who refuse to answer their telephones, we can label the ringing telephone as an *external* time waster (at least potentially, we won't know if it's a time waster until we answer it). Remember, by *external* we mean totally outside of our control. Once we answer it, and discover it's our no-good brother-in-law (the one who wants a $2000 loan so he can invest in pork belly futures), the interruption shifts from external to internal. It's our choice—we can either spend time talking or we can politely hang up. So, while the ringing telephone may be external, the decision to prolong or end the conversation is internal—that is, within our control.

Let's look at another example: Today is Friday and you have to gather all the production figures for the week and make a report to your boss. As you're struggling with the numbers, Agnes Hagglestarter walks up to your desk and starts telling you about her trip to Bermuda. Out of courtesy you switch off your calculator and sit back and listen. At what point did the drop-in visitor go from being an external time waster to an internal one? Again, there are certain rules of etiquette that demand we not ignore people, so when Agnes interrupts, she is an external time waster.

However, when we give in to the temptation and stop to listen, the time waster quickly becomes internal.

In both cases, the initial time waster is external, but our willingness to become involved can make both internal. Further, the amount of time it takes to answer the telephone and explain that we cannot talk now, or to look up at Agnes and indicate something similar, is very short. It's when we surrender too easily to the interruptions—thereby making them internal—that the greatest amount of our time is wasted.

In summary, our definition of an *external time waster* is any time waster that is totally outside of our control. If you have even the slightest control and don't exert that control, then the time waster has an internal cause—you.

Typical Time-Position Internal Causes

Because 80–90% of our time wasters have internal causes, it would be good for us to know what those causes are. The following list, while certainly not exhaustive, does pinpoint some of the most frequent reasons, why we are to blame for our own time-management problems. Read through the list carefully and ask yourself whether or not you may be your own worst enemy when it comes to your time-management problems:

1. *No Established Priorities.* Frequently, supervisors have not determined what is important and therefore what deserves their time and effort. Do you have priorities, or do you take things as they come?

2. *No Daily To-Do List.* Do you make a practice of listing all the things that need doing each day? Most successful managers don't begin a day without first listing all of the important things that need doing.

3. *Attempting Too Much.* Do you take on more projects than you can handle, and then gripe about not having enough time?

4. *Underestimating Time Requirements.* Do you tend to make promises about how long it will take to complete a task and then miss your self-imposed deadlines?

5. *Procrastination.*   Do you put things off until later? Do you try to convince yourself that you work better under pressure?

6. *Unable to Say "No."*   Are you an easy mark? Do people find it easy to get you do their work, or to waste your time? Many people feel uncomfortable saying "no" when a request is made for their assistance, or are afraid to tell drop-in visitors and telephone callers that they're busy and unable to talk.

7. *Poor Organization.*   Can you easily find things in your desk, in your files, and in your department or unit? Or do you waste precious time sending out search parties to locate those files you lost?

8. *Poor Delegation.*   Rather than delegating tasks to your people, do you often handle things yourself, and then spend extra hours on the job catching up on your other duties?

9. *No Clearly Defined Objectives or Plans.*   Do you know where you and your unit are going? Have you and your people spelled out in detail what it is you're trying to accomplish?

10. *Daydreaming.*   Do you catch yourself thinking about the fishing trip you'll be taking next month, instead of figuring out why the Frammit Machine keeps up that incressant gurgling and hissing?

The list goes on and on. Some additional internal causes of time problems are listed below:

Poor organization

Poor listening habits

Too little or too much communication

Making snap decisions

Blaming others

Poor self-discipline

Long hours and fatigue

Poor concentration

Pet personal projects

No time deadlines

Are the Causes of Your Time Problems External or Internal?

Now that we've talked at length about some of the causes of time-management problems, it's time for you to go back over your time record log and evaluate the causes of your time-managment problems. If you have carefully recorded all of the interruptions you had during the three-day period, now you can check to ses if they had external or internal causes.

On the right-hand side of your time log under the heading "Column A" are the letters "I" and "E." Review all of the interruptions you had during the three-day period, determine if they were internally or externally caused, and then circle the appropriate letter in Column A. For instance, if you had a telephone call from your Aunt Tilly, or Zack Clapper came by to shoot the breeze, circle the "I" in the appropriate box. All you're indicating is that you had at least some control of the situation and that any time you spent with the interruption was your choice.

If, on the other hand, you indicated your weekly staff meeting as an interruption , but there was no way you could choose between attending or not attending, then you should probably circle the "E." Remember, though, if you had even the slightest control over a situation you should indicate that control by circling the "I."

Go ahead and evaluate your time record log interruptions.

All finished? You may be surprised by the fact that in most cases you did have at least some control over those things that interrupted you. Most of us have more control than we're willing to admit. Why? Because by admitting to our control, we are eliminating one of our best excuses for not having enough time, and that excuse is that it is somebody else's fault.

No Priorities: Another Cause of Time Problems

Another frequent reason or cause for our time problems is our unwillingness to determine what is important. Most of us recognize the value of setting priorities, but few of us actually take the time to do so; or, if we do, we don't do so as effectively as we should. There are basically three methods for setting priorities.

Two of them are of questionable value, especially to a supervisor. The third method is very valuable, but requires some effort to make it work.

Three Ways to Set Priorities

1. *First Come, First Served.*   This is the traditional "stand-in-line" method of setting priorities. It works very well in the grocery store checkout. Very simply, it means that if you're first in line you'll be checked out first. Unfortunately, it does not work as well in supervising a unit. Imagine a supervisor who lived by this method of setting priorities: "I'm sorry, Bill, I know you think that conflict with our multimillion dollar customer is more important, but Fred here has asked me to help him clean out the pencil sharpener. You'll just have to wait your turn."

2. *Crisis Management.*   This method of setting priorities is actually quite simple to explain. Whoever screams the loudest goes first. It's a little better than the "first come, first served" method, but not by much. A supervisor who uses this method constantly runs from crisis to crisis, and is usually willing to drop one crisis in the face of a larger crisis. This supervisor's co-workers quickly learn that the best way to get his or her attention is to start the building on fire.

3. *Contribution to Objectives.*   This method of setting priorities has a prerequisite: you've got to know what your objectives are. The supervisor who uses this method is goal-directed. He or she knows what it is his or her department is supposed to accomplish and sets priorities by determining which tasks go the furthest in meeting those objectives. With this method, it doesn't matter what task arises first, or which task is the most urgent. Tasks that most satisfy the objectives come first, and all others come later.

When you were completing your time record log, you were recording your activities as they occurred during a three-day period. To really determine how well you prioritized your activities, you should go back and see which activities you did first. Before you do that though, let's differentiate between important activities and urgent activities.

Urgency versus Importance

Suppose you are sitting at your desk doing some long-range planning. It's tough work, but you realize it's got to be done. As you slurp down the final tepid drops of coffee in the bottom of your cup, the telephone rings. What will you do? Answer the phone, right? After you identify yourself you realize it's Manny Gargleknee, the vaccum cleaner salesman. In such a situation most of us would agree that long-range planning is certainly more important than talking to Manny, but at least for that instant when you answered the phone, you put aside the important in order to handle the urgent. The ringing telephone demands immediate attention—and that's what is meant by urgency.

Drop-in visitors also illustrate the concept of urgency. When Louie drops by to discuss the Celtics, he demands your immediate attention—even if you pause only long enough to tell him to take a hike. You see, the real problems begin when we give in to the urgent interruptions at the expense of the important activities.

Things that are urgent and things that are important are not always easy to separate. Some things may be both urgent and important, some things may be one or the other, and some things may be neither. To test your understanding of the concept of urgency and importance, there are five activities listed below. Read the activities and then try to decide which are urgent, which are important, which are both, and which are neither. If an activity is only urgent circle the "U." If it is only important, then circle the "I." If an activity is both urgent and important then circle both the "U" and "I." And, if an activity is neither then leave the letters uncircled.

U	I	1. Straightening your desk
U	I	2. Long-range planning
U	I	3. Drop-in visitor
U	I	4. Fleeing from a burning building
U	I	5. Small talk with a friend

Unless you thought of some extenuating circumstances, you probably responded this way: Number one is neither urgent nor important, even though many of us straighten our desks more frequently than we'd like to admit. Number two is important, but not necessarily urgent. Number three is urgent, but probably not important. Number four is both urgent and important, and number five is neither.

Now that you've had some pratice identifying urgent and important activities, it's time to go back to your time record log and evaluate the activities you recorded during the three-day period. If you'll look at Column B on your time log you'll see the letters "U" and "I." Take some time now to evaluate each of your activities during the entire three day period. Circle the "U" if the recorded activity was urgent, the "I" if important. If the activity was both urgent and important, circle both letters, and if neither, circle neither. Remember, be brutally honest.

If you were honest with yourself then you were very likely shocked by how infrequently you spend your time doing really "important" things, and by how frequently you're involved in urgent things. Take comfort in the fact that you are like most other supervisors, and then take the initiative to read on.

In summary, the causes of time-management problems generally originate from two sources. We may "internally" cause our own time problems by giving in to interruptions, and/or we may be unable or unwilling to effectively prioritize our tasks so as to be sure of handling the important ones instead of the urgent ones. The next step in our time-problem-solving model is determining time-problem solutions.

Step Three: Determining Solutions to Our Time Problems

Setting Objectives and Determining Priorities

The single most effective way to gain control of our time is to determine specifically where we want to spend it, and then absolutely refuse to spend it elsewhere. The only way to do that is to list goals and set priorities. An ancient proverb states: "If you don't know where you are going, any road will get you there."

The first order of business in setting objectives is to sit down with your subordinates, your boss, and anyone else who can help, and figure out exactly where it is your department or unit is going—specifically. The more detailed your goals, the easier it will be for you to set priorities.

Try to think in the long term first. What are the missions of your organization generally? Then, begin focusing attention on your own department's contributions to that mission by coming up with a two-year plan, a one-year plan, and even a six-month plan. Then, when you're faced with 37 things to do, you can determine which ones will contribute most to your plan or mission and let the others slide. One note of caution: do not think you can become a good manager of your time without taking this crucial first step. You can't.

Next, it's important that you deal with your personal time. After all, you have personal ambitions and goals that need attention, too. Where do you want to go with your career? What are your personal goals, objectives, and missions? How can you best reach your goals, and what kind of timetable do you have? For further information, there's a whole chapter in this book dealing with career planning. Take the time to look into it.

Once you establish goals for your department and yourself, you will find it much easier to identify those activities and tasks that bring you closer to a satisfaction of those goals.

Solutions to Some of the Most Common Time Wasters

Because so much attention has been focused on time-management problems during the past several years, several common time wasters have been identified. These include things such as telephone calls, drop-in visitors, meetings, poor delegation, and the like. Since you have probably been victimized by some of these time robbers you may benefit from some general suggestions or solutions. You'll note that after a discussion of each time waster possible internal causes are mentioned which are then followed by possible solutions:

Telephone Interruptions.   It's been said if Alexander Graham Bell were alive today he'd be very old. It's also been said that he wouldn't live much longer because some irate, shell-shocked telephone supervisor would strangle him. Ironically, the telephone, while doing· much to eliminate some of our time problems has caused a whole flock of new time problems,. The same telephone that allows us to transact business at long distances also allows Dexter Bytebelly to call and make a nuisance of himself.

The internal causes of telephone time problems are many. Included are things such as an inability to terminate conversations, no set plan for handling calls, a desire to socialize, a need to be available, as well as many more. To solve these problems, supervisors should develop a plan to screen, consolidate, and delegate phone calls. They should learn to tell callers that they don't have time to talk, and, if necessary, hang up (don't try this with your boss). One excellent method of terminating a phone conversation is to begin talking and hang up in the middle of one of your own sentences. No one would ever think you would hang up on yourself! The caller will likely attribute the problem to the telephone company and try to call back, but in the time it takes him to dial your number you can be in the next county.

Drop-in visitors.   Just like acne and welfare workers, drop-in visitors have a way of showing up at the most inopportune times. You may be inclined to think it's all part of some master plan to force you into early retirement or an asylum, but research has found that the drop-in visitor has no such motive. In fact, one study has shown that such visitors are really rather harmless creatures possessing an intellect somewhat below that of a frozen pizza.

There are quite a few ways that we may unintentionally encourage drop-in visitors rather than dicourage them. The layout of our office may encourage the drop-in visitor (henceforth referred to as a DIV). Our inability to say "no," our fear of offending, our enjoyment of socializing—all make the DIV's visit too pleasant an experience to pass up. Our counteroffensive? To prevent the DIV from getting the upper hand, we should move our desk so that we face away from the flow of traffic. We should remove extra chairs from our offices, or put something in the chairs that will discourage roosting (Doberman pinschers work very well). We need to get rid of the stuffed walleye, the pictures of our trip to Budapest, and anything else that might drag us into an unwanted conversation. And, most importantly, we need to develop the habit of saying "no."

Meetings.   Nobody likes meetings. They're always too frequent and always too long. One Wall Street economist, now exiled in Tahiti, discovered the Inverse Law of Meetings and Sales. Put simply, it states that there is an inverse relationship between the number of meetings an organization has and its sales volume. Hence, if the frequency of meetings in any organization goes up 25%, sales can be expected to plummet 75%.

What causes poor meetings? Usually it's not having an agenda. How many times do you call staff meetings and forget to put together a specific agenda? Do your meetings start on time? How much socializing goes on during the meetings you call? To really get control of the time wasted in meetings, it's essential that there be an agenda, and the agenda should be distributed to meeting partcipants prior to the meting so they can schedule their own time more effectively. Your meetings should begin promptly and end as soon as reasonably possible. You should require your people to stay only as long as their presence is needed. Since there is a strong correlation between the comfort level of the chairs in the meeting room and the length of a meeting, you may wish to try a stand-up meeting. To speed up the meeting even more, you may wish to try a stand-on-one-leg-only meeting, but get prior permission from your physician.

Poor Delegation.   The internal causes of ineffective delegation are usually insecurity, a fear of failure, a lack of confidence in your people, jealousy of a subordinate's ability, among others. If, as you look back over your time record log, you notice a lot of activities that you could have delegated to your subordinates, then you are violating the first commandment of management, and that is to get things done through other people. There is just no way you can hope to do all that needs doing. At some point in time you are going to have to trust in the abilities of your people. Why not begin right now? Do nothing that you can delegate.

Avoid detail work like the plague. Train and cross-train your people so that they can help you to delegate better. Refuse to make decisions for subordinates, and refuse to do your subordinates' work.

Personal Disorganization.   Personal disorganization is without question an internally caused time-waster. Too much junk on our desk, too much mail, a lousy filing system—all make attempts at being an effective supervisor futile. How many piles of paper do you have on your desk right now? Could you locate the Bobwiddle file if you had to? Has an environmental group asked permission to photograph the stacks of paper on your desk for their next "Save Our Forests" poster? If your answer is "yes" then it's time for action. Never allow more than one pile of papers to accumulate on your desk (and try to keep the pile under 13 feet). Tie one end of a rope to a colleagues's desk and the other to your waist and plunge right into those files you've been keeping since the dawn of time. Discard, burn, hack, and dump anything that's discardable, burnable, hackable, and dumpable. In short, get organized.

Procrastination.   There's a temptation to put off a discussion of this time waster until later. Suffice it to say that many a blossoming career has withered because of procrastination. Putting off important things is one of the surest ways of being considered undependable and, even worse, incompetent. How about now? Are any deadlines quickly approaching? Why not save yourself the trauma and pressure and do it now?

Attempting Too Much.   The crunch of time pressures is most frequently felt whenever we discover we've taken on more than we can handle. When you've got to write three proposals, read the Cub Scout leader's manual, entertain the boss, and go to play rehearsal—all in the next 12 minutes—then you've attempted too much. The solution? Change your name and move to Portugal. If that's not feasible than try some of the following: recognize that everything takes 50% longer than your original estimate. Learn to say "no" in 15 languages. Delegate, delegate, delegate. If possible, hire more help. If necessary, take early retirement.

Time-Management Action Plan

Name _____ Date _____

I.   Based on the results of my Time Record Log, and a general assessment of my time-management problems, I have identified the following internally caused time problems:

1.   _____

2.   _____

3.   _____

4.   _____

II. I Plan to take the following actions to eliminate or gain control over the above listed internally caused time problems:

Proposed Action for #1: _____

_____

_____

Proposed Action for #2: _____

_____

_____

Proposed Action for #3: _____

_____

_____

Proposed Action for #4: _____

_____

_____

III. I will have control of these time problems by: ____/____/____

FIGURE 10.3.   Sample Time Management Action Plan

10.19

Step Four: Implementing the Solutions

Unfortunately, the implementing of solutions is the most difficult step in our time-problem-solving process. Why? Because it calls on you to change your habits, and that's difficult. The best way to insure that you will really work on some of your time-management problems is for you to write up a time-management action plan and share it with your boss, your spouse, and your subordinates. Only when we take the time to put our intentions in writing, and then share those intentions with people who will be unmerciful in their ridicule should be fail, will we be successful in changing our habits. A sample time-management action plan is provided at the end of the chapter. Complete it and, if necessary, post it on the bulletin board for everyone to see. You'll be amazed at how difficult it will be to back out once everyone knows what you're up to.

Step Five: Evaluating Your Progress

To be an effective manager of your time is going to take real effort, but the rewards are worth it. If you resolve to become a good manager of your time, and keep plugging away at it, you will succeed. There will be times when it'll seem like you've fallen back into your own ways, but as long as you recognize them as your "old ways" you'll be okay.

After you've had some time to implement your time-management action plan, you'll want to check to see how well you're doing. The best way to do that is to keep a time record log for another three-day period. This time, however, complete Columns A and B after each activity or interruption entry. In this way, you'll be able to make immediate adjustments, and, as you proceed through the three days, you'll begin evaluating each activity and interruption ahead of time, which can only lead to more effective use of your time.

Good luck.

CHAPTER

UNDERSTANDING AND MANAGING STRESS

MATT HENNECKE

You are under stress when you see a "60 Minutes" news team waiting in your office.

You are under stress when you turn on the evening news and the newcaster is showing emergency evacuation routes out of the city.

You are under stress when you come into work and your boss tells you not to bother to take off your coat.

You are under stress when the bird singing outside your window is a buzzard.

You are under stress when your income tax payment check bounces.

You are under stress when your wife says, "Good morning, Bob," and your name is Marvin.

You are under stress when your car horn goes off accidentally and remains stuck as you follow a group of Hell's Angels motorcyclists across the Golden Gate Bridge.

UNDERSTANDING AND DEFINING STRESS

Stress is not new, although we might think so given the attention it's received in recent years. Our ancestors and their ancestors all faced and survived the stress associated with simply existing in a world of change. However, the number and magnitude of changes we're facing in the twentieth century certainly exceed those experienced by past generations. Perhaps that's why researchers, doctors, and business people have suddenly taken notice of this phenomenon called stress. Today stress is recognized as an ever-present danger—a by-product of advances in technology and changes in our economic and social systems. Stress has been clearly linked to the frightening increase in the number of Americans suffering heart attacks and strokes, and to the number of people plagued with high blood pressure. But the physical suffering isn't the whole story. Stress-related illnesses have also caused an economic crisis of huge proportions.

According to the United States Clearinghouse for Mental Health Information, during the last few years American businesses have suffered annual decreases in productivity amounting to more than $70 billion as a result of stress related illnesses. Not surprisingly, stress can cause absenteeism, turnover, and illness—all of which contribute to lagging productivity and, on a smaller scale, make your job as a supervisor more difficult and more stressful. But what exactly is stress?

Stress has been, and will probably continue to be, defined in a variety of ways, but many of us define it by simply recounting some stressful experience we've had in the past. We remember the stress we felt when the deadline for that project was upon us and we were still four weeks behind schedule. Or we recall the stress we felt when we had to give a speech and, as we were being introduced, the guy sitting next to us spilled his raisin and pistachio milkshake all over our notes. We've all experienced similar stressful moments—moments when we wished we could be suddenly transported, complete with a new identity, to another part of the galaxy.

Because stress is such a universal experience and because it is so much a part of daily existence, one doctor jokingly defined it as a "purple heart of an eventful life." A more useful definition, however, might that stress is a response to any change, either actual or potential, that alters a person's biological or mental state.

Stress: Harmful or Useful?

On the surface, our definition of stress may sound a bit frightening. After all, anything that "alters" our biological or mental state has got to be bad, right? Not necessarily. A great deal of attention has been focused recently on the harmful effects of stress, but not all stress is bad for us. In fact, without stress life itself would probably be impossible—and if not impossible than certainly very boring. Why? Because stress is what motivates us. Stress is what gets us out of bed in the morning and gets us to work on time. Stress is what stimulates us to make that extra effort at work that can mean the difference between career success and career failure. Stress is what prompts us and others to tackle seemingly impossible projects in an effort to alter our environment to suit our needs. That's why we build Hoover Dams, Empire State Buildings, and space shuttles. Clearly, every endeavor, every venture of mankind has at its root the exhilaration born of the challenge and stress of living.

Stress can also be enjoyable. Otherwise how do you account for the fact that seemingly normal human beings will stand in line for hours to ride the Skull Masher—a 300-miles-per-hour roller coaster—or subject themselves to horror movies that have no other purpose than to scare their socks off? Most of us like to be scared in controlled, relatively risk-free situations; we experience an emotional cleansing that invigorates us and prepares us for dealing with life's frustrations.

What, then, is the difference between harmful and useful stress?

Quite simple, it seems that stress can be useful and enjoyable as long as it has some sort of outlet—as long as we feel in control of the stressful situation and can redirect the tension and anxiety associated with the stress to some worthwhile project or action. Under such circumstances the stress is consumed by the action. If, however, we experience stress but have no outlet and have no control, then the tension and anxiety may consume us.

The Stress Schematic

Another way of understanding stress is by understanding it as part of a process rather than as an isolated sensation or feeling. Whenever we come in contact with a stressor (which is anything that causes stress) we experience what doctors call the fight/flight response. The fight/flight response is the biological preparation our bodies experience whenever we are faced with a situation that demands action. Our heart rate increases, our eyes dilate, adrenalin is released into our system, our breathing becomes shallow and rapid, our blood pressure increases. Doctors tell us this instantaneous sequence of biological events is nature's way of preparing us to either flee a stressful situation or stay and fight it: Hence the name *the fight/flight response*. Let's look at an example of the response in action.

Lester Gaggle decided one evening to take a walk to the drugstore to pick up a newspaper. He liked walking because it provided him with some exercise. It also seemed to clear his mind of all the accumulated mush that came from functioning in a world full of demanding bosses and incompetent subordinates. It was dark as he made his way down the deserted street toward the lights of the shopping center. He didn't need the walking stick he'd inherited from his now-deceased uncle, but he liked carrying it with him anyway—it made him feel in control of things. A thick breeze was blowing and occasional flashes of lightning were doing battle in the distance. Suddenly Lester heard a menacing growl behind him. He whirled around, the hair on his neck at attention. Standing 15 feet away, teeth barred in a hideous snarl, was a Doberman pinscher.

At that instant, Lester was experiencing the fight/flight response. His heart was racing, his blood pressure was on the rise, and his circulatory system was awash in adrenalin. In a matter of seconds he was physically and mentally ready to either brain the dog with his walking stick or leap into the nearest tree.

Obviously in Lester's case the fight/flight response was a welcome reaction to the danger he was suddenly facing. He needed the abrupt acceleration of this body's systems to enable him to react swiftly and decisively. But what if it had been a false alarm? What if Lester had imagined the growl and when he turned around in the darkness had mistaken a lawn ornament for the Doberman? Then all of his body's defenses would have been on alert, but there would have been no situation demanding action. That's when stress becomes dangerous to our health. That's not to say our bodies cannot tolerate large amounts of stress; they certainly can. But when our bodies are continually subjected to excessive amounts of stress, and especially when there is no energy-consuming action we can take as an outlet, then our bodies begin to break down. It's like racing an automobile's engine but not going anywhere. Eventually, if we race it fast enough, and frequently enough, we're going to throw a rod or piston. Unfortunately, the fight/flight response has only limited usefulness in today's society. Oh sure, it'll help us if we happen to meet a mugger in a dark alley, and it'll prepare us for quick action if the house catches on fire, but those aren't frequent occurrences. Unlike our ancestors who needed the fight/flight response on almost a daily basis to fight the Indians or run away from the grizzly, we seldom require it. But that doesn't mean it isn't triggered every time we face a stressful situation. Let's look at another more likely situation involving Lester Gaggle.

On the Friday following Lester's incident with the neighbor's lawn ornament (which by the way he smashed into 47 pieces), he found himself in a heated argument with Clancy Fester, the plant safety inspector. Clancy was concerned about the exhaust tubing on the Blastdamper and wanted Lester to shut it down so he could inspect it more closely. Lester was furious. He had a quota to meet and no greenhorn safety inspector was

STRESS SCHEMATIC

FIGURE 11.1. Stress Schematic

going to order him around. Besides, he'd shut down his Blast-damper three times already this week for no other reason than Clancy's "concerns." In all three cases nothing had been found wrong.

The fight/flight response can be triggered by virtually any strong emotion, or any demand that we might face. In Lester's case he is again experiencing the fight/flight response, but this time it is a combination of the anger and time deadlines under which he is working. Now he may wish he could knock some sense into Clancy, and he may even feel like running away from the situation, but both actions are frowned upon in a civilized society. Punching out a safety inspector does not win a person the admiration and respect of his or her employer. So, what does Lester do? He fumes, he seethes, and under his breathe he curses like a sailor, but he gets no real release from all of the pent-up energy and stress he's experiencing. With no lawn ornaments handy, all Lester can do is feel distress, and distress can ultimately lead to illness. The stress schematic in Figure 11.1 illustrates Lester's predicament and, sadly, the predicament of modern humans. You see, like Lester, we frequently experience the fight/flight response but we infrequently can vent the energy it produces. The result? Heart attack, stroke, high blood pressure, and more.

DETERMINING THE CAUSES OF STRESS

Many things can cause us stress and elicit within us the fight/ flight response. For instance, you probably experienced a certain amount of stress when you became a supervisor. Like most supervisors you may have had misgivings about your ability to supervise others, and during those first few weeks you probably noticed that your subordinates had their doubts, too. And, once things settled down a bit, you certainly experienced the stress associated with your new role. You were no longer one of the "guys" or "girls" and your relationship with your old buddies was probably never quite the same.

One of the first steps in understanding and managing stress involves diagnosis. By identifying the source of the stress we're experiencing, we can focus our stress-reduction efforts more precisely and, as a result, be more successful in reducing our stress to more manageable levels. There's also a hidden benefit in determining the causes of our stress: the mere process of identifying and categorizing stress into certain types can, by itself, help reduce stress levels. Like the lion who is less threatening and deadly when he is caged, stress can actually become less threatening and deadly if we can classify it into certain specific categories.

The Stress Model

As the stress model in Figure 11.2 illustrates, stress originates from two basic sources: there is a relationship stress and non-relationship stress. Relationship stress, as its name implies, originates from the interaction of people with whom we've formed relationships. This might include boss-subordinate stress, husband-wife stress, parent-child stress, and the stress that could potentially develop in any other relationship we form. Non-relationship stress, on the other hand, is defined as stress that originates from all other sources. Long lines, a flat tire, illness, severe weather—all would be examples of non-relationship stress.

In addition to the two sources of stress, stress has two basic

STRESS MODEL

	Relationship	Non-relationship
Short-lived	Category A Stress	Category B Stress
On-going	Category C Stress	Category D Stress

FIGURE 11.2.   Stress Model

durations: it can be either short-lived or ongoing.[*] Short-lived stress is usually very intense, but relatively brief in duration, and its impact upon us subsides rather quickly. Ongoing stress, though usually less intense, is of longer duration. Its impact may be felt for months, years, or a lifetime.

According to our model, then, all stress falls into one of the following four categories:

Category A: Short-lived, Relationship Stress

Category B: Short-lived, Non-relationship Stress

Category C: Ongoing, Relationship Stress

Category D: Ongoing, Non-relationship Stress

Let's see how well the model works as a tool for understanding stress, by considering the stressful situations Lester Gaggle experienced in our earlier examples.

When Lester did battle with the yard ornament, what kind of stress do you think he was experiencing? Category A, B, C, or D? Since he was experiencing stress from a source with which he had no relationship, and since the stress he felt was very intense but of short duration, his stress probably fell into category B.

Let's try another one. What kind of stress would Lester have

[*] John D. Adams, *Understanding and Managing Stress: A Workbook in Changing Life Styles*, (San Diego: University Associates, 1980), 15.

been experiencing if the owner of the lawn ornament (who had also been Lester's neighbor for five years) had come running out to see what all the ruckus was about? Then Lester would probably be experiencing category A stress.

What category of stress would Lester's confrontation with Clancy Fester, the plant safety inspector, be? Now this one may be a bit tricky. Lester has a relationship with Clancy, that much is clear. What's not so clear is whether animosity and associated stress between the two has been going on for some time or is infrequent and short-lived. If Lester and Clancy have been continually at each other's throats than we may be witnessing category C stress. If, however, their anger is infrequent and short-lived, then theirs may be category A stress.

To give you some additional practice at using the stress model, try to determine the stress category of each of the following stressful situations:

1. Your car breaks down in the middle of the highway during rush hour traffic. This is a category _____ stressor.

2. Your son keeps getting in trouble with the law. He's been arrested this time for driving while under the influence of alcohol. This is a category _____ stressor.

3. You and your boss just don't seem to be able to get along. He never tells you what kind of performance he expects. This is a category _____ stressor.

4. The anchorperson on the evening news talks about the level of destruction should there be a nuclear war. This is a category _____ stressor.

5. You are getting married tomorrow. This is a category _____ stressor.

6. Your company has moved to a neighboring state. This is a category _____ stressor.

7. Crime in your neighborhood has been on the increase for the last several years. This is a category _____ stressor.

8. A snowstorm has left you stranded in the airport over the holidays. This is a category _____ stressor.

9. You had an argument with your best friend and now you feel terrible. This is a category _____ stressor.

10. Your mother-in-law enjoys visiting the kids so much that she decides to move in with you. This is a category _____ stressor.

Answers

Situation 1.   This would be a category B stressor unless your car has been acting up for several years and you absolutely refuse to get a new one. Then it might be a category D stressor.

Situation 2.   This is a category C stressor. This is an ongoing progblem with your son.

Situation 3.   Your response here would depend on whether you felt this to be a short-lived or ongoing stressor. It sounds like the latter, so it would be a category C stressor.

Situation 4.   This is a category D stressor. The threat of nuclear war is an ongoing, non-relationship stressor (unless, of course, you have a relationship with the stress source).

Situation 5.   This is a category A stressor. The act of getting married is short-lived; staying married might be considered an ongoing, relationship stressor.

Situation 6.   This one is interesting. On the surface we may call this a category B stressor. However, it is very likely that the move will break up some close friendships resulting in some category A stress. A and B would both be correct.

Situation 7.   This is a category D stressor.

Situation 8.   This is a category B stressor. If we're stuck in the airport with our seven kids, then it's also a category A stressor.

Situation 9.   This is a category A stressor.

Situation 10.   You might wish this were only a short-lived stressor, but it may very well become an ongoing stressor. So category C would be one possibility. Your answer to this one obviously depends on your relationship with your mother-in-law.

Now that you're familiar with the stress model, you can use it as a tool for diagnosing the stress you're currently facing. A little later in the chapter we'll look at some ways of handling the four categories of stress. But first, let's look at some of the things that can happen to us if we don't learn to manage stress.

OUR REACTIONS TO STRESS

Only in recent years have researchers learned of the frightening link between stress and illness. Yet study after study confirms their worst fears: excessive stress can so weaken the body's defense that it becomes easy prey for all kinds of ailments. And, if that's not frightening enough, further studies have shown that stress is often responsible for a variety of mental disorders as well.

While reactions to stress will differ from person to person, there are a number of ailments that seem to show up time and again in persons suffering from excessive stress. These telltale reactions to stress are of two varieties: physiological and psychological.

Physiological Reactions to Stress

Physiological is a fancy word describing the biological activities and processes of our bodies; in other words, it describes what goes on in our bodies' organs, tissues, and cells. It probably shouldn't surprise us that stress affects our biological systems, but we may be surprised by just how serious some of the stress-producing diseases are. The following list of potential physiological reactions to stress, while certainly not complete, does illustrate the need to keep stress within manageable limits:

1. Heart attack
2. Stroke
3. High blood pressure
4. Ulcers
5. Nausea, diarrhea, colitis
6. Skin problems
7. Respiratory problems
8. Headaches
9. Sweaty palms
10. Back problems
11. Tics
12. Tense muscles

Psychological Reactions to Stress

Intense, sustained levels of stress can also affect us psychologically—and by *psychological* we mean the mental processes. Stress-induced psychological ailments are not only less well understood, but they are frequently more difficult to treat. The following list represents some of the potential psychological reactions to stress:

1. Depression	6. Irritability
2. Anger	7. Insomnia
3. Fatigue	8. Anxiety
4. Phobias	9. Apathy
5. Loss of appetite	10. Moodiness

STRESS-REDUCTION TECHNIQUES

What can we do about stress? Well, most of us are already doing things to reduce stress. As small children we probably sought stress reduction in the arms of our parents; and as we grew older and started feeling the effects of more and more stress, we probably replaced some stress-reduction habits and developed others.

As mentioned earlier, there are many different reactions to stress, but we noted that all stress reactions fall into two broad categories: physiological and psychological. Interestingly, the best-known methods for reducing stress also fall into these same two categories.

Physiological Stress-Reduction Techniques

You'll remember that we defined *physiological* as descriptive of those things that have to do with the body, that is the biological processes. Well, it so happens that there are several physiological ways that we can deal with stress, some of which are healthy and some not so healthy. Let's look briefly at the unhealthy physiological stress-reduction techniques, and then take a more detailed look at some excellent physiological ways of handling stress.

Unhealthy Approaches to Stress

Some of the unhealthy physiological ways people reduce stress are smoking, taking both nonpresciptive and prescriptive drugs, over eating, and overdrinking. While for many people stress-reduction means a cigarette or a drink, doctors have long questioned the advisability of merely trading one risk situation for another. While smoking and drinking may temporarily reduce the stress levels, they have been linked to other serious maladies of both a physical and social nature. Smoking, for instance, increases the likelihood of cancer and cardiovascular diseases, while the unrestrained use of alcohol has been tied to pneumonia, liver disease, and other disorders.

Nutrition

One physiological way to reduce the harmful effects of stress, or at least better prepare our bodies for the onslaught of stressful situations, is through good nutrition. A well balanced diet can be effective in handling all categories of stress, but because it is a long-term solution, it is especially effective against category D stressors.

Unfortunately, ours is a society comprised of convenience foods which are often loaded with sugar, fats, salt, chemicals, and calories. A word of caution: if we need a degree in chemistry to read the label on that processed soybean dip, then we may be in trouble nutritionally. If, however, we take the time to eat fresh vegetables and fruits, lean meats, high fiber breads, and so forth, then we can be the proud owners of a finely tuned biological machine that will give us years of trouble-free service.

Exercise

Exercise, like good nutrition, can help us withstand the constant bombardment of life's stressful events. It too is effective against all categories of stress, but is particularly good against category C and D stressors. Jogging, swimming, racquet sports, basketball, cycling—are all healthy ways to diminish the harmful effects of stress. How much exercise is enough? Doctors tell us that to provide cardiovascular conditioning, we should engage in aerobic exercise at least three times a week and for at least 20 continuous minutes. Anything less than that won't do much for the heart and lungs.

Psychological Stress-Reduction Techniques

Just as there are physiological ways to counteract the harmful effects of stress, there are also some psychological stress-reduction techniques. The following are examples of some of the most widely used ones:

The Negotiation/Avoidance Approach

The first of the psychological techniques involves negotiating with or avoiding those people or situations that cause us stress. Now, obviously, avoiding potential stressors may not be easy because, short of becoming a hermit or dying, it's not going to always be easy to escape from stress. However, we shouldn't overlook the possibility of steering clear of those situations (category D stressors) or persons (category C stressors) who are frequently the source of our stress. Another solution, especially with category A stressors, is to be more willing to discuss and negotiate an amicable settlement of our problems. For instance, if your boss is making unclear demands which are increasing your stress levels, then probably the best way to handle the situation is to sit down with your boss and discuss the problem. Get it out in the open. Let your boss know that you're feeling pressure and stress and then try together to find a solution.

Support Networks

As you're probably aware, one of the greatest sources of harmful stress is other people (both category A and C stressors). It seems we are constantly at odds with someone. If it isn't the boss, it's the kids; and if it isn't the kids, it's the neighbor (you know, the one whose lawn ornament was demolished). But, while other people are often the causes of our stress, other people can also help us through those stressful times. Support networks are simply close friends and relatives in whom we can confide whenever we feel ourselves under too much stress or on the brink of a nervous breakdown. By cultivating relationships with other supervisors, the neighbors, and other acquaintances, you are building a support network that will, as its name implies, provide support when you most need it.

Recreation

Hobbies can be extremely useful to us in getting and keeping control over our stress-ridden lives. If you like golf, then try to get on the golf course once a week. If you like shooting baskets, weaving baskets, building things, or simply reading, then do those things as frequently as needed. Hobbies often provide a means of temporary escape that somehow make the world and its frustrations more tolerable. Hobbies seem to work best against category C and D stressors, though their stress-reducing capabilities spread to include category A and B stressors as well.

Counseling

When we find ourselves feeling the effects of too much stress, we shouldn't overlook the possibility of seeking professional or semiprofessional assistance. Counseling is particularly effective when you're experiencing category C or D stressors. If, for instance, your job is causing you stress, then you may need some career counseling. If your marriage is the cause of stress, then marriage counseling may be needed. In either event, by seeking advice and counsel you have taken an important first step toward effective stress reduction.

The Relaxation Response

The benefits of meditation and mental muscular relaxation have been known for some time. For centuries nearly every culture on earth has practiced some form of relaxation technique designed to reduce tension and anxiety and improve preformance. One such technique called the relaxation response is summarized below. You'll find this technique helpful in dealing with all four categories of stress.

1. Sit in a comfortable position in a quiet place.

2. Close your eyes.

3. Beginning at your feet and progressing slowly up to your face, deeply relax all of your muscles. Concentrate on each muscle and consciously relax each muscle fiber.

4. Begin breathing through your nose. Concentrate on the steady flow of air passing in and out. Then, as you continue breathing through your nose, silently begin repeating the word "yes" (or any other one-syllable word) every time you exhale. Continue doing this for 15 to 20 minutes.

5. When time is up, sit quietly for a few more minutes.

Recent research has confirmed the beneficial effects of the relaxation response. The response will not only relieve us of excessive stress, but has also been shown to permanently reduce elevated blood pressure in certain individuals. One word of caution, however: check with your physician first before beginning to practice the relaxation response.

Stress, as we've noted, is a by-product of a changing world, and is, therefore, as inevitable as change and certainly as challenging. But stress, like change, can be managed. Its symptoms can be seen, its causes diagnosed, and its remedies applied. As a supervisor, though, your responsibility to understand and manage stress may extend beyond you to include your subordinates, your family, and your friends. Perhaps this chapter will help both you and them find the way to that understanding.

PRODUCTIVITY CONSIDERATIONS

CHAPTER

12

THE CHANGING ORGANIZATION

JOEL RAMICH

The American organization is changing. In an effort to improve productivity, institutions of all types are making fundamental changes within the workplace. For the first time, many institutions are changing the way in which work is structured. The interrelationship of the individual and the organization is being examined and, in many cases, redefined.

These changes represent a distinct break with past practice. Traditionally, productivity growth has been viewed primarily in business terms—applications of advanced technology, more effective use of capital, and more efficient management techniques. The new organizational approaches focus instead on maximizing the human potential.

The new approaches may directly affect individuals at any level throughout an organization. However, those individuals at supervisory levels will almost always be involved in an important way. Indeed, it seems difficult to imagine any organizational effort directed at people-productivity in which the supervisor does not have a critical role.

This section will help the supervisor to understand the changing organization, the new approaches it has fostered, and the role of both the organization and the supervisor in dealing with these approaches to improving productivity.

THE TRADITIONAL ORGANIZATION

Conditions Existing at the Time

The key resource in early industrial America was capital. Once in business, companies benefited from a general lack of competition, stable markets, and stable supply sources. Products were manufactured by hand or by means of an unsophisticated, mechanical technology.

Workers were generally uneducated and unskilled. They were hired on a temporary basis. Many workers were members of strong ethnic communities which placed a high value on family, church, and work.

The Drive for Efficiency

Operating within these conditions, early organizations saw the need and opportunity to optimize labor efficiency. Frederick Taylor provided an ideal means through an approach that became known as "scientific management." This approach was based on the belief that the best way to achieve maximum efficiency was to simplify work, create permanent work stations, and have the product to be worked on move on a conveyor system. Simple, repetitive tasks could be endlessly repeated by workers who would require a minimum amount of skill, intelligence, and training.

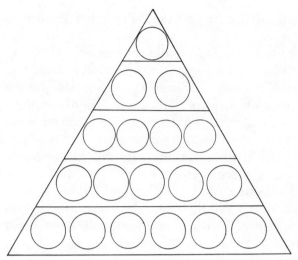

FIGURE 12.1. The Traditional Organization

One more thing was needed, namely, an organizational structure that would meet the requirements for operating the scientifically managed company. This was found in the traditional organizational approach used by the church and the military. It's structure can best be depicted as a pyramid (see Figure 12.1). Direct reporting relationships exist through multiple levels stretching from the top to the bottom of the organization.

Employing scientific management principles within this organizational structure, companies tended to exhibit some common characteristics. Among these were the following:

Extreme division of labor,

Long chains of command,

External controls over behavior,

Disdain for worker innovation,

Productivity from mechanical leverage,

Separation of production and quality control.

Role of the Supervisor: Push for Production

The role of the supervisor within the early organization could not have been more clear. Simply put, the supervisor was to assure production. The means for doing so? Here too there was a clear message: maintain control. Despite the highly routinized nature of the jobs, it was believed necessary to carefully watch workers to insure they were meeting production. The concept known as "span of control" had its beginning during this time. It was applied to prevent supervisors from being saddled with more workers than they could effectively train and control. Along with the responsibility for assuring production and maintaining control, the early supervisors had almost absolute authority over workers during working hours.

Role of the Worker: Production and Conformity

The role of the worker in the early organization was, of course, expected to fully complement that of the supervisor. Survival within the organization was dependent upon production and conformity. Workers were usually expected to learn only one simple job. That job was to be performed endlessly, day after day, month after month, in accordance with set production requirements. In the traditional military style, orders were given by the supervisor and the workers were expected to obey. By and large, variances were intolerable and innovations were scorned. The organization sent an unmistakable message to each of its workers: when you come to work, leave your brain at the door!

WHY A CHANGE WAS NEEDED

Introduction

The traditional organization was remarkably effective. The application of its basic principles was clearly responsible for much of the productivity gain throughout the industrial world. As an organizational form it was easy to understand, communicate, and administer.

With all this going for it, it is not surprising that many organizations have continued to use the traditional structure throughout the years—in many cases with excellent results. Nevertheless, in industry after industry, a number of important issues have caused managements to reexamine their use of the traditional organization approach. Three of these issues are discussed below:

United States Productivity Concerns

There has been a great deal of concern in America regarding the country's productivity growth rate during the past several years. In the early 1980s, this growth rate slowed to about 2%. At the same time, the productivity growth rates for Japan and several European countries were substantially higher. Many of the effects of America's relatively low productivity growth rate have been documented by the press: loss of ability to compete in world markets, loss of jobs, and decline in the standard of living.

However, perhaps even more significantly the concern about productivity has caused institutions of all types to reexamine the way in which they operate. It was obvious that many foreign companies were far more productive than their American competitors. It also became obvious that these companies were organized much differently. Many American managers began to question the value of traditional approaches and to develop a willingness to consider new approaches as well.

Changing Work Force and Attitudes

The work force of today is a far cry from that of early industrial America. Over the years, there have been substantial changes in the makeup and attitudes of the average worker. (Figure 12.2 provides a comparison of the work force of the 1900s and that of the 1800s.)

Predictably, there was a clash between the values of the new work force and the traditional organizational structures used by many institutions. Workers were bothered by the rigidly con-

1900s	1980s
Mature	Younger
Experienced	Less time in job
Uneducated	Better educated
Unskilled	More highly skilled
Male-dominated	More women
Low expectations	Higher expectations
Work ethic	Values fulfillment/ growth

FIGURE 12.2.   Comparison of Work Forces: 1900s & 1980s

trolled, bureaucratic environment they found in the workplace. Those working in highly controlled work systems even questioned the nature and structuring of jobs. As an expression of their dissatisfaction, workers rebelled. This rebellion took the form of poor performance, turnover, absenteeism, drug abuse, and sometimes even sabotage. Again, managers found reasons to reexamine the organization, its relationship to the individual, and the structuring of the work.

Changing Technology

During the past several years, rapid technological changes have taken place throughout American society. A clear trend toward more and better information has been established. A computer-based technological revolution has taken place in the office and factory through microcomputers, electronic offices, personal computing, robotics, and CAD/CAM (computer-aided design/computer-aided manufacture). Change itself has become the "constant." As a means for dealing with change, many people have found the traditional organization to be ineffective. This was the final major issue which drove the search for new approaches.

THE NEW APPROACH

Introduction

What has been called the new approach is, of course, not really new at all. A variety of organizations have effectively used many of the related principles for years. In the book *In Search of Excellence*, authors Peters and Waterman offer observations regarding many of America's excellent companies. Without fail, these companies are shown to exhibit a strong orientation toward people, which has often been present for decades. Mutual trust and respect are evident throughout all levels of these organizations. Oftentimes there are full-employment policies, extraordinary amounts of training, employee involvement, and meaningful reward and recognition systems at all levels. Unfortunately, however, too many American organizaions appear to use traditional approaches rather than those used so successfully by top companies.

What, exactly, is the new approach? It may be viewed as a many-faceted effort aimed at maximizing human potential for the purpose of improving the organization's output. Usually it involves moving away from an extremely traditional organization. Often it includes involving employees in decisions affecting their work. The work itself is sometimes analyzed and restructured. Rewards and recognition at times form some element within the approach. The variations are endless, and so are the ways in which the approach can be outlined and explained. The remainder of this chapter will be devoted to an explanation which centers around the objectives, forms of improvements in the workplace, and benefits of the new approach. At times, various aspects of the new approach may seem confusing to the reader. This confusion can be minimized by keeping in mind the primary goal of virtually all aspects of the new approach, which is simply to encourage each employee to bring into the workplace the brain which was required to be left at the door in the traditional organization.

Objectives

Efforts to use new approaches to improve an organization's output appear to often focus around one primary objective chosen from three possibilities: quality, productivity, or quality of work life (QWL). Various types of employee involvement, work redesign, and rewards are tools that may be employed as part of meeting the chosen objective. Although an organization may choose only one objective, it seems clear that quality, productivity, and QWL are strongly interrelated. Nevertheless, there are differences in terms of the focus and results that can come from an organization's use of each of the objectives. This segment will highlight these differences.

Improvement of Quality

In organizations where improvement efforts are focused around quality, the idea of "doing it right the first time" usually receives a primary emphasis. At all levels, employees are encouraged to hone in on the *prevention* rather than the *detection* of defects.

Many of these efforts have been influenced by the philosophies and techniques of W. E. Deming, Joseph Juran, and Philip Crosby.

Comprehensive quality programs usually have a key person designated as quality director, use various forms of quality teams, involve workers in a direct way, and utilize a wide range of communication and training efforts to implement and sustain the program. Using quality as a focus has the important benefit of providing a way of thinking about work which can be extended to every task in the organizaiton.

Improvement of Productivity

In general, organizations focusing objectives around productivity improvement are concerned with improving the ratio between output and input. This often causes them to focus efforts on improving the overall effectiveness of individuals and the organization in measurable ways. A variety of training, employee involvement, communication, work redesign, and reward tools may be employed. Such tools have often shown positive results. However, at times organizations pursuing a productivity objective may be tempted to take actions which conflict with the concepts of the new approach. For example, cost-cutting measures such as laying off people are likely to have a positive short-term impact on the productivity of the organization. In the long term, however, such measures are likely to have a negative effect.

Improvement of the Quality of Work Life (QWL)

The most narrowly focused objective of the three usually tends to be improvement of the QWL. In many organizations, the primary focus is to enhance the job satisfaction of each employee. A particular source of concern is the employee doing fundamental, day-to-day work within the organization.

It appears that organizations which focus on quality or productivity objectives as described above tend to accomplish many QWL objectives as a by-product. Indeed, for organizations which have a solid record of people-oriented management practices, a QWL effort may prove unnecessary. For organizations taking the first steps away from the traditional approaches, however, an objective focused on QWL improvement would appear to be the best choice.

Improvements in the Workplace

New approaches to maximizing human potential have resulted in a number of fundamental improvements within the workplace today. These improvements have taken the form of specific techniques which have been organized below into the categories of employee involvement, work redesign, and rewards and recognition. It should be noted that the three categories used are by no means distinct. There is a great deal of overlap among each of the three. Nearly every modern institution has experimented with one or more of these techniques at some time or another, often with mixed results. However, many top companies have reported great success in using a number of the techniques simultaneously. An analysis of the approach used by these organizations proves to be instructive. It reveals that, among other things, these organizations have used one or more of the objectives described above to unify and focus the improvement effort. Apparently this

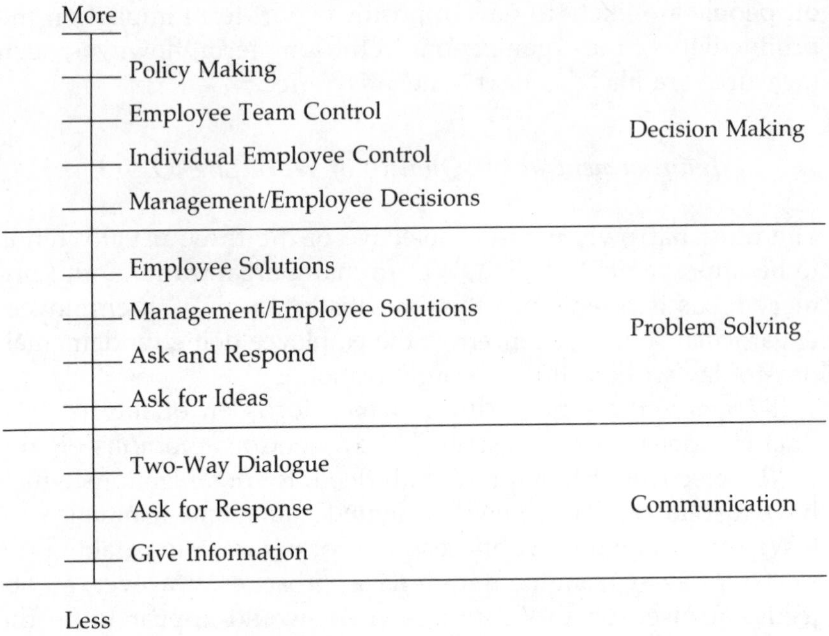

More

—|— Policy Making

—|— Employee Team Control

—|— Individual Employee Control   Decision Making

—|— Management/Employee Decisions

—|— Employee Solutions

—|— Management/Employee Solutions

—|— Ask and Respond   Problem Solving

—|— Ask for Ideas

—|— Two-Way Dialogue

—|— Ask for Response   Communication

—|— Give Information

Less

FIGURE 12.3.   Employee Involvement Scale

has helped them to integrate and coordinate these techniques in an effective manner.

Employee Involvement

What Is Employee Involvement?   Employee involvement (or participation) is a systematic effort to encourage people to become a part of planning and decision-making activities that concern them and their work. The concept tends to be defined and applied within a very broad context and range of circumstances. Figure 12.3 provides a scale to illustrate various degrees of employee involvement.

What Makes Employee Involvement Work?   R. E. Walton has theorized that as people master the primary tasks of their jobs, there develops what he calls a "human resource surplus." People at all levels are mentally capable of doing more higher-level tasks.

If these people are given an opportunity, they will, in fact, do more.

Employee involvement attempts to free up this surplus. Unlike the situation in the traditional organization, it offers the worker an opportunity to use his or her brain and exercise an element of control within the workplace. It recognizes the employee as the one who knows the job best and it seeks to make use of this knowledge to bring about improvements.

Forms of Employee Involvement. As illustrated in Figure 12.3, there are different levels and forms of employee involvement. The most basic level is simple communication. A higher level of employee involvement includes problem solving. Finally, the highest level leads to actually participating in decision making. Examples of each of the three levels are provided below. When reviewing these examples, it is important to keep in mind that these levels are loosely defined and in many cases overlapping.

Communication. Without question, a basic starting point for employee involvement is communication. This may take on a number of various forms, from casual informal chats to highly formal, structured presentations. Eventually, a two-way dialogue is established and information sharing becomes a basis for moving on to higher levels of involvement.

Problem Solving. Problems relating to various aspects of the business or work environment serve as the focus for a range of involvement efforts. At a basic level, a management-controlled suggestion system may be used. Higher levels of employee involvement are achieved when formal teams are organized to work on planning and problem-solving tasks which had not previously been a part of their jobs.

Certainly the most highly publicized form of problem-solving team is the quality circle. The original concept was developed by the Japanese industrial community in the early 1960s. The use of quality circles grew rapidly in Japan during the 1970s and it was estimated that eight million Japanese employees were involved by 1982. Beginning in the mid-1970s, the use of quality circles in the United States has also experienced rapid growth.

What is a quality circle? In general, it is a small (4–12) group of people, usually from the same work area, who come together voluntarily in a formal team to discuss quality problems, investigate causes, recommend solutions, and take corrective action. This definition should make it easy to identify a quality circle. However, oftentimes there appears to be a fuzzy distinction between a quality circle and other types of involvement teams.

Decision Making.   The highest level of employee involvement takes place when employees have a legitimate role in decision making within an organization. In some cases, quality circles or other involvement teams can provide this opportunity. Other forms may include joint labor-management committees or jointly administered suggestion programs. In some rare cases lower-level employees may be members of a policy committee or the board of directors of the organization.

More common forms of involvement in decision making take place when employees are provided with an opportunity to exert control over their workplace—either as individuals or in teams. This can only occur in situations where the work has been appropriately designed.

Work Redesign

Workplace improvements have not been limited to providing more involvement for the employee. In some cases they have included fundamental changes in the way the work itself is structured and completed. Four examples of this so-called work redesign are provided below.

Job Enlargement.   This technique involves adding tasks at the *same* level of work. For example, a job that consisted solely of machining parts may be "enlarged" by adding responsibilities for setting up the jobs and sharpening the required tools as well. (See Figure 12.4.)

Job Enrichment.   The technique of job enrichment also adds tasks, but a different manner than job enlargement. Whereas job enlargement can be described as "horizontally loading" job ele-

Adding Tasks at the *Same* Level of Work

Old Job   New Job

1. _____   1.

2. _____   2.

(P) 3. _____ Tasks   3.

4. _____   (P) 4. Tasks

5. _____   5.

6.

7.

FIGURE 12.4.   Job Enlargement

ments, job enrichment introduces the notion of "vertical loading." In job enrichment, the tasks added provide more decision making and variety. Often tasks used to enrich a job are those usually reserved for higher levels or staff (for example, quality control). Job enrichment is used to maximize the individual's talents and give more autonomy as well as responsibility. (See Figure 12.5.)

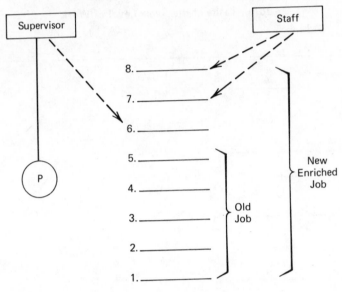

FIGURE 12.5.   Job Enrichment

Work Teams.   In many respects, the notion of a self-managing work team can be viewed as an extension of the job enrichment approach. The first focuses on the individual job, whereas an autonomous work team implies the "enrichment" of the whole group.

A goal of work teams is to provide members with greater feelings of self-management and understanding of the work processes. Opportunities for learning, growth, accomplishment, and rewards may be by-products.

Work teams are sometimes labeled *autonomous* or *semiautonomous*. These terms distinguish the degree of their decision-making power and authority.

In practice, a work team may exhibit any or all of the following characteristics:

Members are trained to do several or all tasks of the team

Members rotate through the various jobs

Team decides:

How the work will be performed

Job assignments for each of its members

Work schedules

Leadership structure

Composition of its members

Pay rates

Quality and quantity of output (within certain guidelines)

Flexible Assignments.   A number of techniques for reconciling the needs of the organization and those of the individual worker have found their way into today's workplace. In the traditional approach, the organization's work was accomplished within rigidly set guidelines. These guidelines determined who performed the tasks, how the tasks were done, and when they were done.

Organizations have come to recognize that many such guidelines are unnecessary. The organization's work can often be accomplished within a more flexible framework. At the same time, the job satisfaction of employees can be improved by providing a less structured work environment.

There are any number of approaches being used to provide flexible assignments for employees. Two of the most significant appear to be flextime and job sharing. Flextime requires each employee to be present at work during certain core hours each day (for example, 10:00 to 3:00) and to put in a certain number of hours each week (usually 40). However, the employee is allowed to set his or her actual work schedule, provided the ground rules are observed. For example, under the guidelines outlined above, an employee who has difficulty getting up in the morning could opt to change his or her work schedule from 8:00 to 4:00 to a more personally acceptable one such as 10:00 to 6:00.

The second form of flexible assignment is job sharing. Applying this concept results in a change in the traditional one-to-one relationship of people to jobs. In other words, four jobs may be held by a total of five people. Using this approach, workers' personal needs can be accommodated and the organization can better plan for and deal with extended periods of absence by employees (for example, childbirth).

Rewards and Recognition

Introduction.   The final element of the new approach to be considered is that of rewards and recognition. The thrust of the rewards and recognition element differs in some key ways from those of the other two elements described above.

Employee involvement seeks to improve the organization's productivity by using the employee's brain to solve problems and make decisions. Work redesign seeks to improve the organization's productivity by changing the way the employee's work is structured and completed. The rewards and recognition element, on the other hand, answers the fundamental question "what's in it for the employee?" The argument is simple. If the new techniques cause the employee to work more effectively and produce more, and therefore result in improved profitability of the organization, why shouldn't the employee be compensated? Putting aside a raft of possible counterarguments, it seems clear that many organizations have concluded that the more productive employee should, in fact, receive more compensation. The trend toward providing such compensation has resulted in the rewards and recognition element becoming an important improvement within the workplace. However, this element often provides something beyond simple compensation. It serves as a key motivator as well.

People are tied, through various profit-sharing methods, into the successes and failures of the firm. Personal and organizational goals often become similar and overall effectiveness increases. Examples and definitions of various techniques and programs are provided below.

Group Profit Sharing (Gainsharing).   According to O'Dell,

Gainsharing plans are broadly defined as programs designed to involve employees in improving productivity through more effective use of labor, capital and raw materials. Both employees and the firm share the financial gains according to a predetermined formula that reflects improved productivity and profitability. The emphasis is on group plans as opposed to individual incentives. [O'-Dell, 1981: 36]

The three major forms of gainsharing plans are Scanlon, Rucker, and Improshare.

Scanlon Plan: This is organization-wide productivity improvement plan designed to increase productivity through greater efficiency and reduced costs. The basic elements of the plan are the philosophy and practice of cooperation, the involvement system, and formulas to measure increased productivity and distribute bonuses (Lesieur, 1958: 1–17).

Rucker Plan: This is a productivity gainsharing program that measures economic productivity as the index of the overall effectiveness of a work group. Its goal is to maximize the output value of production (value added) for a given input value of payroll (Scott, 1973: 41).

Improshare: Invented by Mitchell Fein (1974: 3–4, 26–27) the name is an acronym for *improved productivity through sharing*. Past average productivity determines the base productivity factor (BPF). The BPF is multiplied by standard hours to produce Improshare hours. The actual hours required to produce acceptable results minus the Improshare hours can create a bonus which is split 50–50 by management and workers.

Individual Rewards. Another common technique for compensating employees for improved performance is by means of individual rewards. These vary widely in terms of the form in which they are given and the requirements for their use within a firm. Some common examples include suggestion awards, stock awards, and cash bonuses.

Additional Rewards. Gainsharing and individual rewards represent important, easily identifiable means of compensating and motivating members of an organization. More subtle, but perhaps just as powerful, are what may be called additional rewards. These include job security, promotion, and recognition.

Job Security. Although not apparent at first, job security may be the most basic and vital of all rewards. Without job security, it is difficult to imagine any employee being willing and able to put forth a real effort toward improving the organization's output.

On the other hand, the most productive, motivated work forces can often be found in companies with long-standing policies of full employment.

Promotion. Another less than obvious form of reward is promotion. Again, promotional opportunity can be a powerful incentive for driving the employee toward higher productivity, learning, and growth.

Recognition. Clearly, recognition is an element in reward systems of all types. However, beyond that, recongition seems to have a distinct place in most comprehensive efforts to improve effectiveness. The general thrust of these activities is to create a positive culture in which effort is put into highlighting the good things people do, in contrast with pointing out and punishing that which is not acceptable. The idea is that recognition and incentives for accomplishment are powerful motivators of behavior.

Any number of recognition approaches are used including employee-of-the-month awards, write-ups on bulletin boards, public recognition of accomplishments, and the giving of small momentos. Indeed, as Peters and Waterman have observed, top companies look for endless ways to use incentives. (Peters and Waterman, 1982)

SUMMARY

The traditional organization was structured to optimize efficiency within the environment existing in early industrial America. Major components consisted of Frederick Taylor's "scientific management" principles and an organizational approach modeled after that used by the church and military. The role of the supervisor was to push for production by maintaining firm control of the worker. The role of the worker was to produce and conform.

For years, the traditional approach offered an effective means of accomplishing the work of institutions of all types. Over time, things began to change, however. Three issues in particular spurred a reexamination of the traditional approach. These issues were:

Falling United States productivity growth rates,

Problems caused by a changing work force,

Rapidly changing technology.

In response to these and other issues, a new organizational approach has begun to emerge. It is a many-faceted effort aimed at maximizing human potential in order to improve the output of organizations. Oftentimes, one of three objectives is chosen to unify and focus the overall improvement effort. The three possibilities are quality, productivity and quality of work life.

Improvements in the workplace which are the result of this new approach may be organized under three general categories:

Employee involvement

Work redesign, and

Rewards and recognition.

Within these categories, the variety of techniques being used seems almost endless. However, each and every technique being used as part of the new approach appears to share a simple, but key, objective: Encourage each employee to bring into the workplace the brain which was required to be left at the door in the traditional organization.

REFERENCES

Lesieur F. G., ed., *The Scanlon Plan: A Frontier in Labor-Management Cooperation.* Cambridge, Mass.: The Technology Press of M.I.T., and New York: Wiley, 1958.

O'Dell, C. S. "Gainsharing: Involvement, incentives, and productivity." In *AMA Management Briefing,* New York: American Management Association, 1981.

Peters, T. J., and R. H. Waterman, Jr. *In Search of Excellence.* New York: Harper & Row, 1982.

Scott, R. C. "Rucker Plan of Group Incentives," In *The Encyclopedia of Management,* 2d ed., Edited by Carl Heyel. New York: Van Nostrand Reinhold, 1973.

DEALING WITH THE NEW APPROACH

JOEL RAMICH

The preceding chapter provided an introduction to the changing organization: its traditional form, the reasons it began changing, and the new approach it has fostered.

This chapter will focus on the role and responsibilities of both the organization and the supervisor in successfully applying the concepts contained in this new approach. Practical guidelines and examples will be presented as well.

THE MEANING OF IMPROVEMENTS IN THE WORKPLACE TO THE ORGANIZATION

The organization stands to reap significant benefits from the application of workplace improvements. However, these benefits are by no means automatic. They require a thorough understanding of the concepts, careful planning, and meticulous attention to detail. As D. L. Landen (1982: 2) has stated: "Participative management is perhaps the most difficult form of management. It is highly disciplined, controlled and goal-oriented"

Clearly, implementing the new approach will prove challenging to any organization. Following are some of the tools and techniques that are likely to be required in order to make it a success.

Need for a Basic Philosophy

Companies which are successful in implementing workplace improvements tend to do a superb job of developing and communicating a basic philosophy. Sometimes this philosophy is formed around one of the three objectives described in the preceding chapter: quality, productivity, or QWL (quality of work life). The principles contained in a company's basic philosophy should be easy to understand and should be reinforced on a day-to-day basis throughout the organization. The principles may outline a philosophy which relates to the business, people, work environment, training, management system, employee involvement, or any number of other areas. Figure 13.1 provides an example of a basic philosophy as it relates to the first two of the elements within a top company.

People Selection

Overall, people selection seems to assume greater importance in organizations where the culture demands significant levels of involvement from people. It is interesting to note that Japanese companies hire only rookies and provide a thorough indoctrination concerning the company's expectations. One leading United States company with a strong history of employee involvement shows

THE BUSINESS

1. Profitability is necessary to survive.
2. Operation within corporate and legal guidelines is a requirement.
3. Commitment to equal opportunity principles is fundamental.
4. High ethical standards are essential.
5. Highest standards of responsibility of all stakeholders are maintained.

PEOPLE

1. People are basically honest, deserve recognition and respect, want to achieve, and need to control their lives.
2. Their capabilities are usually underestimated and underutilized.
3. They want to know what's expected of them and receive feedback on performance.
4. They need to be treated as adults.
5. Individuals can be self-motivated to adhere to rules, regulations, systems, and methods which the organization sanctions.
6. Open communications are necessary.

FIGURE 13.1.   Declaration of Principles which Provide the Foundation for Maximizing Long-term Excellence in Quality of Product.

job applicants a videotape entitled "What's it really like?" The videotape discusses the many stresses associated with working in an organization in which the new approach operates. The hope is that a percentage of applicants will "de-select" themselves if they come to question their abilities to make the required commitments.

Training and Education

Activities centered around training and education form the foundation for many aspects of workplace improvements. At the most basic level is *skills training*. Before people can be expected to contribute, they need to know *what* to do and *how* to do it. They also must be *able* to do it and they must *want* to do it. Training helps to bring about these conditions by providing employees with the necessary skills, knowledge, and attitudes.

At another level, training and education activities are vital elements in any effort to make and sustain change within an organization. Through educational events, people are given an understanding of the need for change. They are informed about new work behaviors. They receive information on future requirements and directions. Furthermore, training is required for efforts directed at workplace improvement such as employee involvement groups, flextime, or gainsharing plans. Training often provides the special skills required to be effective in implementing with such programs. For example, participants in quality circles are often found to need two particular skills: problem-solving and the ability to participate in group processes. Training can provide the needed skills.

Finally, training and education provide an orientation for new members to the goals and values of the organization. This allows the new approach to be sustained and grow over time.

Measurement

Measurement is a fundamental tool for organizations engaged in comprehensive workplace improvement efforts. This is equally true for both manufacturing and service-oriented institutions. There are at least three important reasons for systematically gathering and reporting information about the work process and its products. These are explained below:

1. *Create Awareness of Productivity/Quality/Service Levels.*   By engaging more people in collecting, analyzing, and understanding measured outputs, awareness is created throughout the operation.

2. *Add Importance to Current and Planned Workplace Efforts.*   The attention devoted to measurement and reporting suggests to people that what they are doing is important and can lead to higher commitment levels.

3. *Provide a Basis for Problem Solving, Corrective Action, or Innovative Activities.*   When used as an assessment tool, measurement can help identify where to take action or look for opportunity.

Organizations must concern themselves not only with the question of *why* they should measure, but also the question of *what* they should measure. There tend to be two issues here. The first relates to the primary objective being pursued. If productivity is the primary objective, then measures will tend to focus on the cost of using certain assets, particularly people. If quality is the objective, on the other hand, measures will often identify the costs associated with failure to produce defect-free work, for example.

As a second issue, organizations must consider the nature of their products and outputs when deciding what it is they want to measure. Manufacturing processes tend to be easier to measure because outputs are tangible and separable. For knowledge occupations, however, measurement is more complex, but still possible. For example: a research and development organization's output might be measured by patents obtained or disclosures issued; a law firm's output could be measured by briefs filed or client hours billed. The point here is that each organization must find and use an appropriate measure.

Before leaving the subject of measurement, it is important to note that installation of a comprehensive system can be difficult and time-consuming. Moreover, it is easy for some organizations to misunderstand and misuse measurements with respect to improvements within the workplace. There are those who believe that if something can't be measured, then it doesn't exist. This often leads to overmeasurement. Systems become so complex that they are nearly impossible to understand and communicate. Measurement then becomes an end in itself, rather than a means or tool.

Additionally, it is important that organizations understand that each and every workplace improvement technique cannot be expected to show immediate, measurable, bottom-line impact. Techniques to improve workers' QWL, for example, often must be undertaken without any proof that they are positively correlated with increased output. At times, it seems necessary for members of the organization to forget about measurement and instead apply the so-called Missouri Farmer's Test: *Does it make sense*?! (See Figure 13.2 for a list of Dos and Don'ts.)

Do	Don't
Select measures which are at the same time meaningful, practical, and understandable.	Select overly complex measures or those which are poorly related to the outputs of the organization.
Communicate both the measures and the results throughout the organization.	Expect the measures to do too much.
	Overmeasure.
Use measures as an assessment tool for identifying problems and opportunities.	Use measures as a weapon against people or projects.

FIGURE 13.2. Measurements: Dos and Don'ts for Organizations

Communications

An increased emphasis on communications is often apparent throughout organizations involved in workplace improvement programs. This includes efforts by managers at all levels to share more information, explain the firm's future direction, and in general be more visible to people throughout the organization. Communications efforts are also aimed at explaining the need for change, describing new work behaviors, measurement systems, and so forth.

All forms of communication may be used, including face-to-face talks, videotapes, and company newspapers. Increased communication also occurs at all levels, ranging from visits by the CEO to brief meetings with first-line supervisors at the beginning of the day.

Along with improved communications from managers, emphasis is also placed on improving communications from employees at all levels. Efforts such as quality circles feature major communications components. Other mechanisms include employee suggestion systems, open-door policies, attitude surveys and hot lines. In general, people at all levels are urged to make expanded two-way communication a part of their ongoing, day-to-day activities.

Union Participation

The abuse heaped upon the worker in the traditional organization was a key to the development of the American labor union. The workers saw a need for an intermediary to push management for decent wages, working conditions, benefits, and job security. The union came to serve this role.

But now the question must be raised: "What is the role of the union within organizations where the new approach operates?" The answer must be: "There is none." Virtually every workplace condition the union existed to remedy has already been eliminated within organizations where the new approach thrives. As a result, such organizations are almost always union-free. Furthermore, a number of major unionized companies which have made comprehensive moves to install the new approach have done so within new, nonunionized plants. Again, union-free status has remained the rule.

All this is not to suggest that where unions already exist, they should not be part of the move toward the new approach. In fact, just the opposite is true. In situations where the work force is already unionized, it seems unthinkable to attempt workplace improvements without seeking the cooperation and help of the union. And experience within the steel and auto industries has shown clearly that both union and management can be winners in cooperative efforts. Experience has also shown that there are key requirements for success. Several of these requirements will be discussed below.

J. E. Christman has suggested there are at least four characteristics or issues of labor-management collaboration that deserve early recognition (Christman, 1982). Each of the four is listed and described below:

1. *The Concept of Joint Involvement.* Although easy to understand as a concept, equal involvement can be extremely difficult to implement. Much of this difficulty stems from past adversarial roles of labor and management. New behaviors often have to be learned and new understandings developed before the joint process can take root and succeed.

2.   *A Commitment to a Long-term Effort.*   For the process to succeed, many changes must take place and many people have to learn new styles. This takes time. The quick fix in an area of fundamental importance to large numbers of people simply is not possible. The temptation to turn to labor-management cooperation for quick results must be resisted in order to lay the proper foundation.

3.   *The Voluntary Character of the Involvement.*   A key requirement is that the involvement in any effort be voluntary—both for individuals and organizations. This includes selection of specific locations, departments, plants, and so forth as places where collaboration should take place.

4.   *The Relationship of This Process to Collective Bargaining.*   This critical issue must be addressed early and clearly to avoid later difficulties. Properly understood, collaboration will take its place with other decision-making structures in the organization without changing or supplanting them.

Christman has provided a useful illustration of how this can be done (Christman, 1982). Figure 13.3 shows a modified version of the three-element approach he recommends. Under this approach, all plant issues, concerns, and problems are referred to one of three decision-making elements. The nature of the issue, concern, or problem determines the decision-making structure under which it is solved. A represents the collective bargaining element. Beneath A are examples of issues which may be dealt with through collective bargaining. B represents the management authority or plant hierarchy. Beneath B are examples of issues which may be dealt with through this element. Finally, C represents the joint problem-solving element. Once again, beneath C are examples of issues which may be dealt with through this element.

It seems clear that organizing a framework around which labor-management collaboration can take place is very difficult. However, it appears to be a vital first step in any comprehensive effort to initiate meaningful workplace improvements within a unionized setting.

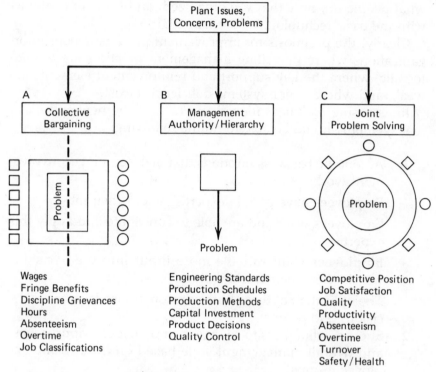

FIGURE 13.3.   Three-Element Approach

Supporting and Managing Change

The literature concerning the application of workplace improvement within U.S. industry is remarkably consistent with regard
to one point. Namely, the shortest route to problems in such efforts is through failure to insure a managerial and organizational
climate able to support and deal with change.

For change is a guaranteed by-product of the new approach.
In the words of organization change expert W. E. Zierden,
". . . human resources innovations invariably alter some part of
an organization and its practices and cut across traditional organizational barriers. . . . They usually involve making changes in

what people do, how they are organized, and how they interact with the basic technology" (Zierdan, 1981: 58).

Clearly, the prognosis for improvement projects is poor in organizations where prevailing management practices are too autocratic, where the key support and reinforcement elements are weak, and where major systems deficiencies exist.

In assessing readiness for moving toward the new approach, management should be able to do the following:

1. Accept the basic assumptions that make employee involvement work:

   Employees have unique expertise about their jobs.

   Employees want and are able to contribute and apply this expertise.

   Employees want to have more input into the decisions which affect their working lives.

   The utilization of these human resources leads to better decisions and results.

2. Show a willingness to change their own ideas, approaches, and overall management style based on input from employee groups.

3. Show a willingness to change (where appropriate and possible) existing policies, practices, systems, and work to foster a climate to support the improvement.

4. Show a willingness to be patient. Significant cultural change within an organization may require 7–10 years to fully implement. Managers must be willing to allow changes to take root and grow before pushing for verifiable results.

5. Provide money and visible support for the effort.

THE MEANING OF IMPROVEMENTS IN THE WORKPLACE TO THE SUPERVISOR

Any and all functions within an organization may be affected when elements of the new approach are installed. The CEO may have to learn a new style of communication. The floor sweeper may be asked to become a member of a work improvement team. Others in the organization may be required to alter their activities or responsibilities. Nevertheless, the most vital role of all seems reserved for the supervisor.

Why is this the case? For most supervisors, the answer is easy. Theirs is a vital role in the installation of any new approach affecting the people who do the work. How could an approach that is directed at maximizing human potential and productivity succeed *without* the wholehearted support of the supervisor? In most organizations, the answers is "it can't." The supervisor must be an integral part of the process.

The preceding segment discussed the meaning of improvements in the workplace to the organization. The following segment will discuss their meaning to the supervisor, as well as the pitfalls to successful implementation that both the organization and the supervisor may encounter along the way.

The Supervisor's Changing Role

Many elements of the supervisor's role have remained the same over time. Supervision is still getting things done through people. Supervisors determine performance standards and expectations. The traditional tasks of planning, organizing, directing, and controlling remain as key responsibilities. The bottom line is still getting out the required product or service.

Nevertheless, workplace improvements have caused significant changes in the traditional role of the supervisor. For one thing, the amount of time required for directing and controlling seems to be shrinking. Within the traditional organization, the push was for production and the focus was on control. The new approach, in contrast, seeks to improve productivity through maximizing human potential. The control is still present, but this time it is internal. The supervisor's role has become one of facilitating, leading, and developing, rather than being first sergeant. These changes may prove most difficult for a supervisor schooled in the old style.

However, sometimes an even greater shock comes when organizations move toward employee involvement. Suddenly the supervisor finds that employees are doing "management work,"—solving problems, making decisions, and presenting findings to top management. The recommendations which are made are being implemented. The bulletin boards are starting to overflow with blurbs describing the successes.

It is not surprising that the supervisor may begin to feel somewhat unwanted and unneeded in such an environment. But this should not be the case. The supervisor still has a vital role. Only the supervisor is positioned to provide the link between the organization's goals and the people who are doing the work. Only the supervisor is able to provide the day-to-day continuity needed to make productivity emphasis a success. But the supervisor needs to be adequately equipped to fill this role. The new approach requires that the supervisor develop certain knowledge, skills, and attitudes. These will be discussed below.

Knowledge, Skills, and Attitudes

Education and training are the normal means by which these abilities are acquired. The organization should provide (and the supervisor should seek) opportunities to satisfy the following needs:

1. *Understand the Basic Philosophy and Objectives of the Organization.* A primary responsibility of the organization is the development of basic philosophies and objectives. A primary requirement of the supervisor is an understanding and commitment to these guidelines.

2. *Understand the Need for Change as It Relates to the Organization and its Objectives.* The supervisor must accept the change goals of the organization and be able to explain the reasons why the organization is making commitments to fundamental changes through workplace improvements.

3. *Understand Both the Concept and the Practical Application of Workplace Improvements.* The supervisor must have a conceptual understanding of workplace improvements as well as a practical sense of "how it looks and feels." This is especially true for those particular workplace improvements the organization has chosen to install.

4.   *Develop Skills for Facilitating, Leading, and Developing.*   The change in the role of the supervisor has resulted in a need for certain specific skills. These may include handling group discussions and processes, facilitating group problem solving, orienting new employees to the organization, and employee counseling of all types. The supervisor should work closely with appropriate staff experts to identify needs in these areas and plan for meeting the needs through internal or external training.

5.   *Develop Knowledge and Skills for Dealing with Technological Changes.*   In many organizations, technological change may have a significant impact upon the job of the supervisor. For example, certain functions of the computer, such as an increased computational ability, will tend to decrease supervisory needs in those areas. However, it will often leave more discretion and allow for better and more specific decisions by the supervisor. Computerized production and inventory information systems, personal computers, robotics, and the like often cause rapid change in the supervisor's role and may result in a need for education and training on almost an ongoing basis.

Communications

Mention was made earlier of the importance of communications in installing and maintaining workplace improvement programs. Included are efforts by managers at all levels to share more information and be more visible throughout the organization. Emphasis is also placed on improving communications from employees at all levels.

In many organizations people are being encouraged to actively seek information, initiate, participate, and provide feedback. One U.S. company has a communication policy which contains the following components:

Multiple communication routes to encourage initiation of issues.

Personal growth and development to be encouraged.

Operating information to flow to the people who need to know to take action.

Problem-solving approach relative to both operational and personal needs.

General business information to be shared to permit intelligent action and decision making.

It seems obvious that such emphasis on continual, two-way communications throughout the organization will have a big impact on the role and activities of the supervisor on a day-to-day basis.

Recognizing and Avoiding the Pitfalls

The observation was made earlier that the new approach represents "perhaps the most difficult form of management." It seems hard to disagree. Workplace improvements are often difficult and time-consuming to implement. Once implemented, they tend to require a great deal of care and feeding. Often the price tag is high and the payback is low, at least initially.

These characteristics suggest that the new approach is not meant for all organizations and individuals. In some situations it just won't work. However, many organizations stand to reap significant benefits from its application, provided they effectively use the tools and techniques outlined at the beginning of the chapter, and avoid certain pitfalls. A number of these pitfalls are discussed below, particularly as they relate to the job of the supervisor.

Poor Environmental Conditions

It appears that certain environmental conditions are important in enabling the new approach to be successfully applied within an organization. When these conditions are absent, problems may quickly arise for the organization and the supervisor.

Robert H. Guest (1982: 15). has developed a list of the necessary conditions. Included are the following:

The organization should be reasonably well run from a management standpoint and management should be competent.

When there is a union, it must be politically strong and democratically run.

Top management (and the union, when present) must have some awareness of, knowledge about, and interest in the new approach.

Using surveys or other means, an assessment needs to be made of management's readiness for change. Included would be the considerations outlined above concerning supporting and managing change.

Those involved must be prepared to take risks.

Management must be prepared to be patient. There must be a commitment to see the process through. The effort must be viewed as something other than a "one-shot" program.

The timing must be right. During times of retrenchment, when job security is an issue, there may be a reluctance to support workplace improvements for fear that certain jobs may be eliminated.

In most organizations, the supervisor appears to have little direct influence in assuring the presence of these conditions. However, this is not to say the supervisor cannot and should not be involved in the process. It is very important to the supervisor that the pitfall of poor environmental conditions be avoided. The supervisor can have an influence by:

Pointing out what the necessary conditions are, if members of the organization seem to be unaware.

Offering to participate in surveys to assess the readiness for change and the organizational and employee climate.

Providing management with valuable insight concerning the feelings and attitudes of employees doing the work.

Threatening Concepts

Provided the pitfall of poor environmental conditions is avoided, a second concern stems from the threat the new concept represents for some people. Among those threatened are supervisors, those supervised, and the union. In each case, the issue is different.

The supervisor may see a move toward greater employee involvement as a direct attack on his or her authority and influence within the organization. As employees learn to solve problems and make decisions, the supervisor's sense of concern may grow. Often this will lead to resistance on the part of the supervisor. This resistance may take the form of a subtle lack of support or open opposition. Either form will prove harmful to the process.

But the real loser is likely to be the supervisor. In the eyes of higher management, the supervisor may be seen as one who is unable to identify with, and support, the goals of the organization. Obviously, this is not a desirable position, nor one which will benefit the supervisor in the long run.

However, beyond that, the supervisor will have missed an opportunity. Employee involvement and other workplace improvements have demonstrated the potential for improving both the output and satisfaction of people at work. The supervisor should not let unfounded concerns stand in the way of the achievement of these goals.

Those who are supervised may also see workplace improvements as threatening, but in entirely different ways than the supervisor. For some, the whole idea of participation may seem manipulative. Just another attempt to "get us to work harder." Others may have a genuine terror of speaking before a group. This terror may be the result of a bad experience years before in a classroom. In any event, it is essential that the organization and the supervisor recognize that participation is not for everyone and that it appears to be most successful when it is *voluntary*.

The union appears to have perhaps the most legitimate reason for feeling threatened by the new approach. Mention was made earlier of the fact that most comprehensive installations have taken place in nonunion settings. Then too, the union often tends to be skeptical of any new programs in which the firm is seen as the main beneficiary of productivity improvements. In order for workplace improvements to succeed within unionized settings. some type of joint involvement appears to be required. This tends to lead to higher trust levels between the union and management and a lessening of initial concerns.

"Schizophrenic" Management

Certain management characteristics can be observed in organizations where the new approach works well:

A consistent management style,

A focus on the long term, and

A shared sense of understanding of the new techniques and their interrelationship.

When these characteristics are present, common or compatible signals are sent to people within the organization. When these characteristics are not present, on the other hand, people in the organization received mixed signals. Management appears to *say* one thing and *do* something else. This can be referred to as "schizophrenic" management. It represents a major pitfall for the organization and a major headache for the supervisor. Some of the symptoms of "schizophrenic" management are described below.

Inconsistent Style.   This symptom is best illustrated by a cynical quip: "Employee involvement is often what the top orders the middle to do for the bottom." The notion that employee involvement can be ordered is nothing less than absurd. Nevertheless, many organizations attempt to do just that—to push employee involvement and other workplace improvement techniques.

Short-term Focus.   Management is often aware that the culture of an organization cannot be changed overnight. Therefore, there is often a willingness to sign up for a long-term effort in which no one pushes for early results. This approach is sound. However, it doesn't always work. Despite earlier promises, certain managers become impatient and begin to push for short-term results. Here again, people end up receiving conflicting messages about what the organization wants.

"Appliance" Approach.   Some organizations use the "appliance" approach to workplace improvements: plug one in and see if it works! This approach fails to recognize the need to carefully integrate workplace improvements and anticipate the effects they will have on the organization's systems, policies, and procedures.

Instead, employees get a message that these workplace improvements are seen as a quick fix to which management has no real commitment.

What steps can a supervisor take when operating within a company where "schizophrenic" management is being practiced? A few suggestions follow:

1. Attempt to learn as much as possible about the way in which the new approach *should* be installed. Focus on articles highlighting companies which have had practical experience—both good and bad.

2. Point out to the boss and any support staff who are involved in the effort (for example, those involved in training and development or organizational development) the inconsistencies that seem to be affecting the local progress of workplace improvements.

3. Suggest that a team take a trip to look at a company which has been successful in installing workplace improvements. Many such teams include a diagonal slice of the organization, so an interested supervisor may be welcomed as a member. Workshops and seminars led by experienced consultants provide an additional option.

4. Discuss the findings and how they might be used to advance the process within the organization.

Unforeseen Events

A final pitfall to be considered here is that of unforeseen events. Included are changes in people, technologies, and economic conditions. The problems created by each of these three situations are outlined below.

Changes in Key People.   Oftentimes the initiation of a comprehensive improvement program is driven by one top individual. This "sponsor" may initiate the effort, make sure that resources are devoted to it, and defend it against attacks from others in the organization. Other members of the organization may become key figures as well, either because of their position, competency, or credibility. Because of their importance, the loss of any one of these key individuals may place the entire effort in jeopardy. In order to minimize the potential for this happening, two actions can be taken by the organization.

First, carefully consider the stability of key individuals *before* selecting a site in which to begin workplace improvement activities.

Second, begin to develop competencies and support among others early in the effort, always looking for opportunities to permeate the principles and approaches throughout the organization.

New Technologies.   The implementation of a new technology may bring about sweeping and radical changes in many facets of the workplace. Included may be modification of physical arrangements, changes in the composition of jobs, changes in the social systems, and both the creating and loss of certain jobs. In order to deal with these changes, it is clear that careful planning and analysis must take place before the implementation of the new technology. This planning and analysis must include the design of the technology itself as well as its impact on any existing workplace improvement efforts.

Economic Conditions.   Despite the best intentions of management, economic conditions can force layoffs, job shifts or budget cuts. It may become easy for key people in management to say, "Let's put the program on ice." To do so, however, may prove fatal. Therefore, it is important to assess how such a decision will be interpreted by people within the organization. Once again, the supervisor can serve a vital role in providing the accurate information needed by the organization during such a critical period.

SUMMARY

The application of the new approach can provide significant benefits for both the organization and its individual members. However, these benefits are by no means automatic. They result from a thorough understanding of the concepts, careful planning, and meticulous attention to detail—on the part of both the organization and the supervisor.

There are a number of tools and techniques which are often used in special ways by organizations as part of their overall approach to productivity improvement. These include a basic philosophy statement, people-selection policy, training and education, measurement, communications, union participation, and management of change.

The supervisor has a vital and changing role within an organization moving toward the new approach. Often the supervisor's role will come to require less time in directing and controlling and more time in facilitating, leading, and developing people. These changes may make it necessary for the supervisor to acquire new knowledge, skills, and attitudes. Education and training may be needed in order to help the supervisor to:

Understand the basic philosophies and objectives of the organization.

Understand the need for change as it relates to the organization and its objectives.

Understand both the concept and the practical application of workplace improvements.

Acquire skills for facilitating, leading, and developing people.

Acquire knowledge and skills for dealing with technical changes.

The trend toward better information and communications throughout all levels of the organization has a big impact on the role and activities of the supervisor on a day-to-day basis.

There are a number of pitfalls which the organization and the supervisor must recognize and avoid. Among these are:

Poor environmental conditions within the organization.

The threat that the concepts represent for the supervisor, the employees and the union.

A "schizophrenic" management style which sends mixed signals to the organization.

Unforeseen changes in people, technology, and economic conditions which jeopardize the effort.

REFERENCES

Christman, J. E. "Labor and Management: Together." Productivity Brief 20, American Productivity Center, December, 1982.

Guest, R. H. "Innovative Work Practices—Highlights of the Literature." In *Work in America Institute Studies in Productivity*. Elmsford, New York: Pergamon Press, 1982.

Landen, D. L. "The Future of Participative Management." Productivity Brief 16. American Productivity Center, August, 1982.

Zierden, W. E. "Managing Workplace Innovations: A Framework and a New Approach." *AMA Management Review*, June 1981.

ECONOMIC CONSIDERATIONS

CHAPTER

CAPITALISM AND PROFIT

THAXTER DICKEY

"There's no such thing as a free lunch." This familiar expression sums up much about economics. It is universally true that our wants are greater and more numerous than our resources. There is simply not enough of everything for everyone to have all that he or she wants. Any everyone faces this truth daily, both as an individual consumer and as a citizen of a nation.

It should be clear that, given this scarcity of resources relative to wants, some means of wisely using these resources must be developed. This wise use of resources is called economics. And national economics exists for exactly the same reason as household economics: to get the greatest possible benefit from the limited resources available. In order to accomplish this purpose, any economic system must answer certain basic questions about the efficient use of limited resources.

14.3

THE BASIC QUESTIONS

There are three basic questions about the efficient use of limited resources: Which resources should be used in producing what goods? How will changes in resource availability and in consumer desires be met? Who should get the products? The first question concerns the use to which limited resources will be put. Remember, only a few of the many things that people might want can be produced from the limited resources which are available. Which of those things will be produced? Furthermore, will the production of those goods be labor-intensive or capital-intensive? How will resources be combined to produce the chosen goods? The second question concerns the adapatability of the economy. Are there mechanisms in the economy for meeting changing circumstances? Suppose population growth slows and less labor is available. Will the economy be able to adapt to this changing availability of a resource? The final question is perhaps most disturbing of all. It concerns the distribution of the products of a society.

CAPITALISM

There are two fundamental ways of answering these questions. One is called "capitalism," or a "market economy," and the other is called a "command economy." In the United States our means of answering these basic questions is capitalism.

Capitalism was born, not created like its alternatives. Communism (and socialism, its more democratic cousin) are theoretical positions created as alternatives to capitalism. On the other hand, capitalism—the older economic system—was not created as a theoretical system, but grew out of the voluntary interactions of people. "But isn't such an unplanned system haphazard?" some may ask. It's not haphazard, and any system which has grown from the voluntary interaction of people is eminently practical.

The language we speak is another example of a practical and workable system growing out of people's needs without some central planning committee to help it along. Just as languages have developed without planning, so too capitalism has developed out of practical solutions to people's needs. And just as grammarians very precisely expound the rules of a language without making those rules, so economists describe what happens in human exchange, not what should happen. In the final analysis, capitalism works regardless of anyone's theoretical understanding of it.

The primary distinction between a market economy and a command economy concerns the ownership of resources. In capitalism, or a market economy, the resources are owned privately. This private ownership of resources means that the owners are allowed to use their resources in their own best interests. Thus, private owners will sell their resources, whether they be land or labor, to the highest bidder. On the other hand, those people who are buying resources for use in producing products—which they in turn sell in the market—will be trying to buy those resources for the lowest price possible.

Capitalism not only allows private ownership, but also free enterprise and choice as well. Consumers are free to buy what they choose, while businesses are free to produce what they choose, and owners of resources—whether of land or of labor—are free to sell their resources as they see fit. But doesn't all this freedom produce chaos in the economy?

Fortunately, there are two other features of capitalism which prevent chaos. They are the price system and competition. The price system is a means of informing consumers about the goods which are available and informing businesses about the goods which are desired. When prices are low, consumers buy. If consumers buy even when prices are higher than cost plus a minimum profit, then other businesses see the consumers' demand and try to earn some of those profits for themselves by producing the desired products. Not only does the price system provide information about the goods and services which consumers want, but it also provides the incentives for businesses to provide those goods.

Businesses produce goods in order to earn a profit. But if they set prices too high, they discourage consumers from buying. However, if profits are high and consumers still want the product enough to pay the higher prices, then other firms will be attracted by these profits. As the number of businesses increase, so does competition for the consumers' dollars, and each business tries to find ways to produce the product more efficiently than its competitors so that it can offer its product for less. The result for consumers is lower prices and higher quality for the goods they want.

If, however, the business is producing goods which no one wants, then the goods will remain unsold even at prices below cost. In such cases, those businesses will either produce other, more highly desired goods or cease to exist.

A similar pattern exists for those who are trying to sell their resources on the market. Here too the informational and incentive functions of the price system operate. The demand for resources is a derived demand, that is, businesses only want resources as they are useful in producing some final product desired by consumers. Whether that resource be labor or land, businesses will not buy it if the cost is so high that it is not profitable to do so. For example, although machines may originally be more expensive than labor, if labor bids the wage rate too high, then management will use the now relatively less expensive services of machines.

The consumer is king in the market, not business or resource owners. The latter earn only as much profit and wage as we allow them by buying their products. It is true that the greatest business is the best servant. The business which best meets the needs of the consumers earns the most profits.

In a similar fashion, the market answers the second question concerning adaptability. It is no secret that consumers' tastes change constantly and that buisnesses are continually trying to anticipate and meet them. If they do not, then they are left holding goods no one wants, while their competitors who more accurately anticipated consumer demand prosper. A business which does not accurately foresee changes in resource availability will likewise fall by the wayside. Thus the price system communicates information to businesses about the changing tastes of consumers and changing resource availability. All that remains is the businesses' desire for profits to bring about efficient adaptation to these changing conditions.

The competitive price system of capitalism is an effective mechanism for answering the first two of the basic questions which must be answered by every economic system. It is amazingly adaptive in coordinating the decisions of numerous consumers, businesses, and resource owners. If you are in doubt concerning the effectiveness of this system, you have only to look about you at the variety of products that you enjoy each and every day. Be amazed at the variety of natural resources and technology involved in the production of even the most common products. Consider the classic example of your pencil. All of the necessary resources and know-how are brought together by the price system in order to provide you with this everyday miracle at a ridiculously low price. It is a further tribute to the effective functioning of the price system that you are not astonished to find your milk delivered to your door each morning along with the local paper, that you never think about the complicated system which brings you your morning coffee and the rubber in your car tires from halfway around the world, that you expect and find all of the groceries on your list at the neighborhood market.

It is amazing that business and profits have so fallen into disrepute in our country when evidence of their usefulness is all around us. Profits amount to less than 10% of the total gross national product (which is the dollar value of all of the final goods and services produced in this country in a year); yet for that small price look at all that we get. Numerous businesses are earnestly seeking the most efficient ways to serve us and to meet our needs. Without the incentive of profit, how else could we get such dedicated service in the effective use of our limited resources? You have only to think of the proverbial inefficiencies of government bureaucracy to decide that the price that we pay to businesses in terms of profits is inexpensive indeed compared to the price we would pay if we lived under a system of government ownership in a command economy.

MARKET FAILURES

All economists agree in principle that it is less expensive to pay profits to businesses than to live in a command economy. But some argue that there are areas in which the market breaks down. For example, how would a market system ever provide for national defense? It probably would not, since the benefits of such defense are not exclusively the purchasers. In other words, if any single person in the country purchases an MX missile system for protection against foreign aggression, then all are protected against such attack. Given the high price of such protection and the fact that anyone who bought such protection would be buying it for everyone else, no one would purchase national defense.

Economic goods, like national defense, are called social goods, and it seems obvious that a market system will not by itself provide for these kinds of goods. Other social goods are flood protection, insect control, and police protection. The provision of such goods, which the market cannot efficiently produce, is the proper function of government.

Another kind of market failure is called spillover effects, or externalities—certain costs which are not included in the market's pricing of the good. An example will make the concept clearer.

The most striking example of spillover costs is pollution. Some industries cause more pollution than others, steel and certain chemical processes are examples. Pollution is costly. It reduces property prices, increases health care costs, and, in some instances, reduces tourism by destroying the scenic beauty of an area. All of these are costs of producing the products. However, these costs are not borne by the business but by the surrounding community. Thus, not all of the costs of producing steel are levied against the steel producers. Consequently, these costs are not passed on to the users of steel products in the price of those products.

These costs are external to the market; they are spillover costs—spilling over to someone other than the producers and the consumers of the goods. Another way to think of the situation is to realize that those who do pay the costs of the pollution—in terms of doctor bills for respiratory illnesses or lost revenue due to reduced property prices and reduced tourism—are subsidizing the polluting industries. They are paying part of the costs of producing the goods. This savings to the producer is passed on to the users of the goods; hence those who do pay the costs of pollution are subsidizing the users of those products. The solution to the problem of the spillover costs of pollution is, of course, to place the costs on the businesses and consumers who benefit from the production which caused the pollution. In this country this is accomplished through pollution standards and taxes on polluters.

The market also fails when a single firm grows large enough to control the market and thus prevent competition. Without competition, a business is free to raise its prices above that necessary for production. This condition is called monopoly and causes considerable concern in some quarters.

It is the intent of every business to find some advantage over its competitors which will give it increased profits. This advantage, for as long as it lasts, will be in some sense a monopoly. These advantages can come about in many ways: discovery of some new technology, favorable location, specialized managerial talent, or especially skilled labor. But these advantages are not permanent. If the lure of profits does not encourage competitors to meet or beat these advantages, or encourage new competitors to eter the market, then the changing taste of consumers will, in time, reduce the advantage to nothing. As a last resort, the consumer's certain protection against the monopolists and their high prices is to weigh the lost opportunities of buying other goods and decide not to buy the monopolists' products.

But is not some kind of government action required in this case? Can we depend on the market? And what is the government's role in the economy?

THE GOVERNMENT AND MONOPOLIES

The government has attempted to control monopolies. This effort has been more vigorous at some times than at others, but a variety of laws now prohibit unfair business practices which reduce competition. Unfortunately though, what the government takes away with one hand it gives with the other.

Patents are licenses given by the government which allow the inventor sole use of his or her idea for a period of 17 years. Although this may seem only fair if we think of a poor tinkerer spending his or her life developing some new technology, it is restrictive to competition. In fact, more and more inventions are the result not of some lonely struggling genius, but of the work of well-supplied research teams working for the more forward-thinking and prominent businesses. How do patents reduce competition? Ordinarily we think of a large number of firms in the same industry as guaranteeing competition, but there are other market qualities necessary to competition. The free flow of technological information is one of them. If information about how best to perform some manufacturing process is monopolized, then the businesses without that process will be operating at a severe disadvantage and are likely to cease operating. With the disappearance of these competing firms, the owner of the secret or protected process will monopolize the market. Government issuance of patents almost guarantees that this will be the case.

Government deliberately creates monopolies in certain industries, especially utilities. It is felt that competition would be more harmful in these industries than helpful. Imagine if you can a city in which several competing telephone companies operate. There will be not one set of unsightly telephone poles and cables, but several, not one telephone book in your house, but several. Furthermore, you could only call friends or businesses who used the same telephone service as you do, unless you subscribed to more than one system and had more than one phone in your home. These kinds of industries are called "natural monopolies." The government restricts competition in these industries by giving licenses to only one company per geographic area.

Of course without competition to keep the prices down and the quality of service up, government must fill another role—that of regulator. Thus arise public service commissions which regulate these "natural monopolies" and determine when and if they can raise their prices. The susceptibility of these commissions to the lobbying efforts of the industries they regulate is inevitable. It is in the interest of the regulated to influence the regulators. In fact these "natural monopolies" are required to inform the commissions of their operations. And it is not surprising that, since they know the business so well, many former officers of these companies become members of the commissions which regulate them.

While the market will quickly erode the monopolist's position in a freely operating economy, it is evident that government-ordained monopolies are permanent and plagued with further regulatory problems. Thus there is probably a need for less, not more, government action in the realm of monopoly control.

GOVERNMENT AND THE THREE BASIC QUESTIONS

There are other, more drastic, areas of government intervention into the workings of the free market economy: the government attempts in certain cases to redress wrongs done by the market to individuals. The third of the three basic questions asked above concerned the distribution of the goods and services produced in the economy.

The market answers that question simply enough: those who pay for the goods and services get them. This method of distributing the products of an economy has several virtues. For one thing, it provides an incentive for those who don't have great wealth to find ways within the economy to increase their wealth. In doing this, however, they are not only helping themselves but improving the lot of all. By efficiently using natural resources, whether their own or others', they are increasing the productive potential of the entire economy, which is to say raising our standard of living.

However, there are some who, by accident of birth, are greatly underpriviledged in the resources with which they enter the market to trade for goods and services. This seems unfair to us and the government, as our agent, attempts to right this wrong—by collecting taxes from those who have and, through welfare payments and social security checks, giving to those who do not have.

Another example of government action of this type is rent control. Apartment rent is too high for some to pay, and in some cases the government has intervened to keep the prices of apartments low enough so that everybody can afford one. The prices are controlled by setting the maximum price which can be charged. This is called a rent ceiling. Unfortunately, as Milton Friedman has frequently pointed out, government actions usually have exactly the opposite effect of that intended. In this case, while the policy was conceived to provide affordable apartments for the poor, it has actually reduced the number of available apartments.

How could this unintended result have occurred? Setting rent controls certainly lowered rental prices, but it also had secondary effects. With prices lower by law, other housing became relatively more expensive, hence the demand for those apartments subject to rent controls increased. With the demand now higher than the supply of available apartments, some means of distributing those apartments was needed. Since prices, being fixed, could no longer serve that purpose, distribution was made on a "first come, first served" basis, or on the basis of favoritism—which encouraged discrimination. And with rent ceilings limiting profits, landowners found other, more profitable investments for their money. So no new apartments were built. In addition, those apartments already standing were unprofitable to repair, so many of them became derelicts and slums. What had begun as an aid to provide apartments for the poor backfired and reduced even further the number of available apartments.

Another example of this perverse effect of "helpful" government interference in the operation of the market is the minimum wage law. Some are underprivileged in the resources they bring to the labor market. Left to itself, the market will determine a wage for these workers based on their profitability. No one will pay these workers more than they are worth. Yet, if the wage rate is allowed to decline, at some point all of these workers will be hired because the work they do can be done in other ways only at greater expense.

Some feel that wages might drop too low, so the government intervenes to help by declaring a minimum wage. This seems to work, for now on one is paid less than the minimum wage (except for those in unprotected jobs). But again secondary effects reverse this seeming benefit. Now it costs more to hire these people than they are worth in production, and the result is less employment for those who were supposed to be helped.

This discussion raises the specter of unemployment, which at this moment faces our nation. Even as I write, Congress is debating the virtues of various "jobs programs." Can we actually succeed in using government policies to end unemployment?

The basis of all jobs programs is government spending. Which activities are undertaken is secondary to the actual spending, although some programs will employ more people than others. Defense spending, for instance, provides fewer jobs dollar for dollar than does public works construction because of the more technical nature of the work. But whatever public works are undertaken, these massive programs must be financed in some way. There are really only three ways: taxing, borrowing (deficit spending), or printing money.

Any of these means of financing a jobs program has secondary effects which cast serious doubts on the effectiveness of the programs. Taxes for instance, whether they be gas tax or income tax, come out of the pockets of consumers and reduce the money available for them to spend. When consumer spending is reduced then the demand for consumer goods goes down and businesses respond to these messages of the price system and reduce production. This means fewer jobs.

On the other hand, if the government borrows money to finance its programs, then it gets its money by crowding out businesses which would have borrowed that money had it been available. They would have used the money for investment (either in replacing present facilities or in expansion). This may not seem so serious, but it has grave consequences, for if businesses do not constantly expand, there are no new jobs for those new workers who enter the job market each year. And without expansion or replacement of existing factories—which are constantly wearing out—our production possibilities are reduced, there are fewer products available for our use next year and the year after, and the standard of living for all steadily shrinks.

Finally, the government can pay for its new programs with the printing press. Printing new money to spend is not a new solution to government money problems, nor is inflation—its inevitable consequence. Other governments in the past have tried to solve their problems by increasing the money supply, but in each case, without increased real production to back up the new money, it lost value after the government spent it; and as it got into the hands of those who thought they were being paid for their resources and labor, it became more and more worthless.

Hardly anyone today needs a lesson in the horrors of inflation. Although some benefit from inflation—principally debtors (and take note of the fact that the U.S. government is the single largest debtor in the country—its most significant consequences are tragic.

In understanding the impact of government jobs programs, it is important to remember our opening statement: there is no free lunch. Government programs must be financed and in most cases the cost exceeds the benefits of the policy.

GOVERNMENT AND SOCIAL REGULATION

The adverse effects of government policies on production are not limited to these examples but are evident in almost all of government's regulation of business. Until the mid-60s, most of government's efforts at controlling business were limited to antitrust regulation and the regulation of specific industries, but with the advent of civil rights, concerns about pollution, and increasing social consciousness came a new form of regulation called social regulation.

Social regulation is concerned with the way goods and services are produced in all industries. Under the heading of social regulation are such alphabetic regulatory agencies as the EEOC, OSHA, CPSC, and the EPA. All of these regulatory agencies have laudable aims, but the costs are high—more than a billion dollars per year in direct costs by some estimates—and their effectiveness is disputable.

Perhaps of more concern are the secondary and long-range effects of these regulations. First of all, these new regulations contribute to inflation since the high cost of complying with these regulations are passed on to the consumer in the form of higher prices. Moreover, this regulation contributes to inflation since it reduces productivity. Time spent in filling out forms alone costs businesses in the U.S. millions of dollars per year and wastes employee time that could be spent more productively.

Government regulation has other adverse impacts as well. Its costs are usually fixed, that is, it costs small firms just as much as it does larger firms and, because they are less able to bear such costs, forces them out of business, thereby reducing competition. It also reduces incentives to innovate. To try out new, perhaps more productive, technology is risky at any time, but with the new regulators watching it can be deadly. For there is a good chance that a new, technologically superior plant will not meet with regulatory approval. Thus it is less risky to continue the same productive techniques.

These adverse impacts have been well documented, yet government policymakers continue to heavily regulate businesses. Remember, there is no free lunch. The aims may be lofty but the price too high. That is the basic law of economics. If there were more than enough of everything to go around, including clean air and fulfilling employment, there would be no need for either businesses or regulators. But there is scarcity and every economy must answer the basic questions: On what do we wish to expend our scarce resources? What will provide the greatest good for the greatest number?

It is surprising that government actions so frequently result in such adverse, even perverse, consequences. Why is this so? Not, I think, because policymakers are either unlearned or deliberately perverse. But, as Henry Hazlitt suggests, it is simply that in an attempt to accomplish some worthwhile goal, policymakers forget that there are secondary and long-range consequences to economic tampering. The immediate problem always seems more prominent, and oftentimes the solution through government policy seems eminently sensible. Although the immediate effects are much more visible than the long-range ones, and the people directly concerned are much more vocal than those who are secondarily affected, these long-range, secondary effects usually have greater impact.

Consider again the effects of some public works program designed to encourage jobs. The program is easy to see. The final product can be pointed to with pride, whether it is a new road or a dam or a building. Equally as visible are the new jobs created. Less visible but just as real are the private projects that went unbuilt because the government absorbed the money for those projects either through taxes or borrowing. Also unseen are those jobs which were destroyed by declining production in other industries due to the reduced consumer demand which resulted from the higher taxes.

THE CASE FOR FREE TRADE

In times of economic stress, as these are, one of the first scapegoats is unfair competition from abroad. The typical argument is that since labor is cheaper abroad or other governments are subsidizing certain industries, our own industries should be protected by quotas or by tariffs (which are simply taxes assessed against imported goods). There is as always some truth to these charges, but the correct conclusions are not the ones so often drawn.

Again, the problem is focusing on the immediate consequences for one group and not seeing the less visible, but nontheless just as real, secondary consequences for other groups: the most visible consequences are those felt by the group which most benefits from the tariffs, while these consequences which are not seen negatively affect a much larger group.

Adam Smith long ago made the case for free trade as plainly as it can be made. As he said, it is obvious that the great majority of the people of a nation are better off if they are allowed to buy everything as cheaply as possible. In this case, what is true of a household economy is just as true of a national economy. It is never wise to try to make at home what you can buy at a lower cost than you incur by making it. The real cost of what you buy is measured in terms of lost opportunities to purchase or to do other things. Thus, those whose occupation pays them $10 an hour would be foolish to forego an opportunity to work at their occupation in order to do for themselves that which they can purchase at a cost of $5 an hour, unless of course there are other benefits involved, such as being with the family or the satisfaction of the work.

On the other hand, a variety of arguments are made for protectionism in the United States, but none of them make economic sense. The infant industry argument, for instance, suggests that as industries are just getting started they cannot compete against mature industries in other countries. This may be true for unindustrialized nations, but for the United States it is ludicrous to argue that we have any infant industries which must compete against mature industries in other nations.

Another argument frequently made for protection of American industries is that tariffs protect jobs in that particular U.S. industry. That is certainly true. But this costs something. (There is no free lunch.) These costs are often overlooked, and they may be more than we would willingly want to pay if we faced them squarely. For here again there are secondary consequences for other, larger groups. We can protect the steel industry or the automobile industry, but only by raising the prices which all Americans must pay for those products.

Protection is bought by placing tariffs on the imported products so that they will not undersell the American-made good. The automobile and steel workers' jobs are saved, but Americans who were forced to pay higher than necessary prices for their purchases have subsidized those jobs. In addition, this extra money they must spend for these protected products is money they now cannot spend for other goods; so production that would have been demanded elsewhere is not, and jobs which would have been created elsewhere are not. We can point to the jobs which have been saved, but no less real for not being seen are the jobs which were lost.

These are not the only negative consequences of trade barriers. We pay for our imports with our exports. Sometimes this fact is disguised by speaking of a favorable balance of trade existing when we have exported more than we have imported. But this makes no sense. What householder would be glad of the opportunity to ship off more of the fruit of his or her hard labor than he or she received in turn? Exports are of no value to us. They provide no comfort, give no nourishment, nor do they make our labor more productive. Imports are useful. Bananas, coffee, watches, television sets, and a myriad of other imports do much to improve our lives. But in order to get these things we must trade with other countries. They do not ship these things to us out of good-will, but to buy our exports with the proceeds from their sales to us. If we fail to trade, if we hide behind "trade barriers," then other countries have nothing with which to buy our exports. And when other countries do not buy our exports, those industries which are heavily export-oriented, such as agriculture and heavy machinery manufacturing, must reduce production due to de-creased demand for their products, with the result that jobs are lost. Tariffs thus have the perverse effect of reducing employment, not increasing it.

Another argument often made in favor of tariffs is that imports will reduce our standard of living by importing lower wage rates. Again this argument has no economic validity; it fails to note that the high wage rates in the United States are determined by the productivity of the American worker, which is still unmatched anywhere in the world. This productivity is largely due to the fact that the average factory worker in the United States is working with $40,000 worth of labor-enhancing machinery. And as long as worker productivity stays high, wages will stay high.

In fact, it is the tariffs themselves which reduce our standard of living. Tariffs guarantee that we pay higher prices for the pro-tected goods, since tariffs are taxes levied on foreign goods to raise their price equal to or higher than that of the American prod-uct. This higher price means that we have less left over from our purchase of these goods with which to buy other goods which would be desirable, and to that extent we have a reduced standard of living.

Furthermore, no such thing as a monopoly can exist in a country which has no trade barriers. In the United States, with only four automobile manufacturers, there is a great peril of monopolistic price-setting, but with competition from foreign auto makers this would be impossible. Competition, or at least the threat of com-petition, is necessary not only to keep prices down but to keep industries innovating and improving, to keep them strong and efficient.

CONCLUSION

It is a strong and vigorous business community that is a nation's greatest resource. Natural resources and an educated populace are important, but without the ability to produce, a nation has no wealth and no hope for the future. And the best hope for an efficient and productive business community is the free market. The informational function of the price system (telling businesses exactly what products people want and which resources are available) and the incentive function of profits (leading businesess to produce those desired goods) and competition (forcing businesses to the most efficient production of those products) assure a nation of the dedicated, efficient, and appropriately directed service of its businesses.

Despite the cynical view of profits held in some quarters, when businesses begin to operate from motives other than profit—no matter how heartwarming those motives may be—then they cease to listen to the information of the price system and consumers are less well served.

To some, this emphasis on profits suggests that greedy businesses gain only as they take advantage of powerless consumers; but so long as economic exchanges are voluntary, both parties benefit, otherwise they would not exchange. However, when a powerful third party such as government intervenes and prohibits certain exchanges, or requires certain exchanges, then the greatest satisfaction of the many is jeopardized. If government requires only those exchanges which would have occurred anyway, then there is no need for intervention in the free market. On the other hand, if other exchanges are required than would have been made, then some benefit has been lost by one or both of the parties. More importantly, the freedom to make one's own choices has been lost. Then must surely come increasing government involvement in every decision we make which has economic consequences: not only what you will buy and what you will sell, but also how much education you will have, which occupation you will enter, and where you will live.

Efficiency of resource use, then, is not the only recommendation for a capitalistic system. All other freedoms are founded in the basic economic freedoms. To use your resources and talents as you wish in your own service, including charity if that so pleases you, and to purchase those things most valuable to you, are basic freedoms without which other freedoms are not possible. There are risks involved in making one's own choices, but this country was founded on the belief that such risks are worth all else. A life of security as a drudge, whether of some individual or of the state, is worse than the most abysmal failure of the free person.

There is no free lunch. The price of freedom is the risk of failure. On the other hand, to ask government to provide us with a riskless society is to trade our freedom for that which is only an illusion. A world without economic consequences is not possible in this life.

REFERENCES

Friedman, Milton, and Rose Friedman. *Free to Choose*. New York: Avon Books, 1979.

Hazlitt, Henry. *Economics in One Lesson*. New York: Manor Books, 1975.

SECTION

7

COMPUTER
CONSIDERATIONS

COMPUTERS, MANAGEMENT INFORMATION SYSTEMS, AND SUPERVISORS

OLICE H. EMBRY

Almost every area of our lives and our jobs has been affected in one way or another by the computer. Understanding how to live with computers and how to make them work *for you* instead of *against you* is very important to supervisors. This chapter will outline some hints to help supervisors better understand the computer's strengths and limitations and how to talk to computer programmers to get what you want from the computer.

WHAT IS A COMPUTER?

Basically, a computer is only a very fast but very dumb adding machine/typewriter. It has to be programmed with a great many detailed steps just to do the simplest of jobs. Because it is so fast, however, this large number of steps can be done in a fraction of a second. It can perform complex calculations, store information, find and display information, and analyze information to either make decisions or alert someone that a decision needs to be made. The computer can do such things as turn conveyer belts on or off, send out letters to past-due accounts, calculate withholding taxes, and order raw materials when needed.

MANAGEMENT INFORMATION SYSTEMS

A Management information system links together various computer programs into a system capable of performing many tasks. For example, one well-known frozen cake company has a management information system that does the following:

1. Receives orders from the sales force.
2. Decides if the order can be filled from existing inventory.
3. Schedules robots to bake more cakes if necessary to fill the order.
4. Moves the inventory to the loading dock on a computerized train.
5. Prints a packing slip and invoice.
6. Subtracts the order from the inventory records.
7. Bills the customer.
8. Records the bill in the accounts receivable file.
9. Pays a commission to the salesperson.
10. Enters the sales in a file used to forecast sales for next year.

This data is used to make production reports, sales reports, warehouse reports, shipping reports, and accounting records. These reports help supervisors identify the best-selling products, the best customers, the best salespeople, and the most profitable items in the product line. Some systems also can keep records of machine downtime and even predict when a machine will be down or in need of maintenance.

MAJOR PARTS OF THE COMPUTER

The computer is made up of components such as keyboards, television screens, or black boxes that are called *hardware* and computer languages or programs of instructions that are called *software*. Hardware items are generally classified as input devices, output devices, memory devices, and central processing units. Software items include *compilers* which are computer languages used to activate the computer, *applications programs* which are the many detailed steps required to do a report or application, and *systems programs* which are instructions used to schedule and manage the computer.

COMPUTER APPLICATIONS FOR SUPERVISORS

The following is designed to illustrate some of the types of applications that supervisors can ask their computer programmers to design.

1. *Production Scheduling and Analysis.* This type of system can be programmed to fit together complicated production schedules like a jigsaw puzzle. Small orders, bunched together with larger orders, can increase the length of production runs. Machine utilization can be increased and downtime or retooling costs can be cut with this type of program. Production peaks can be predicted and more production can be scheduled earlier or later to save overtime expense. Production schedules can take into account raw

material price cycles so that long production runs are scheduled during times when raw material prices are low.

2. *Materials-Requirements Planning, Inventory Control, and Safety-stock Analysis.* One missing part, component, or raw material can shut down an entire assembly line. Safety stocks (a stockpile of inventory to use only when your regular inventory is exhausted) represent a sizable investment for most businesses. The money invested in safety stock doesn't usually earn anything for the firm and would be better off in a bank earning interest or invested in a more profitable project. Computers can help the supervisor operate with less safety stock. The computer can keep track of usage and automatically place routine purchase orders, or notify the supervisor that an order should be placed. The computer can compare the cost of many small orders with the cost of larger but fewer orders that can take advantage of volume discounts but which may cost money to store and a commitment of investment dollars that could otherwise be earning interest. In many businesses, 80% of the sales come from only 20% of the product line. The computer can analyze sales to determine which items are needed most in inventory. The computer can also track inventory levels in other plants or warehouses to minimize the need for high levels of inventory in all locations.

3. *Historical Standards for Piece-Rate Analysis.* The computer can collect large amounts of data over long periods of time and under varying production conditions to improve the accuracy of piece-rate calculations. The computer can also select and determine sample sizes needed to provide a 90% to 95% reliable analysis of certain rates.

4. *Maintenance Patterns and Scheduling for Machines.* The computer can become very good at predicting machine breakdowns and scheduling maintenance during off hours rather than while the work force stands idly by watching. Machine scheduling by computer often eliminates bottlenecks and increases the efficient utilization of the machinery.

5. *Accident Pattern Analysis.* The cost of poor safety can be reduced by having the computer analyze accident patterns. Anal-

ysis often identifies a particular machine, supervisory work group, or work station than can receive attention and greatly reduce accidents.

6. *Materials Control and Flow.*   Getting the right color part or option to the workstation at the right time for each order is a big problem for automobile manufacturers. Computers keep track of which options go on which vehicles and print out instructions to assembly workers. This insures that the right radio and the right color of upholstery get put into the cars exactly as the customers or dealers order them.

7. *Scrap Control and Analysis.*   Scrap in the garment industry is greatly reduced by computers assisting workers to position patterns to get the most efficient use of cloth with the least waste. Scrap and waste control analysis can pinpoint problems with particular machine operators or work processes to reduce scrap costs.

8. *Warranty Patterns and Analysis.*   Computers can analyze product warranty returns to identify production problems, improper tolerances, or particular machines, operators, or work processes.

9. *Personal Turnover and Analysis.*   Despite the many reasons for personnel turnover, patterns often exist. The computer can identify areas where poor supervision may be a problem, or at least predict high turnover periods so that plans can be made to handle or correct personnel shortages.

10. *Cost Control and Overrun Analysis.*   Computers can be programmed to collect and analyze data for cost control bonus programs, cost analysis programs, and to find the reason for cost overruns. Computers can divide overhead costs and give a more accurate picture for pricing decisions. The computer can help the supervisor reward efficient performance.

11. *Equipment Trouble Analysis and Module Replacement.*   Today many plants have computers connected to their production equipment to electronically monitor for trouble. In many systems the computer not only spots trouble, it can also diagnose and type out instructions for maintenance personnel to replace specific parts in the system.

12. *Robot Applications.* Almost any machine that is designed to replace human manual operations could be called a robot. The machines we normally call robots, however, today contain computer circuitry to make them programmable and able to do different jobs. A robotic "arm," for instance, can be programmed to weld a specific part and/or to lift the part and/or to spray paint a part.

13. *Trend Analysis and Seasonal Forecasting.* Sales demand for product inventory, employee turnover, and even equipment breakdowns often follow a seasonal pattern that the computer can plot and use for future projections. With careful scheduling, inventory buildups, shortages, and so forth can be avoided. The computer can help supervisors compare the cost of stockpiling inventory in slack seasons with the cost of overtime or additional hiring during periods of high demand. Equipment breakdowns often follow a cycle so that preventive maintenance can be scheduled or parts replaced before breakdowns occur.

14. *Wage and Salary Administration.* The computer can be used to calculate piece rates and to pick out high quality or high quantity performers for merit raises or bonus pay. Commissions can be paid based on sales orders, or bonuses can be calculated based on production quotas. The computer can be also used to track and equalize overtime.

15. *Personnel Record Analysis and Patterns.* When personnel records are computerized, the computer can be programmed to identify employees with the highest absence rate, tardy rates, and safety problems. It can also identify work groups with the highest turnover, training costs, or grievance problems.

16. *Employee Scheduling, Overtime, Vacation, and Sick Leave Analysis.* The computer can help the supervisor schedule employees for peak periods, slack periods, and split shifts. It can identify employees to go to other work groups to help satisfy peak demands when demand is slack in their own group, and it can equalize overtime. It can identify how many people should be allowed to go on vacation each week and publish a seniority list

for selection of vacation periods. By analyzing sick leave data, it may help the supervisor decide to schedule extra employees on the day after a holiday in order to identify employees with a pattern of taking sick days after a holiday.

17. *Management-by-Exception Applications.* The computer can be used to monitor a huge variety of activities and to notify the supervisor only when problems are detected. For example, when rejects reach a certain point, the computer can identify the problem areas so that management can take action. When equipment breakdowns occur too frequently, the computer can notify management of the problem areas. When inventory gets too low, the computer can produce new orders or notify management. With the management-exception system, the computer is silent when everything is okay and active only when a problem occurs.

HOW THE COMPUTER WORKS AND HOW TO MAKE IT WORK FOR YOU

Input/Output Devices

1. *Punch Card Systems.* The 80-column punched card was invented almost a century ago and is one of the oldest devices used to enter data into the computer. The card is divided into 80 columns like a loaf of bread with 80 slices. Holes punched in specific places on the card are read as a code which the computer interprets as a letter or a number. A one, for example, is represented by a hole in the area of the column reserved for a one. When this hole passes over an electric brush, probe, or a light in the card-reader, a "one" is interpreted by the computer. To represent a 10, two columns are needed and the one and the zero in each column are programmed to be read together for the full number. Many businesses have forms that use blocks to show how much space has been allowed for a specific number. For example, age would probably be a two-digit field since rarely would anyone over 99 be listed. The form would look like this:

1-2.
Age

The small numbers below the blocks are the column numbers that tell the computer clerks which columns of the card are to be used for age.

Numbers entered in the blocks must be *right adjusted,* that is, moved as far to the right as possible. A "5" entered in column two will read as a "5" by the computer, but if a "5" is entered in column one, it may be read as a "50" even though nothing is entered in column two.

When supervisors work with computer programmers to design a system, they must be certain to tell the programmer the largest number that is possible so that enough space on the card will be allowed. In this example, three columns would probably be allowed for age, since an age of 100 is possible and even rare cases have to be handled.

The supervisor also needs to tell the programmer what new things might be added to the program in the future. For example, if information for "weight" is not going to be needed by the computer now, but may be needed by the computer in the future, the supervisor should mention this so that card columns will be reserved for the future addition of "weight" to the program. Punched cards also serve as output devices, particularly if they will become an input device in the next part of a cycle. For example, gasoline companies send their customers a punched-card bill. When the card is returned with a check, a clerk merely puts the card in the "paid stack" of cards to be fed into the computer if the full amount due has been paid. If the amount is different, a new card must be cut or the correct amount entered through a keyboard or other device.

Punched cards also come in other sizes. Some cards are as small as postage stamps and use pin holes to record data. Cards cannot be folded, stapled, or mutilated or they will not work properly. Because of these problems, the slowness of card systems, the cost and bulk of cards, problems with moisture, and so forth, cards are not as popular as they once were.

2. *Magnetic Tape-Reading Devices.* Magnetic tape devices range from the small common tape cassette that uses the same type ¼" tape used in the popular cassette players in cars and homes, to very large special purpose tapes that store the same information that would take hundreds of boxes of punched cards to store. Bits of metal no bigger than a pinpoint are contained in the plastic tape. These bits of metal are either magnetized or not magnetized to store information in a code that the computer can understand. The biggest advantage of tape is that it can store so much data without using much space for storage. The biggest disadvantage is the length of time it takes to wind the tape to the place where desired information is located. The tapes are inexpensive and can be read by the computer much faster than cards. However, care must be taken not to drop tapes or store them in an area where they will become too hot or come in contact with a magnet (such as a magnet in a loudspeaker).

3. *Magnetic Disk, Diskettes, and Floppy Disk Devices.* The problem of quick access to data in the middle or end of a tape is overcome by magnetic disks. These range in size from the diskette or floppy disk, which is about the size of a 45 RPM record, to stacks of disks that are larger than standard LP record albums arranged in layers as in a juke box. Magnetic arms can almost instantly reach in to read a bit of information; this is called "random access" since it is not necessary to start searching at the beginning or at the end of a record. Magnetic disks may be hard like a phonograph record or flexible like a rubber mat. Tiny bits of metal in the disk are magnetized in a code to store figures, words, or instructions.

4. *Optical Scanners.* Optical scanners are now becoming one of the most commonly used methods of input for the computer. Some optical scanners do the following:

a. Read bar codes on grocery and supermarket products.

b. Read human handwriting to sort zip codes on letters.

c. Read the "amount paid" writing on bill stubs returned with payment.

d. Read light beams passing through holes in cards.

e. Read blackened spots on multiple-choice test score sheets.

   f.   Reject parts that are too big or small or do not pass a light test.

One very popular optical scanner uses a light pencil attached to a cassette recorder to inventory grocery and variety store products on the shelf. The cassette tape is limited to a central computer where the inventory record is recorded and new orders are placed.

   5.   *Typewriters and Terminals.* One of the most popular ways to enter information into or receive information from the computer is with a typewriter or keyboard device. Although this is very slow compared with some other input/output devices, more and more applications interact directly with workers through terminals. Automobile assembly lines have terminals that tell workers exactly which cars get which options—such as radios—and which colors are to be used. Clerks make reservations on typewriter terminals and the computer uses typewriter terminals to send form letters to suppliers or customers. Special forms or checks are used in many applications to save time.

   Some keyboards display information on a television screen. It can then be checked and corrected before printing, or only the part needed can be printed.

   Some typewriters use dots to form letters because this is faster than the other methods of typing. "Letter quality" typewriters, however, are often specified for form letters and many customer applications.

   Teletypewriters and typewriters that can be connected to a telephone permit the terminal to be hundreds of miles away from the computer.

   6.   *Television Terminals.* Some computer terminals use Cathode Ray Tubes (CRTs) or television sets to display information, display graphs, or even to play games with users. Some sets can display a multiple-choice question and the user can merely touch the television screen with a finger or a light pen to record an answer. Most television set terminals, however, have a keyboard of some sort attached to them.

   7.   *Voice and Tone Devices.* On some assembly lines, workers can speak certain commands into an overhead microphone, which

will activate or enter data into a computer. The computer can also talk to the worker with recorded messages. Musical tones from telephones are also a very popular input device.

8. *Printers and Microfilm.* Printers are used for output only, although with optical scanners, printing can be read by many computers as a form of input. High-speed printers turn out hundreds of lines of print per minute. Using sandwich forms, the computer can print an address on the outside of a form and, through carbon paper on the inside of the form, print bills, letters, or grades on an inside sheet of paper. Since a print ribbon is used on the address part of the form, the bill, letter, or grade does not get printed on the outside. High-speed microfiche processors produce entire pages of microfilm or microfiche to reduce storage requirements that paper printouts require.

9. *Magnetic Ink.* Banks are the largest users of magnetic ink. All checks, in order to be processed through the United States banking system, must have a magnetic ink bank code printed in the lower left corner of the check. A customer account number may be printed next and the amount of the check is printed in the lower right corner of the check. Since human handwriting must be read and then typed by a human onto the check, the check amount is the most common source of error.

10. *Plotters and Copiers.* Using ink pins on rolls of paper, the computer can output plots of graphs and charts. Some advanced modes of Xerox and other copy machines also can receive signals from computers to produce entire pages of newspapers, photographs, and, of course, letters complete with a company's letterhead.

11. *Other Miscellaneous Devices.* Computers can accept data from old-fashioned teletypewriter paper tape, electric "eyes," floats that tell how much water or fuel is in a tank, and counters that tell how many products have passed on an assembly line. Special robots can sense pressure, light, or temperature—to record data or make manufacturing decisions. The number of special-purpose devices that can be invented for factory use is limitless.

How the Computer Counts

In most of the world, the decimal system is used as the numbering system. *Decimal* means ten and this system came into use because humans have ten fingers.

In an automobile, mileage is recorded on a system of dials on wheels that have the numerals zero through nine on them. When the car goes past nine miles, the wheel goes back to zero and moves the wheel in the next position to one so that two digits, the one and a zero, are required to represent the number "10." Once the car goes past 99 miles, three digits—a one and two zeros—are required to represent the number "100."

Since most computers understand only whether or not a bit in its memory is magnetized or not magnetized, it only has "two" fingers and, therefore, uses a "binary" numbering system. Since the only "fingers" this system has are zero and one, it takes many more digits to represent a particular number. The number nine, for example, is 1001 in binary and takes up four digit spaces inside the computer.

In actual practice, most computers use combinations of the binary system for calculations. Fortunately, computer users do not have to know whether the computer is counting with two "fingers," eight "fingers," or sixteen "fingers" in order to use the computer. This is because we now have computer languages that look very much like English; they encode numbers and machine instructions into magnetized or unmagnetized bits that computers can understand. Some of the more popular languages are discussed in the next section.

Computer Languages

Computer languages, or compilers, enable users to tell the computer what they want done, how to do it, and when to do it. Computers actually only understand whether a bit in its memory is or is not magnetized or whether a hole is in a card or not, and so forth. Computer languages are made of words and phrases that are used to generate the electrical codes that the computer understands.

BASIC (Beginner's All-purpose Symbolic Instructional Code)

The BASIC language, developed at Dartmouth College in 1967, is the most popular beginner's language in the United States. It is easy to learn and is very popular, particularly with personal or microcomputers. This is a segment of a basic program that figures payroll earnings and withholdings:

10 PRINT "What is your social security no."
20 INPUT N
30 PRINT "How many hours did you work this week"
40 INPUT H

Each command to the computer is given a line number to sequence the commands. *PRINT* and *INPUT* are command words in the BASIC language. Whatever follows the word *PRINT* in quotation marks will be printed on a typewriter or television screen to tell the user what information is desired. The command INPUT sets aside some computer memory, and when the user types a number back to the computer, the computer stores the number in this part of the memory. Later in the program it will take the hours worked number stored in the part of the memory that the programmer has called H, multiply it by an hourly pay number it has stored in a part of the memory the programmer has called W, and store the answer in yet another section of memory the programmer has called G for gross pay. This command looks like this:

$$80 \; G = H * W$$

The * sign is the symbol used for multiplication in BASIC.

Later in the program, the computer will subtract the withholding amounts for taxes, insurance, and so forth, and print a check and check stub for the employee. It will also add together the tax and insurance witholding for all employees and send a check and a detailed listing to the tax office and the insurance company. Finally, it will update the employee's yearly-earnings-to-date record so that a W-2 form can be prepared at the end of the year.

COBOL (Common Business-Oriented Language)

COBOL is a very powerful and a relatively old language that actually dates back to 1960 when it was first used by the Navy. It is very close to English and is still the standard language for a great many large firms. COBOL is a lengthy language and requires many detailed instructions to establish and manipulate data files. It is, however, a very efficient language to execute. The following segment of a COBOL program reads a card containing total hours worked and multiplies the hours by an hourly wage to compute gross pay.

```
PROCEDURE DIVISION.
    OPEN INPUT CARD-FILE OUTPUT PRINT-FILE
    READ-CARD-FILE AT END GO TO WRAP-UP.
    FIGURE-PAY.
        MULTIPLY HOURS-WORKED BY HOURLY-PAY
        GIVING GROSS-PAY.
```

In BASIC, this is done with an equation: $G = H * W$. In COBOL, the segments of memory where the variable data is stored can be given names up to 30 characters long. This makes the program longer to write but much easier to understand.

FORTRAN (FORmula TRANslator)

FORTRAN is also an old language dating back to the 1960s; it is useful for scientific calculations. It is very similar to BASIC. Segments of memory for storage of variable data can have names up to six characters long. The following FORTRAN statement also computes gross pay:

$$GROSS = HRSWKD * HRPAY$$

To a programmer, these abbreviations are easier to follow than the BASIC formula $G = H * W$.

RPG (Report Program Generator)

The RPG language uses coded forms to produce specialized reports with very little programming effort. It is a popular language with small companies.

Other Computer Languages

There are dozens of other commonly used specialized languages available in the United States and hundreds of privately developed specialized languages that are used for specific applications for specific firms.

HOW TO TALK TO COMPUTER PEOPLE

Users' Responsibilities

The people who will be using the computer or its output have the responsibility for telling the computer programming staff three key things:

1. How the printout should look or what things the user wants the computer to do.
2. Where the data is that the computer will use.
3. What future additions to the program the user will want in the next five years.

The starting point for the design of a good computer application is actually the design of the end product itself. If the end product is a report, the people who will use the report should be given a printout form (a sheet of paper composed of letter blocks that show how much print can be put on a page) and asked to write out a copy of how a typical report should look. The programmer can then make suggestions or ask questions that can improve the report. The user also is responsible for telling the programmer where the data is that will be used in the program.

One very important responsibility of the user is to tell the programmer what additions to the program will be needed in the future. While a five-year estimate is obviously not expected to be extremely accurate, the user should give a good guess about future additions to the program. For example, in the payroll program discussed above in describing BASIC and COBOL, the user should tell the programmer that a program to write a W-2 form (an annual Statement of Employee Earnings and Federal Withholding that must be given to the government and to employees by January 31 of each year) should be considered for a future addition. The programmer will then know that the data from each run of the program will need to be saved and accumulated so it will not have to be entered again.

If other types of deductions might be allowed in the future, then the programmer will need to make allowances in the program. This keeps the program from having to be completely re-written when new uses are added.

Computer Staff's Responsibilities

The computer staff's responsibilities include:

1. Efficiently designing a program to do what the user wants and yet be compatible with the remainder of the management information system.
2. Testing the program and comparing it with a parallel manual run if possible.
3. Documenting the program so that modifications can be easily made in the future.
4. Preparing instructions for users of the program.

Effective Coordination

The supervisor must understand the detail needed by the programming staff and the programming staff must understand the desires of the user as well as the user's need for simplicity. Many computer applications overwhelm the user with too much information or make the computer application more complicated than the manual operation. There must be respect from both sides for the other side's needs and desires. The computer programmers should thoroughly understand the manual operation before it is computerized. The manual operation must also work well before it is computerized; otherwise, computerizing it only speeds up the mess.

THE STRENGTHS AND WEAKNESSES OF THE COMPUTER

Common misconceptions:

1. *More Computers Mean Fewer Jobs for People.* In most large firms, adding computers has actually resulted in more jobs. The jobs, however, are different: the jobs are for data entry clerks, computer repair persons, and so forth.

2. *Computers Get Work out Faster.* Although computers are extremely fast, they are costly to operate and require a large volume of work to run efficiently. In a manual system, a bill might be received one day and a check might go out the next day. In a computerized operation, bills might have to be accumulated for several weeks in order to have enough volume to justify a run of the computer. A bill paid in one day under a manual system might take two weeks to be paid in a computerized system.

3. *Computers Make Errors.* Actually, almost all errors made are human errors. When a computer malfunctions, it usually stops or prints out garbage and messes up everything, not just one account. *GIGO*—garbage in, garbage out—is an old computer slogan that means that if humans put incorrect data into the computer, they get incorrect data out.

FINDING COMPUTING ERRORS

In order to find errors in the computer process, look first at the input by humans. If the input seems to be correct, see if the same error is occurring on all accounts or runs of the program. If so, then a programming error may be involved and the programmer should be contacted. There is almost always a reason for an error. Simply ignoring it and hoping it will not occur again on future runs almost never works; this usually compounds the problem. When contacting the computer department, be certain to take all information—input and output—with you. Programmers usually must see this to find the error. Simply calling rarely works.

THE HOW AND WHY OF COMPUTER SCHEDULING

As mentioned above, computers require large volumes of work to operate efficiently. Although they work very fast, the reports or work they produce may actually be delayed because of the scheduling process. Once a job is scheduled, it may run in 30 seconds, but may not actually get printed until the next day. Many computer centers have a problem printing out all of the data they run because this is usually the slowest part of the entire process. Long printouts are often purposely scheduled to be run late at night.

In most computer centers, an internal computer program rather than the computer operator, actually schedules jobs on the computer according to some set of rules or priorities in the program.

COMPUTER TERMS

Application Program.   A program written to do a specific job or produce a specific report or form.

BASIC.   (Beginner's All-Purpose Symbolic Instruction Code.) A high-level language that is popular for time sharing and micro-computer or personal computer use.

Batch Processing.   Programs or runs of computer processing that are done centrally at one time.

Bit.   The smallest memory or storage unit in a computer. Usually stores a zero or one.

Cathode Ray Tube.   (CRT.) A television-like screen.

Central Processor.   The main operating unit of a computer.

COBOL.   (Common Business-Oriented Language.) A high-level language resembling English, first used in 1960 and still very popular with large firms.

Compiler.   A computer language that translates commands written in near-English or in formula form into machine commands the computer can understand.

Data.   Numbers, names, orders, and so forth; any information used by the computer.

Data Entry Clerk. Clerks who keypunch data or type data into the computer or into a storage device for input into the computer.

Disc. A magnetic recordlike device that stores information that can be randomly accessed.

Dumb Terminal. A terminal or keyboard with no memory or calculating capability of its own and that depends totally on the computer.

EDP. (Electronic Data Processing.) A common name for computer operations.

Facsimile Transmitter/Receiver. A device that sends or receives pictures or copies, usually over a telephone wire.

Flowchart. A system of symbols that shows in pictures and sequence form the step-by-step process of a program.

FORTRAN. *(FOR*mula *TRAN*slator). A high-level computer language particularly useful for scientific calculations.

Hard Copy. A printed copy rather than an image on a television screen.

Hardware. All of the physical components of a computer system.

Input/Output Device. Any device capable of inputing data into a computer or receiving data from a computer.

Information System. The computer operation responsible for organizing, storing, and retrieving data, making useful reports, and performing specific tasks such as printing orders.

Intelligent Terminal. A terminal or keyboard with some memory, storage, or processing capability of its own that is not dependent upon the computer.

Interactive Terminal. A terminal connected to a computer that enables the user to interact directly with the computer.

JCL. (Job Control Language). A code that controls priority and scheduling of computer input and output.

Keypunch. A machine that punches coded holes in cards.

Magnetic Tape. A magnetizable tape used for input, storage, output, data, or programs.

Menu. A display of questions or choices that enables a user to tell the computer what is wanted.

Microfiche.   A sheet of film that usually contains dozens of pages of data greatly reduced.

Microfilm.   A roll of film usually containing pages of data or information.

Microcomputer.   A small or personal computer built around a small silicon chip.

Minicomputer.   A smaller version of the large computers that simply is not quite as fast or as large as the big computers.

Output.   Any data or information output from the computer in any forms such as print, cards, voice, and so forth.

PL/1.   (Programming Language 1.) A high-level programming language that is supposed to combine the advantages of COBOL and FORTRAN.

Programmer.   A person who writes and tests sets of instructions to the computer to make it perform specific jobs and tasks.

Random Access.   The ability to reach into the middle of a record to access data, as opposed to having to unwind and wind it to a specific location to access the data.

RPG.   (Report Program Generator). A computer language that efficiently and easily generates reports.

Smart Terminal.   Same as intelligent terminal. One with some memory or processing capability of its own.

User-Friendly.   A system designed to be easy to use by those who are not computer programmers.

SECTION

SAFETY
CONSIDERATIONS

CHAPTER

16

THE SUPERVISOR AND SAFETY

MARTIN M. BROADWELL

Since each organization has its own way of dealing with the Occupational Safety and Health Act (OSHA) and other laws concerning safety, this chapter will deal with safety and the supervisor's role in it rather than with the laws governing it. There was a need for supervisors to do things with regard to safety long before safety laws came into existence, so it will be up to the organization to deal with the laws in their own ways. They can do it better and deal with individual peculiarities in their own situations.

What is the role of the supervisor in safety matters? Let's look at the question from two directions: first, some things the role is not, and then some things the role is.

The role is not:

1. Clearly defined in most organizations.
2. The *primary* job of the supervisor but still an important part of the supervisor's job.
3. A police job, to catch every unsafe employee in every unsafe act.
4. A safety engineer's job, to design and reorganize and generally be the expert on safety matters.

The role is to:

1. Create an environment where safety is practiced and respected.
2. Provide motivation among workers for safe action.
3. Provide employee training for job performance, including safety.
4. Inspect equipment, the environment, the working areas, constantly *thinking safety*.
5. Suggest changes in standards, equipment, procedures, practices, and so forth where safety can be improved; then to follow up on the suggestions to see that actions are taken as appropriate.
6. Observe behavior and actions of the employees—watching them work, but thinking "safe" and "unsafe" actions.
7. Provide corrective actions as necessary when unsafe acts are observed.
8. Grow personally in the area of safety and safety knowledge.
9. Conduct safety meetings.
10. Conduct corrective interviews.

Now let's look at some of these things in more detail. When this chapter is over, it should spell out the supervisor's full responsibility for the safety of workers under his or her supervision.

NOT A CLEARLY DEFINED ROLE

Historically, the supervisor's role in safety has been a poorly defined responsibility. Everyone is in agreement that the responsibility is there, but the extent and definition is not clear. Most of the "finger pointing" is done after an accident, but little is done to clarify the role ahead of time in most organizations. The usual idea is that the supervisor will hold safety training and safety meetings, and will be held accountable to some extent when there is an accident—especially one resulting in lost time or one where serious damage is done to equipment; by the same token, the worker is also held accountable for such events. Some make it sound as though safety is the most important part of the supervisor's job, yet most will agree that the supervisor's job is getting the work done (as safely as possible). As we'll see later, it is unfortunate that much more attention is paid to safety after an accident than before.

NOT THE PRIMARY ROLE OF THE SUPERVISOR

The role of any supervisor in any organization is to get the production or service goals of the organization met through the people available. This means that they must:

1. Maximize the use of personnel and other resources.
2. Minimize hazard and risk to life, limb, and equipment.
3. Utilize these resources in a safe environment to produce quality products or services.

What all of this says is that the real role of the supervisor is pretty clearly defined: getting the organization's defined goals of products and services met through the people, money, and raw materials and within the time frame that is profitable for that operation—all within a safe environment. The goal is not safety, but producing things *without being unsafe*. This represents a change from the past when production was more important—so much so that it was expected that there would be *some* accidents, and the goal was to keep them to a minimum. Fortunately, today accidents are considered exceptional and there is little allowance for any at all. We all recognize that some accidents could be prevented. The successful accident-preventing organization is one which constantly *thinks* safety, recognizing that if everyone thinks safety as part of their daily routine, there will be many fewer accidents. Thinking safety, working safely, developing safe habits—safety in general—is a learned way of life, but still not the primary goal of the supervisor.

NOT A POLICE ROLE

In some organizations there is a feeling that the supervisor is there to make sure that the "criminal" (the perpertrator of an unsafe act!) is promptly and properly dealt with. The wrath may be so bad that there will be those who get hurt but suffer the injury in silent torment rather than admit to the accident. It is true that the supervisor must look for and deal with unsafe acts, but catching workers doing unsafe things is not the supervisor's primary role. What the successful supervisor is doing all the time is setting the tone, creating an environment and an awareness of safety to such an extent that the workers themselves are looking for and correcting unsafe conditions and actions. If the safety climate is healthy enough, and there is a correct understanding of the reasons for safety, the workers will be the ones who set the stage for safety. They will even become intolerant of bosses and others who come through the shop or office and commit unsafe deeds such as leaving file drawers open or not wearing safety glasses.

While the supervisor is looking for unsafe acts, he or she is also looking for things that slow production, cause waste, and reduce quality. If there is something that causes the quality of the product to suffer, or keeps the customer from getting the proper service, action must be taken. The supervisor must be quality-conscious, but that isn't the primary function of the supervisor's job. The supervisor must constantly be concerned about waste and take immediate action when there is something causing waste beyond the tolerance level. But concern for waste is not the primary reason for having the supervisor on the job. Safety fits in that same category. Workers must be taught to think quality, service, waste reduction, *and* safety.

To those who are quite aware of safety and the consequences of unsafe acts this sounds a bit too unconcerned. Not so: It's a matter of getting things into perspective and understanding the supervisor's role in the workplace. Just as it doesn't suggest that quality isn't important, or that customer service is of no concern, it doesn't say that safety is something that is caused because there is a police environment.

NOT A SAFETY ENGINEER

The supervisor will never need to become an expert in safety prevention or safety design. There's no way he or she can know all that's needed about job performance, job standards, and interpersonal skills and still understand the intricacies of the equipment and procedures for operating it, from a safety standpoint, to be an expert in it. It is not the role of the supervisor to be able to design a machine or to set operating standards that will make the operation of equipment safe. There are people who do that for a living, people who know the ins and outs of the equipment and safety and safety procedures, and who can keep the equipment safe. The supervisor is not an expert in accident prevention. These are not the skills we look for when we pick a supervisor. The organization usually hires a safety engineer, or the manufacturer supplies information for the safe operation of the equipment. This becomes a case of the right people doing the right thing.

We'll see later that there is *responsibility* for safe operation, but not for designing safety features. There is also a responsibility for observing unsafe conditions or operations and reporting that to the appropriate people, but we'll see that this is where the responsibility ends—if those responsible take the corrective action requested. Again, so that there will be no misunderstanding: There is always a responsibility for safety, but the line must be drawn between being responsible and being the expert. Having made these points about what the job *isn't,* let's now look at what the supervisor's role *is* with regard to safety.

CREATE AN ENVIRONMENT FOR SAFETY

All we know about safety tells us that it prevails most often in an environment where safety is practiced as a matter of *course* rather than as a matter of *threat.* In those places where workers perform their jobs safely from habit and desire, safety is respected rather than disdained. Everyone works safely. Everyone thinks safety. There is a spirit of wanting to be safe. There is a desire to see that no one gets hurt, that the equipment operates smoothly and functionally, without shutdown time. The bosses are as safety-conscious as they ask the workers to be and would no sooner perform an unsafe act than they would allow a worker to do so.

The important thing about such places is that safety is so much a way of life that it is almost not apparent. Those who work in such places don't go around saying, "Look at us; aren't we safe?" If we watch them closely, we see that they do their jobs safely as a matter of course, just as they handle quality or service. They do not do things safely when it is convenient. They do not become unsafe when there is a rush or when no one is looking. If it takes longer to go get an approved ladder, both the worker and the boss accept the time requirement without even thinking about it. Nor do they say, "I could do this job quicker if I didn't have to be safe and go get a ladder, but since I want to work safely, I'll take the time." That's just not the mentality of workers in this kind of environment. Just as a worker would go get a correct size wrench to loosen a nut instead of using a pair of pliers—because the pliers would damage the threads or the nut itself—they would go get the ladder because standing on a box or chair would be unsafe.

The boss's job is to create such an environment that the workers don't see the weekly safety meeting as resting time or joke time. Safety is never a joke in such an environment. Safety meetings are serious times when there is a legitimate discussion on how to save workers from harm or keep the assembly line from shutting down. The workers are as anxious to see movies or hear reports or learn new accident-prevention methods as the management is to show them. If there is union representation, the union is also interested in seeing that safety is practiced and that violaters are dealt with.

The supervisor creates this environment in many ways—the important ones we are discussing here—and by explaining the benefits of safety and doing things by the safety standards. There is no harping about safety or constant threats. Safety is explained as a part of the job, not an occasional thing to practice. When there is training, it is not thought of so much as "safety training" as it is "the way the job is done."

Most importantly, the supervisor is always acting in safe ways— always wearing the proper clothing, performing correct acts, and not making a big show of it. There is no "martyrdom" in doing things safely! If the boss sees water on the floor, then it is wiped up. It isn't a question of who's responsible for getting the water up or who let it spill on the floor—at least until it is up. If a chair is blocking the aisle, the supervisor moves it, then deals with seeing that it isn't there again. All of this comes under the heading of setting the right environment for safety. Only the supervisor can do this.

PROVIDE MOTIVATION FOR SAFE ACTS

Ultimately, the supervisor is concerned with the actions and behaviors of the workers, not just with their attitudes and thought processes. As we've seen, the supervisor's job is to get the job done through others, and the "others" are the workers doing their jobs. This means that a prime responsibility of the supervisor is one of motivating the workers to do their jobs. The process of motivating workers to do their jobs with skill and accuracy, with quality and quickness, is the same process as getting them to do their jobs safely.

The challenge of the supervisor becomes one of finding those things which will motivate workers, then applying the same skill to safety. There are no tricks, just doing what we've learned to do over the years as far as motivation is concerned. For example, we know that workers respond better to positive reinforcement than to negative actions. Threats and discipline—which are necessary at times—are good at keeping workers from doing things, but it will rarely give them a substitute behavior. They'll stop doing something when they are punished, but they won't automatically start doing the correct thing instead. On the other hand, when they are reinforced or "rewarded" for doing something, they're much more likely to repeat that behavior. The obvious thing to do then is to reinforce their good behavior, or, in the case of safety, their safe actions.

Another aspect of motivation is to have employees involved in some of the decision making regarding their own activity. This gives them a feeling of belonging and being in on things. We know that this is very motivating to most workers. If we let them make decisions about their safety, they'll be more committed to whatever action or restrictions they come up with. This is why it's important for them to participate in any safety meetings. It's more than just letting them get involved; it's letting them make decisions, too. If there is a problem or a new piece of equipment being installed or some new procedure being instituted, then by all means we need to get the workers together to discuss ways of making the operations successful. This is a form of recognition, and we can be sure that whatever ideas and suggestions they come up with will be supported by them. They will be more committed to their own ideas than to something we might attempt to impose on them. There may be times when we will need to accept some of their ideas, if they're workable, instead of some of our own, just to insure good support from them.

Another valuable motivation tool that we can use in improving safety is *recognition*. All of us like to be recognized as being good at something—better than others, if possible. The trouble we run into with recognition is that in safety we immediately think of the big sign at the entrance of the workplace announcing that one of the employees is the Safe Employee Of The Month. Considering there may be 2000 employees working in the plant, rewarding or recognizing only one isn't going to do much toward motivating the rest. Even if that employee gets special privileges such as a convenient parking place, the likelihood that the other 1999 will get it next month are pretty slim. It's much more effective when the supervisor offers a pat on the back when he or she sees a good, safe act, or gets a recommendation from a work group for ways of improving safety. The more personal we make the recognition, and the more often we offer it (within limits), the more effective it is. All we have to remember is that, while recognition is a very good means of motivation, it doesn't last very long. If we praise someone for a job done well today, it won't be long until that same worker will need praise again. This is both good and bad: bad in that it doesn't last long; good in that we can use recognition again soon. One fact about recognition is that it is most valuable when seen by others. If we give someone a letter of commendation, it is a good means of motivation, as long as we realize that the letter is effective only when someone sees it. This means that we look for as broad an audience as possible. Putting a worker's name in the organization's newsletter is effective, or putting a group's picture in is even more usuful. It increases comaraderie and competition among others to get their pictures in next time.

TRAIN FOR THE JOB AND SAFETY

Contrary to the popular cliche, practice doesn't make perfect—it only makes *permanent.* It stands to reason that if we expect employees to perform their jobs well, they need to be trained to do those jobs—and the better they are trained, the better they can do their jobs. So training becomes an important part of the supervisor's work. The overall goal is training; part of that training is *safety* training. Just as we make safety a part of the overall job of the worker, we make safety training a part—but not the whole—of our training effort. Since safety is something we practice as well as think, it is learned, hence something we can teach. We have safety classes. We show films, have discussions, get employees involved in training classes, all because we think they can learn something about safety.

The routine is simple: We train employees to do their jobs correctly, and that means safely. If doing it correctly isn't the safest way, then it can't be the correct way. We don't have to emphasize the safety or de-emphasize it, any more than we emphasize or de-emphasize quality or service. This all becomes very important in that it lets the employee see that safety is a natural function of doing the job, not separate and apart from it. This should not be seen as a disinterest in safety. In many ways it is a good way to emphasize that safety is a function of getting the everyday job done, not something that we do as a different part of the job. If we aren't careful, we find ourselves selling safety or defending it, making our position weaker rather than stronger. If we can get in the habit of treating it as a regular standard for the job, letting the employees see that that's the way we see it, then they will more likely accept it the same way.

As we've seen some many times so far in this chapter, we get employees to accept quality and production and service as a regular part of the job—a job done right—so we treat safety the same way. It should be noted, however, that if we fail to point out the safety aspects of the job, then we've done a poor job of training, hence a poor job of supervising. It's not just the safety that's suffering; it's the whole job, for we've not actually trained the employees to do the job correctly. We will (and should) be held accountable for that failure.

For the most part, accidents don't "just happen"; they are *caused*. Most accidents can be prevented, because most are the result of either carelessness or poorly trained employees. Rather than being discouraging, it should be exciting to the supervisor to know that accidents can be prevented by training employees to do their jobs correctly. So what do we train the employees to do, besides just doing their jobs properly? First, that's exactly what we need to do: we first train them to do their jobs correctly. If we're good at that, they'll be a long way toward doing a safe job. The next step is to teach them that there are three kinds of hazards they need to consider:

1.   Equipment hazards,
2.   Environmental hazards,
3.   Employee hazards.

Let's look at each of these and see what kinds of accidents and safety considerations are involved.

1. *Equipment Hazards.* These are the obvious accidents which are caused by the very nature of the machinery or the job. Employees may be pinched or cut; they may get clothing, hair, or even fingers caught or hung up in the machinery. They may get eye injuries from being struck, or something in the job activity may cause an eye accident. These kinds of accidents happen where there are gears, bars, pulleys, sharp edges (including paper), narrow spaces, or things that have pinchers or do some kind of pressing.

2. *Environmental Hazards.* These kinds of accidents or injuries are caused by the nature of the workplace, rather than the equipment, machinery, or the doing of the job. They usually include such things as toxic fumes; obstructions; moving vehicles; drawers; filing cabinets; exposed cords; oil, water, or other liquid spills; steps; risers; heavy objects to be lifted; and so forth. The kinds of injuries are obvious: such things as sprains, cuts, shocks, falls, poisons. Usually these kinds of accidents occur where there is much confusion—lots of people doing lots of things, much motion, activity, and confusion. If it is important to avoid injuries but still have the activity, the key is coordination and having someone responsible for it.

3. *Employee Hazards.* These kinds of problems arise from things worn or used by the workers. They would include things such as loose clothing, shoes, gloves, safety belts, and special tools or equipment such as wrenches, straps, or hand tools. These are things—like the others mentioned—that most often have special rules and standards connected with them; and accidents or injuries are usually due to improper observance to the standards.

Nature of the Training

When training is done to avoid accidents or injuries due to the kinds of hazards described above, there are some specific things to do and specific ways of doing the training. We've already mentioned the need for standards of operation and procedures, as well as a standard of conduct around such hazards. *Everything we do is aimed at getting the employees to do things by these standards.* We should know the standards, teach the standards, and do everything we can to see that employees never get a chance to experience doing the job incorrectly. Even during the training, we do better if we show them how to do the job the right way, rather than let them see it done wrong to demonstrate a point. Many times our training fails because we spend more time telling them how not to do the job than how to do it. We have experiments and demonstrations showing how the improper way will blow up everything, cause failures or damage—and the employees go away remembering all the incorrect ways, which overshadows the simple, correct way.

Steps in Doing On-the-Job Training

There are some proven ways of doing one-on-one training which have been around for a long time and have proven their worth over and over again. The simplest thing to say about them is that *they work.* Here's how it goes:

Step 1. We tell the employee *what* needs to be done, *how* it is done, and if it is important, *why* it is done this way.

Step 2. We perform the operation correctly.

Step 3. The employee tells us what, how, and why, just as we explained it.

Step 4. (Only if the employee tells us correctly:) We perform the task correctly.

Step 5. The employee tells us what, how, and why.

Step 6. (Only if the employee has told us correctly:) The employee performs the task and practices with our supervision.

There is a reason for each of these steps, of course. The main idea is to get the message in the *mind* before working on the *muscle*. Usually we do our training by first and foremost worrying about getting the individual to do the job right as we watch, and not by being concerned with what happens in the head. The typical training we do is to tell the individual what we want done, telling why, show the person, ask if there are any questions, then have the individual *do* it. Most often they do it correctly so we assume they know what and how. But because we've done nothing to put it in their heads, employees soon forget, especially if they don't start practicing right away. We come back a few days later and find that they're doing it incorrectly and say something like, "Don't you remember, I *told* you to do it this way!" The employee in turn feels bad because the memory is jogged, and he or she may say, "Oh, that's right. How can I be so stupid!" The truth is, we all have such an amazing capacity to forget that it's more normal to forget than to remember. If our training doesn't get the employees involved in saying things while they're doing them, they'll forget even more quickly.

The next aspect of training is to be sure to follow up on the training. No matter how well we do, there is always the need to check later and see if the employees are following our training. This is the time to reinforce good performance and get feedback from the employees to see if they have problems executing some of the things we talked about or showed them. Again, we let them tell us what they're doing; we do not show them again. We let them tell us step by step the procedures they're using in doing the job so we'll know what is going on in their heads.

Finally, we remember that our training should be telling them how to do the job, not telling them how not to do it. The bulk of our time is spent letting them hear, see, talk about, and do the right thing, not seeing and hearing all the wrong things that could but shouldn't be done.

INSPECT EQUIPMENT AND WORKING AREAS

So far we've seen that the supervisor has the responsibility to *think* safety. This is most important when just walking around the workplace. The supervisor is always looking, listening, thinking about what is going on. Good supervisors begin to almost "smell" unsafe conditions. Something just doesn't seem right to them; there is a sound that's off, a wheel that's giving off a peculiar sound, a bench or file cabinet or chair that is in the wrong place. For the good supervisor, it is the same feeling as when the line isn't running right or things aren't going well in the office, or a customer is being talked to improperly. There is a sixth sense telling the supervisor that things aren't as they should be. Until the supervisor gets this sense, he or she won't become very good at detecting unsafe conditions or acts. When it does come, the job will be much easier.

Supervisors, as they walk around, are constantly inspecting the work activity, but also talking to the workers and asking for suggestions for improving the operations. The suggestions are taken seriously, encouraged, and rewarded with praise and action if they have merit. The workers will soon see that the boss really cares about the job, about safety, and about their suggestions about the job. It won't be long before suggesting improvements in the job, including safety considerations, will become a natural activity for workers. It is then that we know we are making good progress toward a safe work force! We will now have a group of workers who are *thinking* safety, and that's when we'll start seeing good results in *getting* safety.

SUGGEST CHANGES

It isn't enough that we look for areas of improvement and solicit suggestions from our workers. It isn't enough that we constantly inspect and listen and use our senses. We have to make some effort to get things corrected that aren't correct. While we aren't the safety experts and we can't redesign the equipment, there are people who fall in this category and it's up to us to get the information to them. If we do our job of inspecting, watching, and reporting what we see and hear from the workers, we'll be helping them. We can remind ourselves: "It's our job."

Our job is more than just reporting what we see and hear; we also have the job of following up to see that what we've suggested gets acted upon. We have not removed our obligation just because we filled out a report or sent in a piece of paper. Our job is only complete when we see the action through to completion. It may be that the safety engineers do not feel that the suggestions have merit. They may be right, but we need to follow up to be sure they're coming to that conclusion based on enough evidence, not just putting it aside. It isn't our job to argue with them or try to prove our point. It is our job to see that they give it a fair hearing and provide legitimate reasons if they don't act on it. Above all, they are there to help because they are the experts. They are not our adversaries. The most important relationship we can have is one of closely working with them to solve common problems. This can best be done when we do our jobs and they do theirs, both with the interest of the organization in mind.

It should go without saying, but let's mention one thing about the suggestions we get from our workers: If they have enough interest to make a suggestion, we certainly want them to get the credit for the idea. The best way to kill their interest and convince them we are trying to get all the glory is to make it appear that the good ideas were ours, not our workers'. We can be sure we won't have to worry about future suggestions from them once we've taken the credit for ourselves. Even if the experts don't buy the ideas, we have an obligation to go back to the employees and let them know that we appreciated their interest and hope they will continue to show it.

OBSERVE BEHAVIOR

Another aspect of the supervisor's safety role is simply watching employees at work, looking for safe acts as well as unsafe ones. When we see them doing something that is safe, perhaps cleaning up a spill, closing a door someone else left open, smoothing down a rough or ragged place, we should automatically think about what's happening: An employee is *thinking* safety! It should be commended: nothing elaborate, just a remark like, "Hey, that's good thinking on your part!" Such a remark is just enough to let the employee know that we know, that we care, and that we are glad *they* care.

When we see employees doing something that's not according to safety standards, they are, in fact, not doing their jobs as they should be. It's not just an unsafe act, but poor performance.

We've already seen that the boss isn't a spy out to catch the criminals; but as we look for things being done correctly, we are also aware of mistakes or any behavior that affects the way the job is being done. Unless there is a repeat offender, our first reactions are additional training, reminders that the job is not being done correctly, and suggestions for improvement. If the offense is repeated consistently we obviously need to take action quickly and decisively. As we'll see later when we talk about the correction interview, it is best to have the employee suggest ideas for how such behavior can best be corrected.

As we look about us, we are looking for conditions; at the same time, we are looking for acts. We must always remember that it is not the condition that causes the injury to the equipment or the individual—it is the *act*. No one is injured by grease on the floor or an open bottom drawer of a filing cabinet. The injury occurs when someone slips and falls because of the grease or when someone runs into the drawer. If the grease wasn't there, the fall wouldn't have occurred; if the drawer had been closed, there would be no bruised or cut shins. Remove the condition and we remove the possibility of the act. This is why thinking safety is so important. If we get the employees to think safety, they'll see the possibility of errors or accidents and shut off the source of them.

Obviously, there are going to be some injuries, accidents, and equipment damage because of human error or equipment failure. We will see workers get hurt because they don't follow instructions or use a machine as it was designed to be used. In this case we cannot remove the condition. The condition may be all right for accident-free activity. However, there may be something missing in the environment. The employee may not be thinking safety. To some extent, that would be our fault. We may fail in seeing that all employees are conscious of the need for workmanship. It's the same reason we get disgruntled customers; it's the way we get low productivity and waste raw materials: Somebody isn't thinking as they should be thinking. Taking a shortcut, trying to save time, failing to put a guard up, or not considering the sharp end of a pencil—all lead to injury or damage. It's not carelessness; it's bad thinking or no thinking at all. Our job in these cases is to constantly get the employees to think about doing the job correctly, and keep ourselves always thinking about safety.

We also have a responsibility to see what happened to cause any kind of accident or injury. Usually, organizations have their own procedures for investigating such things, but the immediate supervisor can't shirk responsibility for finding out all about the causes and events as they took place. Naturally, there's no justification for trying to cover up any of the facts or the actions of any of the people involved. Accidents and injuries are too serious to hide anything that might lead to preventing them from happening again. Also, this is not a time for placing blame or pointing the finger at others. The main thing is to see what happened so it can be prevented from happening again.

PROVIDE DISCIPLINE

When unsafe acts occur—and it is human error that results in an unsafe action, *whether or not* injury or damage occurs—there is a need for discipline. It is the supervisor's job to administer this discipline. Discipline is never pleasant; it is most often dreaded, even avoided. But there is a purpose in discipline, and we err if we don't use it. If we do use it, though, it should be used wisely and well. There are some things that only discipline can accomplish, and if it is done correctly it may save a lot of grief and even injury in the future. For that reason, supervisors need to learn to practice good discipline, because it is very much a part of the supervisor's job to engage in constructive discipline.

Among other things, there are at least three things we can hope to accomplish with successful discipline.

1.   We can impress the individual and the others in the work force with the importance of safety. If we don't do it emotionally and with a threatening air of reprisal, the individuals involved will see that we take safety seriously; from now on, they will too.

2.   We can hope to change the future behavior of the individual involved in the problem. No matter how badly we hate to administer discipline, employees dislike it even more. If we handle it correctly, we can leave them with a good attitude about what has happened, but we're really looking to get behavior changed. If this happens, then we did a good job.

3.   We want to prevent future failures on the part of the employees. When employees see one of their group being disciplined, they can easily identify with that person and realize that it could be them. Just as this has its effect on the individual, it has an effect on the whole group. As supervisors we have a good opportunity to take advantage of this feeling by pointing out how the discipline can be avoided. While we have everyone's attention, we can do some effective training, too.

We have to continue to remember that it is the action, not the injury, that caused the discipline. Even if no one is hurt, or there is no shutdown, or there is no damage to the equipment, the action was wrong, hence we used the discipline. Employees need to understand this and can understand it easily enough if we stress correct and safe acts, not just injury prevention and damage avoidance.

GROWTH OF THE SUPERVISOR

We've seen it pointed out clearly that the supervisor isn't supposed to be an expert in safety and accident prevention, but this doesn't mean that the supervisor avoids knowing anything about safety or accidents or how to avoid injury. Good supervisors are constantly trying to improve their knowledge in all areas of the job, including safety. They are also trying ways of increasing their *concern* for safety, and getting their employees more interested in safety. All of this means continued self-improvement, self-study, and participating in other kinds of growth opportunities. They will read and study and reflect and watch and listen and continue to learn. If there are seminars or books or lectures on safety—any aspect—they will attend or participate or take advantage in any way they can. The idea is to grow in every area, including safety.

There's another aspect of the growth pattern of good supervisors. As they see more and more reason to think safety, they will find more and more reason to practice it *off the job* as well as on it. They think about using seat belts in the car, they drive defensively, they recognize the hazards of the road, and they think safety. The same is true at home, on vacation, in the workshop, or in the yard. These supervisors don't put on and take off their safety-thinking hats. They are always thinking about safety— without *consciously* thinking about it. It just becomes that much a part of their lives. Because of this, it isn't much of a problem for them to think about safety on the job. It is this kind of growth that makes the supervisor effective in getting others to think safety too. Safety is truly "a way of life."

Conducting Safety Meetings

If we ask the typical employee how he or she feels about safety meetings, we get something between laughing and crying! In many organizations such meetings are seen as jokes or boring or a time to sleep (through a safety movie), or, at best, a waste of time. Here is the scene that is repeated month after month in many organizations:

The employees straggle in, lethargy prevailing. They are disinterested, show no enthusiasm, plop themselves down in the chairs at the back of the room, and wait for whatever happens. They may get to listen to some figures on lost-time accidents or hear that there has been an award for the "safe employee of the month." The lights are finally turned out and there is another movie shown on some aspect of safety. It will vary from a gory one showing all kinds of bloody scenes, to a very technical film showing the inner workings of some instrument or procedure, to a humorous movie with cartoons. The lights go back on at the conclusion of the film and there is the usual, "Any questions?" of which there are usually none. Then there is the final pep talk about going out there and being safe—or a threat about not causing us to look bad on the next report. The end result? Not much happens in the way of causing people to be more safe.

The only exception to this is when there is a serious accident.

If someone is cut badly, or a life is lost, or even if it's only a serious fire or explosion with no injuries, for a little while there is much interest. At the safety meeting there are questions; the attention is there and everyone wants to know about the details. When they leave the meeting they are talking about the accident, and most likely they will be safety-conscious for a little while. But now it's too late. This may prevent the next accident, but it won't help the one we've just had. It's not very practical to have an accident in order to teach safety. This means that our safety meetings need to be better, just as our whole approach to safety must be the best. Let's see how to run better meetings.

Conducting Better Meetings

The simplest thing that can be done to have a successful meeting is to have a goal before the meeting is even planned. If the idea is to motivate, then there should be some kind of motivating activity; if it is to inform, then every effort should be made to see that all things done are informative, and that the correct techniques are used for informing. If the purpose is to prompt discussion of ways to solve a serious, potential safety problem, then everything should aim at getting productive discussion. If corrective action is being taken because of some kind of violation, then the meeting should be conducive to discipline or correction. Having established a goal and set our sights on that goal, we then begin to plan the meeting with the participants and the goal in mind. As best we can, we inform the participants ahead of time of the goal. If there's a problem to be discussed, we let them know what the problem is, so they can come with thoughts about their problem. If we are looking for solutions, we let them know the problem and the parameters of the solutions, so they'll come in with some suggestions.

If possible, we want to involve the employees as much as we can. It's even better if we involve them ahead of time. This means that we can have them conduct a portion of the meeting, be prepared to speak on certain parts of the problem being presented, and offer assistance in setting up the meetings. We can also have them work in teams to develop certain solutions to possible problems we've encountered. The whole point is that they will have more commitment to those things they've been involved in, and they'll be more likely to have usable solutions when they're asked about things in the future. Another advantage of getting employees involved in the total meeting process (from planning to execution) is that this is one of the best ways to reduce the adversarial relationship that tends to develop over matters like safety. Too often such things like this become "management against labor," instead of a common problem to be solved jointly.

Having set a goal and made efforts to get the employees involved in *their* meeting, the meeting is conducted in a serious way, but not *too* serious. A safety meeting is never a fun-and-games subject, but that doesn't mean that the meetings cannot be conducted in a friendly manner. The key is for the leader to be a leader: positive, assertive, unhesitant in speech. The leader should take charge, say something meaningful, do something meaningful, and end on a note of high confidence. The leader will take advantage of any and every resource available, including (especially) the employees. The objectives have been met when the employees feel they've gotten something that affects them in their jobs, that problems have been dealt with if not solved, that they've been consulted and allowed to offer solutions about their own safety and the safety of the organization, and when they leave resolved to *think* safety.

CONDUCTING CORRECTIVE INTERVIEWS

A final responsibility of supervisors is to deal with those who've committed unsafe acts. Often there needs to be corrective action taken, or some form of discipline. We must remember that the correction comes even when an unsafe act is *observed*, not just when an accident occurs or when there is damage to the equipment or property. There are three purposes of the corrective interview and any subsequent action:

1. Find the reason for the unsafe act.

2. Correct the behavior, dealing with the specific action that took place.

3. Prevent others from committing the same act in the future.

The idea of conducting the interview before an unsafe act results in an accident is obvious. If we talk to the individuals involved and take action (if it is required), then we will have prevented the serious consequences—and perhaps stopped the act from resulting in serious damage to life or limb. We're also preventing others from committing the unsafe act and keeping others from the same fate.

There are those who say, "It's going to take a serious accident to ever get anybody around here to take safety seriously." That is sometimes sadly true, but one purpose of the corrective interview is to call attention to the unsafe act, hopefully to the extent that people will take notice *before* the accident occurs! It shows that management's policy and practice are in agreement. This kind of consistency gets a lot of attention, much more than the often-used "lip service" that exists in some organizations.

Let's look at some steps in conducting the corrective interview. They are simple and easy to use, but very effective if followed reasonably closely.

Step 1. Put the employee at ease. As much as possible, we should try to let the employee relax so that it won't appear that there is a trial going on. Since it is a corrective interview, it isn't going to be easy for the employee to completely relax, nor do we want the person to become so relaxed that the seriousness of the situation is lost. We want to convey a simple message: we can no longer tolerate the kind of action we have seen; therefore we are taking action to see that it doesn't happen again.

Step 2. Explain the situation. This is the time when we aren't going to argue the situation; we're going to point out what we expected and what we actually saw happen. We're going to point out the organization's standards and where these standards have been missed. It isn't a time when we offer an opportunity for debate as to whether or not the policy, standard, or expectation is a good one. It is simply a time when we say this is the way it is.

Step 3. Avoid putting the employee on the defensive. All we have to do is ask "Why?" and we'll be in an argument with the employee, defending the action. A much better approach is to ask, "What do you suggest as a way to prevent this kind of action from happening again?" and, "How can we see that you and others don't repeat it again?"

Some rules:

Support positive suggestions and solutions as much as possible. Employees will be more likely to follow their own suggestions than those imposed on them by others—and most often they're harder on themselves than we would be.

Don't become defensive. There's no reason, nor is this the time, to argue the merits of the rules.

Deal with the standards and the violations. Put all actions in proper perspective to these.

Make sure the employee knows the correct procedure. See that he or she tells us what is right, proper, and according to the rule.

Explain the consequences of continued unsafe acts. Just as this action is timely and swift, so will future actions against violations of safety rules be.

Leave the interview on a positive note. Set a time for review of the worker's actions and a time for commendation when good performance is achieved.

Follow up on the suggestions made by the employee. Use them if possible, commend them to others, reinforce employees who use the new procedures which have been accepted.

CONCLUSION

Safety is a way of life and all should strive to follow it. It is a mental process, however, and that means we have to think safety so that we are safe on purpose, rather than by accident. Safety cannot be turned on and off; it must become a way of life, literally. We are to be safe at home as well as on the job. When we watch our children or people walking down the street, we should be subconsciously thinking "That's not safe to play there or to run that way or to walk on that slick place." This kind of thinking will easily transfer to the job. We will still have accidents, people will still get hurt, equipment will be damaged, and there will be lost time from unsafe acts; but there will be fewer of these and the results will be less serious. That's what safety is all about!

SECTION

PERSONNEL
CONSIDERATIONS

CHAPTER

17

MANAGING HUMAN PERFORMANCE EFFECTIVELY THROUGH PERFORMANCE APPRAISAL

Introduction and Background

STEPHEN L. COHEN
CABOT L. JAFFEE

Portions of this chapter were adapted from the *Managing Human Performance* skills training program published and copyrighted by Assessment Designs, Inc., Orlando, Florida, 1980, 1983. All Rights Reserved.

To say that performance appraisal is undergoing a technological evolution is the human resource management understatement of the decade. Nonetheless, evolution is a gradual process and as such most organizations still have a long way to go to make their performance appraisal systems effective. The purpose of this chapter is to offer an overview of the appraisal process, emphasizing how it can be managed most effectively to produce the greatest return on investment for the organization. This perspective alone, that is, the relation of performance appraisal to improved performance and increased productivity, has done as much as anything to promote and sustain this evolutionary process. With increasing world market competition, organizations have rightfully been concerned with increasing productivity and the need to more effectively manage the cyclical nature of the economy. The demands for more flexibility and professional management practices to meet this need have become more and more apparent. Human resources management has emerged as a critical element in successfully meeting these demands through the more effective management of people. In short, organizations have recognized and continued to notice how critical a role its people will play in the technical evolution that will take place during the remaining part of the century and beyond. Productivity and performance improvement are not just passing fancies. They will ultimately determine which organizations sustain and grow over the next 25 years.

A second perspective yielding an increased awareness of the importance of managing human performance effectively is the evolution of participative management practices into being a more accepted way of organizational life. Despite the United States' claim that it is actually responsible for the "Japanese Art of Management" (Pascale and Athos, 1981: 200), it took a relatively severe economic recession and increased world market competition to open the eyes of American business to the need for a different approach to performance management. Although quality circles and Theory Z practices per se may not be the panacea to this state of affairs, their message is clear. Traditional performance management practices need to be revised if the growing worldwide competitive demands are to be met and conquered.

A third, more humanistic perspective, is the genuine need for employees to self-actualize more than ever before. While unemployment may be relatively high, the majority of our work force has seen many of its lower-order needs (for example, physiological and security) pretty well satisfied, leaving the higher-order needs of self-esteem and self-actualization the object of greater quest. More than ever before people want to know how they're doing, where they're going, and how they're going to get there. In addition, they feel the "right" to know these answers and they are demanding them. As such, it follows that they want to participate in their own work destiny to whatever extent possible and will probably be more productive when they do.

Finally, and in an odd way, the greatest influence on the changing function of performance appraisal in the United States has been the legal perspective added in recent years. Such legislative actions as Title VII of the 1964 Civil Rights Act, the 1978 Equal Employment Opportunity Commission Guidelines on Employee Selection Procedures, the Privacy Act of 1974, the Freedom of Information Act of 1974, and an ever-increasing number of court cases all address the requirements for fairness and nondiscrimination in personnel decision making. And most recently the federal government itself has mandated performance evaluation reform with the prohibition of rankings (1978 Civil Service Reform Act) and insistence on better merit review systems to replace the more traditional ones relying primarily on seniority.

These four changing perspectives on the management of human resources already have had and will continue to have significant impact on changing the human resource tool most used today in evaluating employees—performance appraisal. This chapter and the next will explore these perspectives and their relationship to more effectively managing employees through performance appraisal. The topics that will be covered include a background of the appraisal process, managing human performance for results, the manager's tools in performance appraisal, performance appraisal training, and applications beyond appraisal.

BACKGROUND

Appraisal is not new to organizations or society at large. Indeed, judgments of value or worth are assigned almost daily to things done as well as to people. In the United States, performance appraisal systems being used by business have been largely influenced by systems originally developed in the federal government.

In 1842, Congress passed a law requiring the heads of executive departments to make a yearly report evaluating whether each clerk had been effectively employed or ". . . whether the removal of some to permit the appointment of others would lead to a better dispatch of the public business" (Lopez, 1968). In the years that followed, a variety of evaluation systems were developed, tested, and ultimately abandoned. One system, developed in 1879 for the Pension Office, attempted to measure employees' performances by counting the number of errors they made in a year! Then, as the turn of the century approached, came the military performance rating system that President Benjamin Harrison attempted to mandate for use on the civilian sector, with somewhat unspectacular results.

Performance evaluation systems, however, were more readily implemented in American business than the civil service. While it is not clear exactly which corporation was the first to implement a formal system for appraising employees, General Motors Corporation had such a mechanism for its executives as early as 1918. It was after World War II, however, that an earnest, widely pervasive move toward formal, regularized, written systems began.

By the early 1950s, 61% of organizations surveyed were using some type of appraisal process (Spriegel, 1962: 79). And since then the percentage of organizations using a formal performance appraisal system has been determined to range about 75% (Lazer and Wikstrom, 1977: 8) to 89% (Locher and Teel, 1977: 246). In government settings, 76% of the 50 major U.S. cities (Lahco, Stearns, and Villere, 1979: 113) and 100% of 39 state governments (Feild and Holley, 1975: 146) were found to be employing performance appraisal systems. And while 95% of large businesses (more than 500 employees) was greater than the 84% of small businesses found to be using formal appraisal systems, this small difference points out that indeed performance appraisal has become an accepted management tool in organizations today (Locher and Teel, 1977: 246).

Suffice it to say that well over 90% of organizations use some type of appraisal systems, be it formal or informal. Yet dissatisfaction and problems with these systems appear clear. A 1977 Conference Board report noted that over half of the nearly 300 organizations surveyed had developed new appraisal systems within the last three years (Lazer and Wikstrom, 1977: 9). And in a nationwide survey of 3500 organizations, it was shown that the most often mentioned human resource concern was the appraisal system used (Xerox Learning Systems, 1978). To make matters worse, the procedures, systems, and purposes of appraisal in use today vary widely. While the early uses and currently most frequent uses are for appraising the value or worth of the employee to determine if continued service is justified, more recent uses have included employee counseling, training and development, human resources and succession planning, identifying potential for promotional decisions, job evaluation, legal defensibility against discrimination claims, and of course salary administration. And while administrative uses (for example, salary, promotion, retention, and discharge) appear predominant, the use of performance appraisal in developmental counseling and training is not far behind (DeVries, et al., 1980: 24).

Furthermore, the types of appraisal methods vary widely as well. For example, one recent survey found MBO (management by objectives) to be clearly an accepted practice in many companies, especially for managers in nongovernmental settings. And the higher the management level, the more likely MBO was to be used. Essay or open-ended types of evaluations were the next most prevalent method uncovered, while behaviorally oriented and trait-rating scales, critical incidents, and checklists were mentioned relatively infrequently. However, in state government organizations, rating scales were the predominant method reportedly used, while MBO was not mentioned at all (DeVries, et al., 1980: 19).

In summary, the degree of participation of subordinates in evaluation, an emphasis on results versus behavior, the underlying philosophy of evaluation (evaluation for the benefit of increasing organizational productivity versus evaluation as a personal growth experience for the employee), the format, and the disposition of written reports are some of the elements that have been combined in unique ways to meet individual organizations' needs. So, while there is general agreement within organizations today that some sort of regular employee appraisal is necessary, there appears to be no one uniform method or objective utilized. Perhaps this variance in method is due, in part, to the fact that organizations have identified a multitude of purposes for appraisal. But with its widespread use and long history, why has performance appraisal by and large not worked very well, and why are so many organizations continually reviewing and revising their current systems to make them more productive? It appears that the answer to this question lies in the traditional focus of appraisal, and that as the emerging perspectives have indicated, a new look at appraisal systems is critical if they are to yield positive results. The traditional focus on a final appraisal evaluation at the end of the "year" must shift to that of an ongoing management of human performance if appraisal is to yield the dividends invested in it.

The search for the ideal performance appraisal system has been going on for years, and only recently has the literature begun to define some consistent characteristics of the effective performance management system. Some of these characteristics are:

It is an ongoing process rather than a once-a-year or twice-a-year review.

It is participative in that the employee contributes to the setting of objectives and the reviewing of performance.

It involves two-way communications between employee and boss rather than one-way communications from the boss.

It is a face-to-face system rather than one handled through written communications and forms.

It is based on performance criteria and not personality traits.

It is based on job-relevant behaviors and not unrelated factors.

It is based on the employee's own job performance and is not comparative to other employees doing the same or different jobs.

Its emphasis on positive feedback is the same as on negative feedback.

It offers constructive and specific actions for improving upon weaknesses.

It separates the appraisal of current job performance from potential for future jobs.

All of these points appear to blend comfortably with preferences of employees. The proper components alone, however, will not necessarily result in an effective system. An equally important component is the individual manager who serves as the critical link between the system and the individual employee. The manager is responsible for integrating the employee's individual performance goals with those of the overall organization. This is exactly where most systems fall apart.

The real problem with most performance appraisal system is the manager's responsible for conducting them. First, managers do not effectively communicate to their subordinates the performance and objectives they expect the subordinates to achieve. Second, managers have difficulty observing and assessing the performance of others. Third, managers are unable to effectively document or support their observations of another's performance. And fourth, managers are unable to clearly convey or communicate these observations to their people in a way that stimulates a desire for improvement. Most employees crave such information and need it to make any significant steps toward improving their performance.

Assess, document, and communicate—these are the three essentials of an effective performance appraisal system. Yet few organizations integrate these ingredients into their performance appraisal training and policies. As such, most performance appraisal practices yield questionable results. More adequate appraisal could help to ameliorate the productivity decline.

The quality of the relationship between employee and supervisor is at the heart of employee performance and productivity. Orders for a change in personal job behavior cannot be issued. Instead, a climate must be created in which performance change is possible and rewarding. This process is highly complex and calls for specific skills. Very few managers and supervisors have the necessary skills for effective management without formal training. Effective management of human resources, however, is the bottom line of any solution to our productivity problems.

The focus must be on the interaction between employee and boss, because it is only through honest, personal communication and task assessment and direction that superior performance will develop. Productivity will begin to pick up when employees feel they're participating in setting their objectives—not only for their careers, but for their day-to-day activities as well. Successful development of an employee directly involves the manager. The process of interaction deals with setting objectives for job behavior together—and making such behavior not only goal-oriented and future-oriented, but a matter of day-to-day concern. Successful development of a subordinate means the proper and effective use of a human resource.

The individual benefits to be expected from improved productivity are increased job satisfaction, heightened awareness of the personal values to be derived from the free enterprise system, and a greater feeling of self-worth.

In order for on-the-job performance appraisal systems to work, they must be designed to develop the skills of managers in ways that will make subordinates want to do a better job and be involved in the company's goals. It follows that, when properly motivated, the subordinate will increase personal productivity and, in turn, that of the organization. In spite of this logical position, the development of such a system continues to be difficult for organizations.

The solution lies in a highly integrated, pragmatic, and logical system in which the performance appraisal process can readily fit. The key to the system is that it must be total. All ingredients or components must be in operation if maximum results are to follow. The Managing Human Performance (MHP) Cycle, and explanation that follow later in this chapter provide the framework likely to produce results.

MANAGING HUMAN PERFORMANCE FOR RESULTS

A description of the relationship between managers and subordinates necessary to effectively manage human performance for results is provided in Figure 17.1, The Managing Human Performance Cycle.

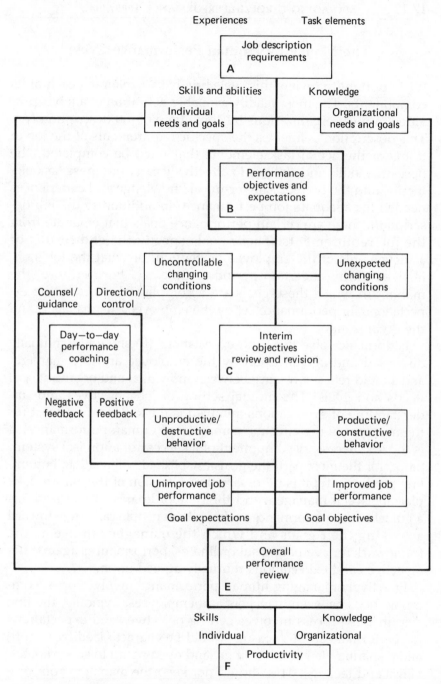

FIGURE 17.1. The Managing Human Performance Cycle

17.11

The Managing Human Performance Cycle

It's important to review this cycle briefly by explaining each of its components. The most readily available definition of a job is provided in most organizations by some type of job description (A). This description delineates the specific requirements of the job in terms of the actual task elements that must be completed, the necessary skills and abilities to effectively carry out these task elements, and the prerequisite technical knowledge and experiences needed for adequate job performance. In addition to the job description, there are certain performance goals that emanate from the job requirements. These goals specify the end results or achievements of the employee on the job, or what the job's objectives during a certain period of time are. Furthermore, the manner in which these goals are accomplished refers to the expectations for performance set by the employee, the manager, and the organization.

Performance objectives and expectations (B) should be mutually discussed and agreed upon by the employee and the manager and should reflect a balance between individual and organizational needs and goals. The mutual setting of job objectives and understanding of expectations involved is the key starting point for the manager in the effective managing of human performance. It is the first necessary component of a successful appraisal system. Since, for the most part, the goals established will relate to bottom-line productivity, it is necessary that a session of this nature take place between managers and their subordinates. It will serve as a guideline for performance within which people can strive toward achieving their goals and which the manager can use as the framework for evaluating subordinates' performances against the objectives and expectations mutually agreed upon.

Effectively managing human performance involves open communications between managers and employees. Typically, the first step in this process involves setting objectives and expectations for performance. This season should be characterized by negotiating, sharing views and feelings, and opening up to subordinates' views and feelings. This should not keep the manager from presenting a specific list of objectives, criteria, and performance standards, but employees should be permitted to do the same. The more open the communications between manager and employee, the greater the likelihood that commitment to achieving the agreed-upon objectives will be shared. Such a commitment will undoubtedly yield greater results.

As can be well understood, even the best-laid plans often go awry. And such may be the case with the agreed-upon objectives and expectations. One expectation that is difficult to accept is that conditions in the world and the job won't ever change. Indeed, it is paradoxical that the only statement that can be made with any degree of certainty about change is that it is a given and one of the few constants in our lives. Knowing this, the manager must be prepared to periodically review the objectives and expectations set, with an open mind to appropriately revising them as directed by unexpected and/or uncontrollable changing conditions. Frequently, the interim objectives review and revision process (C) will be initiated by subordinates who recognize the impact of the changing conditions on their job objectives far earlier than the manager might. The manager should keep an open mind about revising objectives, while maintaining the objectives' legitimacy so that revisions are the exception rather than the rule.

Many organizations have set up elaborate appraisal systems that emphasize the goal-setting component. MBO (management by objectives) has almost become part of management jargon. But one reason many well-designed MBO programs have been unsuccessful is that mutual goal setting and using the attainment of specific objectives as the barometer for evaluating performance is not enough to make the system work. Without question, the most blatantly absent component of most appraisal systems is the informal coaching of employee performance on a day-to-day basis. Without feedback, counsel, or direction, employees cannot all be expected to stay whithin the framework of the guidelines for performance. Continual performance monitoring is the second necessary component for a successful appraisal system.

Day-to-day performance coaching (D) should not necessarily be taken literally, since one of the most difficult challenges as a manager is to strike a fine balance between staying too close to subordinates and giving them the freedom to effectively perform in their own manner and style. However, relatively frequent interaction with subordinates cannot hurt that relationship, if handled judiciously. For those who aren't performing as expected, feedback, guidance, and direction will get them back on the right track. For those who are doing fine, such feedback will not only encourage them to continue their good work, but possibly provide them with ideas for stretching to even higher levels of performance. Just how much interaction with subordinates is desirable and the nature of it will depend on the work characteristics and performance of each. This is the manager's decision entirely, and again, one of the most difficult chores—that is, sensing the appropriate timing for performance coaching. But regardless of timing, there are certain guidelines and skills required for effectively conducting such sessions.

With a clear understanding of the job requirements, mutually acceptable performance objectives and expectations, and frequent and timely day-to-day performance coaching, both productive/constructive job behavior and improved job performance can be expected. Of course, the more feedback is based on accurate assessment and documentation of job-relevant performance, the more constructive this communication is likely to be. But if managing human performance was that easy, the manager's job wouldn't be that challenging. Some people need more day-to-day coaching than others, and even within the upper end of the performance continuum of "satisfactory" to "outstanding," it is likely that certain areas still need development and improvement.

The overall performance review (E) affords the opportunity to provide subordinates with a summary of their performance during the designated period which the review covers. Organizational policies vary regarding how often these formal reviews occur, but typically they are conducted semiannually or annually. The manager's responsibility during this review is to provide subordinates with an evaluation of their performance as it relates to the originally agreed-upon objectives and expectations. In providing this review, it is appropriate to evaluate the subordinates' skill and knowledge levels as they relate to the accomplishment of the objectives. The overall performance review should also be used to discuss areas for improvement in the subordinates' job performance and ways in which such improvement can be achieved.

While the formal review is a natural part of almost all performance appraisal systems, it is frequently misguided and unproductive. But, as the third necessary component of an effective appraisal system, the overall performance review must be conducted properly.

As can be noted from the model's cycle, two things emerge from the overall performance review. First, it sets the stage for beginning the appraisal process again by considering individual and organizational needs and goals, some of which may have changed in establishing new performance objectives and expectations. This, of course, leads to day-to-day coaching, interim objectives review, and finally the formal overall review. The system is clearly integrated and must be in order for effective appraisal to take place. The omission of any component will severely reduce the likelihood of the total system working.

The second thing emerging from the formal review is the actual result of the entire integrated performance appraisal system—productivity. And productivity at the level desired by the individual employee and the organization is a natural result of such a system.

The Role of Ongoing Feedback in the MHP Cycle

The role of the manager in the MHP cycle is mostly designed to be informal and ongoing rather than once a year. Indeed the amount of actual time devoted to establishing and communicating objectives and expectations and reviewing overall performance is minor relative to that spent managing the employee to meet those objectives and expectations over any performance review period. This fact alone supports the more active role of the manager in observing and documenting performance and providing both positive and negative feedback when and where appropriate. Of course, as noted earlier, the key to effective feedback is collecting accurate, job-relevant, and measurable performance samples that reflect actual behavioral observation rather than inference or subjectivity. It must be kept in mind that simply observing and measuring performance does not necessarily influence performance. It is what is done with this information after the measurement that actually can influence performance. This is why feedback is so critical.

Remember also that objectives and expectations that have been mutually established with the subordinate always stand as the yardstick for performance. If care has been taken to *observe* a wide variety of the subordinates' activities, and the observations have been *documented*, giving feedback will be easier and more readily accepted by subordinates. When subordinates are not doing what they are supposed to, or an individual is having problems achieving an objective, then coaching is necessary.

While coaching and reviewing overall performance are both part of the appraisal cycle, there are several differences in the interactions. Coaching is less formal and occurs as frequently as is necessary. Often coaching may occur when an employee comes to the manager with a problem. If the manager is open and receptive, advantage can be taken of this opportunity to help a subordinate. A coaching session should deal primarily with a few specific behaviors that are affecting a particular situation. The purpose in coaching a subordinate is to redirect or change his or her behavior in order to improve performance.

In the overall performance review session, all the subordinate's performances that have occurred over a certain period of time (annually or biannually) in many situations will be reviewed. Waiting until the review session to alert the subordinate to problem areas in performance will be too late to give him or her a chance to improve or correct improper actions. The following comparison chart shows how these objectives are generally outlined.

If coaching and feedback are used effectively on a regular basis, then an overall review will hold no surprises for subordinates. They will know all along how they are doing their jobs and will be more willing to enter into a discussion about overall performance.

Does feedback actually work? This is one of the few questions in human resource management that can be answered definitively. The research and organizational evidence is replete with results

Objectives of Coaching	Objectives of Overall Performance Review
1. To allow open discussion about a *specific problem* area that must be faced.	1. To review *overall* job performance over a specified time period.
2. To provide timely feedback on performance.	2. To measure progress made toward achieving objectives and expectations.
3. To clarify any misunderstanding.	3. To discuss and understand evaluation and ratings of the subordinate's overall performance.
4. To change or redirect behaviors that are unsatisfactory and to reinforce behaviors that are satisfactory.	4. To express continued interest in the subordinate's overall performance.
5. To openly express interest in the subordinate's performance.	5. To set the stage for reestablishment of job objectives and expectations.
	6. To lay the foundation for personal and career development.

showing that properly conducted feedback improves not only on-the-job performance, but morale and satisfaction as well. Furthermore, good, frequent, and constructive feedback motivates employees to not only achieve their goals but to go far beyond them.

THE MANAGER'S ROLE IN PERFORMANCE APPRAISAL

To this point, we have offered a good deal of background on the overall appraisal process and how, if performed effectively, it will result in improved employee and ultimately organizational performance. Before moving on in the next chapter to the tools available to managers for effective performance appraisals and the type of training necessary to provide managers with the skills required in the appraisal process, a summary of the manager's role in this whole process and why it is the manager's responsibility to manage subordinate performance is offered.

Most managers know why it's their responsibility to manage their subordinates' performance. In the end it's their job to produce bottom-line results through people. Authority can be delegated to get things done, but the *responsibility* for getting them done can never be delegated. It's the manager's job to see that work is completed according to the standards set by him or her and by the organization. If this isn't accomplished, barring uncontrollable events, then the situation probably wasn't managed well enough. The responsibility will always be the manager's: to manage the department and the people in it effectively and to keep everything moving toward a goal.

Contrary to popular belief, this doesn't mean keeping everyone happy and being popular. It doesn't help very much to be popular with subordinates in the face of declining productivity of their unit. The answer to "Why is managing subordinates' the manager's responsibility?" is really very simple: *productivity will be raised when done right*—and raising productivity is what management is all about. Of course, numbers are not all there is to productivity. Managing human performance means being aware that people are humans, not machines. Bearing down on people as though they can be accelerated at will, like automobiles, only results in poor morale, lack of cooperation, alienation from the job—even sabotage. On the other hand, learning to work *with* people instead of just *working* them results in the kind of productivity that adds up to the numbers that impress stockholders and consumers.

REFERENCES

Civil Service Reform Act, Pub. L. No. 95-454, 92 Stat. IIII, 1978.

DeVries, D. L., A. M. Morrison, S. L. Shullman, and M. L. Gerlach. *Performance Appraisal on the Line* (Tech. Rep. No. 16). North Carolina: Center for Creative Leadership, 1980.

Equal Employment Opportunity Act, Pub. L. No. 88-352, 78 Stat. 241, 1964.

Equal Employment Opportunity Commission Uniform Guidelines on Employee Selection Procedures. *Federal Register,* 1978, *43* (166), 38290–38309.

Federal Privacy Act, Pub. L. No. 93-579, 88 Stat. 1896, 1974.

Feild, H. S. and W. H. Holly. "Performance Appraisal—An Analysis of Statewide Practices." *Public Personnel Management, 4* (3), 1975, 145–150.

Freedom of Information Act, Pub. L. No. 93-502, 88 Stat. 1561, 1974.

Lahco, K. J., G. K. Stearns, and M. F. Villere. "A Study of Employee Appraisal Systems of Major Cities in the United States. *Public Personnel Management, 8* (2), 1979, 111–125.

Lazer, R. I. and W. S. Wikstrom. *Appraising Managerial Performance: Current Practices and Future Directions* (Conference Board Rep. No. 723). New York: Conference Board, 1977.

Locher, A. H., and K. S. Teel. Performance Appraisal—A Survey of Current Practices. *Personnel Journal, 56* (5), 1977, 245–247; 254.

Lopez, F. M. Jr. *Evaluating Employee Performance.* International Personnel Management Association, 1968.

Pascale, R. T., and A. G. Athos. *The Art of Japanese Management.* New York: Simon and Schuster, 1981.

Spriegel, W. "Company Practices in Appraising Interviewing." *Personnel, 39* (3), 1962, 77–83.

Xerox Learning Systems, *Exchange,* internal communications, Stamford, Conn., 1978.

18

MANAGING HUMAN PERFORMANCE EFFECTIVELY THROUGH PERFORMANCE APPRAISAL

The Manager's Tools

CABOT L. JAFFEE
STEPHEN L. COHEN

In the previous chapter we attempted to give the background of performance appraisal in this country as well as various methods used to appraise people of their performance in organizations. All this fits into a systematic development of a process which starts with goals and objectives and ends with the specific feedback re-

18.1

garding an individual's performance. This chapter emphasizes the tools necessary to perform effective performance appraisals, including forms and scales as well as training for managers and the uses to be made of the information. Overall, this and the preceding chapter provide both an overview and a historical perspective on the process and an in-depth look at how and why it is to be carried out.

PROCEDURES, POLICIES, AND FORMS

As noted in the previous chapter, around 90% of business organizations are estimated to have formal performance appraisal systems (Locker and Teel, 1977: 246), and performance appraisal systems are more likely to be used at lower and middle management levels in an organization than at top management levels. But they are clearly an accepted procedure in virtually all organizations for all levels.

The most often used approach to performance appraisal according to Lazer and Wikstrom (1977: 22) was management by objectives (MBO). In descending order of frequency, essays, behavioral and/or trait-rating scales, critical incidents, and checklists were used. While many different appraisal systems appear to be used, there is a strong tendency to emphasize the rating or description of broadly defined traits rather than specific behaviors.

In terms of the procedures necessary to install a performance appraisal program, it first must be introduced to the organization. This can perhaps be best accomplished through the involvement of respected line managers rather than strictly personnel people. The goal of the installation process is to have employees relate the performance appraisal program to their work.

After the introduction of the program, managers need training in the rationale for the program policies and procedures to be followed in conducting performance appraisal, as well as training in how to set goals and objectives, observe and document behavior, coach, and give performance feedback. Perhaps the most critical step in the process, however, is to maintain it. Managers must be reminded to conduct the appraisals as they have been taught to do, as well as to solve a variety of problems which may come up about the appraisal process itself.

As in the case of all personnel procedures, evaluation becomes critical. The organization must be able to answer questions about whether the intended purposes or outcomes are being accomplished. This may necessitate surveying managers who are using the process, looking at the actual forms filled out in support of the process, questioning employees, or a host of other possible strategies which will help in evaluating the merits of the program.

The approach based most firmly on job-related behaviors is behaviorally anchored rating scales (BARS). This process requires managers to make repeated judgments about actual job behaviors as to their level of desirability. These judgments are ultimately given scale point ratings and used as the basis for judgment about a person's performance. Managers' lack of receptivity to BARS, even though theoretically sound, indicates how cumbersome the system can be. A number of other performance measurement systems that are far less complex make up the majority of performance appraisals used. *Ranking* of employees on certain predetermined characteristics on overall job performance is perhaps the most common. This forced distribution system, which insures that someone must be last, can be further refined by placing employees in groupings according to some forced distribution. The major weaknesses of this system are the lack of good developmental information generated, the difficulty of distributing people according to a predetermined distribution when the numbers may be small, or the fact that employees may actually be performing quite equally.

A very common system involves managers writing summary paragraphs about a person's strengths and weaknesses. These can be only as good as the information gathered. One common system is called the *critical incident method,* in which managers keep a record of all incidents, good or bad, that occur on the job. If done conscientiously, this can provide good information upon which to base an appraisal. The checklist, or graphic rating scale, consists of a form upon which descriptions of a person's work-related characteristics may be listed. The manager is required to place a mark on a scale or select the qualities most or least like the person being evaluated. These systems can also only be as effective as the information being used by the rater. Therefore, if the basis for comparison of people is good, the system will work, but if the information does not allow for adequate differentiation, the system cannot work well.

Management by objectives consists of a manager and subordinate setting work objectives and the standards by which the attainment of these objectives will be evaluated. Essentially this method needs no particular forms, but rather a strategy for boss and subordinate to arrive at reasonable, measurable objectives. This can certainly be done on a blank sheet of paper.

The procedure and policies surrounding a performance appraisal system, as well as the particular forms or scales used to document performance, cannot work without sufficient training necessary to overcome many problems. These may range from managers interpreting factors differently, placing different levels of importance on different factors, and a lack of understanding of the proper information to consider.

THE RELATIONSHIP BETWEEN MANAGER AND SUBORDINATE

Probably the most powerful tool available to managers today is the relationship they share with their subordinates. Taking advantage of this relationship in the positive sense will continue to produce improved performance and an atmosphere of collaboration in which all employees work toward the same goals as the organization's. Making the most of this relationship is not easy. It takes a concerted effort and a true sensitivity to the needs of the employee. What makes this even more burdensome are the changes in employees' work values that have taken place in the last several years and which promise to continue to develop and change in the coming years as society encourages increased independence, advanced technology, improved education, and higher levels of the quality of life. Understanding these changes and what managers can do to work within them will be paramount to managers' success. Let's take a look at some of these issues.

Changes in Employees' Work Values

There have been significant changes in employees' work values over the past few years. Employees want to know where they stand. They're demanding more feedback, they're less willing to work just because it's expected of them, and they're much more interested in seeing how far they can go. Today's employees want a lot more from their organization than just salary. They want—and expect—to find out how they're performing on the job.

Today's employees are taking the initiative by asking for a chance to discuss job performance with their supervisors. They want their supervisors to spell out exactly what's required of them on the job, and they want to help set some of those job-related objectives themselves. They have a lot of questions about their future with the organization, and they're looking for opportunities to develop a real career. They're more interested in achieving, accomplishing, and being recognized for their accomplishments than they are (and this is true) in money, benefits, and other forms of financial compensation.

Today's employees disprove the myths and/or rationalizations promoted by organizations unwilling or unable to face the fact that people do not mind being evaluated if the appraisal system is fair and they understand it thoroughly. This is precisely why employees want to know the rules for evaluation and prefer to help establish them whenever possible.

The key to effective performance appraisal, then, is the open and constructive exchange of information between the manager and the subordinate. Start with the premise that most people want to do good work but don't always know how to go about it. That's why they'll look for opportunities to be more productive, and thus be worth more to their organization and themselves.

What Can Managers Do To Help Employees Be More Productive?

Managers should be willing and able to delegate responsibility; they should know exactly what to do to get better performance from their people without turning them off. They should learn how to associate their own and their unit's performance with the way their subordinates perform. Managers should realize that employees will accept negative feedback if it is constructive and offered in a manner that maintains the employee's self-esteem. Managers should understand that time spent on performance appraisal is well worth the result in improved performance. Finally, managers should be aware that most people are interested in working to improve themselves beyond their current levels and do care about their organization's performance.

In sum, people really do care where they stand with their supervisor or immediate superior—and also care how they stand with others in their unit. In short, they want to know how they fit in and how they contribute to the unit or division as a whole. As a result, managers should be willing to openly communicate with their subordinates. Sometimes, even when managers are convinced that performance appraisals are a great idea, they still have difficulty carrying them out. Strange as it may seem, one of the biggest stumbling blocks to performance appraisal is that many managers simply *don't understand the subordinate's job well enough to evaluate it.* No wonder they don't even know how to tell employees what the job requirements are and what is expected in the way of job performance—much less appraise employee performance.

Other managers who do understand the employee's job are nevertheless simply unable to interpret or communicate a performance evaluation to the employee. And many managers still feel they were hired to do a job, not to be a human relations expert.

OPPORTUNITY FOR OBSERVATION

We have already presented the premise that the foundation of any performance appraisal system rests on those data or information generated about performance. This involves not only specific, measurable objectives and expectations for achieving them, but also provides the key to effective feedback. Later, we will further elaborate on the concept of behavioral observation as we specifically address training in observation, documentation, and evaluation skills. For now, however, we offer a look at one of the manager's other tools for conducting effective performance appraisals, that is, the opportunity to observe performance. In this section some techniques for creating these opportunities are presented, so that more valid and reliable data on your subordinates' performance may be collected. First, the distinction should be made between the casual observer and the trained observer. Basically, this distinction includes three factors: (1) the amount of behavior observed; (2) the purity of the observation; and (3) the relationship of the observation to relevant goals and objectives. In brief, the trained or effective observer notes more job-related behavior, makes certain that observations are based on objective facts rather than subjective inferences, and only records those behaviors that are indeed job-relevant. Since the manager first must have the opportunity to observe in order to make effective or useful observations, he or she must learn how to first make the right opportunities for observation.

Certain job behaviors which may be extremely important from the standpoint of job success and may be observable, relevant, and quantifiable can sometimes be extremely difficult to observe under usual conditions. There exist two alternatives for dealing with this problem. The first solution is to stop searching for those particular behaviors. The second solution would be to do something which would increase the likelihood of those behaviors occurring. The latter strategy is what the present section is about. How does a manager create the conditions that will allow for the observation of on-the-job behavior which is relevant and quantifiable? The answer to this must come from a careful situational analysis and a framework of the following assumptions.

Assumption 1. The manager is responsible for feedback to subordinates regarding their current performance.

Assumption 2. The manager is responsible for feedback to subordinates regarding their potential for other positions within the organization.

Assumption 3.   The manager has an opportunity to evaluate the current environment and determine what skills and characteristics are critical for success.

Assumption 4.   The manager has an opportunity in conjunction with his or her boss to evaluate the environment to which a person may move at some time in the future.

For every given position there are a range of skills and situations in which those skills which will dictate success or failure for the individual are demonstrated. If what is demanded by the task is *not* consistent with the skills of an individual, then even if motivation is high, the individual will not be successful.

The opportunities to observe performance are numerous, but, to help clarify those more readily, the following observation alternatives are offered. In general, there are four observations related to an employee's performance with which a manager should be concerned.

1.   The actual work behaviors as activities related to doing what should be done on a day-to-day basis.

2.   The results of the work behaviors that reflect outcomes or products of an employee's work-related activities.

3.   The long-range consequences of the work behaviors reflecting actions of the employee that are once-removed from the observable results. These observations may include not only third-party reports, but the side effects of the behaviors such as errors, downtime, costs, grievance, turnover, and the like.

4.   The actual achievement of goals which reflect both immediate results and long-range consequences but which can be directly linked to agreed-upon targets within agreed-upon time frames.

In summary, then, creating the opportunities to observe job-relevant behavior is the manager's responsibility and as such requires active participation in this process. A passive approach of waiting until the subordinate presents himself or herself to the manager may not yield enough observations to make performance feedback valid, reliable, or constructive.

LEGAL ISSUES IN PERFORMANCE APPRAISAL

Since the emphasis in employment discrimination for the past 20 years has largely been on selection and promotion, little attention has been paid to the fact that federal law prohibits discrimination in *any* personnel-related decision. This, of course, includes those decisions and issues surrounding performance appraisal, and recent court cases testify that the legality of performance appraisal is indeed confronting organizations frequently. The purpose of this section is to briefly introduce the main thrust of the law as it relates to the task of performance appraisal. The focus will be on what the manager can do to comply with the law, even though much of this compliance is the initial responsibility of those with human resource and/or personnel functions. Nonetheless, it is important that the manager be aware of the issues and employees' rights.

First and foremost it is critical that the spirit of the law be understood. Quite simply, the law surrounding personnel decisions in organizations is intended to do only one thing—protect employees against unfair treatment relative to other employees. Since most unfair treatment has traditionally been directed at minority groups in society at large, the government, through a series of legislative acts, executive orders, and guidelines, has made it more difficult for such treatment to persist unchecked. While this so-called intrusion into the private sector offends many people, it would not have been necessary had there not been so many blatant cases of discrimination taking place both outside and inside the workplace. It is interesting to note that while the intent of the law was to protect traditionally affected classes (for example, minorities, females, handicapped, elderly, and so forth), it has been pervasive enough to protect all employees regardless of race, sex, age, or physical well-being. In the end, only one question need be asked to determine if job discrimination has taken place: were the personnel decisions that were made based on job-relevant information or were other extraneous (irrelevant) factors taken into account? Demonstrated job relevance is the key to the law. Where it can be shown, there is little likelihood that discrimination will be upheld.

Unfortunately, it is not as simple as that might suggest. That is because there are systemic, or in this case organizational, practices which, while not intending to discriminate, in the end affect certain groups disproportionately. That is, the system and the decisions made within it have "adverse impact" on a protected class. Unless an argument for "business necessity" can be used to justify such practices, the law is likely to rule that there must be some remedy for this unfair practice. Many times this remedy comes in the form of affirmative action or quotas to reduce the existing disparity in the work force between groups or classes of people. The whole issue of affirmative action raises the backs of many people who believe that quota systems are inherently immoral, unethical, poor business practice, and not within the spirit of the law. This is an issue that has been and will continue to be debated for years, and it is not the purpose of this section to elaborate on the apparent complexities of such a controversy. Suffice it to say that, regardless of the law, organizations should make the most prudent decisions about their people and these decisions are likely to be most prudent when based on information that relates to the job in question.

What, then, does this all mean for performance appraisal? It means making appraisal-related decisions based on relevant, observable, and measurable data. It means treating all employees on the basis of their job performance only, independent of the extraneous factors mentioned above. It means documenting both the procedures and information on which the decisions were made. And, finally, it means respecting and honoring the rights of employees as both people and workers.

The law affecting performance appraisal, and for that matter any personnel-related decision, can be classified into two general areas: (1) equal employment, and (2) disclosures and privacy. Equal employment statutes have their origin in the Equal Pay Act of 1963 and Title VII of the Civil Rights Act of 1964. The Equal Pay Act was enacted to prohibit pay practices discriminating against one sex even though equal work, skill, effort, and responsibility are required of the other for the same or equivalent job(s). The 1964 Civil Rights Act's Title VII is the most pervasive of all equal employment opportunity laws and covers employers with 15 or more employees. It prohibits discrimination in employment on the basis of race, sex, color, religion, or national origin. It applies to a wide range of employment activities including appraisal-related ones such as promotion, discharge, and compensation. The Equal Employment Opportunity Commission (EEOC) was created by this act to oversee and enforce its requirements. Over the years the EEOC has developed a number of sets of guidelines for conducting fair employment practices. While these are merely guidelines, they have been interpreted as the "law" in a number of court cases. The third major piece of employment legislation was the Age Discrimination Act of 1967 (modified in 1978) which prohibits discrimination against applicants and employees aged 40 to 70.

The second general legal area related to personnel practices involves disclosure and privacy. Basically, two acts have been legislated to deal with this: the 1974 Federal Privacy Act and the 1974 Freedom of Information Act. The spirit of these laws is to protect the individual's rights in order to safeguard against an invasion of privacy. Basically, this means right of access to information collected or stored about oneself, and while specifically set up to protect the public sector work force, the implications for all employees are evident. Indeed, since 1974 many states have passed similar laws, which in some cases are more stringent than those enacted by the federal government. When state and federal law both address these issues, the more stringent of the two generally applies.

The bottom line is that, until recently, performance appraisal has escaped the scrutiny of the courts. But within the last 10 years a number of challenges to organizations' performance appraisal systems have been upheld in a court of law. In general, the courts have found these systems to be invalid, unreliable, and discriminatory. (See Linenberger and Keaveny, 1981; Lascio and Bernardin, 1981; Kleiman and Durham, 1981, for reviews of this litigation). It is anticipated that many more suits of this nature will be filed. Since managers are representatives of their organizations, they are responsible for complying with these various laws in the actions they take. The penalties for noncompliance can range from millions of dollars in settlements to negative employment consequences for the individual manager involved.

Taking the lead in getting its agencies to establish more valid performance appraisal systems, the federal government enacted the 1978 Civil Service Reform Act, which deals specifically with the establishment of performance appraisal systems for all federal employees (excluding CIA, Foreign Service, and GAO employees as well as certain Presidential appointees). It is likely, however, that such provisions will soon be specifically required of private sector employers as well. Very briefly, the act requires an employee to be evaluated only on job-related performance with full knowledge of the performance standards used. In addition, the act states that the appraisals should be conducted and recorded at least once a year.

In summary, certain criteria necessary for a legally defensible performance appraisal system have surfaced from legislation and court cases:

All appraisals should be related to job-specific performance criteria which have been derived from a thorough job analysis of the skills, tasks, and knowledges required to perform the job.

Evaluations and the conditions under which they occur should be relatively standardized from one employee to the next except where type or level of job requires otherwise.

Appraisals should be behavior- rather than trait-oriented and thus based on observable and measurable data.

The appraisal procedures should be outlined in written form and distributed to both raters and ratees.

Appraisals should be examined for evidence of discrimination or bias and corrective action taken through training or other means.

Appraisers should have personal knowledge of and a reasonable opportunity to observe the performance being evaluated.

The results of the appraisal should be reviewed and acknowledged by the person being rated (DeVries, et al.,1980: 77; Holley and Feild, 1982: 398).

Meeting these criteria may not prevent discrimination suits entirely, but it will go a long way to a successful defense should one arise.

PERFORMANCE APPRAISAL TRAINING

One of the most important factors in any system in which performance is evaluated is the training of the evaluators or appraisers. This training must cover a number of factors. The goal of an organization and the responsibilities of each job must be considered before the employee's objectives can be established. These individual goals can be broken down into the different skill categories that the person must perform to meet the goals.

Over the performance period, the subordinate will act in a number of different ways and will be seen in more than one situation. The manager observes the subordinate's work behavior just as it occurs, but may make rating errors. The rating is made up of the work behavior the manager has seen and is influenced by rating errors.

As you see, rating is complex. It begins with determining the organization's goals. Objectives and skills must be defined for each individual in the organization and must be made clear to the subordinate and the manager. Rating errors, such as the halo effect, can interfere with the whole process. Errors contaminate the rating system. However, when we understand the errors and how they occur, we are less likely to make them. This is the major basis and need for training.

Reducing Rating Errors

What are these errors that can affect performance ratings? Let's go through some of the major problems.

1. *Accuracy of Recall.* People differ in how well they are able to remember what they have seen a person do. Probably very few of us maintain accurate and complete notes on our subordinates' performances. Because we lack notes on performance, we may be totally dependent on recall and this, at best, can be faulty.

When there is a lack of documentation, other rating factors enter the picture. If we don't have a solid base of information, we may commit a number of other errors.

2. *Halo Effect.* The subordinate who is being rated is seen by the manager to be much the same on all skills. This is due to being influenced by one or more outstanding characteristics of the subordinate. The manager does not make a distinction between the skills or characteristics of the individual. This holds true in both seeing the subordinate in a positive ("all good") way or in a negative ("can do nothing right") way.

3. *Contrast.* Contrast places a person in the position of being compared. This is unfair, and it is especially unfair if we are supposed to be rating performance according to objectives that have been agreed upon between the manager and the subordinate.

4. *Stereotyping.* When we stereotype individuals we classify or evaluate them in a certain way because of apparent membership in a particular category of people. Common stereotypes are based on the categories of race, religion, and sex. Believing that someone has certain characteristics because they belong to a group of people (females, elderly, Southerners, religious groups, ethnic groups, and so forth) is stereotyping. When a manager holds a stereotyped belief, it is easy to interpret behavior according to that belief. The problem with having this occur in rating is that stereotypes often disagree with reality. An important reason for discussing these problems in rating is that they can cause a rater to give a higher or lower rating than the performance suggests. In all cases, whether these errors have caused a higher rating or a lower rating, they have interfered with a clear consideration of what the person being rated has actually done.

5. *Differences in Standards.* Two managers may see the same behaviors and attach very different number ratings to those behaviors because they have different standards for evaluation. There are many reasons why standards may differ. Two possible reasons are the managers' own needs and their own personality characteristics. If rating standards differ a great deal, it can seriously affect the ratings.

Most of us can remember teachers who were easy graders and others who were hard graders. They had different grading standards. When we establish goals and describe the behavior that is expected in reaching these goals, it helps to establish the set of standards that will be used by the rater. The less clear the goals and the expected behaviors, the more chance there is for the rater to rely on an inner set of standards in determining the rating.

6. *Fixed Impression.* A momentary observation can stay with someone indefinitely. One may have observed someone drop something and formed an impression of the person as careless or clumsy. That impression may stay and become fixed over time. The person is thought of in a way that was formed on the one behavior observed.

7. *The Effects of Time.* The placement in time of an observation can lead to rating errors. This is slightly more complex than the other errors we have discussed because it refers to conflicting observations that occur at different times. Assume there are two opportunities to observe an employee. That is, the employee exhibits different sets of behaviors. Thus these two sets of behaviors clash with each other. Assume that the first opportunity to observe the employee, situation A, puts the individual in a positive light. And suppose that situation B occurs two weeks later and, in this situation, the employee doesn't seem to be as competent. The manager who has observed these two situations may make one of two common errors: (1) the manager may evaluate the employee very positively because the early impression was strong; or (2) the manager may rate the employee very negatively because of the strong influence of the second situation. In either case, the manager is not being objective. Both situations should be taken into account. Having one situation more or less cancel out another situation is fairly common, but during a performance review period one should take into account all the work seen, rather than exclude some observations because of when they occurred in relation to other behaviors.

8. *Projection.* Another factor that can affect ratings of others is called projection. Projection occurs when people allow their *own* characteristics or values to influence their ratings. For example, managers who see themselves as being firm and willing to take a position value this characteristic and believe it makes them good leaders. When they see a subordinate who is also willing to take a position, they will automatically believe that person is a good leader, whether this is actually the case or not.

This discussion of problems that occur when rating is conducted has had one main purpose, and that is to make it clear that one's ratings can be influenced. Once managers become aware that they may be adding meanings to what they see, or that they may be distorting in other ways what they have seen, they have made the first step in correcting these problems. One very effective way of controlling these rating problems has already been mentioned. When we talked about the problem of depending on recall, the need to *document* was mentioned. Documenting behavior can be nothing more than taking notes on what one has seen someone do at the same time the behavior has been seen or shortly afterward. Generally, then, there are two things to do to improve performance evaluation ratings: The first is to observe what subordinates are doing in their jobs, and the second is to keep records on just what has been observed.

Tips for Observing, Documenting, and Rating Behaviors

The following list offers some suggestions for collecting data on subordinates in preparation for a performance appraisal.

1.   Be thoroughly familiar with the skills and objectives that are to be rated during the performance appraisal period. This will permit focusing on the specific behaviors that are related to those skills and thus make ratings more accurate.

2.   Write down the important job behaviors observed as soon as possible, and always include a short description of *when, where,* and *how* they occurred.

3.   Always take notes on (or record) the behavior first. Placing the behaviors into categories, analyzing the situation, and rating the individual should *follow* the actual recording of the behavior.

4.   Be as specific as possible in presenting behaviors and comments to support the rating. Avoid general words such as "good" or "fine." Use clear and specific examples that relate directly to the situation.

5.   Be careful not to allow what has happened in one situation to influence observations of other situations.

6.   Rate each skill *separately*, using only the specific notes that pertain to that skill, and not allowing the rating on one skill to influence the rating on another skill.

7.   Observe what the individual *did not do* in carrying out his or her job responsibilities, as well as what the individual did accomplish.

8.   Be aware that an observation of behavior may be listed under more than one skill. Recognize that a display of behavior will often show more than one skill, and that the skills should be separated before rating.

9.   Be careful about making inferences. Drawing inferences and conclusions should be done only if there are written notes on behaviors which will support these inferences or conclusions.

Observations versus Inferences

Another common problem for observers is confusing actual observations of a person's work behavior with guesses about the behavior. It is necessary to make the distinction between what has actually occurred and the rater's impressions about the occurrence. This is important because impressions and guesses about behavior differ among people, but the observation does not. If a subordinate hands in a report two days late, that is an observation. The manager might conclude, or infer, that the subordinate does not have a high regard for deadlines, or the manager could infer that the subordinate is overworked and cannot get work done on time, or that the subordinate is poorly organized. Each of these inferences or guesses could result in different ratings for the subordinate and could alter plans for training or development in different ways. Which one is true? It's impossible to say without taking other samples of behavior.

Performance appraisal is a vital addition to an organization because it provides important information to the individual, to the manager, and to the organization as a whole. In all cases—for the individual, the manager, and the organization—information that is not based on fact is misleading and can result in some poor decisions.

Only after a manager has a number of samples of behavior can he or she make conclusions about the individual's behavior. This is a goal that we are striving for in performance evaluation—evaluation supported by documentation. If important behaviors are recorded often enough, general statements that represent observed behaviors can be made. These, in turn, will be much more acceptable to the employee because they are evidence of the care a manager may have about the employee's performance.

Understanding Behavior

Underlying all of performance appraisal training is a clear-cut philosophy or approach to the concept of behavior. Understanding behavior and its implications is critical to effective appraisal. There are three major factors that cannot be ignored in order to fairly evaluate performance: the job behaviors must be *observable, relevant,* and *quantifiable.*

1.   *Observable Behaviors.*   In order for any statement containing a judgment to be of value, it must be based on behaviors that can be observed. The reason this is important is because one must come to grips with the fact that what is going on inside a person can never be known. The only information of value in any situation that is job-related is what is *seen or heard.* The search for what goes on inside another person has no value at all when evaluating job performance. Certainly there are differences in what is felt and the way one often behaves, but observed behaviors are important because one can never be certain about a person's feelings. One may only infer or interpret feelings and too often may be in error in relying on that personal judgment. So the first major premise for any performance evaluation program that is fair to all is that *all performance evaluated must be observable.*

2.   *Relevant Behaviors.*   The more relevant any behavior is to the way it needs to be exhibited effectively on the job, the more accurate the appraisal will be. This gives important and specific information that relates to an individual's total performance. Peo-

ple's heights, ways of knotting their ties, colors of their skins, or their sex are all irrelevant when one considers whether or not someone can and does do his or her job effectively.

When speaking of relevant behaviors, one must also consider the situations in which the behaviors are seen. The closer the job situation in which the behaviors occur, the better these behaviors may be counted on to give concrete information that is important for evaluation, development, or effective coaching with individuals.

3. *Quantifiable Behaviors.* For evaluation to be accurate and fair, one must be able to quantify how much of a particular characteristic or skill an individual may have and how much of that skill is necessary to do an effective job. There are very few, if any, qualities that exist on a basis of *all* or *none* for any individual. The skills and behaviors that one typically deals with exist and are observed as degrees—not as the total presence or the total absence of a quality.

As an example, consider leadership. It may be contrary to what many of us believe—a person is either a leader or not—namely, that someone may be a leader some of the time and under certain conditions. In some situations, the person may be a better leader than in others. The questions one would have to ask in evaluating that person would be, "How much and under what conditions is leadership required to do this job successfully?" and "Has this person displayed leadership in the appropriate situations often enough to satisfy the job criteria?"

The quantity of a skill is of crucial importance in job success. It is even more important when one begins to differentiate between individual employees for promotion or development purposes. If, for example, a person is required to work alone most of the time, it would not be as important to develop interpersonal skills since these would not be a high priority. But if the individual was being considered for promotion to a managerial position, then the amount of interpersonal skill necessary for that job would change and become a higher priority.

When working with any appraisal system, the skills and characteristics to be evaluated must be put in terms of observable behaviors, relevantly defined by the elements of the job and quantifiable.

MEASUREMENT ISSUES

Perhaps the primary measurement issue regarding performance appraisal is validity, or the extent to which the measures of performance are related to an employee's job performance. In test development, the three major types of validity are criteria validity, construct validity, and content validity. The first two do not lend themselves to the validation of performance appraisal systems but the third, content validity, may be used. Another term for content validity is *job relevance* and it refers to the extent to which the job performance has been sampled by the performance appraisal system. The three major sources of error regarding this are weighing differences of particular job factors, the inclusion of irrelevant factors, and the degree to which some performance dimensions may be excluded. The effectiveness of the performance appraisal system relies very heavily on its relationship to the actual job and ultimately must be based on this relationship. In many, if not all cases, the only way this can be done is through an accurate job analysis. Basically, there are two major approaches to job analysis. The first emphasizes asking knowledgeable people about a particular position—what is done or demanded in that position—while the second attempts to evaluate the particular characteristics of successful people in the job. Both of these approaches have some merit under different circumstances. So when people talk about the measurement issues involved in developing a performance appraisal system, they really mean the degree to which the measurement approach actually reflects differences in performance. Much of this deals with issues discussed earlier concerning the training of raters.

USES OF APPRAISAL

Wage and Salary

Fairness in the treatment of people is becoming an increasing concern for all organizations. Fairness is defined in the eyes of many by their salary treatment and the organization's promotional policies. In most organizations, the information upon which these decisions are based must come from performance ratings done by superiors. So performance appraisal will play a very important role in wage and salary administration. For most organizations wage and salary administration and performance appraisal provide the ultimate definition of systematic treatment of human resources. All good wage and salary plans are based very strongly on job demands and performance factors. Normally, in most wage and salary plans, points are given for various positions, based on the difficulties associated with certain necessary tasks as well as the problems associated with hiring persons with the requisite background and abilities to perform in the job. Once these points are allocated, wage bands are developed; these may deal with both longevity in a position and performance in that position. Differences in salary come about as a result of differences in an individual's performance measured by some type of formalized appraisal system. So the basis of all wage and salary plans must be the effective measurement and documentation of an individual's performance.

Developmental Planning for Subordinates

A second use of performance appraisal has to do with using the information to develop subordinates. Developing a specific plan for subordinate growth will naturally follow a thorough assessment of the employee's present level of performance. Since this assessment and evaluation is involved throughout the performance appraisal cycle, the manager should be prepared to construct a developmental plan for his or her subordinates. Remember that all plans should be discussed with the subordinate and his or her ideas and desires should be considered and incorporated wherever possible.

Before beginning to construct a plan for the subordinate's development the following questions should be answered:

Does this person really want to develop more?

Is the person interested in more responsibility?

Has greater responsibility been asked for or is more challenging work desired?

Where does this individual want to be in three to five years, eight to ten years?

Is education needed for either technical or experimental advancement?

What is the next most logical move this individual can make with success? When?

Is management committed to fostering growth and development?

What benefit will both the company and individual derive from this development?

The developmental plan for an individual should outline the activities that are considered necessary for correcting specific weaknesses or acquiring skills that are needed for either the employee's present job or potential position. It should include specific activities, tasks, assignments, or learning experiences that are necessary for the employee in order to achieve the desired goal. If possible, include both long-range and short-range goals.

There should be a written plan of progression so that the employee can understand where he or she is going and *why*. The plan should also include a way to monitor progress so the employee will receive feedback on how well he or she is progressing.

The developmental plan will depend on the opportunities that are available within the organization. These are often greater than one might think.

If one wants to determine an employee's "potential" he or she must:

1. Answer the question "potential for what job or class of jobs?"
2. Analyze the employee's past and present job duties.
3. Rate or judge the employee's performance in these past and present job duties.
4. Analyze the job duties or the class of potential jobs.
5. Determine the similarities and differences between the old and the potential job duties.
6. Analyze the employee's skills (strengths and weaknesses).
7. Determine what skills are required for the potential jobs.
8. Determine the similarities and differences between skills of the employee and skills required for the potential jobs.
9. Determine if there are indications (test scores, past performance, assessment center results, and so forth) that the employee possesses high aptitude for acquiring the skills required by the potential jobs.
10. Judge the employee's potential for the class of jobs on the basis of an analysis of duties, skills, and aptitude.
11. Discuss the potential jobs with the employee to learn what he or she feels about the promotion.

Career and Succession Planning

Perhaps all the issues discussed in the previous section very strongly affect the use of the performance appraisal for career and succession planning. If the information contained in the performance appraisals regarding an employee's performance and potential is good, then career and succession planning can be effectively carried out. If the information is incomplete or inaccurate, no amount of well-meaning behavior on the part of a superior will allow a subordinate to deal effectively with career skills and abilities or make informed choices with regard to them. So performance appraisal information becomes the key to so much that goes on within organizations which affects people.

SUMMARY

In summary, then, effective performance appraisal cannot be done without training. Nor can it be done without clarification of what is expected of employees and the basis on which they will be evaluated. The entire process is both time-consuming and difficult to do well, but the rewards truly override the problems. There are many forms and plans, but all of them are only as good as the information they allow managers to generate about the performance of their subordinates. This information, if good, may be used to evaluate, to develop, and to plan employees' careers. The feedback and its various uses are the heart of an organization's functioning effectively.

REFERENCES

Age Discrimination in Employment Act, Pub. L. No. 90-202, 81 Stat. 602, 1967.

Age Discrimination in Employment Act, Pub. L. No. 95-256, 92 Stat. 189, 1978.

Cascio, W. F. and Bernardin, H. J. "Implications of Performance Appraisal Litigation for Personnel Decisions." *Personnel Psychology, 34,* 1981, 211–226.

Civil Service Reform Act, Pub. L. No. 95-454, 92 Stat. IIII, 1978.

DeVries, D. L., A. M. Morrison, S. L. Shullman, and M. L. Gerlach. *Performance Appraisal on the Line* (Tech. Rep. No. 16). North Carolina: Center for Creative Leadership, 1980.

Equal Employment Opportunity Act, Pub. L. No. 88-352, 78 Stat. 241, 1964.

Equal Pay Act, Pub. L. No. 88-38, 77 Stat. 56, 1963.

Federal Privacy Act, Pub. L. No. 93-579, 88 Stat 1561, 1974.

Freedom of Information Act, Pub. L. No. 93-502, 88 Stat. 1561, 1974.

Holly, W. H., and H. S. Feild. "The Relationship of Performance Appraisal System Characteristics to Verdicts in Selected Employment Discrimination Cases." *Academy of Management Journal, 25* (2), 1982, 392–406.

Kleiman, L. S. and R. L. Durham. "Performance Appraisal, Promotion and the Courts: a Critical Review." *Personnel Psychology, 34,* 1981, 103–121.

Lazer, R. I. and W. S. Wikstrom. *Appraising Managerial Performance: Current Practices and Future Directions* (Conference Board Rep. No. 723). New York: Conference Board, 1977.

Linenberger, P. and T. J. Keaveny. "Performance Appraisal Standards Used by the Courts." *Personnel Administrator, May,* 1981, 89–94.

Locher, A. H., and K. S. Teel. "Performance Appraisal—A Survey of Current Practices." *Personnel Journal, 56* (5), 1977, 245–247; 254.

19

EMPLOYEE SELECTION

Job Analysis, Documentation, and Guidelines

FREDRIC D. FRANK
CABOT L. JAFFEE

King Arthur, prior to embarking to battle the Saxons, was faced with an interesting dilemma.* He needed to choose—from among his knights—a personal bodyguard, a person to depend on for leadership, and a messenger who would be a means of communicating and updating the events of the moment. (Please see Figure 19.1.)

*This is a hypothetical example used only for purposes of illustration.

King Arthur

He looks like a bodyguard.

He looks like
a messenger.

He looks like a leader.

FIGURE 19.1.

To select his personal bodyguard, he:

Took the largest people available;

Had them fill out a form which included questions about marital status, because he didn't want a person who would not take necessary risks because he had a family;

Gave each of them a piece of not-so-shiny armor and asked them to interpret what they saw;

And then asked each one directly, "If someone menacingly approached King Arthur, would you protect the king regardless of personal risk?" While the knight answered the question, King Arthur counted the beads of perspiration on the knight's forehead, for excessive perspiration was a certain sign of dishonesty.

To select his leader, he:

Took the people with the most somber expressions on their faces;

Had them respond to written questions which asked them about the history of England up until the present;

Checked with the people whom they had served during their knight apprenticeships to determine their sense of loyalty;

Then asked each of them to imagine that they were in the midst of a fierce battle and that they should think of King Arthur as a knight who was reluctant to do battle. Each of them was given 30 minutes to persuade the knight (portrayed by King Arthur) to do battle. King Arthur, during these simulated dialogues, took note of each of their leadership skills.

To select his messenger, he:

Took the people with the widest smiles on their faces;

Checked with their instructors at the Knight Training Institute to insure that they had done well in school, for good messengers traditionally had been scholastically sound students;

Then, from the same instructors, gained specimens of the knights' written work—not to evaluate the quality of their work, but to check the punctuation because knights who always punctuated properly would always be punctual in delivering messages;

Finally, met with each of them and asked them questions about their families, their hobbies, their likes and dislikes, on the basis of which he selected the most outgoing person of all to be messenger.

King Arthur, although not totally pleased with his eventual decisions, had certainly analyzed differences among the three jobs and had based his choice of selection instruments upon these differences. For his bodyguard he wanted someone who was a large, unmarried, unimaginative, honest soul. For his leader he wanted someone who was a somber, well-bred, persuasive loyalist. And finally, for his messenger he wanted someone who was a smiling, scholarly, punctual extrovert. He used nine different methods for acquiring this selection information, and today, taking some liberties, we would say that the bodyguard candidates were evaluated on the basis of application forms, projective tests, and polygraphs; the leader candidates via paper and pencil testing, reference checks, and assessment centers; and the messenger candidates through academic performance, handwriting analysis, and interviews.

From King Arthur's time until today, selection practices have become more refined, but it is clear that wherever a choice has been made among two or more people for a job, selection practices have been used.

This chapter will address selection practices, dealing primarily with job analysis since it precedes the actual selection process. There is also some discussion of documentation, a necessary ingredient in successful employee selection. Most important to the whole selection activity is an understanding of the guidelines that have been handed down by various court actions and decisions growing out of such actions. This is discussed at length in this section.

SELECTION—WHAT IS IT?

Selection refers to choosing from among a number of available people the person or persons to be employed. It is presumed that such choices are based on information pertaining to each applicant's suitability for the job.

Selection practices are employed by all organizations, but obviously differ. The professional basketball coach who subscribes to a scouting service which provides information on college players' skills and performances, including points scored, rebounds, and so forth, is utilizing a selection practice, just as much as an industrial organization which makes use of college recruiters' input regarding a candidate's decision-making prowess. What is common in these situations is that all the selection practices involve gathering information about a candidate's likelihood of successfully performing in a given job.

PURPOSES OF SELECTION

Selection can serve varied organizational purposes. These include:

Increasing organizational productivity;

Reducing turnover;

Increasing organizational morale (as an indirect result of satisfying other purposes);

Reducing training costs (by better identifying candidates who are likely to benefit from training);

Increasing job satisfaction (by establishing a better match between the individual's preferences and abilities and the organizational needs);

Helping to satisfy affirmative action requirements, for example, hiring of minorities;

Enhancing the overall professionalism of the organization.

RELATION OF SELECTION PRACTICES TO OTHER PARTS OF THE ORGANIZATION

Figure 19.2 is an illustration of how selection practices relate to other functions within the organization. As illustrated in that figure, recruiting precedes selection. Recruiting can take the form of college campus interviewing to entice potential job candidates, advertising, and so forth. Prior to implementation of selection practices, wage compensation studies and job analyses need to be conducted to define job requirements and determine appropriate pay and other benefits. Selection practices are then imple-

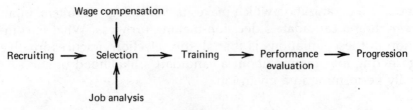

FIGURE 19.2.

mented to choose those persons best suited for the job, consistent with the job analysis findings. Having identified those persons, necessary training is carried out to better insure that the people selected will, in fact, succeed. Once in the position, their performance on the job is periodically evaluated.

As can be seen, then, selection is not an isolated element within an organization. It is also clear, particularly for large organizations, that many organizational resources are linked to selection. These include recruiters, personnel analysts (including those who focus on wage compensation as well as those who focus on job analysis), affirmative action officers, human resource specialists who perform training activities, legal staff, labor relations personnel, labor planning specialists, industrial/organizational psychologists, and so forth. Due to its relationship with other personnel practices, as well as its being a point of convergence for a variety of organizational resources, selection is of utmost concern to organizations.

THE ROLE AND DEFINITION OF JOB ANALYSIS

Job analysis is the cornerstone of proper selection practices. King Arthur, in the example described above, considered differences among the three jobs before deciding what selection practices to use. Similarly, in trying to choose the most suitable person for any position, it is always necessary to first analyze the job, to define the requisite skills, abilities, and so forth, and to analyze how it differs from other jobs.

A job analysis is a set of procedures used to study a job to determine its requirements. From the job analysis, the groundwork is established for determining the most appropriate selection practices.

JOB ANALYSIS METHODS

There is a variety of job analysis methods, including interviews of job knowledge experts, direct observations of the job, questionnaires, and so forth. While there are no mandatory requirements, it is always beneficial to acquire data via many methods, for example, interviews and questionnaires, to make sure sufficient information is gathered.

It should also be pointed out that methodology may vary, depending upon the purpose of the job analysis. While the subsequent development of selection strategy is often a major goal, other purposes of job analysis include the determination of wage compensation practices, training needs analysis, and so forth. Other considerations affecting the choice of job analysis procedure might include the number of people presently in the job, the geographical location of these people, and cost considerations.

DOCUMENTATION

Regardless of the method used, it is strongly recommended that a report be written, summarizing the findings of the job analysis. The report should include a discussion of:

The purpose of the job analysis;

The sample of people used to acquire the information;

Methodology used, for example, interviews, questionnaires, and so forth (and a description of these);

Information analysis, that is, how the information was statistically analyzed;

Results, including:

Key skills, abilities, knowledges;

Education requirements, if any;

Relative weights in terms of the importance of these elements;

Recommended or tentative test plan, that is, what the selection instruments should be (given that the purpose of the job analysis is to establish a basis for specific selection practices).

LEGAL REQUIREMENTS

In reviewing recent court cases where job analysis procedures were scrutinized, Thompson and Thompson (1982) enumerated a list of standards to which there should be adherence. These are:

A job analysis must be performed.

It must be on the exact job for which the selection device is to be used.

The analysis must be reduced to a written form such as a job description, and the job analyst must be able to describe the procedure used.

Data for the job analysis should be collected from several up-to-date sources.

The data should be collected by an expert job analyst,* but the expertise of the analyst is not enough to prove that a "good" job analysis has been performed.

Data collected should be from a sufficiently large sample to be relevant to every position the selection practice is intended to cover.

Tasks, duties, and abilities must be identified and included in the job analysis.

Other terms used by the courts to describe types of information to be identified through job analysis are elements, aspects, characteristics, aptitudes, knowledge, skills, abilities, and critical incidents.

---

*A person trained and experienced in job analysis procedures.

In summary then, a job analysis is necessary to determine the selection practices to be used and is essential for establishing a legally defensible selection system.

CRITERIA FOR EVALUATING SELECTION TECHNIQUES

The remainder of this chapter discusses the criteria for evaluating selection techniques—reliability, validity, and, primarily, the federal Uniform Guidelines on Employee Selection Procedures. Various selection instruments themselves are discussed and evaluated in the following chapter.

Reliability

Reliability refers to the extent to which the instrument provides consistent results. That is, if applicants were to take the instrument on a second occasion, would they get approximately the same scores?

Validity

Validity refers to the degree to which a selection instrument achieves its purpose. There are several types of validity; two of the most often used types are:

Content Validity.   The degree to which the content of the selection instrument resembles the content of the job.

Criterion-Related Validity.   The degree to which scores on the selection instrument correlate with measures of on-the-job performance.

Compliance with Legal Considerations in Terms of Selection Instrument Fairness

To better appreciate the legal considerations, a brief discussion of the Uniform Guidelines on Employee Selection Procedures follows. These guidelines have provided a set of standards to be met by selection systems and selection instruments.

General Objectives of Guidelines

On August 25, 1978, the Equal Employment Opportunity Commission (EEOC), Civil Service Commission (CSC), Department of Labor (DOL), and Department of Justice (DOJ) jointly issued the Uniform Guidelines on Employee Selection Procedures, referred to as *the Guidelines*, to be effective as of September 25, 1978. The purpose of these Guidelines was to establish a unified federal position in the area of prohibiting discrimination in employment practices on grounds of race, color, religion, sex, or national origin. Prior to the Guidelines, the EEOC, CSC, DOL, and DOJ were all responsible for administering and monitoring equal employment regulations, and two different sets of guidelines existed.

In an attempt to end the confusion that existed with regard to federal policies on employment practices, the four agencies adopted a uniform set of guidelines by which they would all abide.

In order to clarify the content of the Guidelines, the EEOC, CSC, DOL, and DOJ published a set of questions that were commonly asked with regard to the Guidelines along with the answers to these questions. One of the most frequently asked questions is, "Who is covered by the Guidelines?" The answer given to this question is that:

> The Guidelines apply to the Federal Government with regard to Federal employment. They apply to most private employers who have 15 or more employees for 20 weeks or more in a calendar year, and to most employment agencies, labor organizations and apprenticeship committees. They apply to state and local governments which employ 15 or more employees, or which receive revenue sharing funds, or which receive funds from the Law Enforcement Assistance Administration to impose and strengthen law enforcement and criminal justice, or which receive grants or other Federal assistance under a program which requires maintenance of personnel standards on a merit basis.

> They apply through Executive Order 11246 to contractors and subcontractors of the Federal Government and to contractors and subcontractors under federally assisted construction contracts. [EEOC, 1979: 11999]

Another frequently asked question is, "Do the Guidelines apply only to written tests?" The answer is:

No. They apply to all selection procedures used to make employment decisions, including interviews, review of experience or education from application forms, work samples, physical requirements, and evaluations of performance. [EEOC, 1979: 12003]

Definitions of Key Terms Contained in Guidelines

For the sake of clarity, some of the terms used in the Guidelines have been specifically defined. These terms and their meanings with regard to the Guidelines are:

(1) *Adverse impact.* A substantially different rate of selection in hiring, promotion, or other employment decisions which work to the disadvantage of members of a race, sex, or ethnic group.

(2) *Substantially different rate of selection.* The agencies have adopted a rule of thumb under which they will generally consider a selection rate for any race, sex, or ethnic group which is less than four-fifths (4/5ths) or eighty percent (80%) of the selection rate for the group with the highest selection rate as a substantially different rate of selection. This "4/5ths" or "80%" rule of thumb is not intended as a legal definition, but is a practical means of keeping the attention of the enforcement agencies on serious discrepancies in rates of hiring, promotion and other selection decisions.

(3) *Compliance with these guidelines.* Use of a selection procedure is in compliance with these guidelines if such use has been validated or if such use does not result in adverse impact on any race, sex, or ethnic group, or, in unusual circumstances, if use of the procedure is otherwise justified in accordance with Federal law. [EEOC, 1979: 12005]

Implications for Selection Procedures/ Adverse Impact and Validity

One of the most significant changes in employment practices that was brought about by the Guidelines is that selection procedures do not have to be validated. That is, if adverse impact does not exist, the selection procedure does not have to be validated, according to the published questions and answers:

Although validation of selection procedures is desirable in personnel management, the Uniform Guidelines require users to produce evidence of validity only when the selection procedure adversely affects the opportunities of a race, sex, or ethnic group for hire, transfer, promotion, retention or other employment decision. If there is no adverse impact, there is no validation requirement under the Guidelines. [EEOC, 1979: 12007]

Thus, unless adverse impact exists, employers do not have to validate their selection procedures. However, unless an employer is positive that adverse impact does not exist and will not exist in the future, it may be advisable to validate the selection procedure.

REFERENCES

Equal Employment Opportunity Commission, Civil Service Commission, Department of Labor, and Department of Justice. "Uniform Guidelines on Employee Selection Procedures." *Federal Register* 43, no. 166 (1978): 38290–38315.

Equal Employment Opportunity Commission, Office of Personnel Management, Department of Justice, Department of Labor, and Department of Treasury "Adoption of Questions and Answers to Clarify and Provide a Common Interpretation of the Uniform Guidelines on Employee Selection Procedures" *Federal Register* 44, no. 43 (1979): 11995–12009.

Thompson, D. E., and T. A. Thompson. "Court Standards for Job Analysis in Test Validation." *Personnel Psychology* 35 (1982): 865–874.

20

EMPLOYEE SELECTION

Evaluation of Selection Techniques

FREDRIC D. FRANK
CABOT L. JAFFEE

This chapter evaluates each employee selection instrument* in terms of its reliability, validity, conformity to the federal Uniform Guidelines on Employee Selection Procedures (legal considerations),[†] and the following criteria:

---

*In providing these reviews of various selection tools, we have endeavored to maintain brevity. More exhaustive reviews are available in other sources.
[†]These criteria are described in Chapter 19.

Personal Effects on Applicants. This criterion focuses on whether the use of the instrument constitutes an invasion of privacy. For example, the use of certain personality tests has been sometimes opposed based on invasion of privacy considerations.

Susceptibility to Faking. This criterion concerns whether scores on a given measure can be faked. For example, in a selection interview, is the interview subject to socially desirable responses deliberately put forth by the candidate?

Reevaluation Considerations. If candidates are reevaluated, is the instrument designed in such a way that results on subsequent administrations of the instrument are not influenced by results from the first administration?

Cost Considerations. To what degree are the costs associated with the instrument, such as costs of materials, testing equipment required, administration, and so forth, reasonable?

INTERVIEW

Overview. The interview, the most widely used selection instrument, ranges in design from very structured to unstructured, from a nondirective to directive approach; and from panel versus one-on-one interviewing. In addition, the training of the interviewer can range from very little to thorough training.

Reliability. Overall, reliability—typically measured through agreement among interviewers—is low.

Validity. If based on a carefully conducted job analysis, strong cases can sometimes be made for content validity. Recent advances, such as performance-based interviewing where short simulations are used in the course of the interview (in which the interviewer and interviewee interact in brief situations resembling those found on the job), make an even stronger case for content validity. Generally, criterion validities are disappointing. Again, the inclusion of simulations in the interview process offers promise for increased criterion validity.

Legal Considerations. Some research studies show that females receive lower evaluations, even though information collected in the interviews is the same for both males and females. Adverse impact has been found with respect to blacks and females.

Personal Effects on Applicants. Since existing law does proscribe what is inappropriate to ask in an interview, in recent years there has been less invasion of privacy, but it still exists to a certain extent.

Susceptibility to Faking. This has always been a problem with interviews, that is, they are often easy to fake because individuals are able to paint the most desirable picture of themselves. The use of simulations, which focus on behaviors, tends to minimize this concern.

Reevaluation. Certainly if one is reinterviewed at a later date by the same organization, the applicant's answers to questions are likely to be affected by the previous interview. The time span between the two occasions will also affect the response, with increases in the time span between the two interviews minimizing the effect.

Cost Considerations. The interview is relatively inexpensive.

Other Considerations. The likelihood of success of the interview process can be increased when:

It is designed and administered in a relatively structured and systematic fashion rather than being informal and inconsistent.

It focuses on job-relevant and observable behavior rather than subjectively generated traits and opinions.

It involves training the interviewer in interpersonal and communication skills as well as in observation and evaluation skills.

It includes procedures for documenting observations obtained rather than relying on total recall.

It provides the candidate with a clear and accurate view of the job demands both in terms of requisite tasks and skills and expectations for performance (in other words, a realistic job preview).

It requires the candidate to demonstrate behaviors, as opposed to relying solely upon self-report.

APPLICATION FORM

Overview.   Application forms are used by almost all organizations. At a minimum, they typically include information regarding the applicant's name, address, previous work experience, education, and references. Applications that contain biographical information—or "biodata" (for example, age)—statistically weighted, gained prominence in the late 1960s and 1970s. The responses are typically placed in a multiple-choice, or short-answer format.

Reliability.   Generally, data yielded through this technique provide consistent results.

Validity.   The use of "biodata" is difficult to justify in terms of content validity. With respect to criterion-related validity, "biodata" moderately correlates with on-the-job criteria.

Legal Considerations.   Statistical keying of items can sometimes result in some legal problems, for example, with regard to items pertaining to tenure, age, marital status, and so forth. Also, different weighting formulas often appear to be necessary for males and females. This is not the case for minority and majority groups.

Personal Effects on Applicants.   Assuming that items on the form do not inquire into personal matters, application forms are basically well accepted.

Susceptibility to Faking.   Research tends to show that "biodata" can be distorted by applicants to provide "desirable" responses.

Reevaluation.   There would be no significant effect of having previously filled out an application form, and obviously this is quite a common practice.

Cost Considerations.   This is a very cost-effective method of acquiring information. It is inexpensive to administer and it is a customary organizational practice.

REFERENCE CHECKS AND LETTERS OF RECOMMENDATION

Overview.   Reference checks and letters of recommendation primarily utilize the judgments of previous employers or supervisors. Since most references and letters of recommendation are characteristically positive, this leads to questions regarding their overall value. This is underscored by recent trends in employers being even more reluctant to disclose negative information due to the threat of litigation.

Reliability.   This has been examined by focusing on agreement between different reference givers, and reliability is quite low.

Validity.   Content validity is sometimes a problem if the reference givers are not very familiar with the job for which the candidate is applying and when there is little correspondence between the previous job and the new job. In terms of criterion-related validity, results have been generally low.

Legal Considerations.   Little information has been collected regarding adverse impact and reference checks, but there is some slight evidence in terms of adverse impact with respect to blacks.

Personal Effects on Applicants.   With regard to privacy issues, it is incumbent upon the hiring organization to not use any personal information which may be inadvertently provided by the reference giver. Therefore, there is some concern over invasion of privacy with respect to this selection practice.

Susceptibility to Faking.   The major concern here is that if the reference giver wishes to falsify information, it is very easy to do so, although verification can sometimes be carried out successfully.

Reevaluation.   This is generally not germane to this type of selection instrument.

Cost Considerations.   While at first glance this approach appears relatively inexpensive, the verification process, which is often necessary, increases the costs significantly.

Other Considerations.

Previous employers may decline to fill out reference forms out of concern over litigation. Telephone references are therefore sometimes more desirable.

Reference checks have value in checking employment history, that is, dates of employment.

Letters which contain specific examples as opposed to merely general statements tend to have more of an impact.

The use of considerable numerical data, for example, length of acquaintance, does *not* have much of an impact.

It is good practice to get written permission from the candidate in order to obtain information from present or previous employers.

ACADEMIC PERFORMANCE

Overview.   Performance in high school, college, or graduate school (provided by grade-point average or GPA) is often used by employers for selection purposes.

Reliability.   Reliability of grade-point average is generally acceptable.

Validity.   Content validity is often difficult to justify on the basis of academic performance, since the content of given courses does not typically resemble the content of specific jobs. Criterion validity studies have not been consistently supportive of academic performance as a predictor of job success.

Legal Considerations.   No research has been directly concerned with academic performance and adverse impact. However, research focusing on GPA as a predictor of subsequent academic success shows significant differences for majority versus minority group GPA.

Personal Effects on Applicants.   Privacy issues are not germane to academic performance as a selection technique.

Susceptibility to Faking. This consideration is not relevant to academic performance.

Reevaluation. This consideration is not relevant to academic performance.

Cost Considerations. Generally, using GPA for selection decisions is relatively inexpensive.

Other Considerations.

In comparing candidates who have attended different schools, consideration must be given to adjusting for school quality. In addition, difficulty of the field of study must be considered. These considerations are often left up to the discretion of personnel departments, which have few guidelines to follow in making these adjustments.

Recent trends in leniency in grading policy creates further questions regarding the utility of academic performance.

POLYGRAPH

Overview. Polygraphs require the job candidate to answer a set of predetermined questions while a recorder monitors physiological indicia such as galvanic skin responses, heart rate, respiration, and, in some cases, low voice frequencies that purportedly lessen under stress. The truthfulness of the candidate's responses is determined by professional analysis of the physiological indicia. The polygraph technique is used by a variety of organizations, particularly where security concerns are critical, for example, a position as a bank teller or police officer.

Reliability. When several administrations of the polygraph on the same candidates are compared, consistency of scores is low. Agreement between two sets of professional judgments (inter-rater agreement) is not particularly high either.

Validity. Content validity is not a basis on which the polygraph can be justified. Criterion validity studies in terms of job selection have not been carried out in an adequate number to provide support for the use of the polygraph.

Legal Considerations.   Not enough data exist regarding scores in the polygraph and adverse impact.

Personal Effects on Applicants.   Because of the nature of questions that are sometimes asked, the polygraph is often considered to be a serious invasion of privacy. Some states have made the use of the polygraph illegal as a selection device.

Susceptibility to Faking.   Some research shows that responses to the polygraph can be faked.

Reevaluation.   Since the measures on the polygraph pertain to physiological indicia which are difficult to voluntarily control, reevaluation effects are not significant.

Cost Considerations.   Costs can be relatively high since equipment is necessary and professional interpretation is required.

Other Considerations.
Results of the polygraph often are significantly influenced by the skills of the professional.

Recent research indicates that, in considering costs and validity findings, the use of the polygraph as a selection tool is severely limited.

HANDWRITING ANALYSIS

Overview.   Handwriting analysis, or the interpretation of personality traits from a person's writing characteristics, has been used in the screening of job applicants. While it is not extensively used in the United States, in Europe 85% of all companies reportedly use it as a hiring tool.

Reliability.   Inter-rater reliability based on handwriting analysis has been quite low.

Validity.   A content validity basis for handwriting analysis cannot be justified. In terms of criterion-related validity, the relationship of handwriting to job success is minimal.

Legal Considerations. There are no available data regarding handwriting analysis and adverse impact.

Personal Effects on Applicants. Depending upon the particular handwriting analyst, interpretations to be made have the potential for being an invasion of privacy.

Susceptibility to Faking. Handwriting analysis is not subject to faking.

Reevaluation. This consideration is not germane to the selection approach.

Cost Considerations. This is a relatively inexpensive procedure.

PROJECTIVE TECHNIQUES

Overview. Projective techniques are tests which require candidates to respond to ambiguous stimuli, for example, inkblots, sentence completion requests, and so forth. In doing so, candidates supposedly "project" onto the stimuli their own feelings, needs, values, motives, and so forth. Projective tests as a selection technique have been especially used for predicting executive success.

Reliability. This is typically gauged through inter-rater reliability where interpretations carried out by two professionals are examined. These studies have not been particularly supportive of projective tests.

Validity. Content validity is not a basis for supporting projective tests, since the content of projective tests does not resemble the content of most jobs. Criterion-related validity studies have generally not been high; they show low correlations with job success.

Legal Considerations. Overall not much data exist regarding the use of projective tests and adverse impact.

Personal Effects on Applicants. Caution needs to be exercised in using projective tests for selection purposes. There is the possibility of delving into personal areas of one's life, which would be considered an invasion of privacy.

Susceptibility to Faking.　Some research indicates that candidates can fake their responses to projective tests.

Reevaluation.　If reevaluated within a short period of time, initial administration could affect the scores on a second administration.

Cost Considerations.　Because projective tests require professional interpretation, costs can often be considerable.

PAPER AND PENCIL TESTS

Overview.　Paper and pencil tests (tests which are administered on paper and which require responses to structured questions, for example, multiple choice) have been extensively used for selection purposes although they have declined in use in recent years, primarily because of legal considerations. Subcategories of tests include:

General intelligence tests

Tests of mechanical aptitude, dexterity, and so forth

Clerical ability tests

Vocational interest tests*

Personality tests

Reliability.　Reliability of paper and pencil tests is generally adequate.

Validity.　General intelligence tests, personality tests, and vocational interest tests typically cannot be supported on a content validity basis. Tests of mechanical aptitude and dexterity and clerical ability tests can sometimes be justified on a content validity basis. In terms of criterion-related validity there is not strong support for general intelligence tests, personality tests, and vocational interest tests as indicators of job success. There is some evidence

---

*Although vocational interest tests are used primarily for career counseling, they are sometimes used for selection purposes.

to support the use of mechanical aptitude and dexterity tests as well as clerical ability tests.

Legal Considerations. Paper and pencil tests have in general been subject to considerable criticism regarding adverse impact. This is especially true for general intelligence tests.

Personal Effects on Applicants. The use of personality tests, and sometimes vocational interest tests, has been associated with invasion of privacy.

Susceptibility to Faking. Research has shown that responses to personality tests and vocational interest tests can be faked, although some tests have built-in detection factors to determine faking tendencies.

Reevaluation. If a short time has elapsed between test administrations, initial administration can affect the results of a later administration.

Cost Considerations. The use of paper and pencil tests is relatively inexpensive.

Other Considerations. Occasionally, careful job analysis is not carried out prior to implementing paper and pencil test procedures. As with all selection approaches, a careful job analysis should first be conducted.

ASSESSMENT CENTERS

Overview. Assessment centers require candidates to participate in a set of simulations or exercises which represent the demands of a job, and the behaviors exhibited are evaluated by carefully trained assessors or raters with respect to job-related skills. Assessment centers are used for promotion purposes as well as for entry-level selection, for example, salespeople, police officers, and so forth.

Reliability. This criterion, primarily measured through interrater (assessor) agreement, has been supportive.

Validity.   Assessment centers, particularly those tailored to or developed with respect to the specific job and organization, have a strong content validity basis. In terms of criterion-related validity, evidence supports the use of assessment centers.

Legal Considerations.   Assessment centers have fared rather well when challenged in the courts. While there is some evidence indicating differences between minority and majority groups' performances, differences are slight when compared to traditional testing instruments, for example, paper and pencil tests.

Personal Effects on Applicants.   There are no serious concerns with respect to invasion of privacy.

Susceptibility to Faking.   Research generally shows that it is difficult to fake assessment center performance.

Reevaluation.   Typically, having previously participated in an assessment center does not materially affect performance in a subsequent assessment center.

Cost Considerations.   Assessment centers tend to be more costly than other selection instruments.

Other Considerations:
Two key elements relating to a successful assessment center are the soundness of the instruments and the training of assessors.

A rule of thumb for assessor training is one day per simulation exercise.

Assessors can be from within the organization (as is usually the case) or outside the organization, and, assuming that the assessor training is adequate, the two groups of assessors will perform equally well.

Assessment centers have been used for a variety of positions including salespeople, entry-level police officers, teachers, instructors, managers, and executives.

Assessment centers have been successfully used cross-culturally, with attention being paid to insure that there is a good fit between the exercise and the culture.

Another benefit of assessment centers is the developmental value—using the information derived from assessment centers for employee development.

OTHER SELECTION APPROACHES

Several other selection approaches are available, but a paucity of evaluative data exist regarding them. Therefore, only a brief description of these methods will be provided.

Miniaturized Training Tests

In a miniaturized training test, the candidate is given job-oriented training materials and evaluation is based on learning performance.* Available criterion-related validity studies indicate some support for this approach, but the primary criterion has been prediction of training performance.

Unassembled Examinations

With unassembled examinations candidates are required to follow structured procedures in assembling a file of verifiable past achievements relevant to the job. These achievements are then evaluated by a panel of expert judges who rate the candidate's potential. This approach attempts to be content-based, but at this point, more research is needed.

Video Samples

With video samples as a selection technique candidates are presented with video (or film or slide) depictions of situations or scenes characteristic of a given job. They are required—either through a structured format, for example, multiple choice, or un-

*This is not to be confused with assessment centers where the focus is on behaviorally-based skills evaluated by trained observers.

structured, for example, essay—to respond to what is presented through the specific medium, for example, a videotape presentation of a sales situation in which the candidate is asked to respond as if he or she were a salesperson.

This approach is content-validity based.

SUMMARY OF SELECTION TECHNIQUES

For reference purposes, Table 20.1 provides an overall summary of the nine major selection tools in this chapter.

OTHER ISSUES

Use of Multiple Approaches

For many jobs, several tools may be used in conjunction with one another, for example, interviews and application forms. In these situations, it is necessary to determine the rules for combining scores on the various tools in order to make employment decisions. Data from the job analysis should provide the basis for the rules for combining scores.

There are several methods for combining data to make employment decisions.

Multiple Hurdles. In a multiple-hurdles approach, each selection instrument serves as a hurdle the applicant must pass before proceeding to the next one. Failure to pass any hurdle results in being denied the job. The assumption is that the factor being evaluated in a hurdle is so important that inability to pass insures that the person will be unsuccessful on the job. In other words, a lack of the factor cannot be compensated for by strengths in other areas. Where multiple-hurdles systems are used, measures of essential factors and/or measures which are low-cost are usually administered first.

Compensatory. In the compensatory approach, candidates have some strengths that compensate for deficiencies. Different combinations of strengths could lead to successful job performance.

TABLE 20.1
Overall Summary of Selection Tools on Eight Factors

	Reliability	Content Validity	Criterion-Related Validity	Legal Considerations	Personal Effects on Applicants	Susceptibility to Faking	Reevaluation	Cost Considerations
Interviews	Q & A[1]	Q & A[2]	Q & A[2]	Q & A[2]	I	I & A[2]	I	H
Application Forms	A	Q	A	I	A	I	A	H
Reference Checks & Letters of Recommendation	A	Q	Q	?	I	I	NR	A
Academic Performance	A	Q	Q	?	NR	NR	NR	H
Polygraph	I	Q	Q	?	Q	A	A	A
Handwriting Analysis	Q	Q	Q	?	I	H	NR	A
Projective Tests	Q	Q	Q	?	I	I	I	A
Paper and Pencil Tests	A	Q & A[3]	Q & A[3]	Q & I[4]	Q & A[5]	Q, L, & A[6]	I	H
Assessment Centers	A	H	A	H	H	A	A	A

Scale: H = Highly acceptable on this factor;
 A = Acceptable on this factor;
 I = Minimally acceptable on this factor, but could be considerably improved;
 Q = Questionable on this factor;
 NR = Not relevant for this factor;
 ? = Not enough information available.

1. More likely to be acceptable when interviewers are carefully trained.
2. More likely to be acceptable when short simulations are included.
3. Tests of mechanical aptitude and dexterity and clerical ability are acceptable. General intelligence tests, personality tests, and vocational interest tests are unacceptable.
4. General intelligence tests are unacceptable; others in this testing category could use improvement.
5. Personality tests are unacceptable; others in this testing category are acceptable.
6. Personality tests are unacceptable; vocational interest tests could use improvement; others in this testing category are acceptable.

Therefore, rejection does not result from discerning one weakness. A selection decision is made only when the candidate has experienced the entire selection process and success is defined as meeting some specified sum of scores on the various selection procedures used.

Hybrid. The hybrid approach uses both multiple-hurdles and compensatory approaches. If a particular factor is considered critical for success, that factor is the first one evaluated. If weak on this factor, the candidate is rejected. If not weak, the candidate experiences the rest of the selection process, and a decision is made at the end of the process, with scores on the various selection procedures added together.

Recruiting Considerations

Regardless of the precision of a selection process, selection problems will surface without a desirable applicant pool. Thus, an organization must have a commitment to implement recruiting procedures when necessary to insure an acceptable workforce. Given the demographics associated with the location of a particular organization, that is, relatively sparse population areas, sufficient numbers of qualified applicants may not exist. This may necessitate the following recruiting steps:

Recruiting, in general, outside the local area;

Visits to schools outside the local area;

Obtaining advertising space in media sources outside the local area;

Advertising within the organization's newsletter to obtain "internal" applicants who otherwise would not have demonstrated an interest in the position.

Literacy

If written materials are to be used during the selection procedure, they should not be so difficult as to exceed the level of written materials found on the job. Literacy tests should be considered as a source of information to determine the extent to which written requirements unrelated to the job preclude entry into the job. In such cases, other means of presenting the material, for example, videotape, should be considered.

Fitness Beyond the Job

Selection requirements for specific jobs are, on occasion, too severe given the requirements of the job. For example, requiring applicants for certain jobs to have college educations may be excessive with respect to the demands of the job, and in fact may be at odds with legal rulings (*Griggs v. Duke Power Co.*, 1971).

The effects of this selection orientation may be significant when viewed within the context of the actual requirements of the job and the environment in which the job is placed. If those with a college education find themselves in a situation where their skills and education are underutilized, considerable dissatisfaction may set in. This reinforces the need for a carefully conducted job analysis.

Role of Personnel Department—Maintaining Standards

Regardless of the selection instrument used, the personnel department must be responsible for the implementation and use of staffing procedures that are consistent with the relevant laws and regulations. Crucial here is training for people who make staffing decisions; this includes some members of the personnel department as well as most managers.

SUMMARY

Personnel selection is complex and critical to organizational success. It starts with a carefully conducted job analysis and is completed with the selection of the best-qualified people. To have a well-developed system of selection practices requires the commitment and professionalism of many people throughout the organization.

PROGNOSIS

Selection practices have advanced considerably beyond the almost total reliance on the paper and pencil tests in the 1950s. In the last 10 years the use of more job-content-related instruments, for example, assessment centers, has met with considerable acceptance from both employees and management, as well as the courts. This trend is likely to continue with increasingly greater innovative use of job-content-related instruments such as video testing.

REFERENCES

Job Analysis

Thompson, D. E., and T. A. Thompson. "Court Standards for Job Analysis in Test Validation." *Personnel Psychology* 35 (1982): 865–874.

Equal Employment Opportunity Commission

Equal Employment Opportunity Commission, Civil Service Commission, Department of Labor, and Department of Justice. "Uniform Guidelines on Employee Selection Procedures." *Federal Register* 43, no. 166 (1978): 38290–38315.

Equal Employment Opportunity Commission, Office of Personnel Management, Department of Justice, Department of Labor, and Department of Treasury. "Adoption of Questions and Answers to Clarify and Provide a Common Interpretation of the Uniform Guidelines on Employee Selection Procedures." *Federal Register* 44, no. 43 (1979): 11995–12009.

Interviews

Arvey, R. D., and T. E. Campion. "The Employment Interview: A Summary and Review of Recent Research." *Personnel Psychology* 35 (1982): 281–322.

Application Form

Asher, J. J. "The Biographical Item: Can It Be Improved," *Personnel Psychology* 25 (1972): 251–269.

Pace, L. A., and L. F. Schoenfeldt. "Legal Concerns In the Use of Weighted Applications." *Personnel Psychology* 30 (1977): 569–607.

Reference Checks and Letters of Recommendation

McCormack, E. J., and D. Ilgen. *Industrial Psychology*. 7th ed. Englewood Cliffs, New Jersey: Prentice-Hall, 1980.

Muchinsky, P. M. "The Use of Reference Reports in Personnel Selection: A Review and Evaluation." *Journal of Occupational Psychology* 52 (1979): 287–297.

Academic Performance

Wise, D. A. "Academic Achievement and Job Performance." *American Economic Review* 65 (1975): 356–366.

Polygraph

Belt, J. A., and P. B. Holden. "Polygraph Usage Among Major U.S. Corporations." *Personnel Journal* 57 (1978): 80–86.

Lyken, D. T. *A Tremor in the Blood: Uses and Abuses of the Lie Detector*. New York: McGraw-Hill, 1980.

Handwriting Analysis

Levy, L. "Handwriting and Hiring." *Dun's Review* 113 (1979): 72–79.

Sharma, J. M., and H. Vardan. "Graphology: What Handwriting Can Tell You About An Applicant." *Personnel* 12 (1975): 65–67.

Projective Techniques

Anastasia, A. *Psychological Testing*. New York: MacMillan Publishing Co., 1976.

Kingslinger, H. J. "Application of Projective Techniques in Personnel Psychology Since 1940." *Psychological Bulletin* 66 (1966): 134–150.

Paper and Pencil Tests

Anastasia, A. *Psychological Testing*. New York: Macmillan Publishing Co., 1976.

Ghiselli, E. E. "The Validity of Aptitude Tests in Personnel Selection." *Personnel Psychology* 26 (1973): 461–477.

Assessment Centers

Frank, F. D., and J. R. Preston. "The Validity of the Assessment Center Approach and Related Issues." *Personnel Administrator* 27 (1982): 87–95.

Jaffee, C. L., and J. T. Sefcik, Jr. "What Is an Assessment Center," *Personnel Administrator* 25 (1980): 40–43.

21

TRAINING AND DEVELOPMENT OF EMPLOYEES

MARTIN M. BROADWELL

Training and developing subordinates is inherent in the job of a supervisor. To say that is to recognize that when we learn the art and skill of delegation, when we learn to appraise people, when we learn how to assign the right people to the right jobs, we'll know that none of these things are really possible unless the people under us have been trained and developed properly. It is evident that most supervisors make some effort at developing subordinates. However, the development is often superficial and improperly done. There is some skill required to be a good trainer, and unfortunately many—if not most—supervisors lack that skill.

That's not a negative perspective, just a well-substantiated fact. In this chapter we'll discuss the steps in training and discover that once we see them, they aren't hard to learn.

We must recognize that there is more to training and developing people than just sitting down and showing them how to do the job. There is preparation, planning, designing, record keeping, and follow-up. More than that, there is the matter of appraising people to see just where development is needed. Training and developing employees also involves career planning and development—determining individuals' potential and the training and job experience needed to get them moving along career paths. This chapter will address all these aspects of training and development.

WHY DO SUPERVISORS TRAIN?

It's not enough to just say that training is a part of a supervisor's job, hence training must take place. There are good reasons why training is done, and they are important enough that we need to look carefully at them. After discussing these reasons, it will be clear that if supervisors don't do their job of training and developing people well, they should be treated as *poor performers themselves.* A person comes to work for an organization and brings some skills, but also brings some potential waiting to be developed. Employees' potentials are, in effect, a kind of raw material or resource. It's up to the supervisor to get the most from this resource. That doesn't mean being a slave driver. All the force and threat and coercion in the world will not enable a person who's untrained and undeveloped to do something, no matter how much potential he or she might have. Potential has to be developed. Undeveloped, it becomes a wasted resource. Developed, it becomes a profitable investment.

When we think about employees coming to us as unskilled and untrained people, we should recognize that training is the only answer to getting the most out of them. It happens all too often that we don't train them until they do something wrong or until they've learned the job incorrectly. At that point we step in with criticism, make them feel badly for doing the job incorrectly, and may even find that the job has suffered. We have an unhappy employee, a job done poorly, and much time wasted, all because we failed to do the training we should have done. If we were caught misusing or wasting any other kind of raw material, we'd be severely disciplined or terminated if we worked for an organization that had the proper attitude toward resources.

We could list a lot of reasons why training and development should be done, in addition to the ones we've mentioned already—increasing production, improving safety records, meeting competition, staying current with technology—but all of them come back to one of two things: either *making more money* if we're a profit-making organization, or *saving more money* while giving more service, if we're a service or nonprofit organization. It's easy to see how we can increase profit or savings by doing a good job of training and developing our people. Employees who can do more than they could when they joined the organization are more valuable. It's the same as getting more than we paid for, getting more use out of the resource than we originally expected. Anytime we can offer more service for the same amount of money, we're going to either make or save money. Anytime we have an employee knowing more about the job to the extent it's possible to produce more, we're going to benefit in tangible ways. These are sufficient reasons for training our people.

DEVELOPMENT RESPONSIBILITIES

We'll make a distinction between training and development by saying that training is the process of making people better able to do a specific task, usually the one they're doing right now or will be doing in the near future. Development, on the other hand, deals with future tasks—using the person's potential to combine skills and talents so that they can do new and different things. Training is usually a quicker process, dealing with the immediate; development is a gradual process, taking place over a longer period of time. To be consistent, we should say that supervisors have both training *and* development responsibilities. Supervisors who are only concerned with the immediate job and the skills required to do it will usually be concerned with training, but do little to develop their people for future activities. Supervisors who have concern for both the employee and the organization are constantly paying attention to both training and development.

How does development come about? It requires an ability to assess potential in employees and know how to bring that potential into reality as soon as possible. Supervisors who work at developing potential find ways to get employees involved in doing things that will help them grow. It may be doing things such as serving as acting supervisor, filling in for higher-rated employees during sickness, or working on a special project that requires some reading or research. Supervisors who are concerned with development are always looking at employees in terms of what they could possibly do, instead of what they are now doing. They think of employees as valuable resources who are never doing all they could do if they were developed more.

That's a very healthy attitude toward organizational resources of any kind, but especially toward people. As we think about it, people are the only resource we have that should be getting *more* valuable as they are used, rather than decreasing in value. A five-year employee should be a much more valuable contributor than a two-year one, and a 10-year employee shuld be much more valuable than the five-year one. Naturally, our goal should always be to develop employees not only to their maximum, but to do it as quickly as possible. This means we're going to have to do some planning, since there has to be the opportunity to use the new abilities once they're developed. That, too, is part of the supervisor's job: providing career opportunities as people become more and more capable of handling more complex and different assignments. While the supervisor may not be able to do all of this without help, there is still the responsibility to keep the organization informed as to the new abilities now available—so the organization can make arrangements to see that the jobs are there when the talent has been sufficiently developed.

HAZARDS OF NOT TRAINING

We've already talked about some of the problems that arise when we fail to train, or fail to train properly. Let's be more specific.

CASE.   A new employee comes to work as a clerk. He has some experience, but none on our kind of word processor. He is a fairly good typist, but totally unfamiliar with our system and our machines. The employee is assigned to work with one of the other employees, a long-term, experienced employee, but one who has no training in how to train others. The training job is considered a chore because the work load is not diminished. There is no particular schedule for the training. The employee asks questions—if any occur to him—watches, does small jobs, and does a reasonably satisfactory job. Gradually the employee is left alone to do assigned work. A few weeks later—at review time— there are good comments about the work, but complaints that some of the simple things are being overlooked and that some shortcuts are being taken that cause trouble. The employee is viewed as a mild disappointment.

What's the problem? We could have predicted what we got. The hazard is that older, experienced employees will overlook the seemingly obvious things and also teach unapproved shortcuts. It's a form of business inbreeding that allows us to perpetuate error and nonstandard procedures. The sad part is that the employee ends up with a poor appraisal and may even believe it is accurate. After all, he may think, there was training, I did have a chance to ask questions, I am doing things incorrectly.

CASE.   A new engineer is hired, with good credentials. Her immediate past experience is teaching in an engineering school. She does not know the particular industry she is now working in, but she is familiar with the technical requirements of the job. The employee is given stacks of manuals, a desk and quiet place, and told to "catch up" on the industry and ask questions as necessary. The employee is eager to be successful, but questions are taken lightly by others, who either try to help—without going into much depth—or who laugh and point out that everybody in the place does that a different way so she shouldn't worry about it! Finally, the employee becomes discouraged. With no guidance, she begins to work on a project without approval, makes some progress, but doesn't please anyone or get any reinforcement. More and more the employee wonders if this was a very good move.

The chances are pretty good that the employee will not leave, since it's already been a big decision to get out of teaching and into business, but the feelings are negative, not positive. There isn't much loyalty to the organization. It's a hard way to begin a new career with a new company.

CASE.   An employee is hired as a supervisor because of unusually good recommendations in previous nonsupervisory jobs in other organizations, as well as good academic and skill-training credentials. There is some resentment that an outsider is getting this job. There is no immediate supervisory training, although the next course is scheduled within six months. The employee tries to assume the role of supervisor, but is told by the manager that others will have to train him since they're familiar with the stock and procedures. The employees don't work very hard at training their new boss-to-be, friction develops, mistakes are made, one subordinate gets mad and resigns, and the new supervisor is rated as a poor selection and offered a demotion. The new employee looks for and gets another job, glad to be out of this environment.

This, or something similar, happens to newly appointed supervisors over and over. Somehow they are expected to know how to be good supervisors without training, just because they were good at a skilled, nonsupervisory task. They're thrown in over their heads, may even be given administrative paperwork and personnel responsibilities—also without any training—and be expected to perform to maximum standards. Sometimes they are viewed as being "on trial"; sometimes the apparent philosophy is to "throw them in over their heads—that's the best way to teach them to swim!" Unfortunately, that's also the best way to drown somebody.

These, and all the other cases like them, are the hazards of not training. The hazards are great because we're talking about the life and goals not only of the organization, but also of the untrained individuals. As we've seen before, it's a poor and flagrant misuse of raw materials.

WHO GETS TRAINED?

It may seem a senseless question to ask who gets trained, but there are some considerations. We have to consider priorities. If not everyone can be trained at the same time, or if we have several untrained people, we have to decide who gets the first time and effort. The answer is fairly obvious: we train where there is the most immediate payoff, then consider the long-range effects of not training others. If it's just that a minor part of the job won't get done or get done as well as it should be, we can let the training of those people or that skill go, in deference to a situation where customers are at stake, or where employees were highly recruited and we want them to start off quickly and well, doing their job with expertise and satisfaction. This may mean that a receptionist or telephone operator gets first attention, because customer image is important. It may mean that a technical employee gets trained quickly, even though the usable production from this person may be some time in coming. As we'll see later, the important thing is that there be a plan and a reason for our training.

WHO DOES THE TRAINING?

We've made a strong case for the supervisor taking the *responsibility* for the training and for training being a part of the manager's role. It should be noted, however, that this may mean that the immediate supervisor doesn't actually do the training. The better solution may be for someone in the human resources or training department to do the training on a centralized basis, or it might be best for a work leader to be assigned the training task. The important thing is for the supervisor to be certain that the training *really gets done*.

When training is assigned to someone else, sometimes there is a tendency to assume that it's done, or that it's done well. We recognize that this just isn't always the case. Somebody needs to be accountable for the *end result*, not just the time that's been put in. It isn't fair to the employee to make an entry into the records saying that training has been done, when, in fact, the training was superficial or poorly done. Someone—probably the immediate supervisor—needs to be responsible for the training so that when a person is certified as having been trained the end product is guaranteed as acceptable performance! That's a big order. It isn't asking too much of the trainers or the supervisors, if the employees are going to be appraised on the basis of having been trained. If we think of training as an investment of time and energy, then we ought to try to get the most return for that investment. Otherwise, we're again mishandling resources.

There are two or three considerations regarding training in a classroom situation or on the job. The main consideration is time: will the training be available as soon as it's needed? Even if the training can be done better in the classroom setting, but no class is scheduled for such a long time that the employee will be doing the job without adequate training for some significant period of time, then on-the-job training will most likely be best. On the other hand, if the classroom training is soon enough, and there is certain laboratory equipment needed to make the training more effective, time doing on-the-job training might be wasted. Sometimes we find that classroom training is available, but the kind of training that's being done is only close to the job situation but too general to be as effective as we'd like. In this case, we have to make a decision whether or not we can do better, even if we have to sacrifice some time and effort of our own. It may be that we can utilize both efforts: take advantage of the generalized training, then get to the specifics on the job. In whatever situation we do the training, we just have to remember that we're looking for the best training, at the best time, to get the maximum use out of the individual being paid to do the job we're training for. Whoever does the training, *it ought to be done well*.

TRAINING POLICIES

When we talk about responsibilities for training, we're really talking about policies. Many organizations fail to develop full-scale policies on matters like training. It's not enough that the policy is that "we believe in training." It's not sufficient to just say that supervisors are responsible for seeing that the people under them are trained. There has to be a firmer statement of objectives, specific actions, and consequences for violation of the policy. For example, in the cases we cited, what will happen to the supervisors of the people not trained? Did they violate policy by not training their people? Will they be held accountable for the results? Will there be any record of this failure on their annual evaluation form? Was there a stated policy that regulated how much training each of these people should have had? Was there a clear enough policy that it could be seen that there was a violation?

This is what is meant by a training policy. It has to be stated, understood, and enforced. Like any organizational policy, it should come from management, not the supervisors or the training department. It's a simple truth that people are likely to repeat those things for which they're rewarded and avoid those things for which they are punished. If supervisors train their people well but it's ignored and they go about their business with no recognition at appraisal time, they will gradually lose interest in good training. However, if they do poorly in their training, their people perform below standard, and they are held accountable for it—either immediately or at evaluation time—then they will probably begin to take more interest in doing better training.

There is no standard for a training policy. Like any policy in any organization, it is a statement of the organization's expectation of its people in the area under consideration—in this case the training and development of people. There are some things it should include, however. Below is a partial list for consideration. Not all organizations will consider these items; some will consider more than these.

1. *New Employees.* Several things have to be taken into consideration with regard to training and developing new employees. We've already talked about much of this. Of prime importance is the matter of when they get the training. There should be a time limit set for training them on specific kinds of things, or a general policy that says something like: "All employees will be trained up to a satisfactory level of performance by the end of two months (or two weeks, or two days)." The policy should express a specific

goal for the training but not be too general. Instead of "all employees deserve and should get adequate training," it should be more like: "Each supervisor will have the direct responsibility for seeing that his or her new employees receive proper training within the time limits designated for that specific job."

2. *Experienced Employees.* While some organizations neglect their newer employees—waiting to give them training until they have learned some things incorrectly—others neglect their longer-term employees. Once they've been hired and trained for the immediate job, they're forgotten as far as training is concerned. The training policy should offer guidance for employees at all levels of experience. Some organizations like to specify the percentage of time, or even the number of hours per day that employees at all levels of experience will get in the way of training. It may break down into segments: for example, employees with one to two years get 5% of their time devoted to training; with two to five years, 2½%; five to 10 years, 1%; over 10 years, two days per year of specific job training. Others like to specify the kind of training being done at different times. Some will actually name courses to be taken at times in people's careers. For some, this is too detailed, but the idea in all cases is to be sure that attention is paid to training for the experienced workers.

3. *Upward Mobility Training.* One goal of training should always be to make people more promotable, better prepared for higher or broader jobs. The training policy should do more than spell out that this is a goal of training; it should specify how and when it should be done. Further, the policy should make it clear what kind of training will be given to which people; it need not name a specific training course, but should say whether the training is for the next job or improvement on the present one. Some will have a policy that specifically states that job vacancies will be filled by people in the organization wherever possible, and that training will be available for the purpose of qualifying people to be considered for the jobs.

4. *Training Payoff.* There are organizations which expect that training will offer a return to the organization, hence they think of it as a means of increasing production, saving money, im-

proving safety, and reducing lost-time accidents. A part of the policy statement will describe how training will offer this payoff to the organization. When training is offered, it is not computed in terms of what the training will cost the organization, but in terms of either what the *failure to train* will cost, or how much return there will be for the time and money spent doing the training. This makes training a much more positive activity and affects the viewpoint of the trainees, the trainers, and the supervisors of the trainees. Management is much more likely to be favorably inclined toward spending money on training if they can see that there is a return to be gotten from the investment. This is especially true if there is a specific clause in the organization's policy stating that training is to be viewed in this manner.

TRAINING PHILOSOPHY

Those who are involved in training, whether they are from the training department or are the immediate supervisor of the trainee, should view training as a means of improving a person's ability to produce. The philosophy should be that people are trained because they either can't do something, can't do it well enough, or are now doing it incorrectly. Training should never be viewed as a chore or an insignificant part of the job, something to do when there is spare time. It is a corrective measure, designed to maximize the utilization of employees' potential. It's a way of getting more and/or better performance for the same or less money. As we've already seen, we are wasting resources when we don't use a person's potential. Training is a way to make use of that potential.

TRAINING IS A SKILL

One problem with trying to establish a successful training program is that most people don't think of training as a skill. They just think that there is a simple process in which someone doesn't know something, somebody else knows it, and the one who knows it tells or shows the other. Most training is done in that fashion—one person telling or showing another. But that's not good training and it's not very skillful training. There are some procedures that make for better training. Some of these precede the actual training process and some of them come afterward.

It's easy to see how we made misguided assumptions about training. After all, who can better train than someone who knows the job better than anyone else? Frequently a new supervisor gets the job because he or she was the best worker, one of the arguments in favor of the appointment being that this person is eminently qualified to do the training of others. We assume that we can somehow clone workers by having this person as the supervisor do the training. However, because training is a skill—and a different skill from that required to do the job being taught—it has to be learned. To think otherwise is like saying, "Joe is such a good lathe operator, let's make him the drill-press operator." There is no more relationship between the two skills of operating a lathe and operating a drill press than there is between one of these skills and training. The difference is that we can tell immediately when a person is a bad lathe operator; we can't always tell when a person is a poor trainer.

As we'll see later in this chapter, there are some logical ways to train and there are some ways that on the surface seem good, even logical, but which do not stand up to scrutiny. Much of the problem hinges on our lack of understanding of how people learn, which we'll examine later. Once we look at people's learning habits, understand how and why they learn and how they retain information, we begin to get a different view of what good and bad training is.

LEARNING BY ADULTS

There are a few things about adult learning that are important to spend some time talking about. First, and probably most importantly, adults vary widely in learning skills. We say *learning skills* because it isn't so much a matter of learning ability or intelligence as it is the skill in learning things that's significant for adults. Some find it difficult to sit in a class, for instance, when it's been years since they've been in a classroom. Others may have difficulty taking tests; some are afraid that they can't learn as well as they used to; some feel they have lost some of their ability to concentrate. All of these things worry them and may, in fact, be a block to their actual learning. The end result of all these concerns and fears may be that each person is quite different from the others—much more so than when they were children.

Another difference in the adult learner that is very significant is the fact that adult learners see learning as a much more important part of their life than when they were children in school. Learning a job is very real, whereas learning algebra may not have been. This isn't to say that they will necessarily learn better or get more enthusiastic about learning. It simply says that the situation is more *significant*, and, in that sense, more important. It does not mean that there is more motivation because it is in the here-and-now or because it has to do with their jobs. Workers being trained may be critical of the way things are taught or what is taught, but they may not be eager to learn the material or skill. Some will, of course, and altogether there will be more interest shown than not shown. But the supervisor must be aware that (1) just because people are adults doesn't mean they will automatically be better learners; (2) just because it is their jobs being talked about doesn't mean that they will be more motivated to learn; and (3) because they are adults and because it is their jobs being talked about, what happens will be significant to them to the extent they will be aware of how and what is being taught.

In addition to adults' feelings about training being different from children's, another thing is certain: if adults are going to get interested at all, it's going to be in something that's dealing with the immediately present situation. They are living and making a living in the here-and-now, so they want to learn things that will help in the here-and-now. If we want to have them quickly lose interest in the training, just tell them, "You won't be using this right now, but someday you probably will." The here-and-now urgency leads to another problem: adults don't handle stressful learning situations as well as children do. They feel the pressure much more, see threats more clearly, and react more quickly to the pressure. This means that we don't have to use large clubs or moderately veiled threats to get their attention. Adults tend to take errors or mistakes very personally, and may either resist learning efforts if they think they are going to fail, or interpret feedback data incorrectly—making it appear as success instead of failure.

PREPARING OURSELVES FOR TRAINING

By now it's obvious where the responsibility lies for good training. We have seen that it is a skill, meaning that we have to know *how* to do something if we're going to be successful at it. We have also seen that preparation should precede the training. In addition to some tangible things that need to be done ahead of time, mental preparation is also necessary. We have talked about recognizing the need for training and the importance of doing it at the right time. This is part of our mental preparation. When we decide to do some training, we psych ourselves up to be sure we do the best possible job. We remind ourselves that the employees we're training will be as good as, but no better than, our training. Their performance in the future will hinge on our ability to train them. Having accepted this, we then pick a time and place that is conducive to a good reception of the training. We make certain that there are no interferences, that we will not be interrupted, that there won't be any kibitzers looking over our shoulders and distracting us. We make sure that there will be adequate time for the training and for any practice and/or questions that might arise. We accept the training assignment with enough diligence that we determine to do it well—including preparing ourselves, the place, and the time frame.

SETTING STANDARDS

Part of the preparation is making certain we know what it is we want the employee to do. This may sound a bit strange, but many times the supervisor isn't exactly sure what the employee is supposed to be doing when the job is being done correctly. There is a general idea, but when it comes down to a firm standard, it may be *too* general. We said in the beginning that we train because a person cannot do the job, cannot do it well enough, or is doing it incorrectly. When we start our training, we need to be able to say what a job done correctly really is like. The easiest way to do that is to ask ourselves, "If the employees were doing the job satisfactorily, just what would they be doing?" This doesn't mean what would they be doing if they were doing an excellent job— better than we have a right to expect—or if they were doing it in a way that few have ever done it. It means that for what we are paying, and for the skills and abilities we listed in hiring them, what can we call a satisfactory job. Having made this determination, we then call this our standard. It's what we train toward; it's what we measure the success of the training by, and, ultimately, it's what we measure the employees' performances by.

PREPARING THE EMPLOYEES

Having prepared ourselves for the training and established standards for the jobs, we now can begin the preparation of the employees who are to be trained. This, too, is an important, pre-training activity. Training shouldn't be viewed as a chore to be done quickly so we can get on to more important things. Neither should it be viewed as punishment or drudgery. Such attitudes as these are easily developed by things the supervisors do and say. When the supervisor says, "Jan, we've got to get this training out of the way before the end of the month," the message is clear enough to Jan: there are more important things to do around here besides training! The supervisor can send the same message with something like, "If we hurry, we can get this in before lunch." It is much more effective to lend it a positive air by showing what advantages there are to being trained: "Jan, we're going to spend some productive time here, with some good training. I think you'll really appreciate the difference it will make in your understanding of the job." We can't make promises of bigger and better jobs, but we can make some "rewards in prospect." We can let people know that training will make them more valuable by saying things like, "When you've mastered this job, you'll be more prepared for learning the next step, the one the experienced people are working on."

Part of preparing employees is setting a time and a place that is convenient for them as well as for the supervisor. They need to know that this training is the most important thing that both *they and we* have to do right now. Once we've alerted them and made the time available, we have to be sure not to let things interfere with our training plans. Nothing short of a disaster should come ahead of this training. This means that we let them know ahead of time when and where the training is to take place—with their concurrence, make it clear why we are having training, what we hope to accomplish, what the benefits are, and then carry all of this out. It is important to let employees know about the training ahead of time so they will be prepared mentally and can think of questions they might have about their job, about why things are done as they are, and why things aren't done some other way.

DOING THE TRAINING

The key to the success of training is good planning, obviously, but all the planning in the world isn't going to make up for poor training. When the actual training is done, it should be done according to some specific procedures. Many supervisors aren't aware of the fact that training is a skill that needs to be learned and practiced. It is something that can be done poorly without either the supervisor or the employee knowing how badly it was done. Only when the employees who are supposedly trained fail to perform do we find out that the training wasn't done properly, and even then we may tend to blame it on the employee rather than on the fact that the supervisor did a poor job. We'll discuss this in more detail later when we talk about follow-up.

There are some indications that virtually all supervisors do a poor job of using effective training techniques in on-the-job or skills training. The thing to remember is that although we're teaching people to do things with their hands, *it's their heads that tell their hands what to do.* Our training must be designed to make certain that their heads have the necessary information to send the proper messages to their hands. This simply means that when the training is over, we won't be satisfied unless we're sure they have it in their minds as well as in their hands, that is, that we've *heard them say* as well as *do*!

The steps in doing on-the-job training are simple and easy to do, but they take a little extra time and many supervisors aren't willing to spend the time to do it correctly. Remembering that we want them to get it in their heads first, we start off by *telling* them what, then how, then why we are doing what we're doing. If there are no questions then we *show* them. The next step is for them to *tell* us what we've said: *what, how,* and *why*. Then—if they've said it correctly—we show them again. Finally, have them *tell* us what, how, and why, and then—if it's correct—we *have them do it*. Notice the effort we've gone through to get into their heads: twice we've shown them; twice they've told us. If, after they've told us twice, they don't have it, then the task is either too complicated or the employee isn't concentrating. We might not know if we just showed them what to do and then had them do it. But by having them explain the what, how, and why twice, we have good evidence that they understand what we've been trying to tell them. The other good part of this is that we've heard them tell us *why* things should be done a certain way and some of the consequences of doing the wrong thing. Usually, supervisors stress these things, never ask the employees to repeat them, then act surprised—even indignant—when employees do the wrong things at a later date.

There is a test of whether we're doing the training correctly: Can we say to the employee several days later, "Don't you remember? You told me the other day to do it this way," or is all we can say, "Don't you remember, I told you to do it this way?" Typically supervisors tend to train people by telling them the what, how, and why, showing them how to do it, then saying something like, "Okay, you try it." Unfortunately, they probably can do it, since it's an immediate feedback and little memory is involved. The supervisor goes away thinking a great training job has been done, the employee may feel the same way, but a few days later disaster strikes: the employee has forgotten some key points of the operation, or performed the job in an unsafe manner. Who gets blamed? The employee, of course!

FOLLOW-UP

After the training is over, after the employees have had a chance to use the information and skills we've imparted to them, there is the need for some periodic follow-up to see how the employees are performing. This isn't exactly an appraisal time; it's a time to smooth out rough places, make sure the employees are still using the instruction we've given them, and see if they have any questions. Many times, even when we've done an excellent job of training and used all the steps discussed earlier, there is still a good chance that there will be areas of misunderstanding or of no understanding at all. An employee can't really know this until the employee has shown strengths and weaknesses by actually doing the tasks assigned.

Supervisors observe, but not in an appraisal stance. It's more informal; it's a "How-are-things-going?" kind of session. In a way, it picks up where the training left off, even if the training occurred some time ago. This is a time for questions such as, "Can I help in any way? How is this working out? Are you having any problems? What's the hardest part of the new activity? Where did I mess up in helping you learn the job?" The idea is to perfect the training, not fault the employee. This is the time to see if the training needs to be improved, too. If supervisors consider themselves as trainers, and consider training as a skill, then they may want to think of the training activity as something they still haven't perfected yet. Each time they do some training, they will want to examine their results to see if they can improve.

RECORD KEEPING

Documentation of the training activity is a vital aspect of employees' career development. There is a serious hazard here, too.

We want to make certain that employees get credit for the training they are getting, but at the same time we don't want them to get it on their records that they've been trained for something that they can't do—especially if the reason was poor training. It's like getting a 53 on a test when the instructor has been a 37! At the same time, we want to keep good enough records that anyone can tell just what kind of training employees are getting. This will prevent duplicative training and will also provide helpful information of the person's ability when considering them for a new assignment. A review of these records will give anyone an instant view of just what kind of training has been done. They will know when the training was done, to determine how current the skill is; they will know who did the training, so they will know who to talk to about any questions or problems; they will know the length of the training and perhaps performance during the training. More will be available in the appraisal records, of course, as far as overall performance is concerned. The training records, usually a part of the personnel file, will give quick access to each employee's training and training needs—if they're kept accurately and current.

CHAPTER

22

PERSONNEL ADMINISTRATION

OLICE H. EMBRY

Personnel administration begins initially in most companies as a one-person staff job to give assistance and occasional advice to line supervisors and managers. The need for uniformity and consistency between departments arises as the firm grows, so personnel departments gradually assume more and more authority for the personnel administration functions. Legal action, government regulations, and union activity usually result in the personnel department's assuming quite a lot of the line supervisor's authority over personnel administration functions.

PAPERWORK AND RECORD REQUIREMENTS OF SUPERVISORS

Most supervisors are initially promoted into their jobs because of superior performance in a classified position or because of superior technical competence or knowledge of the jobs to be supervised. Among the most frustrating tasks facing new supervisors are the paper-shuffling requirements of the supervisory position, the necessity to meet deadlines or due dates, and, often, a lack of clerical help to handle these paperwork requirements. The importance of paperwork requirements, however, cannot be overemphasized. Labor arbitration cases or legal suits have been lost at the expense of millions of dollars simply because of poor records of absenteeism, quality control measures, or disciplinary conferences.

On the positive side, good control of the paperwork required of the supervisor can greatly help the supervisor plan for employee turnover, control costs better, and recognize good performance. It is amazing how hard people will work for recognition even when the recognition is something as simple as a gold star or being first on a production report that ranks supervisory groups according to their productivity.

Payroll Records

Payroll records usually head the list of records required of the supervisor. From these records, however, the supervisor can also keep track of overtime so that it can be equalized. High periods of overtime that are repeated in a pattern can be analyzed so that overtime can often be reduced simply by changing someone's hours, bringing in temporary help, or borrowing personnel from other work groups during peak periods. Excluding peak periods from the vacation schedule can also reduce overtime. Absenteeism patterns, such as workers who only get sick on the day before a holiday, can also be spotted with data from payroll records. Instructions for payroll records that go to the computer, the accounting department, or to personnel are usually well documented with clear due dates and times for submission. Other uses of payroll information, however, often depend upon the supervisor's initiative.

JOB DESCRIPTIONS AND PERSONNEL ADMINISTRATION

Among the primary jobs of management are the tasks of determining the best way of doing a job (engineering it, if appropriate), selecting the best person to do the job, and, finally, training the person to do the job properly. In many organizations, engineers conduct motion and time studies to determine the best way to do a job and to provide standards for piece rates or production quotas. If this is not done by engineers, then it is usually the supervisor's responsibility to at least write the job description for each job in the supervisor's work group.

The job description should list the major duties of the job. This can be done in the order the duties are performed (that is, the employee assembles the product and then inspects it) or according to a time pattern (that is, this report is done at the end of each day, and this one at the end of each month). The description should not be as detailed as a motion and time study but it should be reasonably complete and current. The job description should be used for the following:

1. Preparation of the job specifications (the minimum skills or experience needed to be hired or promoted into the job should a vacancy arise);
2. New employee selection, induction, and training;
3. Performance appraisal.

EMPLOYEE INDUCTION

Nothing gives a new employee a greater sense of security than to know exactly what a supervisor expects. When a new employee is handed a job description and told, "Here is a list of your duties. We are going to train you to do the first three items this week, the next two items next week, and by the end of the month you will know how to do all 12 items on the list." Knowing how performance will be measured and what the performance expectations are is equally important.

In many jobs new employees can be trained initially in a classroom on dummy or simulated training equipment. In most cases, training operators or departments perform this duty. Once this training is complete, a new employee is usually assigned to another employee who acts as a coach to help the employee master the remainder of the skills and duties. In many organizations, however, on-the-job training (OJT) is the primary method used to train new employees. Regardless of the method used, the supervisor is ultimately responsible for the performance of new employees and, therefore, responsible for overseeing their training. Chapters 17, 18, and 21 discuss these responsibilities in greater detail.

In addition to training, new employee induction should include a discussion of work rules and company policies. This is best done by letting the new employee read a new-employee handbook and then discussing the handbook with the supervisor. If an employee can be fired without warning for breaking a particular rule, such as taking scraped materials out of the plant or lighting a match in a restricted area, then the employee should sign a statement signifying that the employee has read and understands the rule. This statement should go into the employee's personnel record.

If a new-employee handbook does not exist, then the supervisor should have a list of items to discuss with new employees. Some examples of items for this list are:

Work and safety rules

Grievance procedure

Sick leave policy and rules

Tardy policy and rules

Vacation policy and assignment procedures

Holidays observed by company

Pay procedures, payday schedules, and related rules

Overtime rules and equalization procedures

Seniority rights, rules, and procedures

Shift or workstation selection rules and procedures

Promotion or transfer opportunities, procedures, and rules

Suggestion plan procedures and opportunities

Employee benefits

Dress codes, rules, or expectations

Union contract or handbook

If possible, employee induction should include a tour of the plant or facility so that new employees can see how their job fits into the overall operation. The tour should also show them such things as the nurse's location or first aid station, designated eating areas or facilities, restrooms, employee lounges or break areas, time clock location, designated parking areas, and so forth.

Most organizations have names for specific work locations, jobs, tools, or products that are confusing to new employees. A dictionary or simple list of these names or abbreviations is a good item for a supervisor to give to and discuss with new employees.

JOB SIMPLIFICATION, JOB ENLARGEMENT, AND JOB ENRICHMENT

Breaking jobs down into simple tasks enables workers to learn jobs faster and to become highly efficient at doing a specific task. Unfortunately, jobs can become so simple that boredom and carelessness increase rejects, scrap, turnover, and absenteeism to the point that the benefits of simplification are offset. When this occurs, supervisors should at least rotate particularly boring jobs so that no one works the job for more than two hours, two weeks, or two months. Where jobs can be combined to make a whole product or unit rather than a simple part, with the employees being held accountable and given credit for their production, the benefits often offset the increased training costs. This is called job enlargement.

Job enrichment occurs when jobs can be redesigned to include more autonomy, responsibility, recognition, and chance for achievement and generally to be made more interesting and meaningful. Although it is not possible to enrich all jobs, experiments with job enrichment programs have generally been successful in improving morale, quality control, and productivity, while reducing absenteeism and turnover.

Repetitious, boring jobs that cannot be enlarged or enriched should, in most cases, be automated.

EQUAL EMPLOYMENT OPPORTUNITY PROGRAMS (EEOC)

The personnel department or an officer of the company is responsible in most organizations for enforcement of EEOC guidelines, policies, and compliance. Supervisors, however, are affected by these activities and may even be responsible for enforcement when the firm has no formal personnel department.

U.S. firms are now prohibited by law from using employment practices (including tests) that discriminate because of race, color, sex, religion, national origin, or age (40–70 is the protected age group). When recruiting and interviewing prospective employees, the supervisor must be especially careful to avoid specifying requirements or asking questions that might be interpreted as discriminating. Marital status is not even a valid question except after employment for purposes such as insurance or tax status.

Although there are exceptions and situations where noncompliance can be defended, this is usually best left to the personnel department. The bona fide occupational qualification rule allows females to be specified for an actress job, a wet nurse, or as an attendant in a women's locker room, but not for a secretarial position. The four-fifths rule states that discrimination occurs if the selection rate for a protected group is less than 80% of the selection rate for a majority group. Therefore, if 10 out of 100 males are hired, at least eight (four-fifths of 10) out of 100 females or other protected groups must be hired to avoid adverse impact.

Just because a job has traditionally been held by a man or a woman or a job has been held by someone fresh out of school, the supervisor cannot automatically exclude or use tests that tend to exclude applicants from protected groups.

EMPLOYEE INTERVIEWING AND COUNSELING

Supervisors regularly interview job applicants, discuss performance appraisals with employees, investigate problems, and counsel employees. Many of these activities are informal or unexpected, with no time for advanced planning. Whenever possible, however, the interview should be planned in advance.

The first step in planning an interview is to determine your objectives in terms of what you want to know or what you want the applicant or employee to know or do after the interview. If the interview is an employment interview, study the job description and application form and write down some questions that you want to ask during the interview. Avoid closed-end questions that can be answered with one or two words such as "Did you like your last job?" Closed-end questions begin with words like *is, do, has, can, will, shall.* Ask open-ended questions that begin with *who, what, when, where, how.* For example, "What did you like most about your last job?" The supervisor can also use statements like, "Tell me about the responsibilities you had with your last job." The idea is to make sure that the applicant does most of the talking. You won't learn enough to make a decision if you do all of the talking. In a counseling interview, it is often necessary to let the employee do most of the talking just to discover the root of the problem. For example, absenteeism is usually a symptom of a problem, just as a fever is a symptom of a illness rather than the problem itself. Listening is usually the most important part of the interviewing or counseling process.

Next, try to find some privacy for the interview. Have someone answer your telephone and avoid interuptions. If the supervisor's workstation is not private, try to find a conference room or go to the cafeteria during off hours to conduct the interview.

Try to make the applicant or employee feel at ease but don't spend a lot of time discussing the weather, traffic, or sports. This doesn't tell you anything. Put the employee at ease by asking a question that can be easily answered. For example, most people can readily talk about their present or last job, so begin the interview with a question related to that.

Maintain control of the interview. If the applicant or employee wanders away from the subject or goes into too much detail, politely bring the applicant or employee back to the subject at hand.

Conclude the interview with a chance for the applicant or employee to ask questions. Let the applicant or employee know what to expect or when to expect a decision. For example, you might say, "We hope to finish interviewing by next Tuesday and we should let you know something one way or another by next Friday."

In a counseling interview, try to come to an agreement as to what you expect to happen in the future and when you and how you expect to follow up the interview or counseling session.

In counseling interviews, try to emphasize and build on strengths. Let the employee clearly know where he or she stands and what actions, if any, are expected in the future. Help the employee form specific goals that are achievable and that will produce the results you desire.

When the interview or counseling session is over, write down the key things you want to remember or follow up later. If an entry is to be made in a personnel record, allow the employee to see it.

WAGE AND SALARY ADMINISTRATION

In most organizations, supervisors have little control over the type of wage and salary system that is used. It is important, however, for supervisors to know how the system works so that they can do the best job possible in administering it. No matter what system is used, the thing that employees want most from a system is fairness.

The simplest method of payment is for output. A commission plan gives an employee a commission, or part of the price received from each sale made. A piece-rate plan measures what a well-trained, hard-working employee can produce and then pays a rate for each unit produced.

A point-factor system tries to decide what factors the firm pays money for and assigns points to each factor. For example, firms expect to pay more for a job that requires a high school education than one that can be done by someone with only a sixth grade education. Factors include such things as experience, responsibility, and hazards. The job description and job sepcifications usually determine how many points are given for each factor. A janitor's job might be awarded 350 points out of a possible 1000 points. A foreman's job might get 600 points out of a possible 1000. The points are then used to rank and group jobs together along a wage scale or curve. The main advantage of this system is the fact that different types of jobs in different departments are compared so that equal pay for equal work is more likely to be given. The job descriptions and specifications are usually written by supervisors so their input into this system is important.

Classification systems are used by the government and many large corporations to group employees into a wage category (for example a GS-6). Standards relating to factors such as the number of people supervised or amount of responsibility are compared with job descriptions and specifications for determination of the category.

A simple ranking system is used by many small and medium companies to determine the wage scale. The best employee or the hardest job in the group is ranked first at the top and then the worst employee or the easiest job is ranked at the bottom. The next-best employee or hardest job is ranked next and then the next-worst employee or easiest job. This continues until all employees are ranked or grouped along a scale.

In most organizations four types of raises are given:

1. Longevity
2. Merit
3. Cost-of-living or across-the-board
4. Promotion

When jobs have been grouped with a point-factor plan or a classification system, there is usually a beginning salary and a top salary for each classification or grouping. An employee who is performing satisfactorily could expect, for example, to move from $5.00 per hour to $6.50 per hour over a five-year period. After five years, the employee is at the "job top" for that classification. This type of raise is a longevity or step raise.

Merit raises are given for outstanding or excellent performance, usually to only the top 15% to 30% of the work group. An employee in the above example could move from the "job top" of $6.50 to a "merit top" of say, $7.00 per hour by doing an outstanding job.

Cost-of-living or across-the-board raises are given because the spending power of salaries may be reduced by inflation or because minimum wage scales are increased by the government causing a realignment of all wage scales.

Promotion raises occur when an employee is promoted from one classification into another.

A single raise may contain some elements of all four types of raises. The supervisor is usually the person most responsible for recommending raises and usually the person most accountable if the system is not deemed "fair."

Raises and pay mean many different things to people. A merit raise is often the strongest form of recognition that the supervisor can use. When poor performance is rewarded at the same level as outstanding performance, morale is usually affected and in the worst situations the best employees often leave.

EMPLOYEE
RELATIONS

CHAPTER

23

GETTING GROUP EFFORT

RUTH SIZEMORE HOUSE

Have you watched a project teeter on the brink of disaster while individuals displayed their individual talents to best advantage? (Or withheld their talents to best advantage, as the case might be?) And have you longed for a way to direct their energies into a single group effort?

A way may be the stuff dreams are made of. But there are *some ways*—some specific methods—that move group effort out of the realm of make-believe and into the realm of reality. In a nutshell: As your staff grows, cultivate group effort by

1. Knowing your people,
2. Complementing group roles,
3. Providing feedback,
4. Rewarding group effort.

And when a problem does develop, prevent polarization of your staff by

1. Naming the problem and encouraging your employees to talk to you about it.
2. Giving employees feedback about effects of the problem on your group's work.
3. Getting your employees to help you remove barriers to group effort and to introduce new choices of behavior.

To illustrate the effects of routine group cultivation or the lack of it, let's look at the case of some technocrats. George is the new supervisor of an engineering department. He's fully confident of the technical ability of each member of his staff. But he's aware of project delays that resulted when his employees failed to pull together as a team. In fact, that's why George was hired. His own supervisor expects him to turn this collection of individual technocrats into a well-coordinated team.

Here's George's staff:

1. *Stan.* A bright young automation specialist, Stan would make a textbook example of the "absent-minded professor." Stan knows a lot and he's perfectly willing to share what he knows. But what he says is often so detailed yet so abstract that listeners walk away in a kind of daze.

2. *Joyce.* The group's secretary, Joyce is almost too good to be true. She's well organized, quick, and capable. But her efficiency sometimes comes across as abruptness. In fact, the rest of the staff seem a little intimidated by her.

3. *Shelley.* She is an outstanding engineer. She began in the drafting department and worked her way through school as she moved up in the company. She has a phenomenal ability to make sense out of a jumble of data—she's a terrific organizer. But in her zest for organization she sometimes bulldozes other people's ideas and feelings without realizing it.

4. *Larry.* The most experienced engineer, Larry is also the most skillful "people person." George senses that Larry may ac-

cept too much responsibility for other people—try too hard to cover for their mistakes or take up the slack on their off days.

5. *John.* He is a young engineer right out of a prestigious university. He's a loner. He seems to resist being "brought up-to-date" on a project by any other staff member.

6. *Mary.* An accountant by training, Mary is bright and quick. But George sometimes feels he has to play "Twenty Questions" with her to get the information he wants. For some reason Mary seems to be holding back.

What a diverse group! Where should George start? What cultivation methods could you use in George's place?

CULTIVATION METHODS

Know Your People

A recent study comparing executives who made it to the top with executives who were derailed along the way concluded: "Ability—or—inability to understand other people's perspectives was the most glaring difference between the arrivers and the derailed. Only 25 percent of the derailed were described as having special ability with people; among arrivers, the figure was 75 percent" (McCall and Lombardo, 1983:31). Don't miss the happy inference that ". . . to understand other people's perspectives . . ." will do more than improve your odds for success on a lone project: it will also improve your long-term odds for success in an organization.

To understand another's perspective is to really *know* that person. How can you start? By *listening* attentively when he or she speaks and by *observing* attentively as he or she works and interacts with others.

To listen attentively you must:

1. First, put your own stream of thought on "hold." You're most likely to succeed at this if you look your employees straight in the eye while they talk and "square away" with them physically. To square away, try to arrange yourself so your eyes are at the

same height as your employee's (easier to do if you're both sitting down). And sit like the Lincoln monument—but with more animation, of course. Keep your feet flat on the floor. (Notice how your body turns away from your employee if your legs are crossed.) And let your arms rest comfortably at your side or in your lap. (Crossed arms can seem like a barrier and "fidgeting" can distract both you and your employee.)

2.   Now concentrate on what your employee is saying as if you will have to repeat it verbatim when he or she is through. Temporarily suspend judgment—don't rehearse the sage advice or the comforting anecdote you might share later. Just listen.

3.   Next, just keep quiet for a few seconds. Don't respond at all until you've counted silently to five or ten. Give your employee the chance to add a "footnote" without feeling pushed, and give yourself a chance for what he or she has said to sink in before you speak.

4.   Finally, summarize what your employee has said in your own words but to his or her satisfaction. At this point it may seem natural to offer some input of your own: advice, instruction, criticism, or reassurance. But each of these is likely to block further communication; each of these is likely to signal the end of the exchange to your employee.

For example, when Shelley virtually explodes with her concern about the data base for some decision, you square away, you concentrate on what she's saying, you let what she's said "sink in." Then you summarize what she's said in a few of your own words: "You think we're moving too far too fast without double-checking our information." You don't cut her short or make light of what she's saying with a remark such as, "Well, time waits for no man— or woman! We've got to do something. I'm not afraid of a few risks!"

To observe attentively:

1.   Notice patterns in your employees' behavior and in their appearance. Who's a morning person? Does anyone actually perk up after lunch? Who likes to work alone? Who would rather get other opinions? Who's always neat as a pin? Who looks like he

combs his hair with an eggbeater? Who takes her lunch hour early? Who's taking a coffee break when?

2. Make it easy for each employee to come in contact with you during some part of his or her daily routine. That may be a snap for those of you who have five or fewer people to supervise—not so easy for those of you who have 10 or more. You can greet some by name as they arrive at work. Say hello to others at coffee break. Walk by workstations or step into offices at other times of day. Wish others a good evening as they leave.

3. Notice changes in individual behavior or appearance. If the change seems to be a positive one, reinforce it. When Stan, who combs his hair with an eggbeater, comes in "all spruced up," let him know he really looks "sharp" (or whatever the "in" word is at the time). That's *not* the same as saying acidly, "Whose funeral are you going to, eh?" If the change seems to be a negative one, be sure the employee has easy access to you in case he or she needs to talk. If Joyce (who usually looks like she stepped right out of *Vogue*) comes in looking bedraggled several days running without approaching you for a talk, approach her. Just say something low-keyed like, "I get the feeling you're having a rough week." Then be silent for the count of 10. If she shows no sign of opening up, then leave her with a comment such as, "Well, I just want you to know I'll be in all afternoon if you'd like to talk about anything." Then be sure to let your secretary or receptionist know you'll be "in" to Joyce even if you're engrossed in some other project.

Complement Group Roles

In order for individual efforts to merge into a single group effort, two kinds of roles (sets of behavior) must be satisfied by members of the group: task roles (behaviors that move the task toward completion) and maintenance roles (behaviors that pull the individuals together into a team).

Task roles include: initiating, seeking information, seeking opinions, giving information, giving opinions, elaborating, coordinating, and summarizing (University Associates, 1976: 136).

Maintenance roles include: encouraging, gatekeeping, setting standards, and following and expressing group feeling (University Associates, 1976: 137).

And some roles contribute to both task achievement and maintenance of the group: evaluating, diagnosing, testing for consensus, mediating, and relieving tension (University Associates, 1976: 137).

The better you know an employee, the better prepared you are to draw on his or her strengths. When a group shows high energy, for example, but has trouble getting the project moving, you might encourage Shelley (a superior organizer) to help get group activities coordinated. Later, if that same group has made great progress on the task but is bogged down with infighting, you can enlist the aid of Larry, a really good "people person." You know that Larry can help get pent-up feelings expressed openly and constructively. Then he can help the group get back on track by summarizing the progress that's been made and the work that's left to do.

The better you know your employees, the better you can fill in the gaps with role behaviors missing in your group. If project members have interpreted group decisions differently several times, it may be up to you to test for consensus and understanding before a staff meeting adjourns.

Your knowledge of group roles, combined with your knowledge of your people, can also have some terrific fringe benefits:

1.   You don't have to be all things to all people yourself; you can draw on the strengths of your staff to move the project along and to pull your team together.

2.   You can identify specific skills to develop in your staff to give them *and* you more flexibility.

3.   You can develop a picture of the specific skills you want in a new hire when you have a position to fill.

Provide Feedback

A recent review of the Hawthorne studies suggests that the improved performance of workers involved resulted not from some mysterious "effect" but from the workers' improved knowledge of results—feedback (Parsons, 1974: 930). And another review of management studies concludes that feedback is ". . . the action lever with the single greatest impact on productivity" (Cummings et al., 1975: 58). (An *action lever* is some characteristic of an organization that can be changed with the reasonable expectation of some desired result.)

Yet, let's face it—most of us supervisors continue to pile heaps of *evaluation* on employees (praise or blame) while serving up only very sparse portions of *feedback*. What's the difference? Well, by definition, good feedback is

Specific,

Measurable,

Goal-related,

Visual when possible,

Immediate.

To hear "Well done!" may be rewarding for an employee. But it doesn't provide the same knowledge of results as "Your sales this month were up 10% from last month. That puts you within $10,000 of your quota for the year. And, as you can see by this chart, it puts the division within $30,000 of its goal for the year."

On the other hand, to hear "You really blew that one!" is only punishing to employees. It gives them no real information they can use to help improve their performance in the future. But they could learn something from, "Acme could have benefited from all five features of our new Model X. But in your sales presentation you mentioned only two. A review of this checklist before your next presentation might help you keep all five features in mind and as a result help you meet your quota for the month."

How about that annual performance appraisal, isn't that enough? Definitely not. In the first place, performance appraisals are usually too general to give an employee concrete information about how to improve. In the second place, helpful feedback doesn't come a year later. It comes right away: right after a sales presentation, in time to make a difference in the very next presentation. Furthermore, appraisals based on peer comparisons can actually be hazardous to performance: any system that "grades on the curve" like some of our college professors used to do is likely to produce" . . . widespread discouragement, cynicism, and alienation" (Thompson and Dalton, 1970: 157).

Reward Group Effort

As your staff works on a project, be sure to reward team effort as well as progress toward completion of the task. How? Well, first you should pinpoint the behavior you're rewarding: ". . . the way you and Larry pooled information"; ". . . the encouragement you each gave after yesterday's setback." Then provide some reward that your staff members are sure to experience as rewarding. Remember that old saying, "different strokes for different folks." (See how often we come back to our original suggestion: "Know your employees?")

And in case you see dollar marks when I use the word "reward," take heart from this response in a survey of employees: ". . . I now have found an employer who believes in me. I feel like a human being again instead of an android typist. I have been handed responsibility without experience and performed superbly . . . just because someone up there had faith in me" (Renwick and Lawler, 1978: 56). In the same survey, employees rated these features of their jobs as the most important:

(1) Chances to do something that makes you feel good about yourself.
(2) Chances to accomplish something worthwhile
(3) Chances to learn new things
(4) Opportunity to develop your skills and abilities
(5) The amount of freedom you have on your job
(6) Chances you have to do things you do best
(7) The resources you have to do your job
(8) The respect you receive from people you work with
(9) Amount of information you get about your job performance
(10) Your chances for taking part in making decisions
[Renwick et al. 1978: 56]

Nonmonetary rewards can come from social interaction, status, the job environment, or job content. Here's an extensive list developed by supervisors and lead performers in a workshop on job instruction.

Social

Certificates of award

Letter to superiors/copy to employee

Letter to personnel file/copy to employee

Parties, showers, picnics, cookouts, and so forth

Award pins

Recognition for good job

Verbal praise, pats on back, "atta-boys"

Attention to person

Passing on compliments

Asking about family, interests, and so forth

Status

Title

Name on desk, door

Furniture

Private/more private office

Status symbols

Business cards

Name and recognition in newsletters

Access to special places

Job Environment

New equipment

Adequate air-conditioning and heating

Ventilation

Less noise

Piped-in music

Private or semiprivate offices
Communication system
Adequate working space
Enough supplies
Less crowding
Office arranged to facilitate doing job

Job Content
Flextime
Choice of assignment
Scheduling own work
Setting own breaks and lunch
Higher-level responsibility
Assignment to special groups and task forces
More access to information
More training
Chance for varied assignments
Chance to specialize
Adequate electrical and office support
Opportunity to help set goals
Having resources readily available
Compliments on work
Sending up their reports to higher management
Change/growth on job
Chance to get more experience

HANDLING A GROUP CRISIS

What about a group crisis? What special action is called for? Let's use George's technocrats as an example.

Apparently John underestimated construction costs on his first project. That's not surprising for someone just out of school.

George wonders why his predecessor didn't catch the problem before the estimate went to the sales department. Based on John's low estimate of cost, the company was awarded a contract. Now it's going to be really difficult to maintain quality without losing money on the job. George believes it's possible, but really difficult to manage.

Yesterday, George held a group meeting in an attempt to tap the brainpower of the entire group. It was a disaster. Shelley exploded at John. John retorted with a sexist remark. Mary—whose input would have been so valuable—closed up like a clam. What should George do now? What could you do to handle this problem situation if you were in his place?

Name the Problem

First, you could name the problem and encourage your employees to talk about it. It may seem like a contradiction to say that the first step of a solution is to name the problem. But when you have listened attentively, observed attentively, and pinpointed a problem, simply naming it—acknowledging it—can clear the air and make room for a solution. Like people, most problems have a first name and a last name: the first name is the feeling that has resulted, the last name is the reason behind the feeling. Bob Carkhuff suggests this formula for giving a problem its full name: "You feel . . . because. . . ." (Carkhuff,1972: 76). If you were George, for example, you might name the group's feeling this way: "You feel like giving up now because it just seems humanly impossible to meet the deadline with all the conflict we've been having around here."

It's a good idea to try out the name on a trusted friend before you share it with the group. You want to be sure it's not judgmental and not emotionally loaded. You would *not* want to give the problem this name: "You feel like copping out because of all the ridiculous scraps you've been having with each other lately."

And it's probably a good idea at first to name the problem to one employee at a time. Otherwise, they may compete with each other for the chance to respond first or loudest and you'll have a skirmish on your hands.

After you've named the problem, encourage each employee to talk to you about it. How? First, just keep quiet for a few seconds. Count silently to 10 or 15 to give the employee a chance to speak up. If the employee offers no reaction, ask a few open-ended questions and allow some time for the employee to respond after each one. Useful questions might include:

What should we talk about to clear the way for a solution?

What do you think has gone wrong?

How do you see the problem?

Before you leave the employee, be sure to introduce some questions that suggest a solution, such as:

What do you think we should do next?

How would things be different around here if they were just the way you wanted?

What do you think we can do to get this project done on time and under cost?

If your employees share their feelings and opinions with you, you're much better prepared to work with them on a solution. If an employee offers neither feelings nor opinions, let him or her know that you are open to his or her input within the limits imposed by the situation. You might say: "If anything comes to mind, I'd surely like to have your input. But Jones insists on having my answer at lunch tomorrow. So I'll have to decide one way or the other by 10:30 A.M.—in time to document my reasons for it."

Provide Feedback

Give employees feedback about the effects of the problem on work. As in the feedback you give during "routine maintenance," try to provide feedback that's specific, measurable, goal-related, visual when possible, and immediate.

In a situation that's likely to be emotionally loaded, it's *especially* important that your feedback *measure* the problem rather than *evaluate* it. Now this example sounds whimsical but it clearly illustrates the difference:

Evaluation	Measurement
His ears look like an elephant's.	His ears are four inches across.

And here's an example suited to that office crisis:

Evaluation	Measurement
That outburst during the meeting yesterday was a fiasco.	The disagreement at yesterday's meeting cost us about 20 minutes. As a result, we couldn't get those plans in the five o'clock mail as we promised.

Don't forget that even during a crisis, *something* may go well. Be sure to notice it with feedback such as: "Even with all the confusion here yesterday, you remembered to give Jones the status report we promised him."

Enlist Employees' Help

Get your employees help to remove punishments for group effort and introduce new choices of behavior.

By this time both you and your employees should have some good information about what's going on and how it's affecting the work. Review the information at hand and see if you can answer these questions: How are employees punished for making a group effort? How are employees locked-in to nonproductive behaviors?

You are likely to find at least a few conditions that present barriers to the group effort you want. Perhaps some people feel punished because group meetings typically run past closing time and make them late for a car pool or for dinner. Perhaps group meetings often degenerate into a "lemon squeeze" where people sound off about the things they don't like without suggesting any constructive alternatives. Maybe one person receives disproportionate praise when a project goes well and others feel neglected. Or maybe a few people receive disproportionate blame when something goes wrong, and they'd rather not get involved.

You're likely to find a few instances of counterproductive behavior by an employee who doesn't know he or she can choose to act differently. Perhaps John backs off from suggestions because he thinks it's a sign of weakness to accept help. Maybe Mary holds back important information because her last boss chewed her out whenever she told him something he didn't want to hear. Could Joyce be so dependent on you because she thinks company policy requires your official approval of all those letters?

When you've uncovered these problems within the problem, use the same approach you've used before:

Name the problem and encourage your employees to talk to you about it.

Give employees feedback about the effects of the problem on work.

Then enlist their help in removing the obstacles you've uncovered. Perhaps you'll need to:

Reschedule meetings so they don't cut into personal time, or get consensus on time limits and then stick with them.

Develop some guidelines with your group for turning a "lemon squeeze" into a problem-solving session.

Use a checklist to be sure you give feedback to all employees who contributed to a successful project.

Be sure your own approach to a problem is oriented toward finding a solution, not toward placing blame.

Model the behavior you'd like John to choose: solicit his ideas and be sure he knows how you put them into action.

Invite Mary to share information when you think she's holding back; and be sure to reward the sharing, whether the news is good or bad.

Encourage Joyce to talk about her choices. Maybe even work through a couple of case studies with her to clarify some ambiguous statements in the policy manual. Help her distinguish between the times she should "go by the book" and the times when her best judgement should be her guide.

Pulling together as a team isn't easy. You can't do it overnight. And it won't happen without setbacks and disappointments. But your effort to build team cooperation " . . . justifies itself . . . as a means of overcoming the limitations restricting what individuals can do" (Barnard,1938: 230). In other words, the whole—your team—will become greater than the sum of its parts.

REFERENCES

Barnard, C. I. *The Functions of the Executive.* Cambridge, Massachusetts: Harvard University Press, 1938.

Carkhuff, R. R. *The Art of Helping.* Amherst, Massachusetts: Human Resource Development Press, 1972.

Cummings, T. G., Edmond S. Molloy, and Roy. H. Glen. "Intervention Strategies for Improving Productivity and the Quality of Working Life. *Organizational Dynamics* 4, no. 1 (Summer 1975): 52–68.

McCall, M. W., and M.M. Lombardo. "What Makes a Top Executive?" *Psychology Today* 17, no. 21 (1983): 26–32.

Parsons, H. M. "What Happened at Hawthorne?" *Science* 183 (March 1974): 922–931.

Renwick, P. A. and E.E. Lawler. "What You Really Want from Your Job. *Psychology Today* 11, no. 12 (1978): 53.

Thompson, P. H., and G.W. Dalton. "Performance Appraisal: Managers Beware." *Harvard Business Review* 23 (January 1970): 149–157.

University Associates. "Role Functions in a Group." In *The 1976 Annual Handbook for Group Facilitators.* Edited by J. William Pfeiffer and John E. Jones. La Jolla, California: University Associates, 1976.

SUPERVISORY SKILLS

Yes, I want to become a member of the New York Zoological Society and get free admission to the Bronx Zoo and the New York Aquarium all year long.

☐ $35 Individual Member   ☐ $45 Dual Member*

☐ $45 Family Member   ☐ $60 Sustaining Member   ☐ $125 Supporting Member

Please print clearly:

FULL NAME _____

ADDRESS _____

CITY _____ STATE ____ ZIP _____

DAYTIME PHONE (____) _____ Required

*Dual Membership is for two adults, no children. List here name of second adult:

_____

Please make check payable to New York Zoological Society and send to: New York Zoological Society, Membership Department, Bronx, New York 10460. For further information, call 212-220-5111.

Join the

New York Zoological Society

and get free adventure all year long.

Travel around the world — from the African plains to the Asian jungle, from the tops of the Himalayas to the ocean floor — all at the Bronx Zoo and the New York Aquarium.

In addition to free admission to the Zoo and Aquarium, you will receive a one-year subscription to **Animal Kingdom,** our bi-monthly magazine, invitations to members' events, and these benefits:

INDIVIDUAL MEMBERSHIP — $35
— free admission for one adult
— 5 parking tickets, 10 ride tickets for the Safari Train, Skyfari, Bengali Express, JungleWorld, and the Children's Zoo
FAMILY MEMBERSHIP — $45
— free admission for two adults and children 16 and under
— 10 parking tickets, 20 ride tickets
DUAL MEMBERSHIP — $45
— free admission for two adults only, no children
— 10 parking tickets, 20 ride tickets
— a membership card issued in each dual member's name
SUSTAINING MEMBERSHIP — $60
— free admission for two adults and children 16 and under
— 10 parking tickets, 20 ride tickets
— private tours of the Zoo by appointment
SUPPORTING MEMBERSHIP — $125
— all the privileges of Sustaining Membership PLUS:
— unlimited free parking
— invitations to special contributing members' events

CHAPTER

24

PROBLEM SOLVING AND DECISION MAKING

LINDA M. LASH

THE BALFORT HOTEL PROBLEM

The Balfort Hotel chain enjoyed a good market position in its region with 80 hotels in a three-state area and over 4000 employees. The net profit margin was only 10%, but the hotel chain had consistently turned this profitability since its founding in 1950. The hotel chain prided itself on its friendly service and kept its prices similar to the well-known national chains that also operated in the area.

The chain was managed by its founder until 1970 when Stephen Balfort retired, and management seemed to change every two to three years as the hotel chain continued to promote from within and hire professional hotel management in an attempt to gain stability in the management ranks.

Since 1968, there had been a quality assurance team whose job was to visit the hotels on a surprise basis and check the condition of the hotels against a comprehensive list of technical items. The check included inspecting 10 guest rooms ready for guests, plus a general check of common areas for safety, image, working order, and so forth. Each hotel received about three inspections per year, and each inspection resulted in a comprehensive technical report with graphs and comparisons with previous visits, other Balfort Hotels, and competitors (the quality assurance team also stayed in competing hotels to gain a comparison). A copy of each report was sent to the manager of the hotel inspected, to the area manager, and to the general manager.

Beginning in 1980, the net profit margin began to slip. The general manager reacted quickly by asking each hotel manager to implement a cost-reduction program. The hotel managers each did what he or she felt was best in the way of cost reduction, with some of them cutting costs on essential guest services.

Revenues and the net profit margin continued to slide downward. The general manager issued strict guidelines on cost control, including some head-count reductions, the temporary suspension of preventive maintenance routines on hotel equipment and facilities, and the cancellation of any image-improvement expenditures.

While cost reductions began to show in the net profit margin, revenues continued to decline. The sales department was instructed to make more sales calls and to sign more small accounts, and the marketing department was set to work to devise and implement weekend promotions, vacation rates, and convention promotions. Further cost-reduction programs were implemented so that more advertising money could be spent.

The sales department began to report more and more complaints from accounts on the condition of the hotels, the service, and billing errors. The staff at the hotels, forced to work in gradually deteriorating surroundings, wear old uniforms, and listen to more complaints about malfunctioning heating or plumbing, grew less friendly and more demoralized. The personnel department was instructed to implement better recruiting techniques in order to hire better staff, and the training department was ordered to conduct training courses to motivate the employees and teach them how to sell.

During this two-year tailspin, the net profit margin continued to decline, revenues declined, market share slipped, occupancy levels declined, and three general managers were hired and fired. Five separate task forces were appointed at various times to identify the problem and solutions.

One of the task forces was sent to the Balfort Hotel in Davis to investigate severe customer complaints and a high turndown level. While occupancy levels at all of the hotels in Davis had been high, the Balfort Hotel in Davis had applied cost-reduction programs exactly as other Balfort Hotels with declining occupancy levels had. The task force obtained copies of the quality assurance reports for Davis and used these as the basis for its report.

In 1983, despite innovative marketing programs, heavy sales activity, and highly visible advertising, the Balfort Hotel chain posted its first loss.

In the now-empty office of the general manager lay three years' worth of unread quality assurance reports which accurately, clearly, and objectively tracked and defined the problem.

BRUCE'S DILEMMA

Bruce joined Stardust Travel as a junior office clerk 13 years ago, just after leaving college. He worked hard to learn the business and enjoyed working for Stardust. Promotions came easily, and he had worked his way up to the position of supervisor of the leisure travel services area of Stardust's office in Trenson. His staff consisted of an assistant supervisor, a secretary, and seven agents and clerks.

With his wife just having given birth to their first child and the progress he had made at Stardust, Bruce had not had much time to think about his future or to discuss any future plans with his family. Promotions thus far had simply happened to him, and he was happy with his progress. He had been supervisor of the leisure travel services area for two years now, and it was about time for another promotion, according to his previous progress. He wondered casually what the next promotion might be. His managers over the years had always looked after his interests well.

One afternoon the Trenson branch manager called all of the supervisors and managers together and told them that he was leaving Stardust that very day to join a competitor and that a new branch manager from Pittsville would replace him tomorrow. Bruce was used to management changes at Stardust and did not view this change as too significant. At Stardust, he reported now to Eva, manager of the consumer services department, and Eva reported to the new branch manager.

A week later, Eva advised Bruce that she was also leaving to work for the previous branch manager at a competitor. Bruce was stunned for a moment but then thought that this might be an opportunity for him to be promoted to Eva's job.

The next day, a friend of Bruce's who worked at Stardust's head office called Bruce and told him that the branch manager of Stardust's small branch in Dorking was retiring and that Stardust was looking to replace her with a young supervisor from one of the bigger branches like Trenson. That night, as Bruce's wife tended to their new baby, Bruce thought about the two possible promotions—manager of the consumer services department in Trenson and branch manager in Dorking. Bruce felt pretty confident that he could do either job and that Stardust would consider him for at least one of the openings. Bruce reckoned that Stardust would begin interviewing the following week and that would give him the weekend to talk to his wife.

The next few days at work were very hectic with peak vacation bookings and the new branch manager trying to learn Trenson's routines and find a house for his family. On Friday morning, Bruce has a brief conversation with the new branch manger. The new branch manager asked Bruce a few questions about houses in Trenson, a few questions about the number of vacation bookings that week, and a question about Bruce's career goals. Bruce answered the questions, giving a fairly lighthearted answer to his career goal of simply moving ahead, and thought no more of the conversation.

Over the weekend, Bruce and his wife discussed the two openings but could come to no conclusion as to which job would be better. On Monday, Bruce decided, he would speak to the new branch manager about his interest in the two jobs.

On Monday, the new branch manager was not in the office, but on Tuesday morning Bruce got to see him. The new branch manager was surprised at Bruce's interest in the two jobs, particularly the one in Dorking since Bruce had indicated on Friday that he had just bought a house in Trenson and hoped to live there quite a while. The new branch manager advised Bruce that both jobs had been filled the day before and that Stardust was unaware that he was interested in either job.

THE CONTINUOUSLY ACTIVE GERUND

It is no accident that the title of this chapter consists of two gerunds—problem solving and decision making. A gerund suggests continuous motion or continuous activity, and that is exactly what problem solving and decision making are all about. The two are continuous business activities that supervisors do daily. How they are done—whether the problem is solved or whether the decision is made correctly—is a critical factor in successful supervision.

In the Balfort Hotel problem, we find a great deal of continuous activity, but the continuous activity does not result in the solution of the problem. The story is unfortunately true, and it is the story of a corporation that failed to correctly identify the cause of the problem. At any level, from the supervisor to the chairman, the problem is best solved if the problem and its causes are correctly identified. The following section on problem solving explores some of the methods, techniques, and critical factors that work best in solving problems.

In Bruce's dilemma, we also find continuous activity, but the continuous activity occurs on different timetables, and the decision to speak to someone is made too late. There are many, many examples in our lives of decisions not made quickly enough—stock not bought or sold at the right time, a vacation not taken at the right time, a phone call not made in time, and so forth. Timeliness is a critical factor in decision making, and a further section explores this and other critical factors in decision making.

PROBLEM SOLVING

Identifying the Problem

Sometimes the problem is easy to identify—you want a mink coat and a Rolls Royce but you don't have the money to buy them—but often it is difficult to correctly identify the problem because:

1.   It is not just one problem; it might be several or many problems intertwined.

2.   It may be costly to identify, for example, require much research, require the purchase of information, require dismantling or interruption, and so forth.

3.   There may not be time to identify it properly.

4.   There may be obstacles in the way, for example, people who do not want the problem identified, laws preventing the procurement of certain information, and so forth.

5.   The problem may involve people's feeling or most-cherished goals, and these are not always easy to obtain or judge.

There are lots of reasons why a problem is difficult to identify. The important thing is to use all of the resources you have or can get—time, staff, money, information—to help you correctly identify the problem.

Dream a While

One of the best ways to help identify the problem is the "dream a while" technique. Sit back with your thinking cap on and ask yourself the key question: "What would the world look like if this problem did not exist?"

Let's suppose your company has asked you to look into a customer billing problem. All you know is that customers are complaining that their bills are wrong. The first step is to sit back with your thinking cap on and ask yourself the key question: "What would the world look like if this billing problem did not exist?" The answer will probably be that no customer complaint letters or calls come in because there are no billing errors. This would lead you in the direction of examining the customer complaint letters or phone call reports to ascertain what errors customers are complaining about.

Let's suppose you have an employee who does not like to perform a certain task and is therefore doing a less-than-average performance when this task has to be done. Sit back with your thinking cap on and ask yourself the key question: "What would the world look like if this problem did not exist?" The answer will probably be that the task would be getting done correctly. From there you can go on to investigate whether the task could be done by somebody else or why the employee does not like doing this task.

Identifying the Cause of the Problem

When we say that it is often difficult to identify the problem, we may mean more specifically that it is difficult to identify exactly what is causing the problem. In the Balfort Hotel situation, the problems of declining revenues, market share, and net profit margin were identified, but the causes were not identified correctly by management.

The causes may be difficult to identify for the same reasons that the problem is difficult to identify and also because it may not be possible to identify how it all started.

A typical problem might have several causes, each of which requires a solution. Billing errors, for example, might be caused by a computer programming error or by a combination of simple human mathematical errors coupled with a few new employees who have not been trained on a certain billing technique. An employee may not like doing a certain task, for example, simply because he or she does not understand its importance and value to the company or because he or she has not been trained to do it well and also gets no recognition or sense of achievement for doing it at all.

Finding a Solution

Pathway to the Dream

Once the problem and its causes have been identified, the solution may be very easy or at least easy to identify. In many problem-solving situations, supervisors find that the most time and effort are devoted to the identification of the problem rather than to the solution. The solution, however, cannot be neglected.

Before mapping out a solution, it is a good idea to quantify the problem—how big it is, how much it may cost to solve, and how much it may cost to let the problem continue. Cost can be considered in pure economic terms, in time or resource terms, or in human motivational terms.

If you can identify what the world would look like if the problem did not exist, it should then be possible to identify the steps to achieve this dream. One successful method is to take a sheet of paper and do the following:

1.   Describe the problem in performance terms—what is not happening or what is happening incorrectly.

2.   Describe what the world would look like if the problem did not exist.

3.   List the causes of the problem.

4.   Beside each cause, list the actions to be taken to resolve it.

5.   Beside each action, list who is responsible to do it, what the due date is, and what the cost will be to take each action.

This should not be lengthy, flowing prose but rather a few key words to identify each of the points.

Evaluating Alternatives

Some problems and their causes may have several possible solutions, resulting in a choice of alternatives. In these situations, decision making becomes a critical part of problem solving since a choice must be made.

A good technique is to list all of the ways you could possibly use to get to the ideal situation, that is, the way the world would look if the problem did not exist. Each of these ways will have advantages and disadvantages as well as costs in terms of pure economic factors, in time or resources, or in terms of human motivation.

Seeing Problems and Opportunities

There are some managers who do not allow their employees to say they have a problem; they allow their employees only to say they have an opportunity. This is a technique intended to dispel some of the negative connotations of the word *problem* and to encourage the positive direction of providing a challenge or opportunity for a creative solution.

Whether you call it a *problem* or an *opportunity*, the identification of a problem is certainly an opportunity for someone to gain a sense of achievement from contributing to the identification and solution of it.

Common Pitfalls to Avoid

There are a few pitfalls to avoid in successful problem solving.

1. If the problem or its causes have been identified incorrectly, a correct solution is very unlikely. Jane was a supervisor with 15 female employees who each wore a company uniform every day. Jane noticed in the past few weeks that her employees had begun to wear their uniforms very poorly. Some of them wore dirty or wrinkled uniforms, some wore excessive jewelry, some wore nonregulation shoes and stockings, some had messy hair and makeup, and some even wore articles of their own clothing with the uniform. One day when Sarah, an employee with only six months of service, was not wearing any part of the uniform except a scarf and a name badge, Jane asked Sarah where her uniform was. Sarah responded casually, saying that she wasn't aware it was that important to be in uniform every day. Jane decided the cause of her problem was that her employees had forgotten how

to wear the uniform correctly. She called the training department and asked them to send an instructor to conduct a training session stressing grooming techniques and the importance of wearing the uniform correctly. The training department sent an instructor who put all of Jane's employees through a one-day session. For a few days afterward, Jane's employees wore their uniforms a bit better, and then the situation returned to its previous state. The punishment for identifying the problem or its causes incorrectly is that you may have to perform the process all over again.

2.   It serves no useful purpose to identify the problem and then not solve it. Howard supervised a staff of 12 clerks whose job it was to process charge card applications, issue charge cards, and input customer data into a computerized data base. The computer system was complex and documentation on how it worked was incomplete. Howard had previously been part of the systems team that designed the system, and this probably had a bearing on his appointment to his current position. After six months in the job, Howard began to identify some of the problems with the system, such as:

Once data was put into the system, there was no way to purge it, even if a customer became inactive.

The system consisted of several files and an update to one file did not automatically result in an update of other files with the same information.

Input documents were not filled out correctly and Howard's staff did not correct errors before input.

Over the next year, Howard's staff members continued to perform their jobs in the same way, and Howard continued to identify the problems—writing memos and reports, some of which went to management.

After a year and a half, the customer-data files were in poor shape with an estimated 50% of the data incorrect or useless. The sales and marketing Department convened a review meeting on the customer-data files, which by that time were resulting in customer complaints and inaccurate marketing and sales statistics. Howard was invited to the meeting and asked to define the problem. Howard assembled all of his memos and reports into one large volume which he presented with great pride. The sales and marketing people were impressed with the size and detail of the problem identification, which contained pages of technical information and technical words not familiar to sales and marketing people. At the meeting they reviewed Howard's document, and Howard gave precise explanations of how each problem occurred. After this lengthy technical review, the director of marketing asked, "How do we solve all of these problems?" All heads turned to Howard for the answer. A critical factor in business success is the solution of problems, which *begins* with the identification of the problem and its causes but which *must* be followed with active solutions.

3.   Problem solving that involves people's feelings and most-cherished goals requires careful handling to insure that the problem and its causes are correctly identified and to insure that the solution comes to pass. Good listening skills are essential, as is the ability to do your own research as opposed to listening to gossip or other people's assumptions. Madelyn was a supervisor who had worked her way up through the ranks in only five years. Madelyn reported to George, along with three other supervisors who had similar responsibilities—Tom, Roger, and Shirley. One day in the employee cafeteria, Madelyn overheard parts of a conversation at the next table between George and Tom. They seemed to be talking about a management opening. Tom was close to retirement, and Madelyn thought she heard them say that Roger was not ready for such a move yet. Then she heard snatches of conversation that sounded like, "No, we'll have to hire from the outside. She's come up through the ranks and isn't professional enough." Since Shirley had been transferred in from another area, Madelyn was sure they were not talking about Shirley but about her. Madelyn checked the job-posting board after lunch but found no posting that seemed to be the one Tom and George were discussing. The next week, Madelyn had lunch with Roger and told him what she thought she had heard. Several times that week over lunch, Roger and Madelyn commiserated together over their plights as a black supervisor and a female supervisor and watched for signs of any openings.

Over the next few weeks, Roger and Madelyn devoted less and less time to their jobs and more and more time to discussing various office events and comments that seemed to point in the direction of both Roger and Madelyn falling out of favor. George began to notice the lengthy conversations between the two supervisors and also the neglected work. George decided to watch the situation for a few days to see if it would return to normal. The next day George had lunch again with Tom, who volunteered the opinion that he thought Roger was upset because he had had to take on some of Shirley's work and that Madelyn, he had heard, had broken up with her boyfriend. It is important in situations like this to pinpoint the performance problem and deal with it openly and honestly to get at the true causes.

DECISION MAKING

Identifying the Decision

Decision making is like problem solving not only because both are continuous business activities but also because a critical first step is identifying the problem to be solved or the decision to be made.

While some decisions are presented simply as two choices or alternatives—for example, do you want vanilla or chocolate ice cream?—some situations which look very complex may be reduced to a series of decisions which will accomplish the goal or objective. In these situations, the "dream a while" technique can be employed to ask yourself two key questions: "What would the world look like if this situation did not exist?" and "What decisions could be made to bring the world to look like this?"

What If

A good technique in decision making is to ask yourself the "what if" question: "What if I decided this way, what would my subordinates, peers, and managers think and what would be the consequences?"

Using the what-if question can lead you to a series of alternatives, each with advantages and disadvantages that can be measured in some kind of cost terms—funding, resources, market advantage, human motivation, and so forth.

The Time Factor

The amount of time available to make the decision is very often a key factor. In a burning building, the decisions to get out and how to get out must be made instantly. The amount of time available also affects your ability to get all of the facts you need to make a decision.

Very few decisions are made with unlimited time and all of the facts. A good technique to practice is to begin getting facts as soon as you know a decision must be made. The idea of delaying the decision until you get more facts is one alternative that can be considered in using the what-if question.

Decision-Making Techniques

The techniques used in making decisions are similar to those involved in the choice of management style:

1.   Will you make the entire decision yourself, will you ask others for their opinions and then decide, or will you delegate the decision-making activity to others?

2.   Will you do research to get the facts or will you ask others to get the facts?

3.   Will you evaluate the alternatives yourself, will you ask others for their opinions, or will you ask others to evaluate the alternatives for you?

4.   Will you make use of brainstorming sessions or quality circles to help you decide, or will you obtain information from subordinates, peers, or managers?

The available time, the skills and knowledge of those around you, and your own style will all affect the techniques you use in decision making.

Living with Your Decision

A decision is not usually wrong when you make it; it only becomes wrong after more facts become available or after the situation changes.

Supervisory or management responsibility includes not just the responsibility for making a decision but also for living with the decision you have made. Whenever you are making a decision, it is always a good technique to ask yourself how you will live with the decision you are about to make. Will there be additional opportunities to alter the direction with new decisions in the future if the first decision proves too difficult to live with? Is there a risk of losing your job or promotional opportunities if you have to live with a decision you are about to make? Will you be able to explain to yourself and others the rationale behind a series of decisions that appear to be inconsistent?

One protective technique that also helps develop your subordinates is to explain your decision as you make it. This helps subordinates learn to make decisions.

A classic example of having to live with a decision is the supervisor who decides to drink heavily at an office party and have an in-depth conversation with his or her manager about career goals. It is a good technique to make decisions in such a way that living with them will not be forever unbearable.

Common Traps to Avoid

In decision making, there are common traps to avoid:

1.   Time pressure imposed artificially by others around you, particularly by subordinates, is a difficult situation to deal with and can be reduced or avoided by questioning and researching the reasons for the time pressure. John, a sales supervisor, rushed into his manager's office and explained that he needed immediate authorization to plan a trip to an important account in three weeks' time. He held out the trip authorization form for the manager's signature, stating that if he booked the flight that day, he could

save money for the company with a special airfare. While on the surface this may seem straightforward, there are usually a few minutes to ask a few questions about the purpose of the trip.

2. Large decisions with large costs and long-range effects are best made carefully. Ruth, a training supervisor, was assigned to find suitable office space for a new training center with two class-rooms and an office. After days of investigating company sites, she found suitable space in another company's office building, but there was another prospective tenant and she would have to get her manager to sign the lease as quickly as possible. Such a decision requires further facts and figures before a costly long-term commitment is made.

3. The short-range and long-range implications of decisions are often difficult to weigh and are susceptible to political angles. Marie worked for several weeks as part of a project team assigned to identify the costs and benefits associated with introducing a new range of home computers for her company. The team was aware that its company's major competitor would announce and display a medium-priced home computer next week in an effort to be first, but that it would not be supported with fast delivery dates, reliability and servicing, or readily available software. The project team was assigned to produce a reliable cost analysis and prediction of whether its company should announce its compet-itive computer around the same time with similar disadvantages, or whether the final product with fast delivery dates, reliability and servicing, and readily available software should be introduced six months later. As Marie and the other project team members worked feverishly in a small conference room, senior managers stopped by, interested in their progress. The vice-president of marketing commented that their company's reputation in the computer field would force consumers to wait for the "right prod-uct." The vice-president of personnel commented that he was afraid some of the development people were going to form their own company. The general manager expressed his confidence in each member of the project team and went on to say how much he wanted to have the edge over his golfing buddy, the compet-

itor's general manager. The vice-president of information services stopped by to chat and mentioned that within 10 months she expected the development people to have perfected a portable personal computer that would retail for under $100. These comments came sporadically as the team worked with market projections, costs, and imagination.

TED'S PROBLEM AND DECISION

Ted joined Romulus 12 years ago at the very bottom and worked his way up to a middle management position, working the last 10 years for Robert. Although Ted now successfully managed the area Robert had managed for years, most people still thought of Robert as the expert in the area and came to him with their questions and requests. Robert also continued to exercise control over Ted's area, sometimes even reversing Ted's decisions and giving assignments to Ted's staff directly.

Because Ted had worked for Robert for many years, he felt comfortable talking to him even on sensitive matters and decided he would try a bit of problem solving by talking to Robert directly.

The two had a good and productive conversation, with Ted explaining his desire to manage on his own with less guidance, and with Robert saying he thought Ted was too sensitive but he would try harder not to interfere.

Nothing much changed, so Ted obtained the names of some job placement counselors and contacted them for interviews. Despite an impressive resume, Ted found that the job placement counselors weren't too interested in helping him find another job. At the end of the third such interview, Ted decided some factfinding was necessary so he asked the job placement counselor what he was doing wrong. The counselor gave him a few tips and, as an aside, pointed to a two-year position he had held during his career at Romulus, telling Ted that the way he described that job seemed to indicate it was the perfect job for Ted.

Ted spent the next few days covering sheets of paper with alternatives, advantages, and disadvantages in an effort to make a decision about his future. He like Romulus and did not want to leave the company, but he wasn't sure how much longer he could tolerate his current position. In between making notes, Ted picked up the telephone and called a senior manager in the area he had worked in two years ago. His old job opened up that very day, with increased responsibilities and pay.

25

COMMUNICATION

The Basic Skill for All Other Skills

ROBERT HAYS

Other chapters in this book will show us a wide array of skills needed by supervisors, such as assigning; managing change, time, and stress; goal setting; training of workers; and many others. What factor do all of these skills share—other than, of course, their importance to a supervisor? Clearly, all other skills depend on communication ability. Whatever else a supervisor does, he or she must communicate. In fact, some experts define *organization* as "a group of people working toward a common goal"; and reaching that common goal depends on communication.

Leading people in a common effort demands that the leader communicate well with them. Failure of a common effort long ago showed communication skill to be the supervisor's most important tool. The biblical account of the Tower of Babel pointed out the disaster resulting from lack of that tool. The Babel contruction project simply fell apart. This failure did not arise from any shortage of materials, money, machines, or methods. Babel failed because the work force could not speak a common language. We can imagine the utter frustration of the crew chiefs and project managers when Babel became a babble of voices!

Organization today depends even more on understanding among its members. John, a maintenance supervisor, did not realize the importance of communication. John should have heard Charlie, one of his leaders, complaining during a break:

"That guy just took one of my group off the job, and that surely irked me!"

"Why?" asked Sue. "He *is* the supervisor, you know."

"Sure," fired back Charlie. "But he holds a leader responsible for getting the work done. And he reassigned one of my carpenters without even telling me. I only found out when I chewed out my carpenter about leaving the work I had assigned."

This type of problem must occur thousands of times daily. Usually the problem does not arise from any lack of knowledge of technical skill. Instead, the problem arises from failure to pass along decisions, ideas, information, or questions. Some problems lead merely to irritation or minor friction. But sometimes failures to communicate well result in disaster—law suits, prosecution, loss of market share, personnel turnover, or even bankruptcy.

Thus we can see the importance of communication. And the importance of this skill implies another fact. Skill in communication is vital to any supervisor's long-range career:

The supervisor whose ideas stay locked up in his or her head;

The supervisor whose subordinates cannot understand his or her instructions; or

The supervisor who cannot convey (sell) ideas to higher management.

Such people will retire on the lower rungs of management's ladder. Worse, they may fall off even the lowest rung. Conversely:

A supervisor who transmits ideas effectively will sell those ideas.

A supervisor who communicates well with workers can apply that ability to planning, training, assigning, and other tasks.

The supervisor who reports clearly and efficiently to higher management attracts favorable attention.

In summary, then, developing communication skill leads to working more effectively, getting work done better, and becoming more promotable.

FACTORS IN COMMUNICATION SKILLS

Before learning particular techniques in communicating well, we must consider the major factors in on-the-job communication:

Selection of a purpose,

Appraisal of the communication climate,

Analysis of the receiver,

Self-analysis,

Choice of timing,

Selection of a method and a medium,

Use of nonverbal communication,

Analysis of content,

Maintaining feedback.

Of course, these factors suggest that the supervisor is sending messages, writing memos, instructing people, making phone calls. However, the last factor—alertness to feedback—implies an equally important role for the supervisor—the role of listener and observer. In fact, as we shall see, some of the supervisor's best communication can come when he or she has mouth closed and eyes and ears open.

This listing of factors will serve as the skeleton for the rest of this discussion. Now let us put muscle on the skeleton by exploring each factor and offering some ideas for improving communication skill.

Selection of Purpose

Surprisingly, far too many supervisors try to send a message before they decide why they are communicating:

Jane would never think of moving one of her people to a different work area without careful plans for moving. She would check with personnel, plant engineering, and all other related departments. Yet Jane's rambling, unplanned memos leave her people wondering, "What on earth was Jane trying to tell us?"

Randy would never travel overnight to his Alabama district without an itinerary. But Randy's unplanned trip reports leave his boss puzzled: "What did Randy's trip really accomplish? His trip report reads like a set of AAA instructions, not a real trip report."

Luckily, we aren't in Jack's clerical group. Since his people don't work in assembly, Jack can pull them off their jobs at any time for a meeting. But Phil, Jack's computer operator, describes Jack's meetings as "a complete waste of time . . . no point . . . nothing gets done."

Renee's communication lacks purpose in a different way. She doesn't waste her people's time. Worse, she wastes the time of higher management. Her phone calls to the main office digress. Consoled by her WATS line, she forgets the value of the other party's time. She even wastes the time and attention of her own boss, with talk that has no goal. If someone urged Renee, "Let's go somewhere," Renee would demand to know "Where?" "Why?" Yet she places phone calls and intrudes on her manager with no sense of purpose.

Appraisal of the Communication Climate

Communication research in recent years has shown the importance of climate to all communication, both on and off the job. *Climate* means "the total of attitudes about the situation in which communication takes place." Climate prompts these questions: What history has management shown in previous messages? What is each supervisor's track record on messages? Do subordinates consider messages to be as reliable and honest as possible? Do supervisors inform subordinates about upcoming changes? Do messages from above meet employees' needs better than the grapevine does?

Climate from the past controls communication. In a favorable climate, subordinates assume management's good intentions and ignore mistakes. In a climate of distrust, hostility, and suspicion, employees will distort even the clearest message and they will unfavorably interpret even pleasant news.

Thus, supervisors who communicate with others will assess the climate:

"How will my readers or listeners probably feel about my message?"

What resistance, quibbles, nit-picking, or hostility do I expect, and how can I avoid these attitudes?"

"Within this climate, how can I best send along my ideas? With whom and when should I communicate?"

Of course, climate both affects and is affected by each message. Therefore, supervisors should wonder:

"How will this message affect the work climate of the future? Will my next message be harder or easier to send?"

Analysis of the Receiver

To state the obvious, the end-user of a message is a human being. Files, phone lines, satellite channels, word processors, and computers can improve the appearance, speed, permanence, and efficiency of movement of messages. But only the human listener or reader can use the messages. Thus the human receiver becomes all-important.

Supervisors who must talk or write should observe that we tend to

Be most interested in that which affects ourselves;

Resist anything which we consider threatening to our ego, status, position, reputation, or security;

Suspect changes, especially if decreed or imposed by people of higher rank or people whom we do not like;

Want a voice in our own destinies, and resent being treated as pawns.

Most important, we humans

See the world through our own attitudes and experiences, in psychological terms *perceptions*.

These principles should suggest to supervisors that each person lives in two worlds: (1) the objective world of reality; most of us agree rather closely on things in this world—forces of nature, laws of physics, dangers of certain activities, and other measurable facts; (2) the perceived world; this world exists in our interpretations and ideas—our own aims, likes, and feelings. We build this world from our own plans and materials.

Let's look at an example. Unlimited Corporation's higher management wants to cut costs by putting in new, numerically controlled tooling, reorganizing departments, and revising duties. Such changes should lead to more competitive pricing, higher profits, and by implication, greater job security. However, Shawn, an operating-level supervisor has some misgivings about Unlimited's new look. Members of Shawn's group have even greater distrust. Note the range of differences in perceptions:

COMPANY PRESIDENT: A great new day for Unlimited!

SHAWN: We supervisors jostle for new positions!

AMANDA: There goes the overtime pay I need!

ZACH: I'm only five years from retirement. Bet they try to chop off the old hands. I won't have time to learn the new jobs!

SAM: Just when I get used to working with Shawn, somebody "turns over the fruit basket"!

HAYLIE: That means the new hires will leave first!

DORA: My husband and I move to different shifts!

HENRY: The brass make themselves look like heroes and get bonuses. At the bottom we get the ax!

In a good climate and with wise management, Shawn can partly answer these misgivings. Of course, the climate at first appears to be the responsibility of top management. But Shawn plays a role in perceptions, too. And far too many supervisors lose sight of subordinates' perceptions. These people-blind supervisors invest all of their concerns in technical detail—specs for the new tooling, diagrams of new flow, sketches of organization charts. Such people-blind supervisors are creating a poor climate.

People-smart supervisors empathize, that is, they try to imagine how their subordinates will view ideas. For example, Shawn should reflect that if he—a supervisor—has some misgivings, his people must wonder even more how the new equipment will affect them. Of ocurse, Shawn can never completely empathize with each of his people. But Shawn should realize that his work equations never balance until the human beings appear in those equations.

Each worker's perceptions come from skills, habits, job experiences, backgrounds, hopes, traits, goals, and attitudes. Of course, the package of perceptions changes with passing time and with new experiences. But the package of perceptions will always affect the worker's ability to understand messages; follow instructions; ask useful questions; provide the supervisor useful information; interpret and apply plans; and make decisions as required.

Self-Analysis

So far this discussion has focused on the receiver and the climate. Such emphasis is proper; too many people overlook the receiver. They think that communication will require only sending out a message, with no attention given to how the receiver interprets the message.

Yet the sender is an important factor, too. The sender must

analyze himself or herself for any strengths or weaknesses. Some supervisors' strengths lie in informal, one-on-one private conversations. Others perform well in talking to groups of passive listeners. Still others excel in guiding a conference group to solve problems.

Appraisal of weaknesses is also important. Jake should realize that he talks too long and therefore never lets his people take part. Irma should learn that she doesn't look her listeners in the eye and that she displays a serious voice mannerism ("you know" almost every sentence). Someone should tell Robert that his phrases, accepted in the oil fields, offend some office personnel. Constance needs to organize her writing to prevent her reports from seeming like literary obstacle courses.

The ancient Greeks upheld the motto "Know Thyself." Today's supervisor follows the same rule before writing, phoning, dictating, conversing, or listening.

Choice of Timing

Many experts on management have pointed to a sense of timing as one of life's vital traits. Surely, knowing when to do what will greatly help in plants, offices, and sites. Let's cite some extreme examples of poor timing. In April, Lori submits her plan for career development in her state agency. Yet in April Lori's boss pays attention to almost nothing except preparing next year's budget. Doug supervises accounting for a small retailer. He, above all, should know when most workers are busy with inventory. He should wait until after inventory to send out his new policies on refunds, exchanges, and claims. Kathy has so many ideas that can't wait. She bursts into her boss's office with her latest—when she is behind in her routine work.

Timing reduces to a simple question: When should this message get to receivers for them to understand and use it properly? An answer to that question depends upon these factors:

Any set deadlines;

The time needed for any action a receiver must take;

The time when the receiver is best ready to pay attention to the message;

The time needed for any coordination;

The time needed for transmission. (Even electronic movement can delay messages, with overloaded circuits, the receiving terminal down, or a receiver busy or not available. Nonelectronic movement, such as mail, can delay transmission even more.)

Selection of a Method and a Medium

Prehistoric people had few ways to send messages: signals or drawings (line-of-sight) and sounds (hearing distance). The inventions of writing, printing, and, more recently, other media for messages allow us many more ways to exchange our messages. However, the range of choices for message sending also burdens us with choosing the best method to meet competition from other messages. And the great increase in message sending vastly increases the "noise"—unwanted messages and distractions.

The prudent supervisor will carefully select the way to communicate from among many ways, or by a combination of these methods:

Orally.   Speech (conversation, phone, p.a. system, meeting, conference, formal interview).

In Writing.   Letter, TWX, memo, bulletin board, chain message, report.

Pictorially.   Pictures, graphs, drawings, samples.

Repetitively.   Sending the same message more than once.

Metacommunicatively.   Communication about a message ("Could you repeat that last statement?")

Connotatively.   Tone (in speech), implication, or choice of words (speech or writing).

Choosing the medium is also essential. Choice of a way to send a message should depend on:

Availability. What the supervisor has or can get.

Importance. Priority compared with other messages.

Cost. Direct charges and value of time.

Permanence. A record for future reference.

Competition. Getting the receiver's attention and cutting past noise.

Suppose that Laura wants to communicate with Amos, her counterpart across the country. She could phone Amos, a low-cost method for a brief message. The phone call would allow them two-way communication. But the call would require Amos to be available. Laura could write a memo at her convenience, for Amos to read at his. But a memo would cost more (in Laura's time) and would offer only one-way communication. In other circumstances Laura may have other possibilities.

Most of us have considered the advantages and disadvantages of various communication devices. However, the following brief table will help remind us:

Medium	Advantages	Disadvantages
Person-to-person	Offers good feedback Can be informal Can be easily arranged Focuses message	Is limited in numbers reached
Phone call	Is cheap and fast Offers long-distance contact Is readily available	Is limited in numbers reached
Meeting or conference	Gives good feedback Emphasizes group unity Troubleshoots ideas Involves participants	Is costly in time Can lead to unexpected results

Medium	Advantages	Disadvantages
Oral presentation	Is efficient in reaching large numbers of people quickly	Is very costly in time For many, may be inconvenient Demands special facilities
Note, letter, or memo	Can be detailed as needed Can be well organized Documents a record Can be prepared at writer's convenience for reading at reader's convenience	Is one-way, with no feedback Is costly to prepare Is slow
Posted notice	Is usually cheap	Offers no feedback May be missed by many

In summary, choosing a method and medium is usually not a complex decision. But the decision does warrant thought.

Use of Nonverbal Communication

Only recently have researchers really studied a type of communication which we have practiced all of our adult lives. We actually send each other messages in many ways besides speaking and writing. The previous discussion suggested some of these, such as the connotative use of words. Now let us look more at types of messages which—even if unconsciously sent—may carry far more meaning than words alone.

Supervisor Jill tries to explain to department manager Alex her problems with scrap and salvage. Jill talks earnestly, and Alex may hear at least some of her words. But Jill senses that Alex is not really listening. How does she know? His body language tells

her. He does not look at her. He does not even face her. He doo-
dles on his desk pad. Finally, he looks at his watch and scowls.

Jill leaves, mumbling, "Show you the rest later."

Alex's voice says, "Thanks, Jill. That was very good to know."

But Alex's body and movements have said, "You're not getting
through to me."

Which messages will Jill believe? If she has studied nonverbal
communication, she may well believe body language.

Nonverbal communication—messages other than words—can
include many menas, singly or in combinations:

Kinesics.   Body position, stance, location, gestures, postures,
movements, contacts; facial expressions; reflexes and rituals
(such as handshakes); eye contacts and glances; nervous responses (coughs and giggles); and nearness to the other person.

Behavior.   Response or lack of response; attention and alertness;
dress and appearance; choice of receivers; selection of priorities
for messages; filtering or obstruction of others' messages.

Competition.   Fighting against or trying to use the grapevine;
struggle against noise.

Environment.   Noise or distractions; location, layout, and fur-
nishings of work space; status symbols (such as parking spaces,
names on doors); separation and isolation; availability of devices
for communicating.

Chronological.   Use of time; promptness or lateness.

Personal.   Rank, title, authority, power, and "clout".

Climatic.   Atmosphere, attitude, values; tension; stress; intim-
idation or openness; consistency and dependability; rewards
or punishments; formal and informal associations; recog-
nitions; general relationships and rapport; activity of grape-
vines.

Much nonverbal communication can be subconscious, for instance, gesturing or scratching. But we can control some nonverbal
messages. A few principles should help any supervisor to make
nonverbal messages reinforce the words he or she uses.

1.   Methods should be consistent with each other. For example, body language should agree with what a speaker is saying. A scowl does not fit with a spoken commendation.

2.   Climate is vital (as already mentioned). If the receiver does not trust the sender, messages dependent on trust will fall on deaf ears or blind eyes.

3.   A combination of reinforcing methods works best. For instance, an open discussion may come before a written summary of a meeting. An advanced summary of a directive may emphasize the openness of the discussion to come later.

4.   Feedback (to be discussed later) gives vital clues to message reception.

5.   Conflict between verbal and nonverbal messages can cast doubt on the verbal message. Actions may indeed speak louder than words.

6.   The face, and especially the eyes, tend to be the best clues to nonverbal communication.

Analysis of Content

Most supervisors realize the importance of what goes into a message. They know that each message must be suited to and must serve the reader or listener. However, a few questions will help remind a supervisor to plan the content of each message carefully:

1.   What does the reader or listener know, want to know, and need to know?

2.   How will the receiver use the message? What is the downstream end-result of the message?

3.   What points may be misunderstood or may cause problems?

4.   At what level should the language be?

5.   What is the best order for arranging ideas?

6.   As a result of sending this message, what will probably happen and what should happen?

A brief example will show the value of planning content. Jo reports to her manager on her trip to check routine safety practices at a pipeline pumping station. Jo could report in strictly chronological order, covering in detail each hour from departure to return. In effect her trip report would prove that she was busy every minute.

Instead, Jo asks herself questions 1. and 5. above. She realizes that her manager most wants to know: "Were safety practices okay at the station?"

Like most writers, Jo needs to make some sort of outline before writing. So Jo scribbles this outline:

Heading.   Date, to, from, subject.

Paragraph 1   Identify trip (dates, place, purpose).

Paragraph 2.   Summarize results (safety practices okay; brief review of recommendation).

Paragraph 3.   Give details of site visit (persons contacted, inspections made, and so forth).

Last paragraphs.   Conclusions and recommendations.

Attachments.   Photos, schedule of safety training.

With this outline, Jo makes sure that her report will be a management tool and not just a supervisor's duty.

Maintaining Feedback

We have already referred to feedback. *Feedback* means "the message(s) sent from the receiver back to the sender." It is both a most important and a most easily neglected step in sending messages. Feedback makes communication a two-directional activity. Openness to feedback comes from a supervisor's recognition of his or her real role—not a broadcasting station sending to passive listeners, but a two-way radio, both sending and receiving. This exchange of messages should at the least tell the supervisor whether the reader or listener gets and understands the message.

The value of feedback comes from the fact that meaning takes place not in the mind of the sender but in the mind of the receiver. A message means what a reader or listener thinks that message means, not what the sender wanted it to mean. Thus, a receiver may get more than, less than, or something different from what a speaker or writer intended. A receiver may "read between the lines," interpret words in his or her own way, place his or her own emphasis on ideas. The receiver filters words, phrases, and nonverbal ideas through his or her own perceptions. And a receiver may distort or omit it trying to read or hear what she or he wants to read or hear.

At lunch one day David casually mentioned to Hal: "We're looking at some minor changes in tool-crib checks." Someone interrupted before Hal, a toolmaker, could seek an explanation. From David's comment, Hal later drew several conclusions. He put his notions on the grapevine during the break and in his car pool later.

The next day, David heard from the grapevine that the company was going to change the area tool-crib system to a central-stores system. The grapevine gave David feedback; feedback directly from Hal would have short-circuited the grapevine.

Feedback can come in a range of ways and times. Any way of sending a message can become a way of returning feedback. Unfortunately, feedback can come at inconvenient times. The busy supervisor may have to ask an employee, "Could we talk about this tomorrow, when you have more time to tell me what you think?" But the busy supervisor will keep that promise.

Neglect of an employee's responses invites disaster (especially in teaching complex or dangerous jobs). No supervisor should simply ask, "Do you understand?" and settle for the glib answer "sure." Thinking about their own feelings will help supervisors to seek feedback. Don't supervisors use their peformance reviews to give workers feedback? Doesn't any supervisor welcome the chance to state his or her own views to higher management? Wouldn't a supervisor reprimand an employee for ignoring squealing bearings or smoking wiring? Why then should a supervisor ignore responses from the tools for doing his or her own work?

A MODEL FOR COMMUNICATION

A model or schematic will help summarize what we have discussed thus far:

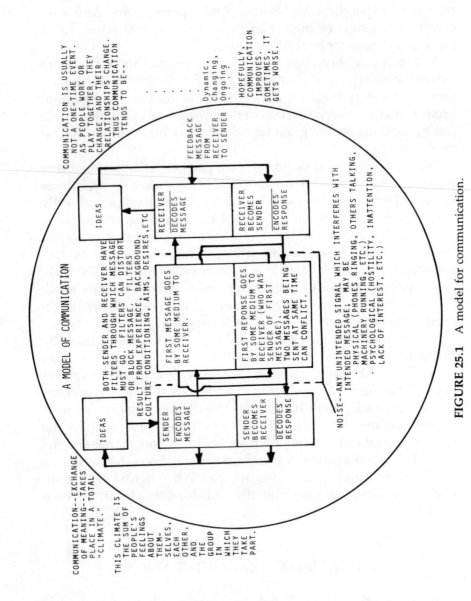

A MODEL OF COMMUNICATION

COMMUNICATION--EXCHANGE OF MEANING--TAKES PLACE IN A TOTAL "CLIMATE."

THIS CLIMATE IS THE SUM OF PEOPLE'S FEELINGS ABOUT THEM-SELVES, EACH OTHER, AND THE GROUP IN WHICH THEY TAKE PART.

BOTH SENDER AND RECEIVER HAVE FILTERS THROUGH WHICH MESSAGE MUST GO. FILTERS CAN DISTORT OR BLOCK MESSAGE. FILTERS RESULT FROM EXPERIENCE, BACKGROUND, CULTURE CONDITIONING, AIMS, DESIRES, ETC.

COMMUNICATION IS USUALLY NOT A ONE-TIME EVENT. AS PEOPLE WORK OR PLAY TOGETHER, THEY CHANGE, AND THEIR RELATIONSHIPS CHANGE. THUS COMMUNICATION TENDS TO BE--

Dynamic,
Changing,
Ongoing.

HOPEFULLY, COMMUNICATION IMPROVES. SOMETIMES, IT GETS WORSE.

FEEDBACK MESSAGE FROM RECEIVER TO SENDER

IDEAS

RECEIVER DECODES MESSAGE

RECEIVER BECOMES SENDER ENCODES RESPONSE

IDEAS

SENDER ENCODES MESSAGE

SENDER BECOMES RECEIVER DECODES RESPONSE

FIRST MESSAGE GOES BY SOME MEDIUM TO RECEIVER.

FIRST REPONSE GOES BY SOME MEDIUM TO RECEIVER (WHO WAS SENDER OF FIRST MESSAGE). TWO MESSAGES BEING SENT AT SAME TIME CAN CONFLICT.

NOISE--ANY UNINTENDED SIGNAL WHICH INTERFERES WITH INTENDED MESSAGE; MAY BE
· PHYSICAL (PHONES RINGING, OTHERS TALKING, MACHINERY RUNNING, ETC.)
· PSYCHOLOGICAL (HOSTILITY, INATTENTION, LACK OF INTEREST, ETC.)

FIGURE 25.1 A model for communication.

25.16

This model shows several facts about communication:

It is two-way.

It involves feedback.

It takes place in a climate.

It must compete against noise.

It filters through perceptions of both sender and receiver.

But this model does not show another feature vital in all super-visory communication: the fact that communication is dynamic.

THE DYNAMIC NATURE OF COMMUNICATION

Change, the rule of life, clearly applies to exchange of messages on the job. Jobs can change with new products, services, equip-ment, materials, and competition. People change, too, with age and experience. And relationships can shuffle as people work to-gether over the years and they themselves change. The organi-zation changes as it grows or shrinks and as people come and leave. Thus, communication alters to different patterns, networks, channels, contents, and climates. Hopefully, change brings im-provement.

Bull has not improved. For one thing, he has not yet learned the value of feedback.

"Gee, Bull," complained Henry, an employee, "I didn't get the word."

"Hey," Bull retorted, "Why weren't you listening?"

Sally, another employee, defended her mistake: "Bull, I didn't know the part belonged there."

Bull sarcastically stated, "When all else fails, then read the di-rections."

Maybe Henry and Sally sometimes do deserve blame for not having paid attention. But Bull seems to face these problems too often. His communication practices are static. Despite the passage of time, his model of sending messages looks the same way it did 15 years ago. His many problems with people should have warned him to explain jobs more clearly.

With the passage of time, not only should Supervisor Bull improve; the entire climate should improve. As senders and receivers work with each other, they should polish their skills in exchanging messages. They should develop a keener sense of timing. They should become more aware of each other's strengths and weaknesses. They should learn to cope better with noise. And they should learn how to watch for each other's perceptions.

Two major devices help in improving communication as time passes. One is feedback, already discussed. The other is alertness to communication problems or failures.

EVIDENCE OF COMMUNICATION PROBLEMS OR FAILURES

"Communication problem" is such a familiar phrase that people almost automatically blame every hardship, lack of success, or mistake on "communication problems." But some problems do not arise purely, or even partly, from poor exchanges of messages. Troubles can arise from bad actions, decisions, or conditions. For example, even the most persuasive builder might not overcome a bad credit history in seeking a construction loan. Many ideas elsewhere in this book will apply to activities which, even though involving communication, are more than matters of sending messages.

Yet communication often fails. Here aresome possible signs of failure in exchanging messages:

Actual results differ greatly from expected results.

A listener or reader asks for a message to be repeated.

A listener or reader asks for more information.

A listener's body language suggests a lack of proper understanding (quizzical look, glances elsewhere, yawns, "fiddling" with some object, hostility shown by crossed arms with clenched fists, reddening of face, vigorous head shaking, and many other signs).

The grapevine says that employees ignore official messages, are confused, or resist decisions.

Employees rely more on the grapevine than on proper channels.

Mail gets no response or is returned undelivered.

A request for information produces no response, poor results, or useless data.

An employee (or, in fact, anyone) tells the sender that he or she is not communicating.

Employees express hostility in such ways as surly responses, sloppy work, or excessive absenteeism.

Employees break into isolated cliques beyond the normal tendency to form friendships.

Employees do not respond to appeals for common self-interest, such as supporting a charity drive.

Employees deride such attempts at communication as an "open-door policy," suggestion box, or house organ.

Many good people quit, transfer, or retire early.

Customers complain of rudeness.

Employees seem to rejoice in the organization's lack of success.

Of course, any of these symptoms may suggest more than mere problems in communication. Some may suggest a need to replace managers, design better products, or change policy. But a wise supervisor will consider poor communication at least a contributing factor.

THE SUPERVISOR AS A LISTENER AND READER

Despite the earlier warning that messages should go two ways, this chapter so far has mainly depicted situations with supervisors sending messages. Now, let us emphasize that a supervisor's best communication may take place when pen (or typewriter) is resting, eyes and ears are open, and mind is alert.

For the good supervisor is both a good observer and a good listener. In fact, one wise manager sums up advice to new shift supervisors: "Get out from behind your desk and associate with your people and find out what's going on!"

Too many supervisors dig moats around themselves. They crave fancier, more isolated work areas. They go to lunch only with other managers or higher-ups or staff. They rely only on reports and memos for their information. They neglect feedback from customers and suppliers, and—worst of all—from their own employees.

Many military leaders have learned to "get out of headquarters and mingle with the troops." But firsthand observation, a supervisor may add a new dimension to his or her knowledge, through

Sensing the tone and attitudes of the workplace.

Learning from the grapevine.

Checking the information gained from reports and memos.

Spotting troubles long before they would have shown up in memos or reports.

Assessing work habits and relationships.

Appraising better the work done by people who cannot write good memos and reports.

Finding potential leaders.

Building a mental file for commending, training, and guiding people.

Most important, personal observation by a supervisor shows that management is interested.

Some supervisors dislike spending much time in their work areas. They welcome meetings elsewhere or gossiping in executive offices. They fear that "familiarity breeds contempt." They point out (correctly) that supervisors are not paid to replace the work force. And, frankly, some are too intent on polishing their images in the eyes of higher management.

However, all of these excuses miss the point. Indeed, the supervisor has higher rank. But he or she is also an employee. Furthermore, to listen and observe does not mean backslapping familiarity or losing respect in "just trying to be one of the gang." Nor do listening and observing equate with taking over workers' jobs.

Watch Larry:

'Twas the night after Christmas, and all through the buildings . . . plumbing was breaking and flooding floors and equipment. (Someone forgot to leave all buildings heated.) Larry called in his crew Christmas night to clean up the mess and repair the plumbing. Larry stayed with his crew all the time, resisting appeals from his family to go home. He had never had a formal course in management, but Larry knew an essential of being a good supervisor: "Thanks," he said, in refusing an invitation to leave for a long meal, "but when my people are here, I am too. That way, I know what's going on."

Larry observes. He considers observing the key to supervisory success. He knows that firsthand data can produce information that is filtered out of reports. Also, a supervisor who has been there can remind higher managers, "I've visited that site." We can learn from Larry a few tips for observing.

Tips on Observing

1. Appear willing to learn, not anxious to intrude.

2. Do enough homework to ask intelligent questions.

3. Probe for understanding. For instance, ask such questions as "What would we do if we got a bad lot of paint?"

4. Know and use employees' names or, if they do not object, nicknames.

5. Watch for things which do not look right, and seek explanations.

6. Follow the rules of the area (such as wearing hard hats and not smoking).

7. Do not bypass lower levels (crew chiefs, lead people, party chiefs). Remember the case at the beginning of this chapter.

8. Unless a crisis or hazard arises, don't interfere. If you must reprimand, try to wait for a better time.

9. Show interest in workers' ideas. One good idea can make a visit worthwhile, and the person who offers that idea deserves recognition.

The Supervisor as a Listener

We have warned that real communication is two-way. We also note that hearing and listening are not the same. Hearing is physical—absorption of sound. Listening is mental—selecting and processing certain sounds. Let us also realize these facts about listening.

1.   Listening must be active. We must be involved in trying to get information, attitudes, ideas, perceptions from other people. We listen *with*, rather than *to* others.

2.   Messages from others filter through two sets of perceptions: theirs and then ours. Thus we do not get all of every message, but we try to get the core of it.

3.   Noise (any unwanted sound) distracts real messages.

4.   A speaker's message is far more than words. It can include body language, pitch, tone, and reactions.

5.   Good listening offers a supervisor many benefits: a chance to assess what an employee really wants the supervisor to understand; a chance to confirm or negate ideas now held; a chance to prove to employees that a supervisor is really concerned.

Some Tips for Listening

Here are tips (some obvious, some not) for good listening:

1.   Listening requires hearing. Minimize distractions. Seek a place where outside lights or motions will not interfere.

2.   Listen and watch for nonverbal clues to what other people mean.

3.   Do not rush to conclusions. The other person may need time to get his or her real message across.

4.   Keep attention focused. We can hear and process at least five times as fast as another person can talk. Use the slack time to ask, "What is Jane really trying to tell me?" "Why does Sam bring up this matter now?" "If I have to write a report on what Harry says, what main points is he making?"

5. Summarize occasionally: "Well, Sue, as I get what you're saying, you think our new work schedule does not fit." This summary checks your understanding.

6. Accept silence; John may be groping for words.

7. When possible, research the subject beforehand. If Ellen wants an appointment to talk about the new plotter, your "homework" pays off in showing your interest. Also, you'll ask better questions. If you need time, ask for—but explain—the delay.

8. Realize that Peggy thinks her ideas are important. So rushing in with "You perhaps don't know about . . ." may turn her off. Besides, she may know something you don't know.

9. Don't let prejudice block your listening. If you continually think. "Jim is bringing in another of his half-baked ideas," Jim's idea can't get a fair hearing. Even if you don't like what Jim says, try to understand him. You can disagree after you know what he means.

10. Show your attentive attitude with your whole range of verbal and nonverbal language.

11. Do not promise more than you can deliver. If you must refuse, do so. Of course, your listener will expect (and deserve) an explanation. Promising an action only to avoid unpleasant confrontation will return to haunt you.

And finally, in the pressure of job demands, others vying for your attention, higher management pushing you, avoid the temptation of cutting off feedback. You cannot always listen at a given moment. Some employees prefer talking to working. Others cannot express themselves well. But your people will find ways to express themselves—if not to you, then to someone else. That other listener may be the shop steward, government agents, customers, other employees, or even top management. You should prefer to be the listener.

A ROUNDUP OF TIPS

Let us close this chapter with specifics, some already cited or implied, others derived from principles discussed.

1.   Communication should occur under the best conditions.

2.   Timing is vital. Questions and answers deserve prompt attention—provided a supervisor is certain of the right response. But wasting higher management's time with trivia can provoke wrath.

3.   Knowing the ground rules (policies, laws, customs, union contracts, decisions) helps to prevent being "caught off base."

4.   Communicating when ill or in a bad mood is unwise.

5.   Homework and thought can prepare a supervisor to cope with questions and hostility.

6.   "Passing the buck" is bad strategy; it undermines a supervisor's authority.

7.   Wise supervisors expect respect and politeness but not fawning, "greasing," or false humility.

8.   Needling people (interrupting, quibbling, playing games, or nit-picking) chokes off communication.

9.   Confrontation is a last resort. Much better is an attempt to solve problems productively.

10.   Accepting constructive disagreement can aid in a search for improvement.

11.   Good strokes (commendations) and bad strokes (reprimands) both have places in urging improvement. But any reprimand should focus on a change in work habits and not be a personal attack. Supervisors should deal with employees as adults and not act like a parent scolding a child.

12.   Supervisors must lead. They cannot abdicate, nor can they dictate (at least not in the long run).

13.   Employees do not demand perfection. A supervisor can admit mistakes or a lack of knowledge. Pretense of knowledge is risky.

14.   The old military saying "Loyalty up begets loyalty down" holds. Blind obedience is absurd. But criticizing higher managers in front of one's subordinates invites subordinates to do likewise.

15.   Irrelevant (not job-related) remarks about race, sex, looks, or age provoke complaints and perhaps grievances and legal action.

16.   Dishonesty breeds itself. Supervisors cannot always tell all they know, but they should avoid lies. False gossip is always dangerous. So is theft of a subordinate's ideas.

17.   Honest commendation pleases anyone, but it must be sincere.

Communicating in writing:

1.   Planning is crucial in deciding when, how, and to whom to send a document.

2.   Analysis of a reader before writing is as vital as choice of destination in planning a trip.

3.   A buffer (good news, an attempt to get on common ground) usually should come before bad news (any idea which the reader will resist).

4.   Before starting a memo or letter, a writer should ask himself or herself.

"What will result from sending this document?"

"Is this the best time to send this document?"

"Who has an interest in this document?"

"What is at stake in this subject?"

"What attitudes will my reader(s) probably take toward this subject? What is the climate?"

"How much credibility do I have with my reader?"

"Would oral communication work better?"

5.   Any writing should serve a reader—should tell the reader what she or he wants or needs to know.

6.   The style, level, length, detail, arrangement, and attachments should fit the intended readers.

7.   Starting with a road-map paragraph or sentence to identify the report and a summary to point out the major ideas will meet most readers' needs. But if the writer expects disagreement, a buffer should usually come before the summary.

8.   Writers enjoy advantages over speakers. Writers can prepare material at their own convenience, use attachments for detail, and edit the final draft.

9.   But writing creates more risk than speaking. A document becomes evidence on the record. Also, writing requires a large investment in time.

This chapter has emphasized one major point: skill in communicating is basic to every other skill in supervision. Communicating well requires planning and careful execution, just as every other supervisory action does.

REGULATIONS
CONSIDERATIONS

CHAPTER

26

THE SUPERVISOR AND REGULATIONS

MARTIN M. BROADWELL

The supervisor is constantly faced with the fact that his or her organizational life is regulated by many things and many people and many organizations. It may or may not cause a hardship. It may or may not be a detriment, or perceived detriment, to the job at hand. In the past several decades, governments at all levels have imposed more and more regulations. Governmental agencies have been created with the specific purpose of regulating the workplace. Society as a whole has seen increased regulation from governmental agencies. However, it isn't just government that is regulating us; we are constantly regulating ourselves with committees, new systems of management which require forms of regulation, and additional appraisal programs which make it necessary for us to be controlled by forms, or procedures, or systems. When we think about our job of "getting the work done through others," we may ask ourselves if, with all the regulations, we aren't trying to get the job done *in spite* of others! What can the supervisor do to get the day-to-day job done, when confronted with all the various impositions, often unrelated to the job, that have been thrust upon him or her? We'll try to answer that in this chapter. Let's start by saying that the easiest thing to do is to realize early and clearly that regulation is a part of the job, not something separate from it. We cannot think of rules and regulations as being different from the job of getting out work. In this chapter we should be able to put regulation in the right perspective, where it belongs, as a part of the everyday activity of doing business as a supervisor.

REGULATION: FACT OF LIFE

It would be impossible for us to make it through the day—any day—without being confronted with some form of regulation. We live in a regulated society. Even the temperature is regulated in the houses and buildings where we live and work. Everything about the building where we work is built by regulation: the heating, the plumbing, the electrical installation, the structure itself—all are regulated. If we drive to work, there are all kinds of traffic regulations, from stop signs and stop lights to speed limits and one-way streets. We may take these for granted, but even here we find that some of them seem overly restrictive. We wait at a light while it is red, easily seeing that there are no cars coming. We creep along in a slow zone when the road surface and apparent safety conditions would accommodate a much faster speed. Yet the restrictions are there. We pay taxes, though we don't always approve of the way they are spent; but the regulations say to pay certain amounts. We go to the pool and find we can't swim because no lifeguard is present, knowing that we can swim better than the lifeguard; but we don't swim because it would be a violation of the regulation.

Why do we tolerate such inconveniences? Usually it is easier to live with them than to change them, and we realize that we often have to have "blanket" regulations because we aren't smart enough to develop regulations that fit all conditions equally well. Of course, when it comes right down to it, we know that regulations are there for a purpose and we respect the purpose, if not the regulation.

WHY REGULATIONS?

There are those who feel very strongly that we don't need any regulation at all, that we'd be much better off if people would just go away and leave us alone and let us do our jobs. In fact, they say, we have too many laws, too many regulations, so we ought to do away with them all and live our lives without outside influence. Few would argue that we don't have enough laws, and probably few would argue that we don't have too many regulations. But why do we have them and how did they come into being? Without getting into politics, let's just say that for the most part the regulations that are imposed upon us are generally the result of our *not* doing what we should have done in the first place—when we didn't have the regulations. Somebody somewhere, at some time, failed to do the right thing by some individual or group of people. It may have been an oversight or it may have been intentionally, but nevertheless the regulation came about because we didn't do what some people felt was necessary to get the job done or to move society along in a certain direction.

Take the matter of coffee breaks, for example. Why do we have to take them at specified times, for specified lengths? Suppose people were left alone to make their own decisions, what would happen? Most would regulate themselves; some would take advantage of the freedom. Most would take a coffee break when it was convenient to get away from the job without having the job suffer. Some would take a break when they felt like it, stay as long as they liked, and let the job go. Some would say, "Well, just punish them and let the rest do as they are now doing." But what is that? It's a form of regulation: As long as you do what we think is right, we won't do anything; when there is a violation of the rule, the action is . . . (which becomes the regulation.) It's been attributed to many people, so we'll just say *someone said*, "If we don't regulate ourselves, we can be sure of several things: (1) somebody else will impose a regulation; (2) we won't like the way they did it; and (3) we probably will never get rid of the regulation!"

There are different kinds of regulations and each exists for a different purpose, or at least serves a different function. Although functions aren't completely clear-cut, let's look at some.

1. *Protect People from Themselves.* People can do strange things to people. They can take advantage of other people. They can show favor to others. They can use their position to cause some to prosper and others to fail to get what is their "right." Whether it be from bias or prejudice, or from ignorance, it still happens, and we have regulations to protect us from ourselves. For example, we make laws and provide regulations that direct that people be hired on the basis of job requirements and individual skills, rather than according to who they are, what they believe, what they look like, or even how old they are or their marital status. This means that we have regulations on such things as fair employment, and equal opportunity, and retirement ages. The regulations also extend after hiring to include upward mobility and affirmative action. How did all these regulations come about? We've already seen that we brought them on ourselves. Somebody somewhere, in some organizations, failed to regulate themselves, so society took on the job. Society takes on the job of regulating because we don't do a very good job of self-regulation.

2. *Protect People from Things.* It is interesting that throughout the ages people have invented and developed things that serve people but that also have the potential to turn against the inventor or developer. The steam engine gave us the power to go faster than we had ever gone before, but then we had train wrecks and trains running over people. The automobile gave us a mobility that made for a great economic society, but it gave us the power to kill thousands of people every year. All kinds of machines have been devised to make, mold, and manage any product we want to make, but those same machines break bones, cut off fingers,

mangle bodies, and damage hearing. There are chemical products that give us materials and conveniences and produce comfort and pleasure unheard of not too many years ago. Those same chemical products and the processes that produce them have the potential of harming the environment in ways unthinkable those same not-too-many years ago.

What do we do about all of this? We develop regulations aimed at protecting people from the things that we've made and developed. We get more regulations because we haven't done a very good job of protecting ourselves from ourselves. Perhaps because we have put more emphasis on end products than on by-products, we need some way to see that legs aren't mangled, that fingers remain on hands, and that the air is breathable. Thus, we get the OSHAs and the EPAs and other regulatory activities. They aren't our enemies, these regulations; they are our protectors. We need them. It's a better place because of them. There are fewer accidents, less lost time, healthier people, and, in the end, greater productivity and profit

Part of protecting people from things includes such seemingly innocuous things as dress codes and regulations on hair styles or hair lengths. It isn't because people are unhappy with the kind of clothes others wear or the way they wear their hair. It's because there are conditions, machines, and circumstances which will harm people if there aren't some regulations. The sign that says "No beards in the refinery area" isn't a protest against beards or hippies; somebody has determined that the gas masks that must be worn in emergency situations won't protect those who wear beards. The same is true for loose clothes or long hair around moving equipment: the machine is not selective in what it chooses to pull through or entangle, so the regulation attempts to protect workers from that nonselectivity.

3. *Protect Things from People.* Like a giant heart, the control room in any large plant offers life to the plant. People are watching dials, reading meters, listening for alarms, looking at displays, observing computer printouts—ready to take immediate action when something goes wrong. The maintenance person fixing the air conditioner in a small office has a tool in one hand, a manual in the other. From one extreme to the other, each is an example of regulation at work, protecting equipment from people. If there

is an error of some kind or a breakdown in the human-made equipment, the control room allows somebody to find out before things get too serious. Each of the control mechanisms is a form of regulation. The manual used by maintenance is a regulation saying, "Do it this way." When a piece of equipment is started up by referring to a checklist, the checklist is a regulation saying that if you do it this way the equipment will work properly. Something as mundane and commonplace as a standard operating procedure is a regulation, as the name implies. Most organizations have something like an SOP. Whatever it's called, it is our regulatory effort to see that equipment isn't wrongfully treated by the people assigned to use it and work on it. It is a very necessary part of the workplace!

4.   *Provide Comfort, Advantages, Equalization, Status.*   As we drive into the parking lot, there is a sign that says, "Reserved for the handicapped." Another says, "Reserved for the Director." Each of these signs is a direct regulation. If we aren't classified as either handicapped or the director, we can't park in those spaces. Why do we have these kinds of regulations? They provide different things for different people. For the handicapped the regulation provides equalization and comfort. It allows those people to compete in terms of the time it takes to get from the parking lot to the workplace. It allows them the comfort of not having to struggle in some way that doesn't offer any advantage to the end product of work. For the director it offers convenience for his or her comings and goings at hours different from the others. It also offers status as an additional reward for having obtained this particular rank. The regulation is necessary because it isn't likely that the workers would voluntarily leave a space for the director or for the handicapped. This isn't to say that they don't believe each should have special parking privileges; they just wouldn't think of it on a rainy day when they were running late.

ATTITUDES TOWARD REGULATION

Perhaps of all the important things to be said about regulations, the most important is that if regulations are accepted by the organization, then, for all intent and purposes, *they are a part of organizational policy*; hence they are not to be treated lightly, ignored, or thought of as necessary evils. Just as we can't pick and choose which policies we like and don't like or will and won't observe, we can't decide that we do and don't like certain regulations. If it is policy, then we not only observe and abide by the regulation, we *support it* as long as it is recognized as something the orgaization wants us to believe in. By now we have seen that there are reasons for policies, procedures, and regulations, so we not only accept them, we back them up, because they are best for the environment in which we are living and working. Being a part of the supervisory team, we are on management's side. We have an obligation to make the regulations work, whether we like them or not, whether we are in favor of them or not, and whether or not we even understand why we have them. Just as we don't always know why top management has certain policies that we have to enforce but we nevertheless abide by them, so we also enforce and abide by those regulations which don't make much sense to us.

Of course, not every regulation imposed on us is unfavorable, stupidly conceived, and designed to make our lives miserable. Most are reasonable, practical, well thought-out, serve obvious purposes, and serve to give us an obviously better work life. Because they are a part of policy, most of them are so much a part of the work scene that we don't even notice them as we go about our jobs; they don't interfere with our functions. We have to watch that we don't object to them simply because they've been imposed by an "outside" source, or for reasons other than increasing production or that relate directly to the job. For the most part, people prefer to control and direct themselves, so there is a natural resentment to being controlled and directed from the outside. Overcoming this natural tendency will help us to more easily accept the regulations—certainly with a more open mind.

What about those regulations we don't like, that we think are perhaps more than just an irritant, that are a hindrance to getting the job done? Do we have to live with them, too? Again, as a part of policy, we do have to accept them, abide by them, enforce them, and discipline those people under us who don't follow them.

However, if we have legitimate reasons for not liking them, or for thinking they are keeping us from getting the job done, there is some action we can take. The organization provides its employees with processes for communicating suggestions up the line. Most places even have avenues for changing policies. Whatever these avenues are, we can use them for channeling our objections to the regulations. If enough people object, or good enough arguments are presented, there is ammunition for management to take steps to change the regulations. Part of our job, then, is to see that top management knows that there are some problems with the regulations, especially as they relate to production, customer service, or employee relations. These things are important to management, and they can act more quickly to institute changes if we furnish them with the information to support the changes. We may not get the results we want, or the results may not come as rapidly as we'd like, but at least we've met our responsibility as a supervisor when we've used the means available to try to get action. We have to remember that most suggestions are turned down—for legitimate reasons—as are most suggestions for changes in policies. However, we still have an obligation to try.

Another factor in our attitude toward regulation is how our employees see us. As we've just discussed, supervisors have a responsibility to support regulations as long as the organization want them supported. This support goes beyond just our own thinking and mental acceptance. It includes our actions with and around our employees. Not only do we enforce the regulations and discipline those who don't follow the rules, we also go on record as supporting them. We make sure that we don't let our employees think a rule is lousy, one that is imposed on us and that we follow even though it makes us miserable. The first time we hear ourselves saying something like, "This is a lot of garbage, but we've got to do it anyway," we should know that we're in trouble! We should be much happier when we hear ourselves saying, "There are some valid reasons for this, so let's stick with the rules," or "Hey, this *is* policy, you know; the organization wants us to do it this way, so I'm sure you all want to do it by the book."

We also must give the employees the same right we ask if they still don't like the regulations: they should be able to use their available avenues for disagreeing or making suggested changes. That's what they do if they don't like a procedure or are opposed to some policy; they should be able to do the same thing if they don't like something about the regulations. Obviously they should get the same hearing that they get about any of their other suggestions or complaints. It is sometimes unfortunate that organizations hide the fact that there are dissatisfactions with regulations. Like any kind of problem, it is usually better to get things out in the open so they can be faced and discussed. Even though the issues aren't resolved, at least they've been talked about and there are no secrets about how people feel. Often just having the opportunity to state a position will make a person feel better. Such occasions give the supervisor a chance to express confidence in management and give support to the policy that has brought about the regulation being enforced. Probably the worst thing that can happen is for a supervisor to band together with the workers and present a "petition" to management concerning the disliked regulation. Such action puts the supervisor in a bad light, reduces him or her to a level not much above the workers, places management in an awkward position, and creates some polarization that will exist for a long time, regardless of how the situation is resolved.

DON'T RUN SCARED

Lets set the stage for regulations: We know that we have a job to do and that there are various procedures we have to follow to do that job, procedures which pertain to the job itself. While these are a form of regulation, they concern themselves directly with the operation, production, or service that is the end product of the job, so they fit into our scheme of things. Superimposed over this scheme now comes an "outside" regulation, one that does not concern itself with the direct function of the job. It may concern who is hired, how the interview is conducted, how the workplace is to look, sound, smell, or be arranged. It may require the addition of equipment or people or the rebuilding of staircases. We see no immediate benefit to the actual assignment we have of getting out the work. Along with the regulation come some ominous threats or warnings that there is a severe penalty for not following it. Words like *jail* and *fines* are bantered about. Classes may be held, memoranda distributed, conferences convened. There is no doubt that implementation is important, and that the consequences for failing to follow the letter of the regulation will be severe. That's the setting; what do we do?

Historically, the majority of supervisors have taken a disdainful or begrudging approach to the regulation but have also feared that the regulation had better be right no matter what. The "no matter what" is often going overboard: hiring unqualified people, getting less than minimally satisfactory information from an interview, cutting off valves sooner than necessary even to meet the requirements, spending additional time overreacting to the slightest apparent deviation from the regulation. They panic, in other words. That's too bad. That's not the way good supervisors act or react.

Good supervisors realize that the job is never easy, that situations are never perfect, that conditions are never ideal, that we never have the right policies at the right times—at least enough of them—and that we rarely have the best people in the jobs they are best suited for. That's just a fact of life. Good supervisors know that; they accept that. Having been conditioned to these facts, they don't panic when one more thing comes along for them to face. They simply study what needs to be done, figure out what needs to be changed and what needs to be added, then get on with the job. They take it in stride, recognizing that their job is to produce with the people they have to produce with, under the circumstances they are faced with, including all the other constraints. What is more helpful to them than anything else is the knowledge that somebody else, doing the same kind of job, under the same kind of circumstances, is getting the job done. "If they can, I can too!"

Part of dealing with regulations—especially those that don't fit our tasks very well—is to be able to run the business with the regulation being a part of it, instead of letting the regulation run the business. When supervisors panic, when they get things out of proportion, they begin to let regulations run their jobs for them, making everything bend around the regulations rather than molding the regulations into the existing job procedures. Good supervisors learn to go to the limit of a regulation if necessary. They know what they can and cannot do under the regulations, and don't stop short of going as far as is permitted. Poor supervisors, for example, may be scared to discipline an employee, or even discharge one, for fear there will be repercussions. They have a legitimate case and they have the documentation. They are within the rules and guidelines set up by some regulation. However, because they fear some problem, they just let the employee get off "this time," thereby creating dangerous conditions later on. They make up obstacles in their minds. They decide that nobody will back them up in their actions. They cite cases from the past where something bad happened when somebody tried to take a similar action—all of which may be quite true. However, they aren't doing their jobs as supervisors if they don't go through the actions *they think best* within the ground rules of the regulations.

There is a fine line between stretching a regulation to the limit and openly flaunting it. We have to keep reminding ourselves that there is a reason for the regulation and that when we push it to the limit, we aren't trying to get away with anything. We're just trying to do our job within the framework of the rules. We aren't trying to bend the rule or even violate the spirit of the regulation. We should be willing to bend over backward to provide the same protection or conditions the regulation is trying to provide. But we aren't going to fall short of doing the job correctly, within the guidelines, if the regulation allows us to do something. This isn't a deviation from how we normally approach other restrictions on our jobs. For example, there is a limit to our authority to make decisions or spend money; these carry serious consequences if we don't follow them, but good supervisors go right to the limit of their authority, spend up to the limit of their authorization—not to flaunt their power, *but to get the job done.* Poor supervisors, on the other hand, will always stop short of going to the limit, and not use all of their authority. Someone has observed that the only way we can know when we reach the ceiling in a dark room is to bump our heads. When a regulation or authorization is not clear, we many have to bump our heads to find where the limit is. The test is: have we bumped our heads lately? If not, we're probably a far piece from the limit!

We've already seen that there are avenues to pursue if we think a regulation actively and actually interferes with getting the job done and fails to protect what it was designed to protect. If we have a legitimate case against the regulation, we pursue it with vigor. We get the facts, document the data, build a strong case, and follow the proper channels with all the enthusiasm and drive we have. If we win the argument, everyone is better off. If we lose, then we've at least tried, and we've made our point. We've documented our ideas and we are on record in case the matter comes up later. We don't use a loss as a reason to pout and fail to do our jobs. When it is over, win or lose, we still try to do our jobs.

One problem we may run into when we're dealing with regulations is that we may actually have some of the biases or prejudices the regulations were designed to overcome. It may not be a prejudice pertaining to people. It may be simply that we want to get the job done quickly, so we don't see the need to follow the regulations on safe risers. If the box or table or chair is steady enough, is handy, and there's an emergency, why worry about going to get an approved riser? We think the rules are too stringent anyway. We don't have to climb up on the line too many times, and we aren't asking the employee to go very high. There's no way a person could be hurt from that little height. These are our own prejudices coming out. They cause us to violate the regulations and we have no excuse for doing so. When something does happen, we have no case. We simply violated organizational policy, and we deserve whatever discipline comes for the infraction.

Another problem we may have as a result of our biases against certain regulations may arise from constantly bad-mouthing them. Maybe we appear to support them; maybe we even deal with employees who don't follow the regulations. We may even make statements about everybody doing just what the rules say. But in our conversations with other supervisors, we constantly complain about the regulations, make fun of them, cast aspersions on them, and generally won't drop the subject. Because we make fun of a regulation, complain about it, have a negative attitude toward it, it gets out of proporation. Psychologically, it's bad for us, because anytime we constantly dwell on something unpleasant, our thinking gets warped a little. We begin to build it up in our minds to the extent that it's too big a barrier to overcome—as we envision it. Sooner or later it will begin to take its toll on our actions and will affect our behavior on the job and with our people. The others we're talking to can't do any more about the situation that we can, so talking to them about it won't do them or us (or the regulation) any good. The admonition of successful, old-time supervisors is: Do what you can to change it—if it needs changing, learn to live with it if you can't change it, *then leave it alone!*

KNOW THE REGULATIONS

Having established that we aren't interested in getting around a regulation that is legitimate and protects something that needs to be protected, what do we do with those regulations that are bothersome but are not going to go away? They don't help or hurt anyone or anything. They're there because of something that's not our concern, but we have to live with them. We've seen that one thing we do is to go to the limit of the regulation. Use all the law allows, take the liberties provided. What this boils down to, of course, is that we have to become moderately expert in the ins and outs of the regulation. We have to know what it says in order to do what it says, but we also have to know what it says in order not to do *more* than it says do. Most regulations are general enough that they apply to everyone, but don't apply *specifically* very well to anyone. They are often confusing, sometimes ambiguous, perhaps not even written very well. There may be too much or too little information. There may be some real questions about just to whom all of the regulations apply. Our job: Learn the regulations as best we can. Become a near expert. Be able to answer questions about them. Look for and remember interpretations of the rules. See what others have and haven't been able to do. If there are rulings on the regulations, read them, or at least become familiar with them.

The person who has the most knowledge of any subject has the beginnings of an advantage over those who don't have as much knowledge. It is often the case that the investigators and/ or enforcers of many of the regulations aren't always familiar with all the aspects of the rules, so they may be operating at a disadvantage when dealing with those who know all the details of them. While the intent should never be to evade the regulation as it is written, when negotiations are appropriate, the person who knows the finer points and has the greater knowledge has the advantage in the negotiations. For the most part, large organizations have to deal with the most regulations; they also have the most professional people to deal with those who question actions taken by supervisors. Nevertheless, successful supervisors have to deal with the regulations every day and can't wait for a ruling every time they take some kind of action. For this reason, it is still a good idea to know what can and can't be done and the ramifications of doing or not doing what the regulations say.

ENFORCE PENALTIES FOR VIOLATIONS

Since regulations are part of doing the job and part of policy, there must be action taken against people who violate the rules, just as for any other infraction. Failure to do this will have serious consequences in many different areas. The disciplinary action we take is like any other, and the same steps should be taken. Discipline serves some very necessary purposes, including providing for changes in the person being disciplined and setting an example so that others will be less inclined to violate the same rules.

The steps in successfully disciplining those who fail to observe the regulations are simple, straight forward, and, when followed, make the job of the supervisor much easier.

1. *Know the Regulations.* We've already talked about the importance of this. We need to know the regulations, know the parts that apply, and be able to explain them. This becomes the standard for us to follow and gauge actions by. This is the guideline that

tells us whether there has been any violation. If we do not know the regulations, there is no way of knowing if there has been a violation.

2. *Let the Employee Know the Regulations.* Before there can be any action taken, we have to know that the employees actually know the regulations, know what parts apply to their jobs, and know what they can do to meet the regulations.

3. *Train to the Regulations.* It's not enough just to tell employees what the rules and regulations are; we must also see that they can actually do the job within the regulations. This may mean training. If so, then we train—before we exercise any discipline. The training isn't complete until we have actually seen the employee doing the job up to the standard specified in the regulation.

4. *Let the Employee Know about a Violation.* When there is a violation, let the employee know immediately that there has been a violation. We can't let the employee go on thinking that the job is being done correctly. If it's the first violation, we may just let the employee know how we feel, let it be known that there has been an infraction, and make this a warning. We do this only if that's the way we handle all of our discipline with all of our employees.

5. *State the Consequences.* If the first violation ends only in a warning, we should make the consequences of future violations completely clear. We make it clear, listen while the employee repeats it to us, then record it.

6. *Set a Time for Review.* Before the warning meeting is over, make certain there is a specific time and date set for review of the employee's action after this meeting. That is almost a sacred meeting, and if possible, nothing should interfere with that meeting. It will be the time when we determine if the behavior on the job has changed, and the time when we give positive reinforcement for good behavior and deal with the poor performer.

7. *Exercise Discipline as Required.* If discipline is required and the time has come to do it, then we should do it immediately. Nothing is to be gained by waiting. This is when our integrity is at stake: Do we stand by our word, having said that we would do certain things if there was a violation of the regulation

again? The rule: Never threaten anything we aren't willing—and inclined—to carry out!

REWARD POSITIVE BEHAVIOR

There are some simple rules for getting people to perform properly. Simply put, people are more likely to repeat those things for which they are rewarded in some way, and quit doing those things that either are not rewarded or are punished. To the supervisor who deals with people who must follow certain regulations, this means that when employees perform well, they need to be reinforced for it. Sometimes this gets mixed up and we find ourselves rewarding the wrong things: An employee violates the rules, gets the job done more quickly than someone else, gets praise for it, and all kinds of incorrect messages are sent. The employee who violates the regulations is rewarded for doing the incorrect thing, so will more likely perform it incorrectly the next time. The employee who did it corectly, without praise, isn't likely to continue to do the correct thing when he or she sees others receiving praise for doing it in a way that is at odds with the regulation. All the reinforcements have been wrong in this situation, and we shouldn't be surprised when things go from bad to worse on the job.

On the other hand, when we give praise to the employee who is performing within the regulations and discipline violations, and let everybody know why we've done both, we send all the correct messages. The employee performing within the rules will more likely repeat the performance and others will follow the example. The person performing badly will not be as likely to want continued discipline, so will make some effort to improve, and others will try to avoid the same discipline. The praise doesn't have to be a big thing. It may be no more than simply a pat on the back and a "Hey, I like the way you did that." It doesn't necesarily have to be a public announcement, but it might help if others know we said it. If we reprimand an employee for a violation, that, too, can be in private, but others should know that some action was taken. Praise doesn't have to accompanied with flags and whistles and drums. It can be done quietly, just letting the employee know that the boss cares, knows, and is impressed. For every "safe employee of the month" there should be many, many more "nice people of the month!"

GET EMPLOYEES INVOLVED

Experience shows that we get a lot more commitment to a regulation from employees when they discover its uses, advantages, and purposes. When we tell them these things, we sound like the boss trying to sell something on behalf of the organization. They think—rightly so—that we are just the mouthpiece for higher management and are obligated to try to persuade them to accept the regulation. On the other hand, if they decide for themselves that there is some reason to the rule, they will accept it more readily. There is some risk involved, because if we turn them loose and let them try to figure out why this regulation exists, they may not come up with the same answer we have. If we give them enough information, they can begin to see the validity of what's happening, and will say so. Honest questions such as "What advantages can you see to such a rule as this?" or "Why to do you suppose such a regulation came into being?" will usually get them thinking in positive terms. It probably helps if we ask in a neutral rather than defensive tone—at least in the beginning. Certainly they will have trouble finding anything good about the regulation if we begin by disparaging the rule, management, or the regulatory agency.

We can also get employees involved in figuring out ways of applying the new regulation. After we establish that it's here to stay and try to get them to determine why we have it, we solicit their ideas for applying the regulations. Let them decide, as much as possible, what we will do to enforce the ordinance. We ask for—and use if possible—their ideas and suggestions. This is a time for open discussion and communication. It is not the time for secrets and keeping things from them that pertain to their jobs. Worse yet, it is not the time to be defensive or negative about the regulations. A good, positive approach will work best. We look for ways to get the regulations working for us, not against us. We learn to think of them as standards, rather than as prohibitions.

As we've seen before, this is the time to let them know that these regulations are a part of the job, that they are policy, and that they are the standards by which we will all be measured.

CONSIDER FUTURE REGULATIONS

Since regulations are frequently enacted because we haven't been self-regulating, we should consider what areas future regulations might address if we don't attack the problems ourselves. This is an excellent time to get employees involved. Share with them the fact that most of the restrictions imposed on us are the result of our not seeing that there was an unsolved problem which we weren't attacking. By having employees involved in looking for other areas where we might be regulated in the future, we make them aware of the reasons for the *present* regulations. We aren't likely to remove any of the present rules and regulations, but we can learn to live with them. The point is, we shouldn't be generating additional openings for *more* regulations. If we are allowing unsafe acts, discrimination, or pollution, we can be sure that sooner or later there'll be some kind of regulation imposed on us. Now is the time to get employees on board with suggestions, ideas, and activities aimed at preventing further restrictions and regulations. We have to be prepared to accept their thinking and try to adhere to their suggestions where we can. We don't have to disrupt the organization or give up existing freedoms. We simply let employees know that we don't want to do things that run counter to health, safety, public welfare, or upward mobility considerations. We want employees on our side looking for ways to prevent outside interference, not against us looking for complaints against us and outside help in overcoming what they perceive as a problem.

CONCLUSION

A regulation, any regulation, is a part of doing a job, not something unrelated to it. It is there for a purpose, which may or may not be legitimate. The reason for the regulation may no longer exist. This doesn't really matter in the long run. It is there, it is to be treated as policy, and we don't have any license to violate it or to look the other way when our people violate it, nor can we spend our valuable time fighting it. Our best course of action is to accept regulations as a part of the daily work assignment, get our people to think of them as policy and work standards, with no more flexibility than other standards and policies might have. Like everything else, the rules represent standard operating procedures—SOP—and should be considered as no more or less than that.

The worst thing we can do is call strong and frequent attention to the regulations, complain about them, let our people know how unhappy we are with them, and overlook those who violate them. We have to be careful not to make the outside-imposed regulation or restriction *bigger than life.* If we remember that management is aware of the regulations and our discomfort with them, we can go on with our business-as-usual approach to the job. Also, we can understand a restriction better if we remember that a restriction is a restriction, wherever it comes from. It is a regulation when top management says, "Because of business conditions we are imposing a 10% budget reduction" (or a wage and hiring freeze). We don't like this, but we don't entertain any idea of violating it. The same is true if an outside source imposes a hiring condition or a work rule. We should no more think of violating this rule than one imposed by management. In fact, when the rule comes to us, it has already passed top management and has its approval, so there is *no real difference.*

Maybe if we worked harder and smarter, we wouldn't have as many regulations as we have. We might even find them removed. But if not, then we continue to work harder and smarter, and do the job assigned to us.

27

FAIR EMPLOYMENT PRACTICES

MATT HENNECKE

What is fair? In order for supervisors to be fair in their employment practices, they have to know what is fair and what is unfair. Unfortunately, the number of laws and regulations governing employment is so vast and the laws themselves change so quickly that most of us are at a loss to understand them, much less abide by them. We hear of discrimination, class-action suits, out-of-court settlements, backpay awards, and sigh in relief that we've been lucky enough to escape untouched. We may be lulled into thinking that those things happen to other companies and other supervisors and that surely they'd never happen to us. Be warned! Unless we take the time to find out what makes some employment practices fair and others unfair, we're walking a dangerous tightrope—blindfolded and without a net. Given enough time, financial disaster for our companies and career disaster for ourselves is likely.

AN INTERACTIVE CASE STUDY

Read the following case study and try to imagine yourself in the leading role. As the case unfolds, keep asking yourself if you are being treated fairly or unfairly. How would you feel if you were treated this way in your own organization? On occasion, you will be required to refer to Figures 27.1–27.5 in order to determine the outcome of an important decision regarding your future, status, and position with the company. So, if you're ready let's begin.

It's Thursday afternoon and you are sitting at your desk contemplating your plans for the weekend. The forecast is for rain, but you're hoping the forecasters miss this call as they missed last weekend's call—sunny and dry! Ha! As your thoughts turn back to the task at hand, you begin worrying again about the financial situation your company is facing—the economy is soft, sales are down, and more layoffs are imminent.

It's difficult to work today when there may be no work tomorrow. Already two of your best friends have been laid off—both have families and house payments. As that whole terrible scene involving them plays itself again in your mind, one frightening fact keeps surfacing: even supervisors can get the ax. You'll know today if your number's up. With a sigh (or was that a shudder?) you turn your attention to your work.

Two hours later in walks your boss. His face is the color of putty, his look a mixture of sympathy and agony. Inwardly you groan as he hands you your check. Attached to the check is an apologetic memo with bad tidings. You've been laid off—indefinitely. Resisting the urge to violently rearrange your office, you bid a somber farewell to your job of 14 years and clean out your desk.

Seven weeks later you are still unemployed. Your search for a new job has been frustrating and nonproductive. You have only one lead and you're keeping your fingers crossed that it comes through. If it doesn't you'll have to sell the television set or one of the kids. Living off the savings and and the unemployment check just won't be possible much longer. You're waiting by the telephone. The Xambofizz Company, with whom you had an interview earlier this week, promised to call at three o'clock and give you the news. All week you've refrained from walking under ladders, spilling salt, breaking mirrors, or stepping on cracks— all in preparation for this moment. The phone rings. You pick it up and . . .

To see whether you got the job, turn to Figure 27.1 and follow the instructions.

If you got the job, congratulations. If you didn't get the job, it's because of your eye color and age. The Xambofizz Company has its reputation to think of and your age and physical attributes just don't fit their profile of a successful employee. If you got the job, you start immediately. (If you didn't get the job, your search continues for two more months before you finally find one. In the meantime, your new car has been repossessed because you've been unable to make the payments.)

Your new job is difficult, but you are determined to work hard so you can get into a supervisory position again. This new job is a step down from the one you had before, but desperation makes even the sorriest job attractive. You were a pretty good supervisor in your last job, but now you'll have to prove yourself all over again with your new boss and new company. You've never been afraid of hard work and now you buckle down to learn the new job backward and forward.

Instructions: Find your eye color along the top edge of the grid below. Then find your age along the left side of the grid. Locate the box where your eye color and age intersect to find out whether you were hired.

	Brown	Blue	Other
16–34	Not Hired	Hired	Not Hired
35–53	Hired	Not Hired	Hired
54–72	Not Hired	Hired	Not Hired

FIGURE 27.1.

After working with the company for eight months, you hear about a management training program being offered by the company for those employees interested in getting into management. Upon further investigation you also discover that the three-week course is required before an employee can even be considered for a management slot. Here's your chance to show your already well-developed skills. You go down to the training department to sign up for the course. As you walk into Matty Schmuck's office you notice a sign posted on the wall: "Space Limited for Management Training Program—Applications for Enrollment Required." You ask Matty for an application and complete it, carefully listing your qualifications and previous supervisory experience.

To see whether you were accepted into the management training program, turn to Figure 27.2 and follow the instructions.

Congratulations and good luck if you were accepted into the program. Sorry, if you didn't make it this time. There will be another class in two or three years. If you weren't accepted, it's because the instructor of the class is left-handed and prefers left-handed students.

You've been with the company now for a full year. You were promised when you got the job that you would be eligible for a salary increase after one year. You wait patiently for your boss to approach you with what you're sure will be good news. After all, your work has been top-notch. Even though you've only been here a year, you're already outperforming Manny Gargleknee—a four-year veteran. You found out he got a 17% increase in salary just last month. Three weeks pass and still no adjustment has

Instructions: Find your sex along the top edge of the grid below. Then find your handedness along the left side of the grid. Locate the box where your sex and handedness intersect to find out whether you were accepted into the training program.

	Male	Female
Right-Handed	Not Accepted	Not Accepted
Left-Handed	Accepted	Accepted

FIGURE 27.2.

Instructions: Find your sex along the top edge of the grid below. Then find your age along the left side of the grid. Locate the box where your sex and age intersect to find out what your salary increase was.

	Male	Female
16–34	3%	4%
35–53	15%	15%
54–72	4%	2%

FIGURE 27.3.

been made to your salary . . . four weeks, five weeks, six weeks; your impatience builds. Finally, after two months of waiting, you go to your boss to inquire about the raise you've been promised. Your boss laughs nervously and then apologizes for his poor memory and assures you your next paycheck will reflect a salary increase.

To see what your salary increase is, turn to Figure 27.3 and follow the instructions.

If you got a 15% increase in pay, well done! You work has been excellent and you'll go far with the organization. If your increase was disappointing, too bad. Even though your work has been excellent, you were either too young or too old to get much of an increase. You see, the company feels that younger employees need to prove themselves over a longer period of time, and that older employees don't usually have many dependents and can, therefore, get by with less.

As you walk back from the cafeteria one day with Melba Marble, the personnel manager, she tells you of a job opening in your department. You question her carefully about the job and discover it is exactly the same kind of position you had where you worked before. You tell Melba of your qualifications and she is impressed. She tells you no one else in the company has had the same experience you've had and that the job is as good as yours. Eagerly and confidently you submit a formal request for the job.

To determine whether you got the promotion, see Figure 27.4 and follow the instructions.

Instructions: Find your eye color along the top edge of the grid below. Then find your handedness along the left side of the grid. Locate the box where your eye color and handedness intersect to find out whether you were promoted.

	Brown	Blue	Other
Right-Handed	Promoted	Not Promoted	Promoted
Left-Handed	Not Promoted	Promoted	Not Promoted

FIGURE 27.4.

If you got the promotion, super! If you didn't get it, sorry. Maybe something else will come along. In a conversation with Melba two weeks after the bad news, she tells you that the job required someone with either brown or green eyes and that the candidate had to be right-handed. That job has always been held by a right-handed, brown-eyed or green-eyed person. You can't break with tradition you know . . .

You've been with the company now for three years, and once again the economy is acting up and the threat of layoffs is haunting you and the organization. Your competence is unquestioned and your performance appraisals reflect the fact that you are the most capable person in your department. You are never late for work and frequently you come in on Saturdays even though it's not required. You're not too worried; after all, your boss has always said you're indispensable. If anyone goes, it'll surely be that lazy, no-good Agnes Hagglestarter. Your boss has already warned her 15 times about her poor performance—and that was just in the last week!

To determine whether you will be laid off, turn to Figure 27.5 and follow the instructions.

If you're still drawing a paycheck, great! If you were laid off, our sympathies. Apparently Agnes is well liked by the people in the department. Surely someone of your talent will be able to get another job elsewhere. If Agnes had been let go, her lack of talent would have made her job search much more difficult.

The interactive case study you've just completed was designed to help you experience the frustration and anger felt by those who

Instructions: Find your handedness along the top edge of the grid below. Then find your age along the left side of the grid. Locate the box where your handedness and age intersect to find out whether you were retained or laid off.

	Right-Handed	Left-Handed
16–34	Laid Off	Retained
35–53	Laid Off	Laid Off
54–72	Retained	Laid Off

FIGURE 27.5.

are subjected to unfair employment practices. Admittedly, the case was exaggerated, and we may be reasonably sure that today people are not discriminated against because of the color of their eyes, or because they are left-handed or right-handed. But discrimination does exist today and is frequently based on equally absurd and irrelevant factors. Rather than considering a person's abilities when making decisions about hiring, training, and promoting, many supervisors still consider race, color, religion, age, and gender. The result? Entire groups of people are discriminated against, usually for things over which they have no control, and that's not fair or legal.

THE HIGH COST OF DISCRIMINATION

While discrimination against people of various nationalities, religions, and races is as old as recorded history, only recently has there been a concerted effort by the United States to outlaw discriminatory practices. On July 2, 1964, Congress passed the Civil Rights Act, which, among other things, made it a violation of law for any employer to discriminate against anyone because of race, color, religion, sex, or national origin. At the same time, Congress created the Equal Employment Opportunity Commission (EEOC) to administer the law. Later, the Office of Federal Contract Compliance Programs (OFCCP) was established. Both agencies were given certain powers for enforcing antidiscrimination laws. But what does this all mean to you as a supervisor? Simply put, it means your company can be punished financially if *you* discriminate against someone. A few examples will serve to illustrate the high cost of discrimination:

United States v. Allegheny-Ludlum Industries. Because it was found guilty of discrimination against minority and female employees, Allegheny-Ludlum Industries was ordered to pay damages for back wages totaling $30,940,000.

Secretary of Labor v. Wheaton Glass Company. Upon investigation, it was found that male selector-packers at Wheaton Glass were paid $2.35 per hour, while female selector-packers were paid $2.14 per hour. Though the company tried to defend the rate differential by claiming that only the male employees were required to lift heavy packages, the courts determined that the "economic value" of the additional duties did not justify the pay differential. Wheaton was ordered to pay $901,062 plus 6% interest per year in back wages.

United States v. American Telephone and Telegraph (AT&T). In January 1973, AT&T was ordered to pay $15 million in back wages and $23 million in raises to 13,000 women and 2000 minority males who had been discriminated against by the company, which placed them in lower-paying clerical jobs instead of higher-paying craft jobs. The total award was 38 million dollars!

MAJOR LAWS AND WHAT THEY MEAN TO YOU

Because you can so easily get yourself and your company into trouble by violating various laws that have been enacted by Congress, it would be a good idea for you to know what the major laws are and how they can affect your supervisory responsibilities. Four major laws are outlined below. By becoming familiar with them, and making a real effort to keep from violating them, you will be on your way to practicing fair employment.

The Equal Pay Act of 1963

This federal law prohibits employers from paying employees of one sex less than employees of the other sex for jobs that require equal skill, responsibility, and effort, and which are performed under similar working conditions. There are exceptions to this law as indicated below:

1.   Seniority systems which allow salary differences based on length of service are allowed.

2.   Merit systems which allow salary differences based on documented and verifiable merit are allowed.

3.   Any system which measures earnings by quantity or quality of production are allowed.

Essentially, this law means that you can't pay Karla Clumpker less money than Rodney Reeler simply because she is female. The law is intended to insure women the same pay for performing work that is basically the same as work performed by men. One note of caution: sometimes similar jobs can have some different duties or even different names and still be considered legally equivalent. That means you're not necessarily safe if your subordinates have different job titles or somewhat different job duties. The question is one of responsibilities and duties. If the job is basically the same, the pay should be the same.

Title VII of the Civil Rights Act of 1964

This law prohibits discrimination in employment on the basis of race, color, religion, sex, or national origin. The broadest of the equal employment opportunity laws, this law governs such areas of employment as recruiting, hiring, compensation, placement, training, promotions, discharges, and nearly everything else you can think of.

The sheer magnitude of this law can and does scare most supervisors. Basically, it means any decisions you make regarding the recruitment, hiring, salary, training, and so forth of an employee must be based solely on nondiscriminatory factors. If Sybil's skills and performance exceed Leroy's then she'd better get that promotion, even if that position has always been staffed by a male. Try to base every personnel decision you make on documented, verifiable performance factors rather than on irrelevant prejudices.

The Age Discrimination in Employment Act of 1967

This law and its amendments prohibit discrimination against applicants and employees because of their age. No decisions regarding hiring, compensation, discharge, promotion, and so forth can be based on the age of the employee.

When that well-qualified job applicant happens to be 64 years old and you hire the less qualified 26-year-old, you may be in violation of this law and your company would be on unsafe ground. Here again, your personnel decisions should be based on job-related qualifications and not age. Even if you know the older job applicant may be retiring in two years, to deny him the job in favor of a younger, less-qualified candidate simply because of his age is not only unfair, it is illegal. Imagine what it would be like to be denied a job because of your age. Not a pleasant thought, is it?

The Rehabilitation Act of 1973

This federal law provides for equal employment opportunity for the physically and mentally handicapped. Under this law, it would be illegal to discriminate against any physically or mentally handicapped person for non-job-related reasons. It would not be considered discriminatory, however, to deny a job opportunity to such a person if his or her disability prevented him or her from performing the job duties.

What this means is that it would probably not be discriminatory to deny the lathe-operator job to the amputee since two arms are absolutely necessary for the operation of the lathe, but it would be discriminatory to deny him or her the specifications-compiler job (a job for which one arm would be adequate) on the basis of his or her handicap alone. Again, the concept of fairness would dictate your action. It would not be fair to place handicapped people in jobs that are beyond their physical capabilities, but at the same time it would not be fair to arbitrarily disqualify them for jobs they could handle.

FAIR EMPLOYMENT PRACTICES QUIZ

Simply knowing the equal employment opportunity laws is often not enough to keep us from accidentally violating them. You see, the laws form the basis of fair employment practices. There are, however, many employment practices that on the surface seem perfectly legal but are in fact illegal. To test your ability to recognize potentially discriminatory employment practices, respond to the following case studies.

Case Studies

CASE 1.   Alvin Messey has an opening for a cashier in his department store. He has asked his assistant Rex Wrecks to write a "help wanted" advertisement for the Philpot Gazette. After struggling with the wording, Rex shows you what he has submitted to the Gazette. You notice he has indicated that a "high school diploma is preferred." Is the wording discriminatory?

_____ YES

_____ NO

CASE 2.   Karla Clodd, one of your best employees, has requested the correspondent position that has just opened. Ordinarily you would be happy to have her in that position, but it requires a lot of travel. Karla has three young children, ages two, three, and five. You're afraid the travel will get to be too much of a hardship for her. Because of your concern for her and her family, you select someone else for the job. Is your decision discriminatory?

_____ YES

_____ NO

CASE 3.   Mookey Klink has been working for you for nearly six years. His performance has been basically satisfactory. A few months ago

Mookey became a member of the Zulu Zappa religious order. Now he is requesting Saturdays off so he can attend religious services. Your business requires all employees to work every Saturday. In fact, when you hire people you tell them that the job will require them to work all day on Saturdays. Can you refuse Mookey's request without violating the law?

_____ YES

_____ NO

CASE 4.   Betty Mannard works in the training department of the SafeTee Security Guard Company. SafeTee provides security guards to several Memphis-based businesses. Betty is always looking for qualified individuals to attend the 13-week security guard training program she conducts. Last week Melfred Boxter, a distribution clerk in the mailroom, asked if he could get into the training program. Because of the nature of the security guard job, Betty always asks potential trainees if they've ever been arrested. Is this practice discriminatory?

_____ YES

_____ NO

CASE 5.   Moses Brown has been working for Buster Schultz for three weeks. Buster is the shift supervisor for the Krushem Construction Company out of Pittsburgh. One day as Buster walks by some of the men who are on lunch break, he overhears Moses bragging about having been dishonorably discharged from the Army. Buster, a veteran himself, decides to check out the story. He calls the personnel office and asks Bertha to check Moses' application. Sure enough, in the space asking whether the applicant was honorably or dishonorably discharged from the services, Moses checked "honorably." Buster confronts Moses and accuses him of lying on the application, and Moses admits to his deceit. Buster reminds Moses that lying on an application is grounds for dismissal. Can Buster fire Moses?

_____ YES

_____ NO

CASE 6.   Lula Scrimp has been Tom Megunn's bookkeeper for three years now and has done a pretty good job. Lula is Tom's prime candidate for a management trainee position he wants to fill. Lula is currently making $950 a month, and the starting salary for a management trainee is $1,200 a month. Tom wants to give Lula a shot at the management trainee job, but wants to try her out at a trial salary of $1100 a month. He talks to Lula about the job and the salary, and she excitedly agrees to Tom's conditions. Has Tom discriminated against Lula if she agrees to the salary?

_____ YES

_____ NO

CASE 7.   Larry Masterson, who is mentally retarded, applies for the bin-sorter job at Melburn Solar. Even though Larry seems capable of handling the job, Omarr Fisbit, the recruiter for Melburn Solar, is afraid he won't fit in with the other employees—that they'll make fun of him. As a result, Omarr turns Larry down for the job. Was Omarr in violation of equal employment opportunity law?

_____ YES

_____ NO

CASE 8.   Zapp Electric Company is looking for a customer service clerk to handle the phone in the customer service department. Robert Ohmm is interviewing Andrea Watt for the position. Because the bus service in town is poor, and Zapp Electric is located in an industrial park several miles from the nearest subdivision, Robert asks Andrea if she owns a car. He's concerned about how she will get to work. Was Robert's question illegal?

_____ YES

_____ NO

CASE 9.   After carefully reviewing the qualifications of the four candidates for the Southeastern Management Development Program, Elma Floot selects the best-qualified candidate, Terri Koote. Terri's performance appraisals have all been very good and she is by far the best of the candidates. Gabb Eastfrik, another of the candidates, claims he has been discriminated against because of his race and threatens to charge Elma with discrimination. Can Gabb formally charge Elma with discrimination?

_____ YES

_____ NO

Answers to the Case Studies

ANSWER TO CASE 1.   Yes, the wording is very likely discriminatory. A high school diploma is not a bona fide occupational qualification for the cashier's position. A person without a high school diploma may be quite capable of handling the basic mathematics and skills needed for the job. By requiring or even "preferring" a high school diploma, you may be unfairly discriminating against certain ethnic or social groups. When writing advertisements, avoid educational requirements that are not absolutely crucial to the performance of the job.

ANSWER TO CASE 2.   Yes, your decision is discriminatory. Inquiries by an employer about family status, number of children, and so forth are illegal, as are any employment decisions that are based on such factors. It is discriminatory to assume that having young children will keep Karla from performing her job satisfactorily. Most employers would not bypass a male for a promotion because of the number and ages of his children. To bypass a female on such grounds amounts to sex discrimination.

ANSWER TO CASE 3.   Yes, you may refuse Mookey's request. Under Title VII of the Civil Rights Act, employers may not discriminate against people on the basis of religion. At first glance this may appear to be a violation of that law. However, if attendance at religious services constitutes a genuine hardship for the employer's business, then the employer may legally refuse to allow time off. An important fact to note is that the employer in this case made a special point of telling all prospective employees of the Saturday work requirement.

ANSWER TO CASE 4.   Yes, the practice is probably discriminatory. No employment or personnel decisions should be made on the basis of arrests. An arrest is not the same thing as a conviction and is therefore irrelevant.

ANSWER TO CASE 5.   No, Buster cannot legally fire Moses. The fact that Moses lied on the application is irrelevant. It is considered discriminatory to ask questions about honorable or dishonorable service records either on application forms or during interviews.

ANSWER TO CASE 6.   Yes, Tom has discriminated against Lula. If the starting salary for a management trainee is $1200 a month, then Tom will be in violation of the Equal Pay Act if he attempts to pay Lula less.

ANSWER TO CASE 7.   Yes. Omarr violated Larry's rights under the Rehabilitation Act of 1973. The courts would reason that what the other employees think of Larry is irrelevant and cannot be the basis of an employment decision.

ANSWER TO CASE 8.   Yes, Robert's question was illegal. Whether Andrea has a car is irrelevant. If Robert feels that Andrea is qualified for the job, then he should give it to her and let her worry about getting to work on time. Questions pertaining to automobile ownership have been found to discriminate against certain groups of people.

ANSWER TO CASE 9.   Yes, Gabb can formally charge Elma with discrimation. Any employee may bring a charge against his or her employer, whether or not it is well-founded. Being charged is one thing, being judged in violation of the law is another. In Elma'a case an adverse judgment is unlikely since she made her decision on the basis of documented performance.

HOW YOU CAN AVOID DISCRIMINATION

Depending on how well you did on the quiz, you may be frustrated by how difficult it is to avoid discrimination. After all, asking a potential employee whether she has a car seems safe enough, and asking a person whether he's been arrested seems legitimate on the surface. How can we be expected to know what is and what is not legal when there are so many fine points to the law? As supervisors, do we need to keep several attorneys on call? Hopefully not. There are a few principles we can keep in mind that will go a long way toward keeping us both honest and out of the courts.

Principle 1: Be Objective in All Personnel Decisions

Try to avoid using vague, subjective words or factors when making personnel decisions. Words like *ambitious* or *bad attitude* can only get you into trouble. When taking notes during an interview, only write down factual, objective information. For instance, noting that the person you are interviewing for the plumber's job has worked as a plumber's assistant for three years is specific, objective, and measurable. To note that the person has a "bad disposition" is not specific, not objective, and not measurable. When conducting performance appraisals, follow the same principle. Note the measurable, objective facts and not your feelings and biases. Then, when a salary increase needs to be made, you'll have specific, measurable facts on which to base your decision.

Principle 2: Consider Only the Job and Its Requirements

To require a college degree for the grocery-bagger job is obviously going beyond what the job really demands. Whenever you are faced with finding the right person for a job, take the time to pinpoint exactly what qualifications and requirements are demanded by the job. Are dictation skills essential for the secretarial job? Perhaps, but you'd better make sure. Is a driver's license necessary for the trucker's job? Probably, but again you'd better be certain. The point is, you can only legally require what the job itself requires. It shouldn't matter if the person is black, blue, white, ugly, fat, skinny, lumpy, or smelly—if he or she can do the job, handle the promotion, complete the training program, or whatever, then that should be all that matters.

Principle 3: Avoid Requirements That Adversely Affect any Group of People

If a requirement for a job is applied the same way to everyone, it may still have an adverse effect on minorities or females. For instance, if Bubba Jackson decides he will only hire people with military experience to work in his chain of gun stores, then his decision would have an adverse impact on females since far fewer females have military experience than do males. Since military experience is not essential to running a gun store, Bubba could be accused and judged guilty of discrimination. In one of our earlier case studies, an interviewer asked a job candidate whether she had a car. Again such a requirement would be unfair and probably illegal because minorities are more likely not to have cars than nonminorities. Requiring a car when it is not crucial to the job has an adverse impact on minorities and is therefore discriminatory. Be sure to think carefully about how any requirements you place on job selection, promotion, salary increase, training, or termination may adversely affect one group of individuals in comparison with another group. If a requirement singles out a particular group, then it is probably illegal.

Principle 4: Know the EEO Laws

In this chapter we've looked briefly at the EEO laws governing personnel decisions. Take the necessary time to go back and review those laws whenever you are about to make a personnel decision. By knowing the laws and being sensitive to the principles of fairness, you should be able to recognize potentially discriminatory situations and avoid making any major mistakes.

CONCLUSION

As a supervisor you do not have the right to decide whether you will be fair in your selection, promotion, salary, or other employment practices; and this chapter was not written to present a case for being fair. Instead, this chapter was written merely to introduce you to and make you aware of your legal and ethical responsibilities to all of your employees. It was written to illustrate the high cost of being unfair and the obligation you have to yourself, your company, and your employees to make decisions that are in the best interests of everyone involved. True, the laws are sometimes ambiguous, and it can be frustrating and time-consuming for a supervisor to have to be so careful about making employment decisions, but we should remember the principles of fairness and applaud the laws that help us to remain true to those principles.

SECTION

13

PERSONAL CONSIDERATIONS

28

THE SUPERVISOR AND SELF-DEVELOPMENT

LINDA M. LASH

"Ask *not* what your country can do for you; ask what *you* can do for your country."

Few of us have forgotten these immortal words spoken by John F. Kennedy as President of the United States of America. The words were spoken in the political environment of an elected leader trying to spark optimism and hope among voters and taxpayers who faced inflation, poverty, unemployment, and the threat of nuclear war.

The words grew to be immortal not only because they were spoken by a young and popular leader, brutally assassinated before he could deliver all of his promises, but also because they found application outside the political arena—to personal situations, to religious causes, to patriotic feeling, to corporate life.

Development of employees to meet corporate goals and to satisfy the individual's needs is a key topic in today's corporate environment and a central topic for many books, training courses, and films. The focus, however, is often on the supervisor's or manager's role in developing his or her subordinates.

For the corporate world, and for this chapter, John F. Kennedy's immortal words might be restated:

> Ask *not* what your country can do for your development; ask what *you* can do for your development.

The following pages contain the 15 most frequently asked questions about self-development and offer thought-provoking considerations to use in dealing with yourself (and others) on the issue of self-development.

1. What is really meant by self-development?

The dictionary offers generous help in defining the word *self-development*. A good example from *The World Book Encyclopedia Dictionary* is: "make better, fuller, more useful, etc."

In everyday life, we use the word to describe a housewife's taking a course in healthful food preparation to better plan family meals as well as to describe schoolteacher's spending the summer recess in India experiencing transcendental meditation for his or her own peace of mind.

The business and working world takes a narrower view of the word, with management feeling that *self-development* is an activity which makes an employee a better, fuller, more useful contributor to the achievement of corporate goals.

Many companies provide internal training programs to develop employees. Examples include:

1.   Job skills training that provides employees with specific skills to do the job.

2.   Management skills training that provides human management skills training to newly promoted employees or to employees being considered for promotion.

3.   Conceptual skills training that offers employees training outside of their routine job duties to stimulate their development as members of the organization.

Many companies also provide the opportunity to receive this same training externally at company expense or to attend external training programs or educational courses that contribute to employee development.

But self-development in the business world extends beyond formal training and educational courses. Self-development and learning happen in each of the following situations as well:

1.   Management trainee or apprenticeship programs bring in young persons or university graduates to work alongside experienced or skilled employees to learn the business. In addition to the obvious development of the trainee or apprentice, the experienced or skilled employees can also develop his or her coaching and communication skills.

2.   Company relocation and job transfer or rotation policies can offer development opportunities for employees to learn and do various jobs in different disciplines, in different locations, with different people.

3.   Special project assignments outside routine job duties offer developmental opportunities to employees to learn new skills.

4.   Organizational change and technologial innovations offer employees continuous opportunities to develop new skills.

5.   Managers who take the time to explain their decisions and coach and counsel employees provide development opportunities daily to those they are in contact with.

There are many more situations which offer self-development opportunities. Each time we encounter a new situation, each time we deal with an old situation in a new way, each time the world around us changes, self-development can happen. Making it happen is the responsibility of a person to himself or herself. We can sit back and let others deal with new situations, we can continue to deal with old situations in the same way, we can try to ignore or insulate ourselves from changes around us, and we can let our minds and bodies stagnate. Very few of us do that.

Self-development could be defined more loosely as learning or encountering something new, thinking about it, and putting this new information to work for yourself in some useful way. Self-development could include each of the following:

1.   Taking a computer appreciation course outside working hours to better understand the automation that is taking place in your office and in your children's school.

2.   Taking up jogging in the morning to help you feel more fit at work and at home.

3.   Trying a new Korean restaurant when you've never eaten Korean food before.

4.   Participating in a company training course on making, effective presentations to help you in your job.

5.   Volunteering to participate in a quality circle at your company.

6.   Volunteering to help organize a cancer-fund drive.

7.   Having a conversation on supervision with someone who does your job in another company.

8.   Having a conversation on eating habits with a foreign visitor.

9.   Reading IBM's latest product announcement.

10.   Reading the latest status report from Three Mile Island.

11.   Asking a city council representative the reasoning behind the latest city ordinance ruling.

12.   Asking your manager the reasoning behind his or her latest decision.

Self-development can include all of these activities and many, many more, covering a wide variety of topics, disciplines, and situations. The one thing they have in common is that they are something a person does for himself or herself. While the corporation may send you to a training course or give you a special project to do, what you get out of it depends upon you.

2. Who is responsible for my development?

There is one school of thought that says our development is the responsibility of our parents for the first six years of our lives and that for the next 12 years the responsibility is shared between parents and schoolteachers with scout leaders, church school teachers, camp counselors, and others also making a contribution. After that, responsibility for our development may be transferred into the hands of university professors with contributions from sorority or fraternity housemothers, dormitory counselors, and so forth. After that, corporations are responsible for our development until we retire, when the government, retirement homes, and our children take over.

The profound and valuable impact that each of these persons and institutions makes on our development cannot be denied. Nor can we deny the age-old saying, "You can lead a horse to water, but you can't make it drink."

A major part of the responsibility for our development rests with ourselves. Parents, schoolteachers, governments, and corporations bear the moral and social responsibility for giving us the *opportunity* to develop ourselves; we bear the responsibility for taking advantage of the opportunity and also for creating the opportunity when they fail.

In addition, corporations are generally guilty of the charge that they provide the opportunity for us to develop ourselves not purely out of social and moral responsibility but also out of profit motives. They develop employees to meet corporate goals. How each corporation sees the development of employees as meeting corporate goals may be radically different from corporation to corporation, and that is yet another reason why employees must consider that they are personally responsible for their own development. One corporation may see its role as providing specific job skills training to train employees to do the jobs it needs done. Another may hire only those with the required job skills and provide no training at all. Another may elect to use job rotation and on-the-job experience to develop employees. Yet another may send all management candidates to a lengthy university management program. Another might provide a complete range of internal training programs at all levels, coupled with job rotation and frequent relocations and transfers. Another may have a special project-team concept where all candidates for promotion work as part of a special project team. And another might offer internal programs and courses on elective, off-duty time to improve basic reading, writing, mathematical, analytical, or computer skills.

Supervisors who consider themselves responsible for their own development will tend to do some of the following:

1. Participate in elective company training courses they view as important to their own development.

2. Participate in company training programs that their managers view as important to their development.

3. Participate in off-duty courses and activities that might contribute to their own development.

4. Discuss their development needs during performance appraisals and other conversations with their managers and follow up on agreed actions.

5. Make contact with other professionals in their field and join professional organizations in their field.

6. Read books, magazines, and newspapers about subjects that could contribute to their development.

7. Apply for internal transfers and relocations that could contribute to their development.

8. Volunteer for special projects that could contribute to their development.

9. Volunteer to work with management trainees or apprentices to help them learn the business.

10. Volunteer for assignments that they or their managers view as important to their development.

11. Submit useful suggestions and ideas to company quality circles or to company employee-idea programs.

12. Take up a hobby or sport that contributes to their own development or that allows them to establish rapport with other supervisors and managers.

13.   Offer solutions to company problems.

14.   Accomplish their objectives, do a good job, and present their accomplishments in a favorable light.

15.   Encourage and help others to develop themselves.

The critical thing is to do something as opposed to nothing, to take advantage of every opportunity for self-development, and to create opportunities where none seem to exist.

3.   How can I determine what areas I should develop myself in?

People are very often the harshest judges of themselves, and a group of good supervisors left alone to make a list of what areas they need development in will tend to produce lengthy lists.

A good way to identify areas requiring self-development is to discuss ideas openly with your manager during the performance appraisal process. This is one of the central issues that should be part of a good performance appraisal.

If performance appraisals are done infrequently, you can discuss the areas requiring development with your boss at any appropriate moment. One good opportunity is at the completion of an assignment or objective. Whether the completion was a resounding success or a dismal failure, you can always ask what could have been done better and what skills should be worked on in order to do better the next time.

With the popularity of assessment centers, psychological testing, in-basket exercises, self-evaluation quizzes, and increasingly open discussions between manager and subordinate, there are many easily available ways for a supervisor to identify areas that require development. The key is to determine which of these areas are the most important ones for the achievement of the supervisor's own goals. Below are some of the ways that the list of areas requiring development can be organized by priority:

1.   The performance appraisal process remains one of the best ways, since managers are the ones most familiar with their supervisors' work, strengths, and weaknesses. A good discussion between manager and supervisor can produce a list of the areas

requiring development in order by priority as well as identify the specific activities to support the development.

2. Supervisors with specific career goals in mind can look at the people holding the positions they would eventually like to have and make a list of the skills those people have. Supervisors can then make an honest list of the skills they have and compare this with the list of skills that those in their career-goal positions have. Any missing skills can be identified in this way, and supervisors then have a list of the key skills they need to develop to get the positions they want.

3. Supervisors can identify their own missing skills by engaging in a bit of historical analysis. They can list on one piece of paper the successful activities, personal or business, that they have done in the past year or more and the skills they believe were most critical in those successes. On a second piece of paper, they can list the activities which were not so successful. With some careful thought, they should be able to list the missing skills that caused the activity to be less than successful. They can then look at each missing skill and ask themselves, "If I had this skill, could I do my current job better or could I get the promotion I want?"

4. How can I control my career development?

Career development does not generally happen by accident. It is the result of identifying where you would like to go and taking the necessary steps to get there. Taking the necessary steps may involve identifying the areas requiring development and acquiring those skills which you and your manager agree are critical to your own progress. Taking the necessary steps may also involve relocation or transfer to get to the eventual goal.

Supervisors who want to control their own career development may do the following:

1. Discuss their goals openly with their managers so that their managers can help them attain their goals.

2. Discuss their goals with other managers who can help them attain the goals.

3. Volunteer for special projects or work assignments that lead them in the direction of their goals.

4.   Apply for transfers, relocations, or promotions that lead them toward their goals.

5.   Identify and develop the skills that they and their managers agree will help them attain their goals.

6.   Complete current assignments, work projects, and objectives successfully so that promotion can be considered.

7.   Help others take the necessary steps to attain their goals.

Some flexibility must be maintained. If, for example, an opportunity not on your list of necessary steps appears, you must be able to assess quickly whether this new opportunity also leads toward your goal.

5.   *My manager won't let me attend any courses. How can I develop myself?*

Attending training courses or educational courses, internal or external, to acquire needed skills or knowledge is an important part of self-development. A good supervisor who is devoted to self-development should continue to discuss participation in relevant and necessary courses with his or her boss and also with the personnel and training departments to obtain permission to participate. Most of these courses do increase skills as promised in their statement of objectives, and in some companies, participation in these courses is mandatory for promotion.

If participation in courses is not possible, there are other methods. Internal and external courses of value almost always have stated objectives and brief descriptions of the course content. Details for external courses are published in brochures or catalogs that can be easily obtained by writing or calling the company offering the course. Details of internal courses can usually be obtained from the training department. Once the details of the course are obtained, they can be studied to see if there are other ways to obtain the same skills or knowledge elsewhere:

1.   If a textbook is used in the course, it may be available at the local library or in a bookstore.

2.   The same course or a similar one may be available from a local college, university, or technical institute outside of normal working hours.

3.   A book on the same subject can be recommended by a librarian at the local library.

4.   Course handouts and materials may be obtained on loan from other supervisors who have attended the course.

Taking action on one's own helps in the development process and demonstrates to management that a supervisor is indeed serious about self-development.

6.   I've never really had a proper performance appraisal. How do I go about developing myself when I'm not sure where I stand now?

It is difficult to know where you're going and how you're going to get there if you don't know where you're at now. If your manager cannot give you the opportunity for a proper performance appraisal discusison, you will have to do your own. Here are some ways:

1.   Look back over the year and try to write down the activities and work assignments you did that your manager or other managers appeared to be pleased with. If you have trouble determining which activities management was pleased with, try to think of any work which had to be redone by you or somebody else, any reports which you feel certain were never read, or any activities which no one wants to talk about. These were probably the less successful assignments. On the positive side, think of any work which your colleagues or subordinates said was good, any activities someone thanked you for, or any reports which appeared to have been read by a number of people and acted upon. These should be the more successful assignments.

2.   Review all facts, figures, and dates. Did you produce the numbers you were supposed to produce? Did you meet the dates you were supposed to meet? Write down each one and, if your performance did not meet the targets, write down why it didn't.

3.   Put yourself in your manager's position for a moment. If you were your manager over the past year, would you have been pleased with your performance? What deficiencies do you see? Were any dates or targets missed? Was there any conflict or problem?

4. Think of your colleagues and subordinates. If they had to evaluate your performance, what would they say and why? Would they view you as a capable supervisor? Would they say you met all dates and targets? What skills would they say you should work on?

If you can give yourself an honest appraisal of where you're at, and the facts and figures support your opinion, you can then identify what areas need improvement. Be careful to put your list of development areas in order by priority, considering the priorities your manager and other managers would assign first, those you would assign first, and those your colleagues and subordinates would assign first.

7. *There aren't any openings ahead of me. Why should I develop myself?*

There are quite a few reasons:

1. The fast pace of technology, death, a sudden promotion, the sale of your company to another, a sudden termination, or a sudden change in the economy all could open the position ahead of you without a moment's notice. You would want to be ready for the unexpected.

2. Technology might suddenly do away with your job—at your company or in the entire industry. You would want to be prepared with other skills to find another job.

3. A management change or corporate takeover might cause you to be fired suddenly. You might want to be prepared with additional skills if you suddenly have to find another job.

4. A very attractive opening in another division or company might come up suddenly. You would want to be prepared so that you could be considered for this surprise opening.

5. The fast pace of technology might change your current job so that you are no longer able to do it. You would want to be on top of developments in your field and be ready to change with the job.

There are many other variations of these extreme but certainly realistic situations, and they might even happen slowly, without your being aware of the changes. There is an old saying: "To fail to prepare is to prepare to fail."

8.   *Nobody takes me seriously here. I'll have to go to another company to develop myself.*

If you have worked your way up through the ranks at your current company, you might fall victim to the long-term employees who still think of you in one of your starting or lesser roles. This is a difficult syndrome to overcome, and many supervisors in this situation who have transferred to other divisions or other companies will vouch for the fact that you can indeed rid yourself of it by changing jobs.

If you do not want to move to another company or another division, there are some things you can do:

1.   Take yourself seriously. Develop the skills and areas that you honestly feel need developing, even if you have to pay for training or education yourself. Put your new skills to work in visible ways.

2.   Be patient with long-term employees who still view you in your starting position and block your full participation in their exclusive club. If you can, learn a sport or hobby that they enjoy and use it to establish rapport by asking their advice on a particular aspect of it. If a work assignment brings you in contact with any of these people, make sure the work you do then is particularly brilliant but not antagonistic.

3.   Remove the trappings of your previous lesser positions, such as dress, hobbies, and lesser status symbols. Dress for your new position or your next promotion, use the amount of office space accorded to your new position, learn to speak about a hobby or sport that others at your level enjoy.

If you continue to take yourself and your own development seriously over a period of time, chances are that others will begin to take you seriously, too.

9.   *How can I go about developing myself when I work in a discriminatory environment?*

It is a fact of life in our society that people have prejudice—against people of a different race, against people of a different sex, against people of a different religious belief, against people of a different sexual preference, against people who belong to a different club, against people who dress differently, against people who attended a different university, against people who enjoy different sports or hobbies.

While there are laws against certain kinds of discrimination and while most companies offer development opportunities to all employees, prejudice may affect a supervisor's ability to capitalize on all of the developmental opportunities.

As a first step, you should insure that your company is not violating any discrimination laws. Secondly, you should be sure that you have the correct facts about all development opportunities available to employees. The personnel and training departments should be able to help with these steps. Job openings should be posted, for example, and details of training courses and their prerequisites should be available.

A logical next step is a discussion or performance appraisal with your manager to identify the areas requiring development and to agree upon actions to take for your development. Be sure to follow up on any actions you are supposed to take, and then make sure your manager takes any actions he or she agreed to. If your manager does not provide all of the help you feel you need, carefully select another manager in your company or in another company who can provide additional counsel and guidance.

Apart from the racial, sexual, religious, and age discrimination barred by law, other types of discrimination exist and may be very difficult to deal with. An example might be a company management training course which is essential for promotion, but for which a manager declines to nominate a supervisor—giving as a reason that the supervisor cannot be spared for that time period (with an underlying reason being that the supervisor does an average job but did not attend a recognized university and probably, in the manager's view, should not be considered for promotion at this time).

If we look at the game of baseball for a moment, we know that the pressure on a batter is greatest when the bases are loaded with a tie score in the bottom of the ninth inning and the count is two strikes, three balls. Contrast this situation with that of a batter who has just stepped up to bat in the top of the second inning and whose team leads four to zero. For the first batter, his manager, his teammates, and the team's fans will tolerate nothing less than a good performance—a walk, a base hit, or a home run. For the second batter, the same group of people will accept any performance—a strike, a ball, a pop fly.

If you as a supervisor are completely different than the people you work for, the pressure is on you for nothing less than a good performance, and you can probably identify with the first batter. If you have no differences or only a few, there is less pressure on your performance, and you can be compared with the second batter. While we all agree that discrimination and prejudice are unfair and should not exist, they do in fact exist. While individuality and personal beliefs should not be sacrificed unwillingly, there are ways to reduce the impact of differences or to lower the count against you. While it is not practical to undergo a sex-change operation or take four years off to attend a better university, there are some ways to reduce the impact of differences:

1.   You can downplay any stereotypical habits. For example, a female supervisor could refrain from powdering her nose and applying lipstick during a business meeting with male colleagues.

2.   You can avoid the obvious practice of a different habit while at work. For example, a smoker who attends a management meeting with nonsmokers might refrain from smoking during the meeting.

3.   You can learn to discuss a popular sport or hobby so that you can participate in informal conversations with other supervisors and managers.

4.   You can focus your conversation on business accomplishments and issues and refrain from initiating conversation on topics which you know are hotly controversial. For example, a supervisor might walk into a room of other supervisors and managers and ask how the latest work project is going rather than ask whether everyone agrees that the United States should bomb Israel.

If you want people to accept you, you may have to make a few subtle, temporary changes such as these to relieve the pressure. Once you have established rapport with other supervisors and managers, they may more easily accept and even appreciate your differences.

10.   *The union and seniority control promotions here. What's the use of developing myself?*

Development is often used in the context of a person developing himself or herself for a promotion or a bigger job. However, self-development could be undertaken for any of the following reasons:

1.   To do your current job better, thereby attaining more recognition, more of a bonus, a larger merit increase, a more secure feeling, and so forth.

2.   To keep pace with technological innovation and organizational change which might change the nature of, and skills required for, your current job.

3.   To be ready just in case the unexpected happens suddenly such as a break in traditional promotion methods.

4.   To be ready for sudden disasters, such as the shutting down of your company or the discontinuance of most jobs like yours in the industry.

The most certain thing in today's world is change, and it happens so quickly that it is difficult to predict the exact nature of the change. Changes in the business world often spread quickly to the personal world and vice versa. Fortunately, people are not dogs, and older ones can learn new tricks. Learning-skills may be rusty, but they never disappear entirely.

If you feel locked in by union and seniority promotion practices, you may want to use that time period in your life to concentrate on your personal development—learning to restore furniture, taking up art appreciation, learning to use your son's personal computer, or any number of things that give you a sense of achievement. If your work life does not provide the opportunity to satisfy achievement, social, or other needs, you can satisfy the same needs outside the work environment by engaging in an activity which might provide you with a different view of your working situation.

11.   I think my manager is wrong about what areas I should develop myself in. What should I do?

As long as you report to your manager, it is your manager who will evaluate your performance and recommend you for promotion. Thus, your manager's opinion of what areas you should develop yourself in cannot be lightly dismissed. The following should be considered.:

1.   Do you have the time to develop yourself both in the areas your manager feels are important and the areas you feel are important? Can one activity develop you in both areas?

2.   Consider why your manager is specifying each area you should develop yourself in. Does your manager have a different view or different knowledge that would allow him or her to see needs that you are unable to see? Could there be corporate plans or opportunities you are unaware of?

3.   Is there a way to obtain other opinions? Can you talk to someone in the personnel or training departments? Can you talk to another manager in your own company or in another company?

4.   Can you go back to your manager and discuss your development needs again, asking why your manager feels strongly about these areas?

5.   The local library may have information about nearby assessment centers or about self-evaluation tests and quizzes that can help you verify which areas you require development in. These could be helpful to you.

12.   My manager is really good at developing people and has looked after my development for years. I don't really have to do anything except what my manager tells me to do, do I?

Supervisors who have managers who consistently guide their development are indeed fortunate, but there are some cautions to be exercised:

1.   Remember that self-development is somehting you do, not something your managers does for you. A good manager will provide the opportunity, but a good supervisor must make the

most of the opportunity. Be sure you understand what each rec-ommended developmental activity is supposed to do for you, and make sure you obtain the maximum benefit from each opportunity.

2. Every now and then, it may be beneficial to insure that your manager is doing the right thing for you. Look around the rest of the company and make comparisons. Is your manager sending you to every available training course, while others do not go, because you are the "favorite"? Is your manager sending all of his or her employees to every available training course, while other departments do not do the same, and is this likely to lead to criticism from senior management of your department's function?

3. You may have to face a day when you work for a new manager. Will the new manager see you only as the old manager's "favorite"? Will the new manager be able to look after your development as well? Will you be able to look after your own development?

If you do work for a manager who is good at providing opportunities and coaching you on your development, make the most of this opportunity. Watch and study your manager's techniques and try to apply them to your subordinates. Make them a part of your own management style.

13. I'm happy right here in this job. Is there something wrong with me that I don't want to go any further?

Any organization needs a balance between employees who want to move ahead and employees who want to stay where they are. An organization with too many people who insist on moving ahead may not be able to keep the majority happy or may lose employees to other companies. An organization with too many people who want to stay where they are will find promotional candidates in short supply and may have to recruit externally.

Being happy in your job is very important. When you consider the number of hours you spend at work each day, each week, each year, it is quite a sum of time to spend doing something.

Being unhappy with this activity can be depressing and can affect your health, your family, your life. Being happy in your job is productive and useful and can lead to a happy and healthy personal life as well.

There is one caution, and that is simply that our world changes often. The possibility of your job being eliminated, your job being changed dramatically, or the people you work with changing must be considered as real, and the happy job you have might no longer exist.

14. I'd like to change careers completely, but how do I do that at my age?

There are many examples of people who successfully make a complete career change. Consider the career longevity of a professional football player who chooses that career with the knowledge that he will most likely have to begin a new career at age 35.

Changing careers requires planning effort and detailed research into what the requirements are and how you can go about satisfying them. Opinions and guidance from others are important, as well as self-confidence and dedication to your goal.

If you would like to change careers but you are not sure what career you would like, consider the following:

1.   Do you really want to change the type of work you do or would you be happier doing similar work in a different place, with different people, with different salary and benefits, in a different office?

2.   With the choice open, it is best to find out which careers pay the most, offer the most security and opportunity for advancement, would take you at your age, are reasonable to learn, and so forth. The placement office of local schools and universities will be able to help, and your own company's personnel department may have information.

3.   Do you want to remain with your current company and pursue a different career or do you want to change companies? If you want to stay with your current company, there should be a wealth of guidance and information available—from your man-

ager, from the personnel or training departments, from other employees. If you want to change companies, visit the employment offices of other companies you think you would like to work for and obtain information about them.

Once you have chosen a specific direction, or if you already have a direction in mind, it is best to get the facts and support you need:

1.   Find out everything you can about your chosen field—what companies are good to work for, what the salaries are likely to be, what kind of preparation (training, education, and so forth) you will need, how to apply for the jobs you want.

2.   Talk to trusted friends and family about your plans so that you can gain their commitment to support you in your efforts.

3.   Take stock of your financial situation to see exactly how you will make the move financially.

4.   Make a list of activities you will need to do, and shape them into an action plan with target dates and costs.

5.   Review your action plan with someone who is able to advise you of its practicality—your manager, a guidance counselor at a local school or university, someone who has made a similar decision, your local pastor, a local civic leader whom you know, and so forth.

6.   Before you put your plan into action, check to see if there is any way to "try out" your skills or attitudes in your chosen path. Can you take an evening course on the subject to see if you like it, or can you talk to people who hold jobs in your selected field?

With a sound direction and a solid action plan, you can attain your goals with the added ingredients of confidence, perserverance, dedication and support from those around you.

15.   If I do a good job, I'll get a promotion, won't I?

Doing a good job—meeting deadlines, achieving targets and objectives, accomplishing goals and assignments—is usually an essential ingredient to being considered for promotion. It is not, however, the only ingredient; and doing a good job does not guarantee promotion.

Getting the promotion you want is more often a combination of the following ingredients:

1. Doing your current job well—meeting deadlines, achieving targets and objectives, accomplishing goals and assignments.

2. Insuring that your manager and other managers know you are doing your current job well and that they appreciate and value your work. (More specifically, meet your targets and deadlines on those projects which you know these managers consider most important.

3. Developing and displaying some of the skills that will be needed in the job you want.

4. Insuring that your manager and other managers are aware of your goals and that they support them.

5. Conducting yourself in such a way that others around you (subordinates, peers, managers) believe you will be able to do the job you want (for example, by helping others to attain their goals, volunteering for key assignments, dressing and acting in ways associated with higher-level jobs, undertaking self-development activities).

While much office gossip is devoted to the people who get promoted because of who they know or with whom they have special personal relationships, the majority of promotions happen when people concern themselves with all five of the criteria listed above.

INDEX

6

INDEX

Team building:
  maintenance of, 7.11–12
  technical, 7.9–11
Technical supervision:
  positive outlook in, 7.8–9
  is it special?, 7.4–6
  supervisor's role in, 7.6–8
Technical teams:
  building, 7.9–11
  communicating with, 7.12–13
  maintaining, 7.11–12
Technology:
  change in, 12.8
  new, 13.19
Testing, in training effectiveness, 2.17
Time:
  identifying problem causes with,
    10.5–7
  identifying problems with, 10.3–5
  problem-solving model of, 10.3–10
  procrastination using, 10.18
  wasters, 10.15–19
Time management:
  determining objectives for, 10.14–15
  identifying problem causes in,
    10.5–7
  identifying problems in, 10.3–5
  problem-solving model in, 10.3–10
  in retail industry, 5.15–16
  setting objectives for, 10.14–15
Time problems:
  external or internal?, 10.11
  identifying, 10.3–5
  internal, 10.9–10
  model for solving, 10.3–10
  lack of priorities causing, 10.11–12
Traditional organization, 12.4
  conditions of, 12.4–6
  role of supervisor in, 12.6
  role of worker in, 12.6
Training:
  doing, 21.16–18
  experienced employees, 21.10
  following up on, 21.18
  hazards of not, 21.5–6

new employees, 21.9–10
pay for, 21.10–11
philosophy of, 21.11
preparing for, 21.14
preparing employees for, 21.15–16
presupervisors, 2.4–12
for QWL, 13.3
record keeping in, 21.18–19
retail supervisors, 5.9–12
setting standards for, 21.14–15
technical/professional people,
    7.15–18
for upward mobility, 21.10
who gets it?, 21.7
who does it?, 21.7–8
why?, 21.2

Unenriched jobs, 6.10
Unions:
  climate with, 4.2
  discussed in presupervisory training,
    2.7
  using leadership with, 4.4
  working with, 2.18, 13.7–8

Wages, 4.16
  administration of, 22.8–9
  and benefits, 4.16
Work:
  redesign of, 12.14–17
  teams, 12.16–17
Worker:
  change in attitude of, 12.7–8
  change in makeup of, 12.7–8
  role of, in production, 12.6
  role of, in traditional organization,
    12.6
  selection of, 13.2
Work ethic:
  change in, 12.7–8, 18.5
  lack of, 6.15
Workplace:
  improvements in, 12.11
  meaning of improvements in,
    13.10–19
  poor conditions in, 13.14–15